Tribes and State Formation
in the Middle East

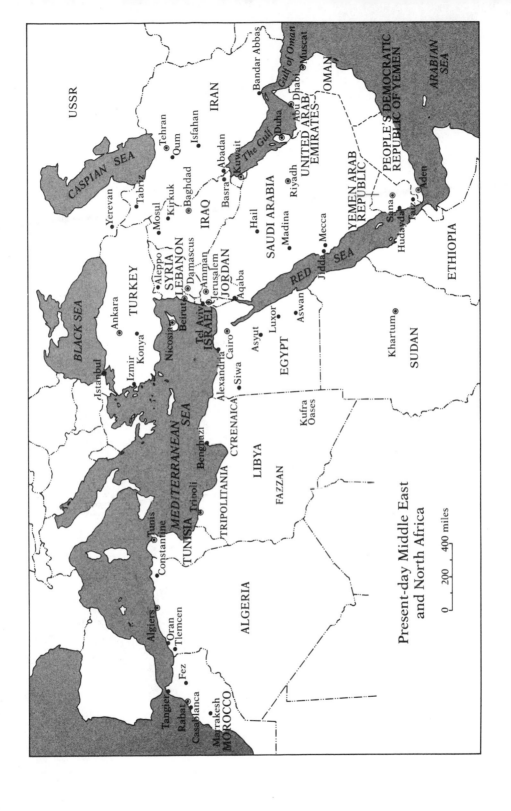

Present-day Middle East
and North Africa

Tribes and State Formation in the Middle East

EDITED BY

Philip S. Khoury
and
Joseph Kostiner

UNIVERSITY OF CALIFORNIA PRESS

Berkeley   Los Angeles   Oxford

University of California Press
Berkeley and Los Angeles, California

University of California Press, Ltd.
Oxford, England

© 1990 by
The Regents of the University of California

Library of Congress Cataloging-in-Publication Data

Tribes and state formation in the Middle East / edited by Philip S.
Khoury and Joseph Kostiner.
    p.   cm.
  Proceedings of a conference sponsored by the Massachusetts
Institute of Technology and Harvard University.
  Includes bibliographical references.
  ISBN 0-520-07079-8 (alk. paper). — ISBN 0-520-07080-1 (pbk.
alk. paper)
  1. Middle East—Politics and government—Congresses. 2. Tribal
government—Middle East—History—Congresses. 3. Tribes—Government
policy—Middle East—History—Congresses. 4. Islam and state—
Middle East—History—Congresses. I. Khoury, Philip S. (Philip
Shukry), 1949–   . II. Kostiner, Joseph. III. Massachusetts
Institute of Technology. IV. Harvard University.
JQ1758.A2T75 1990
306.2'0956—dc20   90-35640
                                               CIP

Printed in the United States of America
2 3 4 5 6 7 8 9

CONTENTS

vii

FOREWORD

Roy P. Mottahedeh

Some historical subjects remain unrecognized until they are discovered; some need to be rediscovered every generation. When Professor Philip Khoury and Dr. Joseph Kostiner came to the Center for Middle Eastern Studies at Harvard University to propose a conference on tribes and state formation in the Middle East, I immediately felt that the moment had arrived to rediscover this perennial subject or, at the very least, to recast it in the light of the considerable work by anthropologists and historians of recent decades who have studied tribes and states in specific Middle Eastern contexts.

The subject is perennial for many reasons. It is considered central to the question of the formation of settled communities in the Tigris-Euphrates valley six thousand years ago. It is implicit in the categorization of human societies given in the Qu'ran (49:13) "O mankind: We created you from a male and a female and made you into peoples and tribes [*qaba'il*] that you may know each other. Truly, the noblest of you in God's sight is the most pious among you: God knows all and is aware of all." The categories of both tribe and government power are central in the thinking of the subtlest and most significant premodern Islamic social thinker, Ibn Khaldun (1332–1406).

For a while, however, tribes were relegated to the background in global discussions of Middle Eastern societies and their governments, since the tribe seemed to be a disappearing, premodern unit, and colonialist regimes were suspected (often rightly) of playing with tribal identities in an attempt to divide and rule. As the authors of this volume amply show, tribes cannot be relegated to the background in a proper historical picture of the Middle East any more than can urban market economies or the *'ulama'*. The persistence of older forms of social identification in new settings is as much a feature of contemporary Middle Eastern history as it is of contemporary European history.

It is an honor to be able to dedicate this volume to the memory of Malcolm Kerr, who combined dedication to the scholarly understanding of the Middle East with a commitment to the furtherment of education in that region to a degree that is an inspiration for us all.

IN MEMORY OF MALCOLM KERR

Albert Hourani

I am pleased that this volume is dedicated to the memory of Malcolm Kerr, for two reasons. First, he was associated with Harvard at one point in his career, and he was well known to several of the volume authors, was much loved, and is mourned by all who knew him. His death left behind a memory of intelligence, wit, an austere charm, and a heart of crystal.

My own memories of him go back almost fifty years and cover most of his life. I remember him first of all as a small boy in his parents' home in Beirut, where his father was a professor at the American University; he was slim, active, polite, neatly dressed, almost unnaturally clean for a small boy. Twenty years later he spent a year at St. Antony's College in Oxford, on his way from the American University of Beirut to UCLA, where he had been given an appointment. He and Ann lived in a very cold house, which may have been bad for his health, but his Presbyterian stoicism enabled him to bear it. It was a year of reading and reflection, marking a moment of transition in his intellectual life; a year, also, when he and Ann made close friendships, with Elizabeth Monroe and others as well as with ourselves. He deserves a small footnote in the history of the college, because it was he who persuaded us to break with the absurd convention that one could invite somebody else's wife to dine at High Table but not one's own. "If I can't bring Ann, I shall not dine," he said firmly, and we changed the rules.

Then I remember several visits to UCLA. The last one was for the Levi della Vida Conference in 1979. I stayed once or twice at his beautiful house in Pacific Palisades, which may have reminded him of his parents' house at 'Ayn 'Anub in the Lebanese mountains, with Los Angeles spread out on one side and a bare mountain on the other; I seem to remember waking early and seeing the wild deer come down from the mountain to eat the roses in the garden. These were the years of a happy family life and fulfillment as a teacher, director of the Von Grunebaum Center, and for a time a dean. It may have been a surprise to those who did not know him well and were thinking only of the normal pattern of an academic career that he should have left UCLA to go back to the American University of Beirut as president in a time of civil war and just at the moment of the Israeli invasion of 1982, but those who knew him well understood that for him there was no promotion beyond Beirut.

My last memory of him is of his visit to England in the summer before he died. He came to Oxford, and we gave a party for his friends. He seemed to have changed a little: he was less outspoken, more wary, rather sad. It was as if the shadow of what was to come had already fallen across his path; but I am sure he would not have wished to be anywhere at that time except the American University of Beirut, the place of his childhood and now the place of his duty.

The second reason for which I am pleased that we are commemorating him may not seem so obvious. There does not, at first sight, appear to be much in common between the subjects that preoccupied him and those we are discussing here. He was a political scientist, and a very good one, with unusual historical depth. His works are few, but of high quality: three books—*Lebanon in the Last Days of Feudalism* (a translation of an Arabic chronicle of the war of 1860), *Islamic Reform*, and *The Arab Cold War*—and a number of articles, including one of great importance on "Arab Radical Notions of Democracy." They show a combination of conceptual clarity and detailed knowledge and are among the basic writings I have put into the hands of those who wish to understand the Arab World.

If we look beneath the surface of what he has written, we can find a concern for the ways in which societies and cultures express themselves in the forms of political and social action. He believed that the ideas and creeds that mold a culture should not be regarded simply as the product of social forces but should be taken in their own right and judged in themselves, and that they give a specific nature to social and political processes. In his book *Islamic Reform* I find this statement, which is also a profession of faith:

> The theme of this book follows from the assumption . . . that the significance of a set of abstract social ideas may be at least partly dependent on their intellectual worth: on their coherence, profundity, insight and learning, and sincerity of purpose. This may seem at first glance an unexceptionable proposition, but in actuality many people today are em-

barrassed by it. In this age of foreign aid and cultural exchange programs, where all cultures are equal and none are more equal than others, critical evaluation of other people's beliefs seems arrogant and tactless. Worse yet, modern sociological theory makes critical evaluation seem unsophisticated. . . . It directs our attention to the life situation of those who propound or accept certain ideas, and away from the content and quality of the ideas themselves, reducing them to a forlorn status among the host of dependent variables by which the social process is scientifically explained. The sociologists may, of course, be right, in which case we are only moving bones from one graveyard to another.

One of the questions that is discussed in this volume is that of the ways in which the beliefs, ideas, and practices we call Islam have molded the process of the formation of tribes and states, and perhaps we can learn something from Malcolm Kerr's profession of faith.

ACKNOWLEDGMENTS

Philip S. Khoury and Joseph Kostiner

This volume has its origins in the Conference on Tribes and State Formation in the Middle East held in Cambridge, Massachusetts, in November 1987. Its sponsors were the Massachusetts Institute of Technology and Harvard University, where it took place. Funding was provided by Harvard's Center for Middle Eastern Studies and MIT's Center for International Studies, Technology and Development Program, and Middle East Program. We are grateful to Roy Mottahedeh of Harvard and Myron Weiner and Nazli Choucri of MIT for securing this funding.

The editors wish to thank Isenbike Aricanli, Edmund Burke III, John Esposito, Fuad Khuri, Gideon Kressel, Gerald Obermeyer, James Piscatori, and Theda Skocpol for participating in the conference. Although their contributions are not found here in print, they were of considerable value to the making of this volume. To the other participants, whose contributions form the bulk of the volume, we are grateful for the readiness with which they accepted our suggestions for revisions and for the promptness with which they submitted their essays. We are also indebted to Lisa Anderson, Thomas Barfield, and Bassam Tibi for preparing essays specially for the volume. We especially wish to thank Lois Beck and Albert Hourani for their incisive comments on the introductory chapter.

We are grateful to Helen Ives for her meticulous typing of the entire manuscript, Paul Furtaw for his editorial assistance, Supreo Ghosh for assisting in the compilation of the bibliography, and Bronwyn Mellquist for her skillful copyediting. The strong encouragement and support provided by Lynne Withey, our editor at the University of California Press, is greatly appreciated. Our largest debt is to Roy Mottahedeh, whose intellectual guidance and support enabled us to undertake and complete the project.

Introduction: Tribes and the Complexities of State Formation in the Middle East

Philip S. Khoury and Joseph Kostiner

In recent years anthropologists, historians, and political scientists have discovered fruitful opportunities for intellectual exchange and even collaboration in their efforts to understand continuity and change in different societies. Historians and political scientists have turned to the concepts and tools of anthropology to examine certain questions the written record has failed to address. Similarly, anthropologists have taken greater cognizance of the importance of studying the historical record to understand the contemporary cultural and socioeconomic phenomena they encounter in their fieldwork. Today historical research based on documents and anthropological inquiry based on personal observations increasingly complement one another. Such scholarly interactions, as difficult as they are to sustain, have become indispensable to the study of Middle Eastern states and societies.

This volume brings the disciplines of anthropology, history, and political science to bear on a topic that none is adequately equipped to address alone. Although the study of tribes and states has long been a preserve of Middle Eastern anthropologists, historians and political scientists have always had more than a marginal interest in the role of tribes in the construction of major political systems and institutions. Several contributions to this volume vividly illustrate the variety of ways in which the three disciplines have begun to interact. They reach beyond limited historical case studies, narrow legalistic analyses, and anthropological microstudies of specific communities by combining the study of socioeconomic and cultural change with that of political and institutional development over a long historical span.

The focus on tribes and state formation in a Middle Eastern context is significant for at least two reasons. First, for long periods of

1

history large parts of the Middle East were not effectively dominated by the imperial states that otherwise ruled the region. Although tribes played a significant role in the creation (and, with some exceptions, disintegration) of such Islamic empires as the Umayyad, Abbasid, Fatimid, Ottoman, Safavid, and Qajar states, they also populated and dominated at various times vast areas of the Middle East that did not come under effective Islamic imperial authority; such areas included the Iranian and Turkish plateaus, the Syrian desert, the Arabian Peninsula, the Upper Nile, and the deserts, mountains, and plateaus of North Africa.[1] Only since the midnineteenth century have tribal populations in these areas begun to be incorporated, at different speeds and with different rhythms, into the modern states that grew up in the Middle East and North Africa. But, as some of our contributors suggest, tribes did not necessarily cease to exist because states were formed. Even when tribal forces contributed to the formation of states in regions as different as Iran and Morocco, they might remain much as they were in spite of state formation or they might just as easily become different kinds of tribal entities. In fact, it was not uncommon for the very process of state formation to encourage already existing tribes to reach an accommodation with the state authority in order to retain their autonomy or to create new tribes that might organize themselves around other, more dynamic loyalties, especially those associated with ethnicity, thereby enabling them to oppose the state and even seek independence from it.

A second significance of the volume is that it contributes to the efforts of social scientists to bring the "state back into political analysis."[2] Political and institutional studies of Islamic states in the Middle East belong to a long historiographic tradition, dating at least as far back as the fourteenth century and the writings of Ibn Khaldun. However, studies of state formation in the Middle East that are concerned with the state as an autonomous political actor that both instigates and reflects social change are few in number and of recent vintage.[3] Their inspiration derives in large part from the intensive examinations by scholars of state formation in Europe, Latin America, and, most recently, the United States.[4]

Discussions of state formation in the Middle East, however, pose certain difficulties that are not easily resolved. To start with, the term *state* is associated with modern European conceptions and institutions that do not necessarily correspond to Middle Eastern realities, even in the late twentieth century. Ali Banuazizi and Myron Weiner have written that "the state implies a sovereign authority, a sovereignty based upon both consent and coercion. The state is associated with a particular bounded territory over which it exercises a monopoly of coercive authority. Legitimacy implies myths and symbols which provide a kind of ideological rationalization and justification for this monopoly of coercive authority."[5] But in the Middle East, the monarchs, military officers, and other elites that have come to power in the twentieth century have faced varying degrees of difficulty in building exclusive monopolies of coercive authority and control largely because they have been unsuccessful in developing the forms of popular legitimacy necessary to support their rule. As a consequence, they have faced opposition and resistance from a variety of social and political forces, including tribes, as the history of Afghanistan in the 1980s would suggest.[6] At the same time, however, the very process of state formation across the Middle East and North Africa during the last century has led to the voluntary or forced breakup of traditional forms of tribal authority and the erosion of old tribal loyalties; the result has been the emergence of new groupings and movements that retain certain tribal characteristics but that are also heavily conditioned and shaped by other factors, including class, ethnicity, and even nationalism.

The important point to underscore here is that the contributors to this volume approach the historical relationship of tribes and states from several different perspectives that suggest a certain tension in current scholarship on tribes and state formation. This tension is reflected to some extent in the different approaches or slants adopted by some of our historians, on the one hand, and several of our anthropologists, on the other. Whereas all agree that there are no examples of a "pure" tribal society in the Middle East, Ira Lapidus and Joseph Kostiner, both historians, adopt a nuanced evolutionary approach in seeking to explain how and why certain tribal societies lacking the dominant political and institutional characteristics of states metamorphosed over the *longue durée* into states. Richard Tapper and Lois Beck, both anthropologists, generally take exception to the notion of an evolutionary sequence in which tribes are precursors of the state; they are more concerned with the coexistence of tribes and states over time and with how far each can be defined in terms of its relations with the other, rather than with the transformation of tribes into states. Indeed, they suggest that although many tribal systems were part of states and manifested certain state structures, rarely were they transformed into states. Bassam Tibi and Lisa Anderson, both political scientists, adopt a third approach. They are mainly concerned with the identity and structure of Middle Eastern states; they demonstrate how tribes and tribal modes of behavior have exerted influence on the collective identity and decision-making processes of states.

Ultimately, the volume provides an examination of the definition, function, and interrelationship of tribes and states at different times and in different parts of the Middle East, and of the cultural and ideological assumptions behind the different usages of the terms *tribe* and *state* in the specific context of Middle Eastern society and Middle Eastern scholarship. Our contributors examine the continuous interaction of tribes and states, changes in that interaction over long spans of time, the similarities and differences those changes produced across the Middle East region, and the reasons tribal structures and systems continue to be viable in contemporary times, when comparatively powerful Middle Eastern states dominate the region.

When considered as ideal types, there seems to be an incompatibility between tribes and states, particularly nation-states, as Tibi suggests in his essay. Tapper has noted elsewhere, for instance, that "tribal groups in Iran and Afghanistan are conventionally viewed as historically inveterate opponents of the state," and this same view has applied to much of the Middle East.[7] As ideal types, tribes represent large kin groups organized and regulated according to ties of blood or family lineage; states, by contrast, are structures that exercise the ultimate monopoly of power in a given territory. In this normative typology, states require loyalties of a more complex kind than ties of kinship can provide. In Emile Durkheim's words, states are based on a kind of "mechanical solidarity," that is, on the cooperation of a multiplicity of ethnic, economic, bureaucratic, and political groups.[8] To become states, therefore, tribal societies must undergo tremendous changes; basically, they must radically alter their tribal ethos.

The problem with such ideal typologies is that they fail to express a much more complex reality. They adopt a definition of tribes and states, and posit an understanding of their relations with one another, that historical and contemporary evidence from the Middle East fails to corroborate. As Tapper notes, the typology of tribes assumes, for instance, that their members are essentially pastoral nomads and "isolated groups of 'primitives,'" when, in fact, tribes in some regions have been "settled cultivators who had little or no leaning to pastoralism or nomadism." Whereas in western Iran nomadic tribal groups, including some Kurds and Shahsevan, were prevalent, in eastern Afghanistan there existed settled tribal groups, such as the Pathan.[9] The typology also posits that tribes historically have been "remote from contact with states or their agents" and have existed in a relationship of opposition to each other, when, in fact, "tribes and states have created and maintained each other as a single system, though one of inherent instability."[10]

Because the term *tribe* has been used to describe many different kinds of groups or social formations, a single, all-encompassing definition is virtually impossible to produce. Tapper's essay in this volume underscores the problem of definition by illustrating not only the myriad ways the term has been used but also the ways anthropologists and historians have misused it. He has suggested elsewhere that it is most advantageous to examine tribes at their different levels of organization, "from camp to confederation," and by the different kinds of processes that affect them at each level. He offers some helpful hints in that regard:

> *Tribe* may be used loosely of a localised group in which kinship is the dominant idiom of organisation, and whose members consider themselves culturally distinct (in terms of customs, dialect or language, and origins); tribes are usually politically unified, though not necessarily under a central leader, both features being commonly attributable to interaction with states. Such tribes also form parts of larger, usually regional, political structures of tribes of similar kinds; they do not usually relate directly with the state, but only through these intermediate structures. The more explicit term *confederacy* or *confederation* should be used for a local group of tribes that is heterogeneous in terms of culture, presumed origins and perhaps class composition, yet is politically unified usually under a central authority.[11]

Albert Hourani suggests in his essay that tribes owe their solidarity not to kinship per se but to "a myth of common ancestry." Other contributors to this volume argue that tribal solidarity was often based on a much more complex set of loyalties than kinship, actual or mythical, especially under twentieth-century conditions. Political, social, cultural, ethnolinguistic, and territorial bonds could produce tribal solidarity. Tapper points out that some tribes in Iran never subscribed "to an ideology of common descent, organising as explicitly political local groups with a common leadership." Most tribes, however, "ascribe[d] common descent to all those who, by whatever means,...acquired rights in the territory"[12] they inhabited. The ideal typology of tribes has also failed to consider that tribes could exist in different ecological systems, that some could be nomadic and others sedentarized, and that they could even have different ethnic origins. Sometimes tribal segments, such as clans, coalesced on their own initiative into tribes;[13] at other times tribes might literally be created through state intervention.

In separate studies Dale Eickelman and Paul Dresch have catalogued the various limitations of kinship analysis, more specifically segmentary-lineage theory, as a means for distinguishing tribes from states. Their emphasis is on such features of tribes as cultural distinctiveness and political autonomy and not on segmentation (which posits that members of a segment or kin group are expected to come to the aid of their fellow group members against other groups, in a system of "balanced opposition") and tribal egalitarianism, as emphasized by earlier generations of anthropologists.[14]

Similarly, the ideal typology of the state has been subjected to considerable criticism by historians and political scientists of the Middle East who are no longer satisfied with the notion of the state as a single, monolithic entity that exercises the ultimate monopoly of power in a given territory. They prefer to depict the state as one of a number of social formations whose structures and functions do not necessarily correspond to the model of the modern European state, on which the ideal typology is based. Roger Owen, for one, warns us that although the term *state* "carries with it multiple associations of thingness, or Leviathanness, encouraging us to think of *it* as a single entity, of *it* 'penetrating' something called society, of *it* having capacities, of *it* inhabiting a different area of space from the people it seeks to manipulate and control," its "reality . . . is much more complex, more fluid and much more difficult to conceptualise."[15] Ronald Cohen suggests that "the state refers to any and all variations in power, authority, structure, and values that support the organizational framework of society."[16] For Tapper, "the existence of territorial frontiers (however vaguely defined), a central government (however weak and limited in its aims) and a heterogeneous population, are enough to define the state. In these terms some confederacies constitute states, while some states operate on the basis of tribal ties, or, in the form of empires, recognise the autonomy of other states and tribes within their territories."[17]

In these and other new definitions of the state, state power, state legitimacy, and judicial sovereignty in a demarcated territory are implicitly regarded as aspirations. All states aspire to such features, but in reality the degree to which they are successful in acquiring them varies. Their legitimacy and territorial sovereignty can only be defined as partial. Different groups within the state or regional and international powers can limit the state's strength in these two spheres. Joel Migdal emphasizes the diversity of society; it is "a mélange of social organizations" in which "the state is one organization

among many."[18] Gabriel Ben-Dor suggests that the state's effective-
ness depends on the historical, cultural, economic, and political circumstances in which it finds itself at any given time. The strength or
viability of the state, that is, its "stateness," can change over time in
terms of its ability to govern, enforce laws, and accommodate pluralism, social mobility, and political representation.[19] Hence, as their
level of stateness changes over time, states accommodate tribes in
varying degrees of social integration and political participation. As
tribes also change over time and form a variety of social categories
within a state, they maintain varying levels of autonomy and subordination. Tribes and states thus form a dialectical symbiosis: they
mingle and sustain each other; each part changes owing to the other's influence; and sometimes they seek to destroy one another.[20] The
nature of this dialectic emanates not only from tribal military prowess and political organization but also from tribal values and life-
styles and the wide range of influences they exert on society. Even in
the absence of a common definition of *tribe*, some scholars seem to
agree that as a collective, tribal society possesses what Fuad Khuri
calls a "cultural substance,"[21] namely, a typical mode of behavior
and a value system, or what Tapper calls a "state of mind." Because
values and beliefs exist in the abstract, they can have more lasting
endurance than the changing ecological and social conditions faced
by a given tribal society. Tribal values therefore exist and can influence state and society even if their bearers do not subscribe to a single, clear-cut definition of themselves.

In short, the picture that emerges is much more complex than the
one that is ascribed to ideal typologies of tribe and state. In their relations to states, tribes have acted in various ways. At times they have
fit into the fragmented societies of Muslim empires by linking distant centers to one another through the provision of important mercantile and military services.[22] At other times, they have hardly fit at
all into the wider social and political systems associated with Islam,
especially as manifested in cities.[23] Occasionally, tribes have interacted with other tribes to form states or, more commonly, with states
to form other kinds of states. Moreover, tribes are just as likely to resist states by acting as antistates as they are to coexist with states.[24]
It is these different permutations that interest the contributors to
this volume.

Let us first look at the circumstances in which tribal societies acquire more stateness, namely highly centralized political features
that are embodied in statelike institutions. Some anthropologists
and historians have addressed this question from an evolutionary

perspective that emphasizes the formation of chiefdoms (also referred to in this volume as chieftaincies) in tribal societies. Chiefdoms may be viewed as one type of intermediate political formation
between tribes and states, incorporating some features and institutions of both. Allen W. Johnson and Timothy Earle have written that
chiefdoms "develop in societies in which warfare between groups is
endemic but becomes directed toward conquest and incorporation
rather than toward the exclusion of defeated groups from their
land." Chiefdoms are therefore not sudden creations, nor can they be
explained by a single causal factor. This perspective suggests that
they evolve gradually and in response to changes in the size of population, wealth, and production and in their degree of political and social stratification.[25]

A chiefdom is a relatively homogeneous confederacy by comparison to more organized states, which are higher political forms on the
evolutionary scale. But it may also exhibit a certain degree of hetero-
geneity in terms of its origins, culture, and class composition. It is a
power-sharing partnership involving pastoral nomads on the margins of cultivation, semisedentarized (especially agriculturalist)
tribesmen, occasionally urban dwellers, and a ruler or chief domi-
ciled in a town or in the countryside. In a chiefdom the nomads and
semisedentarized tribesmen are expected to refrain from internal
disruptions and to contribute military forces for protection and expansion. In return, town dwellers are expected to provide these rural
forces with access to marketing and organized religion. The chief's
function is to supervise the partnership. In chiefdoms the bonds between the chief and society are not necessarily institutionalized;
they tend more often to be based on personal or ad hoc arrangements. In such circumstances the various societal segments of the
chiefdom, notably the tribes, remain intact and still enjoy a considerable degree of political maneuverability and cultural and economic autonomy.

Underlying this evolutionary approach is the notion that chiefdoms are based on a segmentary division of society, in which tribes
or tribal segments are bound together by a common identity based
on kinship. The problem with this approach is that chiefdoms cannot
be defined by kinship alone, given that the chief or ruler is central to
the existence of the chiefdom. In depicting chiefdoms considerably
more attention must be paid to their leadership systems and political processes. Clifford Geertz and Fredrik Barth, among others, have
suggested that political motives expressed in symbolic language and
practices are more important than kinship and segmentary lineage
in the creation and maintenance of chiefdoms.

One vital characteristic of chiefdoms, therefore, is the status and role of their chiefs. Tapper has suggested that for a tribal leader to become a chief, he must first combine a certain "moral authority" over his fellow tribesmen with the ability to deliver a "continuous flow" of goods and services to his other followers. "To retain his wider leadership," however, he must eventually establish a "hereditary dynasty" or acquire "recognition by a more powerful ruler as the legitimate, official leader of his followers."[26] Here it is important to examine the different economic and social systems that tribes inhabited in order to understand their development into chiefdoms. Tribes that became chiefdoms usually had to be comparatively well-off; they had to produce a regular surplus that could "support a class of leaders" and at the same time attract the interest of more powerful rulers or heads of states, who could offer these leaders official recognition in return for state access to, or control over, a share of the surplus. Some tribes that became chiefdoms had, according to Tapper, a "long history of at least nominal subordination to surrounding states: Ottoman, Safavid and Qajar rulers insisted on a measure of administrative control over the tribes, however indirect," using official recognition of "chiefships to this end."[27] Essays by Ernest Gellner and Steven Caton focus on the reasons and ways tribes and tribal leaders contributed to the formation of chiefdoms, including the needs to combat seasonal hardships, mediate feuds, distribute the surplus, and expand the territory by conquest.

Another characteristic of chiefdoms, underscored in the essays by Gellner and Ira Lapidus, is the importance of religion to their maintenance. Religious ideology could enhance the legitimacy of the ruler or chief by granting him religious or saintly authority; moreover, infused into the ideology of the chiefdom, it could strengthen existing bonds between ruler and ruled and provide a raison d'être for a chiefdom's expansion. Religion, however, was not always important in the creation or maintenance of chiefdoms. Most of the chiefdoms that arose and fell in the Arabian Peninsula and North Africa over the centuries were not distinguished from their rivals or enemies by religion. The rule or mediation of the "saints," therefore, was an exception, although an important one.[28]

Caton, in his essay, evaluates different modes of analysis scholars have adopted in examining the relationship of tribes and chiefdoms by highlighting the central features of each, from the Marxist mode to segmentary-lineage theory. He also critically examines Ibn Khaldun's assumptions and relates them to anthropological studies that are accepting of these assumptions, in particular those of Gellner. Tibi's essay complements Caton's by critically examining lit-

erature in political science on tribes and states. Lapidus enumerates
the frequency of chiefdoms throughout Islamic history and suggests
that many of the conquest movements that resulted in the creation of
empires owed their success to the resourcefulness and expansionary
drive of tribal chiefdoms. Thomas Barfield's essay offers an interesting glimpse into the differences between ecological conditions in Inner Asia and in the Arab Middle East; these differences help to
explain why the Turkish and Persian tribes of Inner Asia generated
larger and more durable chiefdoms. Here we may add that chiefdoms in sub-Saharan Africa were also more durable, though not necessarily larger, than those in the Arab Middle East.[29]

Although tribes might coalesce into chiefdoms, they rarely were
long-lived or durable entities. The principal problem faced by chiefdoms was how to endure the powerful fluctuations and disruptions
that occur over time in any human society. In the absence of a strong
central authority, clearly defined territorial boundaries, and population with a cohesive value system, chiefdoms could hardly cope with
dramatic upheavals and change. Several essays in this volume suggest that their fragility was inherent, for two reasons.

First, there was the unstable nature of the chiefdom, with its weak
or nonexistent institutions. It served only limited purposes—
shouldering existential hardships and minor territorial expansion.
Only a minimal government and a fragile alliance among tribes and
between them and their chiefs undergirded the chiefdom. Beyond
this, the spectrum for instability was vast. Because the bonds between tribes in a chiefdom and their chief were personal and ad hoc
in nature, they could be rendered defunct or rescinded any time one
party deemed the partnership unsatisfactory. Tribes might defect
from the alliance, or they might withhold recognition of a particular
chief or openly defy him; at the same time, chiefs could manipulate
tribes and play them against one another. Consequently, chiefdoms
were unstable entities with limited staying power.

A second trait that created difficulties for some chiefdoms was
their tendency to expand. Barfield places greatest emphasis on the
existential necessities that urged chiefdoms, particularly in Inner
Asia, to fight one another and expand by conquest. Lapidus posits
that either a fundamentalist or a Sufi (mystic) brand of Islam loomed
behind expansion. There is no real contradiction in these two kinds
of explanations, however; it was not uncommon for conquests for
control of trade and agriculture to be intertwined with expansionary
drives in the name of religion. No less a student of tribe-state relations than Ibn Khaldun argued that tribal solidarity (*'asabiyya*) was

most effective in the establishment of alliances and as a force of conquest when it was infused with religious ideology.[30]

During expansion, and especially after it peaked, the anomalies of many a chiefdom surfaced as their minimal and unstable governmental arrangements proved unfit to cope with the challenges of expansion. The most serious challenges posed by the acquisition of new territories and peoples were the need to regulate the culture, economy, and political life of newly conquered areas, to integrate them into the dominant administrative system, and to keep the entire realm from disintegrating after the peak of expansion was reached and the anticlimactic routinization of life set in. An Ibn Khaldunian apocalypse, in which tribal 'asabiyya eventually undermined the chiefdom, haunted chiefs. Thus, chiefs with a vision of longer-lasting edifices turned to new strategies. They needed to replace the precarious foundations on which expanded chiefdoms rested with new ones. H. A. R. Gibb's analysis of the evolution of government under the Umayyad Caliph Hisham (724–743) offers a typical characterization of the evolution of chiefdoms into states. After years of expansion, Hisham had to channel the expansionist forces within his domain by directing their energies toward state building; he had to strengthen the institutions of the Islamic Empire to enhance its stability and thus extend its duration.[31] Although only partially successful, Hisham provided a model for ambitious chiefs. Their mission became one of overcoming the limitations of chiefdoms by transforming them into more fully developed states.

It was when chiefdoms established themselves in cities and drew on urban financial and human resources that they became something different. Expansion led to the incorporation of new populations, territories, and sources of wealth in a chiefdom; consequently, tribal society became increasingly stratified. In such circumstances political and economic power might become centralized in the hands of the chief and emerging regional elites, who were often linked to him by a mix of kinship and socioeconomic ties. The demands of warfare, distribution, and trade created the need for centralized control, as distinct from centralized management.[32] Occasionally, chiefdoms became imperial states. In time, rulers became stronger than their tribal allies. They established new, more centralized institutions to administer their enlarged territories. They replaced tribal forces that conquered these territories with standing armies. They began to emulate the imperial traditions and practices of earlier non-Muslim empires, such as Byzantium and Sasanid Persia. Lapidus illustrates how Islamic empires from the Umayyads to the Ottomans and Safavids evolved in this fashion. Gellner stresses the critical role of military-administrative elites (his *"mamluk* solution") in the evolution of chiefdoms into imperial states. Because these slave elites were not bound by kinship or blood ties, they could be completely loyal to their rulers and hence were instrumental in maintaining control and in expanding the frontiers of large states such as the Ottoman Empire. Lapidus again highlights how Islam continued to function as a force for empire building, which gave empires both ideological legitimacy and a sense of continuity with their tribal past. Governments became more bureaucratic and militarily centralized. But the dynastic nature of their leaderships still required consultations with next of kin at the highest governmental level. Interestingly, these empires housed a mix of tribal formations. In fact, both tribes and chiefdoms were more likely to coexist and coevolve with states and empires than they were to evolve into states and empires.

One pattern of state formation involved tribes on the margins of the different imperial states in the Middle East. In the peripheral desert and mountain regions, where central government could not reach, autonomous tribal organizations not only survived but were even granted semiofficial recognition by the imperial government. At different times, such tribal confederacies dominated Kurdistan, the Arabian and Syrian deserts, and the desert and mountain areas of North Africa. Although their distance from the centers of these empires allowed them sufficient autonomy in which to develop their own independent governing structures, the most successful among them became only chiefdoms and not fully developed states, whether in Arabia, along the Upper Nile, or in North Africa. They engaged in conquests, which they justified occasionally by religious motives. These were typically articulated by a religious reformer who emerged from within the tribe or connected with it. Prominent examples include the first Saudi state (1744–1822), the Mahdiyya in the Sudan (1881–1898), and the Sanusiyya in late nineteenth- and early twentieth-century Libya. As a consequence, they formed what Barfield calls "regional states." These states were rarely long-lived, however; inevitably, they ran up against the superior forces of the imperial state on whose frontiers they had established themselves. Some regional states were destroyed; others found only limited opportunities to consolidate their expansion and never became anything more than chiefdoms. Because they remained isolated from Ottoman and European imperial influences, these chiefdoms were not inspired to transform themselves into something else.[33] Paul Dresch's essay demonstrates in the case of the Yemen imamate that such tribal formations or polities did not develop according to a linear process. The local chronicles he exploits suggest just how ephemeral the Yemen imamate was. In the absence of any recognizable forces of stability, the imamate tended to take form and then disintegrate quite rapidly. Dresch's analysis would seem to have applications in other regions of the Middle East and North Africa where tribes existed on the margins of large imperial states.

Tribal formations not only existed in those areas beyond state control but were also prevalent in rural districts over which the state could adopt a form of indirect rule.[34] Tapper has written that "stronger rulers would control the tribes by nominating leaders, keeping chiefly members as hostages, establishing marriage alliances between chiefly and royal families, executing dissidents, or fostering dissension between rivals for leadership or between neighbouring tribes." In such circumstances tribes might accept indirect rule, resort to armed resistance, or try to avoid central control by relocating or reducing their production to a bare subsistence level so as to dampen the state's interest in extending its authority.[35]

These vast, pluralistic imperial states were obliged to accommodate within them different religious and ethnic communities, professional organizations, and groups bound by ties of region and descent. Indeed, group identity was shaped by the ties of particular communities to the different religious, professional, regional, or descent-bound groups that were characteristic of these empires. Imperial states such as the Ottoman Empire and Safavid (and later Qajar) Iran were characterized by a shifting balance of power between tribal and ethnic groups, on the one hand, and bureaucratic and slave institutions, on the other. The tension produced by this shifting balance could at times be creative, though it could just as easily be destructive.

As the twentieth-century successor states emerged from the Ottoman Empire, the tension between tribes and central government could still be detected, though it was expressed in new ways. In the regions over which the imperial state had exercised effective rule (Turkey, Syria, Palestine, and, to some extent, Iraq and Libya) or where European colonization replaced that rule (Algeria, Tunisia, and Egypt), the foundations of the modern states were built on the old imperial framework of institutions or on the new colonial order.[36] In addition, tribal formations still persisted as chiefdoms, particularly in the desert and mountain peripheries where they remained beyond the reach of the Ottoman and Iranian governments and where they continued to thrive and to maintain the traditional cultural basis for their group identity. For instance, the Ottomans adopted a policy in the last decades of the empire to sedentarize the nomadic and seminomadic tribes by force or by financial inducements in order to bring greater stability and state authority to the countryside. Britain, France, and Italy not only encouraged this policy in the former Ottoman territories they occupied but also enhanced it by playing the countryside against the towns, and the nomadic and seminomadic tribes against the new, urban-based nationalist elites. This policy could be seen most vividly in the case of the British in Iraq and Transjordan in the years between the two world wars, but it is also apparent in Syria under the French.[37] By the time that most of the newly independent states had emerged in the aftermath of World War II, such policies had actually helped to preserve and even reinforce certain tribal societies. Consequently, as newly independent states attempted to impose their hegemony, they faced considerable difficulty bringing central government to all corners of their territories. Not surprisingly, the urban-based nationalist elites who came to govern these independent states retained the generally hostile attitude toward the tribes that earlier generations of town dwellers had expressed, one that spoke in pejorative terms of the "tribal problem" and that deemed the tribes unruly and "savage" and therefore in need of rapid incorporation into the state system.[38]

Beck's essay underscores the persistent tension between tribes and states and the new ways it expressed itself in Iran. She illustrates how the Qajar and especially the Pahlavi governments used the military might of the state to weaken autonomous and sometimes rebellious tribal groups. To impose state authority over the countryside, these governments even created "tribes" by combining different rural groups. Moreover, they commonly turned tribal leaders into government agents. But governmental dependence on tribal infrastructures in the armed forces and in the tribal areas only served to bring greater vitality to tribes and tribal identities.

Beck illustrates how the Pahlavi dynasty in Iran harbored a perception of the modern state and sought to introduce reforms in the areas of education, finance, and economic infrastructure. The Pahlavis also propagated a nationalist ideology, one that regarded tribes as backward elements that stood in the way of the state's efforts to control remote areas of the country and impose a national identity throughout Iran. The Italians, as Anderson suggests, regarded the tribes of Libya in much the same manner as the Pahlavis did those of Iran. Kostiner shows in the Saudi case that the tribes were part of a formidable expansionary force on which the Sa'ud family depended until the process of consolidation required them to be subjugated by force to a centralizing, urban-based administration. In Yemen Dresch describes how the Imam Yahya set out to strengthen his rule by reinforcing his family's grip on the state's provinces and by taking hostage family members of recalcitrant tribal chiefs.

The important point these contributors all underscore is that the new states failed to form completely centralized bureaucracies and therefore a monopoly of authority. The transition period from empires or chiefdoms to modern territorial states was either too short or too abrupt and uncomfortably fashioned from European models of state formation. Consequently, the new states still reflected certain tribal habits and had to accommodate a certain measure of tribal power. In Iran, Saudi Arabia, Yemen, and Libya, tribes constituted the main element in the peripheral areas of each country. In Yemen the tribes were strong, autonomous forces that played a major role in determining the outcome of the civil war in the 1960s. In Saudi Arabia and Iran, tribes suffered military defeat, yet they still maintained considerable control over their internal affairs. Tribal chiefs in Iran even became the linchpin of regional administration in rebellious peripheral districts.

In the decision-making sphere, patrimonial practices evolved in several Middle Eastern states. The absence of centralized planning, administrative appointments based on kinship ties, and ad hoc taxation arrangements characterized the situation in Saudi Arabia, Libya, and Yemen until the 1960s. Pahlavi rule in Iran was considerably more institutionalized, though it was not free of domestic societal pressures, including tribal ones.

The new states that emerged in the twentieth century had to adapt to borders that had not previously existed. Encouraged by the European powers, several states signed treaties among themselves in the 1920s and 1930s demarcating these borders. Nonetheless, the frontier territories became particularly difficult to administer; their inhabitants were not willing to surrender their autonomy to a new central authority that wished to establish sovereignty over them. Moreover, neighboring states also treated the inhabitants of these frontier regions as part of their own constituencies or as agents through whom to extend their influence into the other state. Frontier areas thus became hubs for domestic and interstate rivalries, in which local tribes were often found maneuvering among the surrounding governments. Territorial sovereignty as such hardly developed in Saudi Arabia and Yemen until the second half of the twentieth century, when frontier disputes began to ease.

The new states described in this volume have been unable to develop fully integrated communities along the lines of the European nation-state. Tibi suggests in his essay that throughout much of the Middle East the term *nation-state* is only a nominal cover for a mélange of ethnic groups and tribes with different kin-based, regional, and linguistic and cultural identities. Governments clearly have attempted to integrate these groups more effectively by introducing new means of transportation and communications to bring society closer together and by applying a uniform law and religious doctrine to establish general norms of public behavior. In Iran, new dynamics have altered the structures of some tribes, created other tribes, and made some tribes adopt the dominant ethnic and cultural identity of the state. In Saudi Arabia, the royal family has become a cluster of tribal segments; it is heavily intermarried and bound by its elite interests, but it has not been completely successful in imposing a single, unitary identity upon Saudi society. The state identities that emerged after mid-century in Iran, Saudi Arabia, Yemen, and Libya have been based more on "compliance" with the state's existence rather than on modern legitimizing forces.

Several Middle Eastern states have experienced over the past forty years dramatic, even revolutionary changes that have greatly enhanced state formation and altered tribe-state relations in particular. In Iran, Saudi Arabia, and Libya such changes were generated by rather sudden infusions of vast oil revenues, which encouraged rapid urbanization, the spread of modern education, and even industrialization. In Yemen, Libya, and Iran there were revolutions: in Yemen a military coup in 1962 led to an internal war that lasted almost a decade; in Libya the military coup of 1969 sparked substantive ideological and social changes; and in Iran the Islamic revolution of 1979 destroyed the ideological foundations of the Pahlavi state. New social and economic formations and ideological commitments replaced traditional parochial loyalties and sentiments. But the values of tribal society kept affecting states. Indeed, from the perspective of the state, modernization and rapid social change were often counterproductive in that tribes were given a renewed role through their participation in the conflicts these changes inevitably produced.[39]

The essays in this volume illustrate that behind each case of state formation special circumstances loomed: massive European, Turkish, or Arab intervention and sometimes occupation, world and regional wars, and the economic changes and upheavals caused by Western imperialism and vast oil revenues. These forces changed the rules of the game for chiefdoms, forcing them either to strengthen their state functions or dissolve.

Some chiefdoms even established administrations that embraced specifically defined territories, integrated rival segmentary groups, and created the foundations of state legitimacy. Kostiner, Anderson, and Dresch demonstrate that state building was a dialectical process: brief periods of sweeping change were followed by longer periods of adjustment and absorption. Saudi conquest and expansion in the 1920s, the rapid injection of oil wealth in the 1970s, and the introduction of a populist-nationalist ideology in Qaddafi's Libya in the 1970s (which was also accompanied by vast oil wealth) were such sweeping periods of change. The establishment of central and centralizing governments coupled with new opportunities for economic growth and social mobility not only created some movement toward national integration (more in Saudi Arabia and Libya than in Yemen) but also strengthened the territorial integrity of these states. In some instances ethnolinguistic loyalties expressed in the new language of modern nationalism supplanted traditional forms of tribal authority, as in Iran; these new loyalties at times undergirded expansionary states, and at other times they formed the basis of opposition and resistance to states.[40] In other instances tribal and sectarian identities mixed to form subnational movements; the 'Alawis of Syria, as Tibi illustrates, are such a tribe-sect. For the first time the forces of urbanization, modern transportation and communications, and nationalism created new forms of social interaction and bonding. But, as we have suggested, these same external forces encouraged not only state formation but also tribal formation within these states, which could preserve and even strengthen older tribal loyalties. As Beck and other contributors to this volume posit, tribal formation was much more likely to coexist and coevolve with state formation than tribes or chiefdoms were to create states.

Bursts of rapid change were often followed by protracted periods in which adjustments and accommodations to these changes could take place. Here tribalism could play a significant role. Tribal groups, after all, were among the autonomous elements at whom the centralizing and modernizing reforms initiated by the state were directed. Their tendency was to try to slow the reforms down in order to maintain their autonomy. By reasserting familiar tribal traditions and practices, tribes buffered society against the abrasive waves of change. Although they could not nullify reforms, they could help to modify them and thus render change more acceptable to society. "Primordial groups," to offer a variation on a Geertzian theme, not only disturbed the formation of new states; they also helped these states undergo change by providing a practical and symbolic counterbalance that eased the process of state expansion. The ways this happened differed, of course, from country to country. In Libya and Yemen, where governments could not dismantle the tribes, they had to compromise with them at the policy-making level. In Saudi Arabia the patrimonial values of tribalism constitute the bases for group identity and enable both rank-and-file tribesmen and the royal family to preserve that identity. For example, both have been able to employ tribal practices to shortcut bureaucratic procedures.

New forms of patron-client relations have grown up in these states. They play an important role alongside bureaucratic practices in facilitating the distribution of goods and services among the population and in harnessing popular political support behind leaders. Such relations are rarely based on ties of kinship alone but rather are a mix of kinship, class, and political interests.

It is important to reemphasize here that tribal societies rarely formed modern states, though they were often significant contributors to Middle Eastern state formation. Indeed, many Middle Eastern states today still contain tribal societies within them, but tribal states as such do not exist in any meaningful sense of the term. Rather, tribes are one of several dynamic forces that have contributed to state formation. In the Middle East, tribes might be forced to reach an accommodation with the state simply to survive; they might apply leverage on the state to enhance their opportunities vis-à-vis other competitive groups or organizations living within or alongside an expanding state system; or they might try to resist incorporation within the state system and, if successful, even create their own independent governing institutions.

States that contain, or coexist with, tribal societies have encountered difficulty developing the efficient administrative machineries and compelling ideologies necessary to achieve legitimacy. Instead, they have depended heavily on physical and psychological coercion to expand their control. Although such states have acquired powerful repressive apparatuses, tribal practices have provided a practical and symbolic counterweight to state coercion. The degree of legitimacy attained by many Middle Eastern states has depended on the government's ability to establish broad, effective societal coalitions in the service of state ideology. To draw on Alexandre Passerin d'Entrèves, states that seek to incorporate tribal societies wish to create an arrangement between government and society that converts "force into authority," that is, to minimize the abrasive effects of governmental power on society.[41] Rather than framing the contract in terms of sovereignty and natural rights, however, it is framed in terms of tribal concepts relating to the distribution of power among the tribes and between them and the central government.

Unlike the imperial states of Europe and the Middle East, tribal societies have not generated highly developed theories of statecraft. Even the theory of the caliphate, as epitomized by al-Mawardi, is not directly applicable in tribal societies. Although there has been an absence of theory, tribal societies have nonetheless evolved over the centuries their own ways of legitimizing themselves through the formation and management of coalitions.

Hence, modern states that have emerged in societies in which tribes are not marginal have left a special mark on the Middle East. They have not conformed to models of state formation as known in the West because they have not developed the kinds of legitimizing institutions and ideologies that have been common in the West. Similarly, tribal societies have not evolved into modern nations as in Europe or in certain parts of the Middle East itself, as Tibi suggests in his essay. Nor have tribal societies assumed the classical characteristics of the Islamic *umma*, or community of believers, which transcends the concept of the tribe.[42] Rather, they have been built on a series of coalitions that formed over long periods of time and occasionally also generated the institutions of central government. Here the formation of chiefdoms was a much more common occurrence than the formation of states, but even these enjoyed rather limited life spans.

This volume aims for a fuller understanding of the complexities and particular patterns of state formation in regions where tribes have exercised significant influence. One of its central concerns is the continuing viability of tribal structures and systems in contemporary times, within contemporary nation-states. It offers some hypotheses and answers as to why these polities have managed to survive and what impact they have had on modern states. And it points out directions for further research on this important topic.

NOTES

1. As Hodgson has noted, these regions were not hubs of civilizations. Marshall G. S. Hodgson, *The Venture of Islam* (Chicago, 1974), 2:69–78.

2. Ghassan Salamé, Introduction to Salamé, ed., *The Foundations of the Arab State* (London, 1987), 1:1. Also see Peter B. Evans, Dietrich Rueschemeyer, and Theda Skocpol, eds., *Bringing the State Back In* (New York, 1985).

3. For example, Richard Tapper, ed., *The Conflict of Tribe and State in Iran and Afghanistan* (London, 1983); Gabriel Ben-Dor, *State and Conflict in*

the Middle East (Boulder, Colo., 1983); Lisa Anderson, *The State and Social Transformation in Tunisia and Libya, 1830–1980* (Princeton, 1986); John Davis, *Libyan Politics: Tribe and Revolution, Society and Culture in the Modern Middle East* (London, 1987); John Wilkinson, *The Imamate Tradition of Oman* (Cambridge, 1988). The plenary session of the Twenty-third Annual Meeting of the Middle East Studies Association of North America, Toronto, 15–18 November 1989, was devoted to new ways of thinking about the state in the Middle East.

4. For example, Theda Skocpol, *States and Social Revolutions* (Cambridge, 1979); Charles Tilly, ed., *The Formation of National States in Western Europe* (Princeton, 1975); Evans, Rueschemeyer, and Skocpol, *Bringing the State Back In.*

5. Ali Banuazizi and Myron Weiner, eds., *The State, Religion, and Ethnic Politics: Afghanistan, Iran, and Pakistan* (Syracuse, 1986), p. 7.

6. Banuazizi and Weiner, *State, Religion, and Ethnic Politics*, p. 8.

7. Richard Tapper, Introduction to Tapper, *Conflict of Tribe and State*, p. 4.

8. See the discussion by Ernest Gellner, "Cohesion and Identity: The Maghreb from Ibn Khaldun to Emile Durkheim," in Gellner, *Muslim Society* (Cambridge, 1981), pp. 86–98.

9. Tapper, Introduction, p. 47.

10. Tapper, Introduction, pp. 4, 8.

11. Tapper, Introduction, pp. 6, 9.

12. Tapper, Introduction, p. 66.

13. Tapper defines a clan as "a group of people, part of a larger nation or ethnic group, who claim common ancestry, though without necessarily being able to trace it." A clan "may be seen as the cultural or ideological dimension of tribes and their sections, when they are politically-defined groups." Introduction, p. 10.

14. Dale F. Eickelman, *The Middle East: An Anthropological Approach*, 2d ed. (Englewood Cliffs, N.J., 1988), pp. 126–150; Paul Dresch, "The Significance of the Course Events Take in Segmentary Systems," *American Ethnologist* 13 (May 1986); Paul Dresch, "Segmentation: Its Roots in Arabia and Its Flowering Elsewhere," *Cultural Anthropology* 3 (1988):50–67.

15. Roger Owen, "State and Society in the Middle East" (Plenary address to the Twenty-third Annual Meeting of the Middle East Studies Association of North America, Toronto, 15–18 November 1989). The editors wish to thank Dr. Owen for permitting us to quote from his address.

16. Ronald Cohen, Introduction to Ronald Cohen and Elman R. Service, eds., *Origins of the State* (Philadelphia, 1978), p. 2.

17. Tapper, Introduction, p. 11.

18. Joel S. Migdal, "A Model of State-Society Relations," in Howard J. Wiarda, ed., *New Directions in Comparative Politics* (Boulder, Colo., 1985), p. 47.

19. Ben-Dor, *State and Conflict*, pp. 1–34.

20. Maximal stateness means a centralized, bureaucratized administration that permits little autonomy for tribal groups; it means that the society

acknowledges the state's legitimacy over a clearly demarcated territory with established frontiers and that it is fully assimilated into a single nation, with the state being the embodiment of the society's collective will. Minimal stateness, by contrast, means a highly decentralized state authority that permits vast autonomy for tribal groups who do not accept state authority over the territory within the specific borders claimed by the state and who do not subscribe to the same ideological precepts that the state wishes to impose on the society. In the Middle East, because the degree of stateness varies widely between maximalist and minimalist, interactions between states and tribal groups also vary widely. In general, however, modern state identities are considerably diluted in comparison to those in Europe because they remain based both on ascriptive, parochial loyalties and on categorical, national ones. This is bound to be the case where political coalitions among tribal segments are fostered by intermarriage but also are influenced by state-initiated integrative policies, such as the application of a uniform law, religious norms (even revivalist norms), and a national ideology to the society as a whole. See Migdal, "Model of State-Society Relations."

21. Khuri made reference to "cultural substance" in the brief paper he presented to the conference that led to this volume.

22. Hodgson, *Venture of Islam*, 2:62–151.

23. Eickelman, among others, has taken issue with Gellner's theories accounting for "how presumably acephalous and egalitarian tribes organized by segmentary lineages coexisted with the inegalitarian and stratified social order of the cities and states of the [Middle East] region." Eickelman, *Middle East*, pp. 137–138; Gellner, "Political and Religious Organization of the Berbers of the Central High Atlas," in Ernest Gellner and Charles Micaud, eds., *Arabs and Berbers: From Tribe to Nation in North Africa* (London, 1972), pp. 25–58; Gellner, "Flux and Reflux in the Faith of Men," in Gellner, *Muslim Society*, p. 185.

24. Eickelman, *Middle East*, p. 130.

25. Allen W. Johnson and Timothy Earle, *The Evolution of Human Societies: From Foraging Group to Agrarian State* (Stanford, 1987), pp. 21–22.

26. Tapper, Introduction, pp. 54–55, 57.

27. Tapper, Introduction, p. 60.

28. Tapper notes that in Iran and Afghanistan, when religious leaders were able to unite large groups into confederacies, "the hope of material gain and the absence of material cause for conflict" were often more important factors than religious ideology. Introduction, p. 50.

29. Eickelman, *Middle East*, p. 130.

30. This is one of the main theses presented by Ibn Khaldun in *The Muqaddimah*, trans. Frantz Rosenthal (Princeton, 1967).

31. H. A. R. Gibb, "The Evolution of Early Government in Islam," in Gibb, *Studies in the Civilization of Islam* (London, 1962), pp. 34–45.

32. Johnson and Earle, *Evolution of Human Societies*, pp. 244–245.

33. Yitzhak Nakash, "Fiscal and Monetary Systems in the Mahdist Sudan, 1881–1898," *International Journal of Middle East Studies* 20 (August 1988):365–385.

34. It is doubtful that tribal formations existed in the main urban centers. Certainly, kinship units were (and are) important in cities, but what was lacking was precisely the kind of authority we have associated with chieftainship. In cities, chieftainship only came into being in a condition of political anarchy and social disintegration. Beirut in the 1980s is one contemporary example of city-based chieftainships.

35. Tapper, Introduction, p. 54.

36. See Albert Hourani, "The Ottoman Background of the Modern Middle East," in Hourani, *The Emergence of the Modern Middle East* (London, 1981), pp. 1–18.

37. For example, Hanna Batatu, *The Old Social Classes and the Revolutionary Movements of Iraq* (Princeton, 1978), pp. 63–152; Mary C. Wilson, *King Abdullah, Britain, and the Making of Jordan* (Cambridge, 1987), pp. 85–102; Philip S. Khoury, "The Tribal Shaykh, French Tribal Policy, and the Nationalist Movement in Syria between Two World Wars," *Middle Eastern Studies* 18 (April 1982):180–193.

38. Tapper has written that "the general view of tribal society among contemporary writers of the nineteenth and early twentieth centuries opposed it to settled urban society, the civilised Islamic ideal. While the city was the source of government, order and productivity, the tribes had a natural tendency to rebellion, rapine and destruction, a tendency which might be related to the starkness of their habitat and its remoteness from the sources of civilisation, and also to the under-employment inherent in their way of life. Such a view has some justification, but it is superficial and oversimplified." Introduction, p. 6.

39. Milton J. Esman and Itamar Rabinovich, eds., *Ethnicity, Pluralism and the State in the Middle East* (Ithaca, 1988), pp. 3–24.

40. Banuazizi and Weiner, *State, Religion, and Ethnic Politics*, pp. 3, 19–20.

41. Alexandre Passerin d'Entrèves, *The Notion of the State: An Introduction to Political Theory* (Oxford, 1967).

42. Joseph Kostiner, "State and the 'Crisis' of Legitimacy in the Arab World" (Paper presented to a joint session of the Emile Bustani Middle East Seminar at MIT and the Harvard Center for International Affairs Middle East Seminar, Cambridge, Mass., 7 April 1988).

PART ONE

Historical, Anthropological, Methodological, and Comparative Perspectives

Tribes and State Formation in
Islamic History

Ira M. Lapidus

The title of this essay, "Tribes and State Formation in Islamic History," is wonderfully ambiguous. It is not clear what any of the key words mean. What I would like to do is discuss a certain type of rural social organization commonly called tribes, but which is better described as chieftaincies, in relation to states and empires in the greater Middle East (that is, the Middle East, Inner Asia, and North Africa) from the beginning of the Islamic era to the nineteenth century. First, I would like to make some general remarks about the *longue durée* in Middle Eastern history to indicate the framework in which I see the relations of tribes or chieftaincies and empires. By the Islamic era Middle Eastern patterns of tribe-empire relations already had a history reaching back to the fourth and third millennium B.C., when neolithic village communities evolved into societies on the scale of temple-city, city-state, and empire, and agrarian-urban-imperial societies came into being. By then Middle Eastern societies were organized around a tripartite structure of parochial units (lineages, villages, tribes, or chieftaincies), religious associations, and empires. On the eve of the Islamic era the region was divided into two imperial realms, the Byzantine and Sasanian empires, whose populations were each organized into several Christian churches and other religious collectivities and into smaller local units on the scale of family, lineages, or small clientele and residential groups. In this period there was a clear differentiation of empire and religious bodies, though the authority of rulers was based on religious charisma and entailed a considerable degree of control over religious institutions.

The Islamic era represented profound continuities and equally profound changes. In this era the basic institutional framework of

past Middle Eastern civilization—the tripartite arrangement of
tribal, religious, and empire collectivities, and the sedentary-
agricultural and city-commercial economies—were taken over in
toto. At the same time the Islamic era generated new variations on
the older institutional structures, above all, a new religious culture
and new political identities.

These redefinitions proceeded through three principal phases.
The first was the early Arab-Muslim empire (seventh to tenth centuries), which set the cultural norms for the new civilization. The second was the age of the Turkish migrations and Saljuqid regimes of
the eleventh and twelfth centuries, in which these cultural ideals
were translated into the framework of a mass society. By then the
bulk of the Middle Eastern population had been converted to Islam,
and the processes of forming an Islamic identity, Islamic religion,
and Islamic forms of state and community were largely complete.
The third and final phase was the reorganization of these Islamic
Middle Eastern societies into their definitive premodern forms under the Ottoman and Safavid empires and the several Islamic states
of the sixteenth to nineteenth centuries.

At the same time that Middle Eastern societies were acquiring
their Islamic identity, the twin processes of Islamization and state
formation spread from the Middle East proper into the peripheral
regions of Arabia, North Africa, and the steppe lands of Inner Asia.
The Arab and Turkish migrations induced state formation and the
spread of Islam in areas that hitherto had not been organized as
state or imperial societies. These new regions became integral parts
of a greater Middle Eastern Islamic society, organized on the tripartite institutional framework of tribes or chieftaincies, religious associations, and empires. I shall briefly introduce each of these institutions.

The concept of tribe is unclear and controversial. The word is
used to refer to a kinship group, an extended family, or a coalition of
related families. It may refer to the elite family from whom some
larger confederation gets its name, to a cultural, ethnic, or other non-
familial social group, or to conquest movements of pastoral peoples
without regard for the internal basis of cohesion. I will not take a position about the meaning of tribe except to make clear that I am not
talking about small-scale family groups, cooperative herding, or village communities but about political entities that organize fragmented rural populations—be they small kinship or clientele groups
or ad hoc alliances of individuals conceived as an extended family—
into large-scale alliances. Such large-scale political entities may be
conceived by their members in terms of a common mythic ancestry,

but usually the leadership is defined in terms of patriarchal, warrior, or religious chieftaincies. In the Middle East, chieftaincies are generally found among pastoral peoples, though this type of social structure is also present among semisedentary, mountain, and even peasant populations. Although I may use the word *tribe* for convenience, it should be clear that tribes in my sense are not familial or ethnic groups but political and religious chieftaincies whose composition varies greatly.

The second type of collectivity in the Islamic era was the religious associations. These were made up of the followers or devotees of an *'alim*, a Sufi, or some other holy man who was an inspired teacher and exemplar for his group. Such associations were generally local, but they were commonly affiliated into larger networks such as the *madhdhahib* or schools of law, theological schools, Sufi *turuq*, and Khariji or Shi'i sects. In Muslim societies we do not find a hierarchical organization of such groups, though the authority of certain master teachers may become widespread. Religious associations were in principle separate from state or imperial regimes, having different personnel and a different ethos from that of the state elites. In many instances, however, states managed to achieve some kind of control over their operations.

The third principal institutional feature of Middle Eastern societies was states or empires. Middle Eastern empires in this period were commonly organized by conquering or other military elites. They administered the regions they controlled through a combination of bureaucratic and quasi-feudal means—the *iqta'* being the most common form of decentralized fiscal administration—and were legitimized by a combination of Islamic and non-Islamic symbols. Almost every Middle Eastern regime cultivated its identity as a successor state to that of the Prophet in Medina or as a regime serving an Islamic religious purpose; at the same time, each patronized an artistic and cultural style that established its cosmological-universal, cosmopolitan-cultural, or patrimonial claims to legitimacy.[1]

These collective structures were systematically interrelated. Although tribes and empires represent, in one sense, an evolutionary sequence, once the sequence had been fully realized, the issue became one of the construction, deconstruction, and reconstruction of tribal chieftaincies and imperial entities. Ever since the third millennium B.C. empires have been the most encompassing collective bodies. Tribes had a large role to play in Middle Eastern societies, but they almost always played their part in the context, or under the umbrella, of empire regimes. By the Islamic era tribal populations constantly interacted with state-sedentary communities and were integral elements of a more encompassing system. Even tribal societies in Inner Asia, Arabia, and North Africa, outside of state domains, entered into regular exchanges with the imperial societies and were strongly influenced by the political, economic, and cultural forces radiating from the state centers. Though tribal chieftaincies from the periphery might repeatedly conquer the imperial-sedentarized Middle East, they would themselves evolve into states and be integrated into the larger civilization.

In cultural terms, the Islamization of the greater Middle East also led to a reformulation of tribe-state relations in Islamic terms. From the fourteenth to the nineteenth centuries Sufism became a common organizing mechanism for Middle Eastern rural populations, especially in North Africa and Inner Asia, and gave them and the empire-organized societies a shared, albeit differently understood, cultural framework to articulate the complex relations among them. I stress this point because it is misleading to look upon Middle Eastern societies as primarily tribal or to think of empires as a derivative or secondary phenomenon. In fact, we are dealing with a system involving two types of political and cultural entities, often on the same territory, competing for power and legitimacy.[2]

To better understand the chieftaincy-empire system, I want to examine a few basic modalities of this relationship: (1) the organization of conquest movements leading to state formation in stateless regions or to the reorganization of states in regions that already have a history of states or empires; (2) the transformation of conquest states into routinized states or imperial governments; and (3) the relation of routinized or institutionalized empires to the tribal populations within and outside their boundaries.

CONQUEST MOVEMENTS

The first modality is the organization of fragmented rural populations into conquest movements. In spite of the use of the term *tribal* in describing them, conquest movements in Islamic Middle Eastern history have little to do with kinship. For many of us, the nature of tribal solidarity, the character of tribal leadership, and the ideological or conceptual basis of tribal unification have been defined by Ibn Khaldun. Ibn Khaldun gave us the concept of *'asabiyya*, tribal bonding or the sentiment of group solidarity that results from kinship, blood ties, and common descent. This natural sentiment, grounded in the impulse to provide mutual help, leads to the banding together of Bedouins to fight for survival and domination over others. Their solidarity is reinforced by chiefs who promote internal harmony, fortify the group will to power and royal authority, and direct it outward to the aggrandizement of its interests. Though *'asabiyya*, in Ibn Khaldun's view, is a kinship phenomenon, religion is critical to its expression. Arab peoples in particular need religion to achieve the levels of *'asabiyya* essential to conquest and royal authority because their natural savagery ordinarily inhibits cooperation. Religion enables them to restrain themselves and cooperate in a common cause. It supplements family loyalties to create wider, more encompassing solidarities.[3]

Despite the authority of Ibn Khaldun, if we look empirically at Middle Eastern conquest movements, we find that kinship was a secondary phenomenon. Such movements as the Arab, Fatimid, Almoravid, Almohad, Safavid, and other conquests were not based on lineage but on the agglomeration of diverse units, including individuals, clients, religious devotees, and fractions of clans as well as perhaps lineages and clans. The diverse elements were united in one of two principal ways. Among Arabs who did not accept political hierarchy and whose leaders were required to be mediators, the most common form of agglomeration was religious chieftainship under a charismatic religiopolitical leader. The elite religious cadres, ruling subordinate units, were bound together by religious commitment or ideology. In such movements there was an uneasy tension between the religious and prereligious bases of organization.[4] Among Turkish Inner Asian peoples who accepted hierarchical rule and recognized dynastic rule, the most common form of leadership was the warrior chieftaincy supported by a lineage, clan, or *committatis*—a band of warriors who in turn won the allegiance of other such warrior units and thereby dominated a subject population. Tribes were in effect the creatures of religious or political elites. Genealogical factors may have been important in the constitution of clear-cut aristocratic groups, in small participation kinship units, or in theoretical self-image, but they were not significant in the actual organization of the larger movements.

The paradigm for the first type is, of course, the Arab conquests. We commonly think of Arabian society on the eve of the conquest as having been built around extended families or lineage groups, but despite the existence of this concept in the minds of Arabians, there is in fact no evidence of large-scale genealogically defined tribes. H. A. R. Gibb and M. A. Shaban have cogently argued that Arabian tribal confederations were creations of the post–Arab conquest garrison cities. The movement of a large Arab population and its sedentarization in the garrison towns and cities of the Middle East broke down old family and lineage structures. To meet the insecurity of the garrison towns, to cope with the stresses of a changing society, and to compete successfully for power, Arab populations became ever more self-consciously Arab in identity and ever more formally organized in terms of the tribal models provided by their culture but not found in their social experience. The garrison cities gave us the ad hoc alliances conceived as the tribes of Qays, Yemen, and other regions.[5]

In pre-Islamic Arabia, rather, we find collectivities of clans such as the Quraysh, who were not organized under patriarchal leadership but were unified by a *mala*, or representative council of chiefs, and by shared religious affiliation with the *haram*, the sanctuary of Mecca. Mecca was thus a shrine-based, rather than a strictly tribal, community. The confederations of Ghassan and Lakhm were not tribes but monarchies, built on Byzantine and Sasanian political support and governing smaller units, perhaps clans. In Yemen there was a long history of monarchical rule over subordinate or vassal tribal auxiliaries. The principal mechanisms of large-scale organization in sixth-century Arabia, then, were conciliar or monarchical rather than patriarchal or genealogical.

Furthermore, the early Muslim *umma* was not based on lineages or tribes alone but was composed of several different elements. First were the *muhajirun*, the Meccans who left their kin in order to cleave unto Muhammad and migrate with him to Medina. There were the *ansar*, the first Medinians who accepted Islam from the Prophet and who were followed by several of the Medianian clans. In Medina there were also individual émigrés, dissident groups, and fractions of clans from other parts of Arabia who left their people to join the Prophet. Eventually the *umma* included the converts made from among the aristocratic clans of Mecca and the various tribes in western Arabia who became allied to the Muslim community. Thus, the components of the *umma* were disparate, including individuals, groups without a lineage basis, and clans with a definite tribal affiliation. The underlying unifying concept of the community was religious, though there were strong undertones of lineage appeal owing to the fact that the concept of *umma* was fused with concepts of tribal alliance; the image of the religious chief was identified with that of the traditional clan shaykh. The early *umma* was built on an undifferentiated tribal religiopolitical identity and an undifferentiated religiopolitical leadership.[6]

The history of conquest movements in North Africa confirms the fact of religious, rather than kinship and lineage, *'asabiyya* as the basis of conquest movements. In North Africa long-standing Berber concepts of kinship, lineage, and tribal identity had not led to conquest movements and Berber-based state formation. Instead, it was Roman influence in Tunisia and in the coastal zones of western North Africa that provided the region with its spotty history of organized states and urban development. It took the Arab conquests, Arab elites, and Muslim concepts to supply the authority and the ideology for the first wave of Berber state formation in what is now southern Tunisia, Algeria, and Morocco. Kharijism in the case of the Rustamids, Shiʻism in the case of the Idrisids and Fatimids, reformist Islam in the case of the Almoravids and Almohads, and Sufism in the cases of the Saʼdians and ʻAlawis show that Islam could be used for the unification of fragmented populations. Repeated religious movements played a critical role in the Islamization of the region, facilitated the spread of the Maliki school of law and of Sufism, and helped give a political-territorial identity to Morocco. This is not to say that all North African state formation was entirely based on religious movements. The Aghlabid and Hafsid states were based on imperial ʻAbbasid and Almohad authority. There were also nonreligious coalitions led by the Zirids, the Hammadids, the Zayanids, and the Marinids.[7]

The Almohad case illustrates the importance of religious leadership, rather than tribal kinship, for a conquest movement. In this case the central authority was based not on lineage charisma but on religious purity. Claiming descent from the Prophet and professing to be the promised *mahdi*, Abu ʻAbdallah Muhammad ibn Tumart followed the precedent of the Prophet and modeled his life on that of Muhammad. He preached the necessity of returning to the true Islam—the Islam based on the Qurʼan, *hadith*, and the teachings of the companions. He affirmed a unitarian view of God, defended the Ashʻari theological position as opposed to anthropomorphic views, and called for a high standard of Muslim morality and the strict application of Muslim law. He was hostile to music and to the unveiling of women.

Ibn Tumart found his supporters among settled Masmuda Berbers. These supporters included his disciples, *tolba* or preachers, and *huffaz* or students, as well as the populace of Tinmal, his capital city, which was not a tribal group but a diverse sedentarized population with many disciples from elsewhere. The kinship groups comprised in this coalition were Ibn Tumart's own family, the Hargha, and fractions of the various principal tribes of the Atlas region drawn from the Hintata, the Gadmiwa, the Sauda, and others. It later included Sanhaja as well as Zenata Berbers. This coalition was made without regard to conventional kinship, lineage, or tribal concepts of

solidarity. Like the coalition of the Prophet Muhammad, the Almohad movement represented a fusion of clan, religious, and political
identities rather than lineage *'asabiyya*.[8]

A third example is the Safavid movement, which arose in very different conditions. This movement originated in northwestern Iran in
the thirteenth century in the context of widespread and destructive
nomadic Turkish and Mongol invasions, the ruin of towns, and the
decline of state protection. Sufi preachers and shamans took the
lead in organizing the population of western Anatolia, northeastern
Iran, and northern Mesopotamia. They performed miraculous cures,
manipulated occult forces, and claimed a religious authority based
on esoteric knowledge vouchsafed through direct revelation or the
interpretation of magical texts. They taught their battered followers
that a savior would come to redeem ordinary people and that the
qutb, the pillar of the saintly world, would provide a haven for the
oppressed. These Sufi teachers promoted the veneration of tomb
shrines, some of them of contemporary origin, others reviving earlier saint cults. They organized *khanaqa*s or *zawiya*s, which became
a refuge for distressed populations. These shrines were taken over by
the descendants of the founding saints, who thereby became administrators and the heads of local political communities.[9]

The Safavid movement was typical of these developments. The
founder, Shaykh Safi al-Din (1252–1334), began by preaching the purification of Islam. His son, Sadr al-Din, turned the movement into a
hierarchical and propertied organization, expanding the family com-
pound in Ardabil, providing it with residences and schools, and organizing a hierarchy of missionaries, students, and novices. The
Safavids at first claimed Sufi authority and were affiliated with
Sunni Islam, but they later declared a Shi'i allegiance. Shah Isma'il
(1487–1524) proclaimed that he was descended from the seventh
imam, the seventh descendant in the Safavi line, the incarnation of
Khidr, the bearer of ancient wisdom, the messiah, and the possessor
of both temporal power and mystical rulership.

In the fifteenth century the Safavids took advantage of the
breakup of the Aqquyunlu regime to turn from preaching to militant
action. Shaykh Junayd, Sufi master from 1447 to 1460, was the first
to gather his followers and lead them in the jihad against Christians
in Georgia and Trebizond and then against the Muslim states, which
he denounced as infidel regimes. From Asia Minor and northern
Syria came persons identified by the names of districts, which suggests that they were not members of lineage or kinship groups but
soldiers and adventurers from specific regions now given political
organization by the Safavid order. From Iran came Turkish, Kurdish,

and Luri-speaking pastoralists, peasants, artisans, and middle-level lineage chieftains, who joined the Safavids to oppose the more powerful local lords. In addition, Shaykh Junayd married into the families of local princes to form military alliances and recruit large-scale tribes to his cause. He recruited his followers among both individuals and local tribal (or, as they are called in Inner Asia and northern Iran, *uymaq*) chieftains. The principal recruits were called Qizilbash after the distinctive red headgear that showed they were the disciples and warriors of the Safavid house. Thus, the Safavid movement united individuals, clientele groups, and *uymaq*s into a unified force that eventually conquered Iran. This case is interesting because it is relatively rare for conquest movements in Turkish societies to be organized under religious leadership. Perhaps here Sufism met the special needs of the heterogeneous populations of northern Iran and eastern Anatolia.[10]

A second basis for the organization of conquest movements was nonreligious—warrior authority commonly found among the Turkish populations of Inner Asia, northern Iran, and Anatolia. Some critical examples are the Qarakhanids, Saljuqs, Ottomans, Uzbeks, and Kazakhs. Turkish societies in Inner Asia, like Arab societies, were conceived in kinship and genealogical terms, but the actual units of social organization were based on loyalty to successful warrior chieftains. The status of a chief was earned by victory in battle; authority depended on success in the struggle for power, though chieftaincy in Turkish societies might also have had a religious component. The Sufi *babas* who led Turkish warrior bands in the conquest of Asia Minor and the Balkans represented a variant type of warrior chieftaincy combined with religious appeal. Success showed the hand of God.

The chief was supported by his warrior clients, his family, and other, lesser chieftains and their followers and families. The support of these lesser chiefs was won by success in war and by delicate negotiation. The chief used this core of military support to overwhelm townsmen and peasants, collect taxes, and establish a territorial government. This type of chieftaincy, called an *uymaq*, was in effect a state regime, though the leading families tended to identify themselves in genealogical terms. *Uymaq*s were generally unstable, however, because they were based on the personal prowess of the chiefs and the loyalty of semi-independent warriors who constantly calculated their relative advantage, bitterly competed for leadership, and regularly rebelled against the dominance of the greater chieftains.[11]

This type of formation is also important in the origins of the Ottoman Empire. The founder of the Ottoman dynasty was not a lineage chief but a successful frontier warrior who won the support of frontier freebooters, *ghazi*s, and even Byzantine defectors, whom he united by their shared interest in conquest and in service to himself. The Osmanli dynasty and tribe were formed out of these warrior loyalties. Neither family, language, nor religion were critical in the early organization of the empire. Only later did the Ottomans replace this type of warrior tribe by a state system of administration.[12]

Other Inner Asian confederations, such as the Golden Horde, its offshoots in the Crimea and in the Volga region, the Uzbeks, and the Kazakhs, were similarly organized. They, too, were coalitions or hordes formed under the authority of warrior elites backed by a confederation of families who took their identity from that of the dominant chiefs. Islam came at a secondary stage in the history of these societies. It helped consolidate the identity of khanates, hordes, and *uymaq*s but does not seem to have played a critical role in their origin. Thus, *'asabiyya* in Inner Asia was based neither on kinship nor on religion but on predator solidarity. Only successful chiefs won the opportunity to legitimate themselves in tribal, patrimonial, or imperial terms.[13]

Thus, so-called tribes and tribal conquests show little evidence of kinship as an important factor in state formation and much evidence of religious, or chieftaincy, and warrior solidarity. Although there are other factors in the agglomeration of conquest movements, from our point of view religious and warrior solidarity are the critical factors in the major historical cases.

FROM CONQUEST MOVEMENT TO STATE REGIMES

The next issue is how conquest movements were transformed into empires. The critical feature of this transformation was the differentiation of conquest movements into separate tribal, religious, and political collectivities. The first aspect of this process was the displacement of the conquering tribal forces by a new government. Tribal leaders were supplemented by administrative-scribal cadres commonly drawn from the subject or conquered populations. Tribal armies were routinely supplemented and even replaced by newly recruited forces expected to be more dependent on, and loyal to, the rulers. This was the case for the Umayyad-'Abbasid, Fatimid, Almoravid, Almohad, Saljuq, Ottoman, Safavid, and other Middle Eastern regimes.

The Umayyad-'Abbasid empire gives us the paradigmatic case. The position of the caliph as military and administrative overlord of a large empire inevitably changed him from a religious patriarch of a small community into an imperial ruler. The transformation of the conquest movement into an empire was furthered by the creation of client military forces and routine fiscal administration. Umayyad military policy aimed for almost a century at replacing the general *levée en masse* of the Arabs with selected client forces, whether Arab, Berber, Iranian, or Soghdian. The 'Abbasids completed the process by demobilizing the Arab masses in favor of politically reliable armies. Free soldiers were replaced by dependent slave and client forces. The 'Abbasids first depended on the Arab troops who had brought them to power, then on Persian regiments from the Transoxanian principalities, and finally on Turkish slave forces. Apart from Bedouin auxiliaries in Mesopotamia, Arabs were removed from the caliphal armies. The state military apparatus was no longer identified with the tribal armies that had conquered the empire, and the remnants of these armies became part of the subject population.[14]

Similarly, the Umayyad and 'Abbasid caliphs displaced Arab shaykhs in favor of administrators drawn from the former Byzantine and Sasanian bureaucracies. The tax-collecting bureaus were used to strengthen the financial and political position of the caliphate at the expense of Arab tribal elites. Thus, the 'Abbasids replaced Arab rule with a kind of coalition government in which eastern Iranian, Iraqi, Nestorian, and Baghdadi Shi'i scribes shared power with Turkish military slaves.[15]

There were similar tendencies in the history of other conquest movements. The Fatimids replaced their Berber tribesmen with Turkish and Sudanese slaves and a Coptic Egyptian administrative apparatus. The Almohads added to their Berber forces Arab, Turkish, Kurdish, and black slave troops as well as Andalusian scribes. In these cases the original Berber conquerors were not entirely displaced, but a balance of power more favorable to the rulers was created by the recruitment of more diverse forces.[16] In Iran a similar pattern was followed. The Safavids destroyed the original Qizilbash supporters of the dynasty and replaced them with a Georgian slave army. They also integrated Persian functionaries into the administration. Still more ruthlessly and successfully did the Ottomans replace the *ghazi* Turkish warriors with slave janissaries and the most centralized and efficient of all Middle Eastern bureaucracies.[17]

The second principal feature of the transformation of conquest movements into empires was a change in the concept of the ruler and the principles by which his rule was legitimized. As charismatic religious leaders (or their immediate successors) gave way to emperors, the successors continued to claim divine authority, but they also progressively adopted the monarchical panoply of the regimes they had conquered. The Umayyads incorporated Byzantine art, architecture, and ceremonial style into the caliphal identity. Their coinage and the monumental architecture signified that they were successors not only to the Prophet but also to the emperors of Rome and Constantinople. Similarly, the 'Abbasid caliphs became patrons of science and philosophy and translated Pahlavi and Hellenistic literatures, as well as becoming patrons of Islam, to signify their legitimacy in historic Middle Eastern terms.[18] A similar evolution from religious to monarchical identity was characteristic of the Almohads. 'Abd al-Mu'min was titled *amir al-muslimin* and caliph of Ibn Tumart. The first successor of Ibn Tumart no longer claimed full personal authority to define religious doctrine but rather a caliphal or executive role.

The Safavid and the Moroccan Sa'dian and 'Alawi cases were somewhat different. In these cases the rulers also moved from the purely personal toward institutional forms of authority, but they still maintained their claims to personal religious charisma. In the Safavid case the claims of the Sufi master to direct divine inspiration were allowed to lapse, though the concept of the ruler as the descendant of the seventh imam, and the principal authority of Shi'i Islam, was held intact until the end of the Safavid era. At the same time, however, the Safavids cultivated, assiduously and brilliantly, the historic images of Iranian monarchy. Safavid manuscript illuminations and architecture consolidated the place of the dynasty in the history of Iranian kings of kings. Safavid authority, then, was built on both a lingering charismatic personal appeal and a thorough assimilation to Iranian forms of monarchy.[19]

The Moroccan cases resemble the Safavid in the sense that the Sa'dian and 'Alawi sultans also combined the concept of descent from the Prophet and Sufi *baraka* with an institutional form of sultanal authority. These rulers had important ritual roles at Muslim holidays and shared in the national veneration of Sufi saints, but they were also regarded as caliphs, as executors of the Prophet for the defense and administration of the community. They were caliphs and imams as well as *sharifs*, *walis*, and *mujtahids*.[20] In Morocco there was an unusual perpetuation of personal authority within the conquest movement into an institutional monarchy; but in general, state formation effected changes in the symbolic and ideological identity of rulers and brought about an evolution from personal to institutional forms of leadership and from religious to political forms of authority. The great leaders of the religious movements were succeeded not by charismatic saints or Prophet reformers, but by *khalifas*, deputies, and executors who combined their original religious authority with the inherited routinized forms of Middle Eastern monarchies.

The third aspect of the routinization of conquest movements was the formation of separate state and religious institutions that defied their ideological claims. We have already seen how the Ummayad and 'Abbasid rulers took on increasingly secularized functions and identities. At the same time, the religious and spiritual heritage of the Prophet came to be embodied in his companions and their disciples rather than in his caliphs. Teaching of the Qur'an, reflection on legal and theological issues, moral preaching, and devotional activities were diffused throughout the community of loyal Muslims rather than concentrated in the caliphate. Private scholars and holy men came to be the bearers of the religious aspect of the Prophet's legacy. Around these holy men clustered small groups of devotees who gradually developed into organized schools of law, theological sects, Shi'i communities, and, later, Sufi lineages and brotherhoods.

In the eighth and ninth centuries the caliphate and the emergent communities of scholars and holy men were locked into a struggle for religious authority. The 'Abbasid caliphs continued to claim a divine authority and the right to determine the boundaries of true faith and punish heretics and deviants. Al-Ma'mun (813–833) came into direct conflict with the scholars as a result of his effort to make the doctrine of the createdness of the Qur'an an obligatory Muslim belief and assert his authority over the religious teachers. This effort was resisted by the Hanbalis; the caliphs were forced to concede that the doctrine of the created Qur'an was not official Muslim belief and that they did not have the authority to define such belief. This concession marked in effect the recognition of religiocommunal life independent of the caliphate. The emergence of an autonomous, segmented, and sectarian Islamic religiocommunal life separate from the state marks the onset of the differentiation of state and religious institutions.[21]

The differentiation of conquest movements into separate religious and state institutions was repeated in other cases. Such a differentiation marked the Almohad regime. 'Abd al-Mu'min did not claim the personal authority of the founder. Later Almohad rulers abandoned the early doctrines of the movement and eventually renounced them completely in favor of a return to Maliki law. They gave up the effort to create a purified Muslim community, accepted the existing Maliki legal establishment and the popular cults of saints and Sufis, and ratified the already established structures of Muslim religious life. Thus, a unified religiopolitical movement integrated itself into the conquered society by accepting the existing differentiation between state and religious elites and associations.[22]

Similarly, the Safavids built up the cadres of a routine Shi'i religious establishment. Ithna-'ashari Shi'ism was proclaimed the official religion of Iran, and messianic Shi'i claims were set aside. The Safavids imported Syrian, Iraqi, and Arabian Shi'i scholars to administer a new system of courts and schools. To sustain the new official religion, Ithna-'ashari Shi'ism was imposed by a wave of persecutions that has little or no parallel in other Muslim countries. The Safavids destroyed their messianic-minded Shi'i followers, eliminated Sunni 'ulama' and Sufi holy men, and made the Shi'i 'ulama' the sole representatives of Islam in Iran.[23] As with the 'Abbasids, the Almohads, and other Muslim regimes, religious and political authority were in practice, if not in theory, differentiated. Parallel institutions built around distinct elites had emerged. The routinization of a religious-conquest movement had led again to the separation of religiocommunal and state elites and collectivities.

The conquest movements based on warrior chieftainship rather than combined religiopolitical authority did not, of course, go through this process of differentiation. From the outset, rulers in the Turkish tradition saw themselves as patrons and protectors, perhaps even managers, of religion but not as personal repositories of religious knowledge or spiritual power. Many Turkish rulers sought patrimonial, cosmopolitan-cultural, and cosmological legitimation for their kingships and became patrons of the existing schools of law and Sufi brotherhoods. The conquest movements based on warrior 'asabiyya easily accepted the already developed imperial sedentary pattern of separate state and religious institutions.

Thus, conquest movements represented relatively less differentiated societies in which family or group solidarity, religious affiliation, and warrior leadership were closely identified. Armies and administrations were scarcely distinct from the totality of the male warrior population. Conquest, however, led to the transformation of chieftaincies into empires—to the specialization of military and administrative functions, the separation of religious and political authority, and the transformation of religious or warrior leaders into emperors.

TRIBALISM IN STATE-ORGANIZED SOCIETIES

The third and final phase is the relationship of fully formed, routinized imperial governments to chieftaincies. For the purposes of this part of the analysis, I will choose illustrations from the history of the

Middle East in the sixteenth to nineteenth centuries. In this period, major conquest movements ceased to occur, and the relations of tribes and states stabilized.

Two major geographical and political constellations emerged. The first was the Ottoman Empire, which ruled the Balkans, Anatolia, the urban areas of the Fertile Crescent, lower Egypt, and coastal North Africa. In the empire the central state triumphed over its tribal components. In the midst of the fourteenth-century conquests, the Ottoman dynasty was already developing the state apparatus, using Saljuq and Byzantine models, precedents, and even personnel. The Ottomans built up slave infantry and artillery forces and a centralized administration. They brought the *'ulama'* under state patronage and eventually under state control. At the same time, Sufism was spreading among the nomadic and pastoral Turkish populations of eastern Anatolia. Sufi leaders spearheaded the Ottoman conquests and opposed the consolidation of a bureaucratic administration. Eastern Anatolia, like northwestern Iran, was a breeding ground for Sufi revolts that espoused messianic beliefs. The high point of this agitation was coincident with the rise of the Safavids. For example, in 1519 a Sufi preacher named Jelal took the name of Shah Isma'il, claimed to be the *mahdi*, and organized Turkish cultivators and pastoralists to oppose the state. The sixteenth century brought further and frequent revolts in the name of Jelal. However, the Ottomans progressively defeated these movements and established a long-lasting political control over most of their territory. With a vast region under state control, tribal formations remained alive only on the Ottoman periphery, in eastern Anatolia, the North Arabian desert margins of the Fertile Crescent, Arabia, Upper Egypt, and the southern zones of North Africa.[24] It is noteworthy that the great religious movements and tribal societies of the eighteenth and nineteenth centuries—the Wahhabi, the Sanusi, and the Mahdist (Sudan)—are located in these peripheral regions.

The second constellation was found on both the eastern and western flanks of the Ottoman Empire, in Safavid Iran and 'Alawi Morocco. In these areas the state shared political power with effective rural chieftaincies. As distinct from the empire, substate formations in Iran (the *uymaqs*) and Morocco (Sufi-led movements) were extensive and strong enough to rival the state authorities—indeed, at times strong enough to gain political dominance.

In North Africa territorial states were organized in tandem with the consolidation of a Sufi-led rural social organization. With the collapse of the Almohads, North Africa took on a new configuration of state and society. North African states, such as the Marinid and the Hafsid, were based on political institutions passed on directly from their Almohad predecessor. They were supported by client-slave and mercenary armies, a small household bureaucracy, and a coalition of tribal forces. These states developed a new relationship with religious notables. They surrendered the previous claims to direct religious authority and accepted the 'ulama' and Sufis as the bearers of Islamic legitimacy and as intermediaries in the government of society. Thus, the Saljuq and Egyptian Ayyubid-Mamluk type of Middle Eastern Islamic institutional structure was recreated in the west. Parallel to this state consolidation was the spread of Sufism. Inspired by developments in Spain and the eastern Muslim world, Sufism took root throughout North Africa, and Sufi-led communities became common among rural populations. The way was paved for the development of a balance of power between states and religious chieftaincies and a culturally integrated system of state and tribal societies.[25]

Algeria and Morocco provide variant illustrations of how this type of balance was worked out. The Algerian regime was based on a Turkish janissary elite that directly ruled the regions of Algiers, Constantine, Mascara, and Titteri. Within the directly administered zone, local beys commanded a janissary garrison and auxiliary forces and nominated the qa'ids, who controlled the local tribal leaders, levied taxes, settled disputes, and presided over the markets.

Outside of these zones of direct administration the population was organized under the authority of intermediary religious and other chieftains. The Turkish regime actually helped create a tribal structure by consolidating smaller groups into tribes and appointing local chiefs as leaders. It helped transform a small-scale, rather egalitarian, kinship-based society into a hierarchical society linked to the central polity. Nonetheless, in some regions local chiefs maintained their autonomy and were confirmed in their local power. Many of these chiefs were Sufis who were accorded official respect, endowed with mosques and tombs, and appointed to judicial positions and to assignments of land and tax revenues. The Algerian state used the Sufis to maintain an indirect suzerainty over the rural Algerian populations. Only in the early nineteenth century did the relationship between the Algerian regime and the Sufi orders break down. Between 1800 and 1830 sporadic rebellions were led by the Darqawa, the Qadiriyya, and the Tijaniyya brotherhoods in protest of excessive taxation and the reliance of the deys on Jewish, French, and English merchants for financial support. Thus, Sufi-led rural communities could function either as transmitters of state authority or as organizers of resistance to state authority.[26]

The consolidation of the Moroccan variant of state- and Sufi-led rural societies goes back to the Marinid-Wattasid era. In that period the state was built around a coalition of Arab and Zenata Berbers; it centered around a small household administration at Fez Jadid and extended to the countryside by the recruitment of elite tribal forces. The Marinids attempted to cultivate good relations with the *'ulama'* as a further basis of their authority. At the same time, the failure of the Marinid regime to resist Portuguese incursions promoted Sufism as the organizing authority for movements of local self-defense. Sufis became the leaders of rural coalitions and used the mechanism of the *tariqa* to create large-scale territorial organizations. Through the *turuq* numerous *zawiyas* could be linked together on the basis of a shared religious genealogy and shared forms of worship.

Much of the history of Morocco can be described in terms of the oscillation of power between the two poles. In the absence of an Ottoman pattern of institutions the Moroccan sultans ruled by means of a household administration and a coalition of Makhzan forces; but they legitimized their authority by combining the *baraka* derived from Sharifian descent, dynastic inheritance, and elective authority conferred by the Makhzan tribes, the *'ulama'*, and the army. At the same time, they claimed the caliphal position as executors of Muslim law and of *'ulama'* as well as Sufi Islam. The 'Alawis also attempted to control the Sufi brotherhoods. They took up the right to confer on the Sufis spiritual titles and material benefits such as land. Sultans were often able to intervene in Sufi succession disputes and thus to assert their authority over the *zawiyas*. In return, Sufi brotherhoods often acted as agents of state authority in the countryside; at other times they were antagonistic and resistant. In this highly decentralized system both power and authority were dispersed widely throughout the society, requiring incessant negotiation and manipulation.[27]

The Safavid regime affords another example of a system of relations between a central government and a tribal society. In the Safavid case the authority of the sultan was analogous to that of the Moroccan sultan. He possessed Sufi *baraka* and personal charisma combined with caliphal functions defined in terms of responsibility for the maintenance of Shi'i Islam. In the Safavid case, however, the monarchs seem to have lost much of their personal charisma and to have cultivated a much stronger imperial identity expressed in Iranian and cosmopolitan cultural terms. The state was further based on a rather strong, centralized slave army and on a relatively weak bureaucracy concentrated in the royal household.

The territory of Iran was parceled out to subordinate *uymaq* principalities. Beneath the level of the Safavid state Iran was actually or-

ganized into *uymaq* chieftainships, which ruled over subject clans,
tribal affiliates, and towns and villages. *Uymaq* chieftains based
their power on a warrior clientele and control of local resources, but
they also were formally recognized by the Safavid government and
received subsidies, allotments of infantry, and rights to collect taxes.
The struggle for power between the state and *uymaq*s reached a crisis in the late sixteenth and early seventeenth centuries. Shah 'Abbas
sought to centralize military and administrative power, control tax
revenues, and promote a royal economy centered in the capital city
of Isfahan. The program of state centralization often led to the con-
fiscation of estates administered by *uymaq* chiefs, but generally
royal influence was used to tip the balance of power against great
magnates in favor of lesser chieftains who would ally with the shah.
Shah 'Abbas succeeded in reducing the power of the great *uymaq*
chiefs without actually changing the basic structure of the political
system. His effect on the *uymaq* system was profound but not decisive. Upon his death the Iranian state continued to function by virtue
of the shifting balance of power between the Safavid regime and its
uymaq subordinates and rivals. Iran was essentially a Safavid suzerainty over a society organized into regional *uymaq* states.[28]

Thus, we have two zones of Middle Eastern political organization:
a vast core region, in which central imperial power was predominant
and rural chieftaincies were confined to the periphery, and flanking
zones, in which rural chieftaincies were integral to the political system. In all regions empire-chieftaincy relations may be characterized
in terms of certain political and religious factors. First, all populations were part of a state-centered political system, but states in
practice were not absolutely dominant in their own territories.
Power was commonly shared with organized political communities,
especially in rural areas. States and rural chieftaincies confronted
one another as organized entities, and there was usually an open
struggle for power between the two types of political organizations
within the same territory. In this struggle states had the advantages
of reverence for the authority of the ruler, ability to exert military
force, control of access to economic resources such as markets, and a
bureaucratic apparatus for taxation. Tribal populations had on their
side geography, mobility, a warrior population, and flexible capacity
for organization.

States ordinarily attempted to subordinate and dismantle rural
political structures and bring them under state control and taxation.
Where these efforts failed, states could manipulate rural populations by actually organizing them into tribal entities. States
supported or even appointed cooperative chieftains to govern seg-

mentary groups and incorporated the notables into the ruling elite. They rewarded cooperative chiefs with administrative appointments, honors, and bribes. Otherwise, they used the notables as negotiating intermediaries. In cases where notables remained autonomous, states coerced them as best they could and accepted whatever degree of autonomy they had to. In each region there were differences in the bases of state power, the extent and character of rural chieftaincies, and the historic ebb and flow of power between center and periphery. Ecological and demographic factors were very important in this balance of power. Mountain and desert regions tended to favor tribal autonomy; the plains and sedentarized regions tended toward subordination.

These routinized political relations also gained a cultural component as Islam became the idiom of state-rural relations. In many areas, between the fourteenth and nineteenth centuries, Sufism became a principal mechanism of economic organization, tribal agglomeration, mediation among segmentary groups, and resistance to, and collaboration with, state authorities. In the thirteenth and fourteenth centuries Sufism played a great part in the expansion of Islam into India and Anatolia. It was particularly important in eastern Anatolia, northwestern Iran, and parts of Transoxania in the fourteenth through sixteenth centuries and in North Africa from the thirteenth to nineteenth centuries. It was never an important rural force in the Arab Fertile Crescent.

The eighteenth and nineteenth centuries brought a new wave of Sufi leadership in the organization of segmentary populations. The rise of what is variously called reform, *islah, tajdid,* or neo-Sufism inspired Sufis to take charge of segmentary populations in the Sudan (Khalwatiyya, Sammaniyya leading to the Mahdis), Libya (Sanusiyya), and North Africa (Tijaniyya, Qadiriyya, Rahmaniyya, and other reformist movements). The diffusion of Sufism among segmentary populations was, of course, not limited to the Middle East. In Saharan and sub-Saharan Africa, *insilimen* or *zawaya* lineages claiming Arab and Sharifian descent mediated among, and organized, the desert and Sudanic populations. In Mauritania Shaykh Sidiya al-Kabir played, par excellence, the roles of Sufi, legal scholar, *qadi,* mediator, economic organizer, and political chieftain. In Transoxania we find *evliadi* lineages among Turkmens, and *mir*s, *khwaja*s, and *sayyid*s among Uzbeks and other Inner Asian peoples.[29]

Sufism was adopted by tribal peoples because it served as a condensed symbol of their complex political situation. It established the authority of outside individuals or nontribal families who could serve as arbitrators and unify small groups for shared economic or political projects. In its local saint and shrine versions, which focused on local holy men and lineages, Sufism established a parochial religious identity distinct from that of the state and the urban *'ulama'*. It was well adapted for this purpose since, in ideational terms, it conveyed a more universalistic concept of the social order; in organizational terms, individual holy men and lineages could mediate at the local level, and the *turuq* could integrate dispersed populations over wide territories. Furthermore, Sufi Islam served to symbolize, on the one hand, the opposition of tribal peoples to empires and urban forms of Islam and, on the other, their potential and actual integration into the structure of empire societies and the universal brotherhood of Islam. It expressed the complex mixture of antagonism and cooperation that marked the relations of tribes and states.

CONCLUSION

Since ancient times the normal structure of Middle Eastern societies has been a tripartite organization of parochial groups, religious associations, and empires. Consolidated regimes have for several millennia maintained a routine relationship involving both conflict and cooperation with subordinate but politically organized populations. This structure was periodically challenged by the rise of conquest movements, usually in the peripheral regions of Arabia, North Africa, and Inner Asia. These conquest movements integrated segmentary groups by reverting to an undifferentiated type of political and social structure. Successful movements, however, generated empires and rapidly evolved into the ordinary patterns of differentiated Middle Eastern societies. Tribal, religious, and state structures again became separate institutions, though some ambiguity remained about the boundaries between them and the relationships among them. Over the centuries Islam became the almost universal metaphor of social organization and political legitimation and the ideological basis of empire-chieftaincy relations. It served symbolically as a mediating factor in the organization of tribes and as a unifying factor in their relation to the rest of society.

The twentieth century has brought great changes, and it seems doubtful that such systems can continue to exist except in vestigial forms. Militarily, administratively, and technologically, strong states seem to have put an end to the political prospect of large-scale tribal mobilization. They have appropriated modern forms of moral authority—nationalist, socialist, or Islamic—that deny the legitimacy of intermediate autonomous political forces within their territories. The empire-chieftaincy systems of the past have given way, and are giving way, to new forms of political and social organization and new concepts of social solidarity and political legitimation.

NOTES

1. On the overall evolution of Middle Eastern and Islamic societies, see Ira M. Lapidus, *A History of Islamic Societies* (Cambridge, 1988).

2. On historic relations of tribes and states in the Middle East before the Islamic era, see William M. McGovern, *The Early Empires of Central Asia* (Chapel Hill, N.C., 1939); René Grousset, *The Empire of the Steppes* (New Brunswick, N.J., 1970); Owen Lattimore, *Inner Asian Frontiers of China* (New York, 1951); X. de Planhol, *Les fondements géographiques de l'histoire d'Islam* (Paris, 1968).

3. Ibn Khaldun, *The Muqaddimah*, trans. Frans Rosenthal, 3 vols. (New York, 1958), 1:247–327.

4. Three contemporary works have been particularly important in shaping my view of the interrelation of tribal societies and religious elites: E. E. Evans-Pritchard, *The Sanusi of Cyrenaica* (Oxford, 1949); Ernest Gellner, *Saints of the Atlas* (Chicago, 1969); Charles C. Stewart, *Islam and Social Order in Mauritania* (Oxford, 1973).

5. M. A. Shaban, *Islamic History*, vol. 1 (Cambridge, 1971).

6. On pre-Islamic and early Islamic Arabian society, see Eric Wolf, "The Social Organization of Mecca and the Origins of Islam," *Southwestern Journal of Anthropology* 7 (1951): 329–355; J. Chelhod, *Introduction à la sociologie de l'Islam* (Paris, 1958); W. M. Watt, *Muhammad at Mecca* (Oxford, 1953); Ira M. Lapidus, "The Arab Conquests and the Formation of Islamic Society," G. H. A. Juyboll, ed., *Studies on the First Century of Islamic History* (Carbondale, Ill., 1982); J. Ryckmans, *L'institution monarchique en Arabie méridionale avant l'Islam* (Louvain, 1951).

7. For North African conquests and state formation, see J. Abun Nasr, *A History of the Maghrib* (Cambridge, 1971); A. Laroui, *The History of the Maghrib* (Princeton, 1977); H. R. Idris, *La Berbérie Orientale sous les Zirides* (Paris, 1962); H. Terrasse, *Histoire de la Maroc*, 2 vols. (Casablanca, 1954); R. Brunschvig, *Le Berbérie Orientale sous les Hafsides*, 2 vols. (Paris, 1940, 1947). On Kharijism, see T. Lewicki, "La répartition géographique des groupements Ibadites dans l'Afrique du Nord au Moyen-age," *Rocznik Orientalistyczny* 21 (1957): 301–343; "The Ibadites in Arabia and Africa," *Journal of World History* 13 (1971): 51–130.

8. J. F. P. Hopkins, "The Almohade Hierarchy," *Bulletin of the School of Oriental and African Studies* 16 (1954): 93–112; R. Le Tourneau, "Sur la disparition de la doctrine Almohade," *Studia Islamica* 23 (1970): 193–201; W. M. Watt, "The Decline of the Almohads," *History of Religions* 4 (1964): 23–29.

9. For a seminal overview of the formation of Sufi movements in Iran, see Marshall G. S. Hodgson, *The Venture of Islam* (Chicago, 1974), 2:493–500; Jean Aubin, "Etudes Safavides," *Journal of the Economic and Social History*

of the Orient 2 (1959): 37–81. A. Bausani, "Religion under the Mongols," in J. A. Boyle, ed., *Cambridge History of Iran* (Cambridge, 1968), 5:538–549.

10. On the origin and rise of the Safavids, see R. Savory, *Iran under the Safavids* (Cambridge, 1980); M. Mazzaoui, *The Origins of the Safawids* (Weisbaden, 1972); Z. V. Togan, "Sur l'origine des Safevides," *Mélanges Massignon* 3:345–357; E. Glassen, "Schah Isma'il: Ein mahdi der Anatolischen Turkmenen?" *ZDMG* 121 (1971); H. Sohrwede, "Der Zeig der Safevidin ein Persian," *Der Islam* 41 (1965): 95–213; V. Minorsky, "The Poetry of Shah Isma'il I," *Bulletin of the School of Oriental and African Studies* 10 (1942): 1006A–1053A.

11. On the *uymaq*, see James J. Reid, *Tribalism in Society in Islamic Iran* (Malibu, Calif., 1983); "Rebellion and Social Change in Astarabad," *International Journal of Middle East Studies* 13 (1981): 35–53; "Comments on Tribalism as a Socioeconomic Formation," *Iranian Studies* 12 (1979): 275–281; John Smith, "Turanian Nomadism and Iranian Politics," *Iranian Studies* 11 (1978): 57–83; R. Loeffler, "Tribal Order and the State: The Political Organization of Boir Ahmad," *Iranian Studies* 11 (1978): 145–171; G. K. Garthwaite, "Pastoral Nomadism and Tribal Power," *Iranian Studies* 11 (1978): 173–197.

12. R. Lindner, *Nomads and Ottomans in Medieval Anatolia* (Bloomington, Ind., 1983).

13. For references to Inner Asian social structure, see note 2. See also L. Krader, *Peoples of Central Asia* (Bloomington, Ind., 1963); *Social Organization of the Mongol-Turkic Pastoral Nomads* (The Hague, 1963).

14. On early Islamic military organizations, see Patricia Crone, *Slaves on Horses* (Cambridge, 1980); Daniel Pipes, *Slave Soldiers and Islam* (New Haven, 1981).

15. There is no general account of 'Abbasid administration: see D. C. Dennett, *Conversion and the Poll Tax in Early Islam* (Cambridge, Mass., 1950); D. Sourdel, *Le vizirat 'Abbaside*, 2 vols. (Damascus, 1959–1960); R. Sprengling, "From Persian to Arabic." *American Journal of Semitic Languages and Literatures* 56 (1939): 175–224, 325–336.

16. On North African state organization, see Abun-Nasr, *History of the Maghrib*; and Laroui, *History of the Maghrib*, passim.

17. On Safavid state organization, see Savory, *Iran under the Safavids*, pp. 179–212; R. M. Savory, "Principal Offices of the Safavid State," *Bulletin of the School of Oriental and African Studies* 23 (1960): 91–105; L. Lockhart, "The Persian Army and the Safavi," *Der Islam* 34 (1959): 89–98. On the Ottoman military system, see H. Inalcik, *The Ottoman Empire: The Classical Age* (New York, 1973).

18. On the concept of the caliph as emperor, see Oleg Grabar, *The Formation of Islamic Art* (New Haven, 1973); Patricia Crone and Martin Hinds, *God's Caliph* (Cambridge, 1987); H. A. R. Gibb, "Constitutional Organization," in M. Khadduri and H. Liebesney, eds., *Law in the Middle East* (Washington, D.C., 1955), pp. 3–28.

19. On the Safavid theory of monarchy, see A. K. S. Lambton, "Quis Custodiet Custodes: Some Reflections on the Persian Theory of Government," *Studia Islamica* 5 (1956): 125–148; 6 (1956): 125–146. On Safavid art and ar-

chitecture as a source of the image of kingship, see S. C. Welch, *A King's Book of Kings* (London, 1972); S. C. Welch, *Persian Painting: Five Royal Safavid Manuscripts of the Sixteenth Century* (New York, 1976).

20. On the Moroccan concept of monarchy, see Laroui, *History of the Maghrib*; C. Geertz, *Islam Observed* (New Haven, 1968).

21. On the separation of state and religious institutions, see Ira M. Lapidus, "The Separation of State and Religion in Early Islamic Society," *International Journal of Middle East Studies* 6 (1975): 363–385; *History of Islamic Societies*. See also Crone and Hinds, *God's Caliph*.

22. See note 8.

23. On religion and state in Iran, see N. R. Keddie, *Roots of Revolution* (New Haven, 1981); H. Algar, *Religion and State in Iran* (Berkeley, 1969); S. Arjomand, "Religion, Political Action, and Legitimate Domination in Shi'ite Iran," *European Journal of Sociology* 20 (1979): 59–109; "Religious Extremism (Ghuluww): Sufism and Sunnism in Safavid Iran," *Journal of Asian History* 15 (1981); H. Algar, "Some Observations on Religion in Safavid Persia," in T. Naff and R. Owen, eds., *Studies in Eighteenth Century Islamic History* (Carbondale, Ill., 1977), pp. 287–293.

24. On the Ottoman Empire, see Inalcik, *Ottoman Empire*; H. A. R. Gibb and H. Bowen, *Islamic Society in the West*, 2 vols. (Oxford, 1950, 1954). On the Jelali movement, see William J. Griswold, *The Great Anatolian Rebellion, 1000–1020/1591–1611* (Berlin, 1983). On Sufism in Ottoman society, see J. K. Birge, *The Bektashi Order of Dervishes* (London, 1937).

25. On Tunisia and the Hafsid regime, see Brunschvig, *Berbérie Orientale*. For the structure of post-Almohad North African states, see Abun-Nasr, *History of the Maghrib*; Laroui, *History of the Maghrib*.

26. On the Turkish regime in Algeria, see P. Boyer, *L'évolution de l'Algérie Médiane* (Paris, 1960); *La vie quotidienne à Alger* (Paris, 1964); R. Gallissot, *L'Algérie pré-coloniale: Classes sociales en système pré capitaliste* (Paris, 1968); J. C. Vatin, "L'Algérie en 1830," *Revue Algérienne* 7 (1970): 977–1058.

27. On the Moroccan state and Sufism, see Geertz, *Islam Observed*; V. J. Cornell, "The Logic of Analogy and the Role of the Sufi Shaykh," *International Journal of Middle East Studies* 15 (1983): 67–93; J. Drague, *Esquisse d'histoire religieuse du Maroc* (Paris, 1951); R. J. Jenkins, "The Evolution of Religious Brotherhoods in North and Northwest Africa," in J. R. Willis, ed., *Studies in West African Islamic History* (London, 1979), pp. 1, 40–77.

28. On Safavid suzerainty and the *uymaq*s of Iran, see notes 10 and 11.

29. On reform movements, see John Voll, *Islam: Continuity and Change in the Modern World* (Boulder, Colo., 1982); F. Rahman, *Islam* (Chicago, 1979), pp. 193–224. On the Saharan and sub-Saharan lineage system, see C. C. Stewart, *Islam and Social Order in Mauritania* (Oxford, 1973); H. T. Norris, *The Tuaregs: Their Islamic Legacy and Its Diffusion in the Sahel* (Warminster, 1975). On the Sanusi, see E. E. Evans-Pritchard, *The Sanusi of Cyrenaica* (Oxford, 1949). On Evliadi among the Turkmens, see V. N. Basilov, "Honour Groups in Traditional Turkmenian Society," in A. S. Ahmed and D. M. Hart, eds., *Islam and Tribal Societies* (London, 1984), pp. 220–243.

Anthropologists, Historians, and Tribespeople on Tribe and State Formation in the Middle East

Richard Tapper

In recent decades Western historians and anthropologists have come closer together in common endeavors to reexamine both Western and Third World society and history.[1] A welcome feature of this trend has been the willingness of each kind of specialist to learn from the other in studying the tribal peoples of the so-called Fourth World. In most cases a lack of documentation gives the anthropologist precedence, but various tribal peoples have participated in the economics and politics of states and empires long enough and actively enough to have left a considerable mark in the archives, even producing their own chronicles. In such cases anthropologists and historians are on equal ground; the former have "done history," scouring archives and chronicles as well as oral narratives for information to provide depth to their accounts of social and cultural change. Historians, not content with the often meager "facts" to be established from such materials, have enriched their interpretations with ethnographic, theoretical, and comparative insights from anthropology.

The cooperation has not been all roses. Whereas anthropologists have not always been as careful and critical as they might be in their use of sources, historians have sometimes employed anthropological theories or concepts that are outmoded, inappropriate, or controversial. Not least among these are the concepts of "tribe" and "tribalism." These terms refer to a category of human society whose study was once regarded as the prerogative of anthropology, yet anthropologists themselves have notoriously been unable to agree on how to define them. Small wonder, then, if historians, and for that matter political scientists and others interested in "tribal society," have differed widely in their understanding of the terms. Similar problems attach to the concept of "state," which might be said to be more the concern of political scientists and historians. If interdisciplinary dialogue and cooperation are to be fruitful, it would seem essential not so much to attempt to agree on definitions (the experience of anthropologists has shown this to be a tedious and indeed futile enterprise) as to examine the assumptions behind different usages and indeed the sources from which they derive.

There are several general theoretical issues associated with the "problem of tribe" and the related problem of "state formation." How far are tribal systems necessarily segmentary, egalitarian, decentralized, autonomous, and hence opposed to the state as the source of inequality, central authority, and government? How far are tribes defined in terms of their relations with states—and vice versa? Are tribes precursors of the state in an evolutionary sequence, or, as several writers have suggested, are they creations of the state?[2] Does the state arise from social stratification, or is social stratification the result of state formation? What is the role of tribes in processes of state formation—specifically in the combination of disparate elements, the development of hierarchical inequalities, and the centralization of government—that leads to the formation of confederacies, "protostates," or "secondary states"?[3]

The diversity of social, economic, cultural, and political forms to which the terms "tribe," "tribal," and "state" have been applied in the Middle East—as great within that region as anywhere else in the world—touches centrally on these issues, a discussion of which can best be approached, I suggest, through a consideration of definition and usage. In this essay I examine first the main conceptions of tribe current among anthropologists, the usages of the term in academic and administrative treatment of Middle Eastern society, and the semantics of various indigenous terms that have been translated as tribe; I say less about state, not because it is less problematic, but because the issues are more adequately covered in other essays within this collection. Then I attempt to throw some light on the problems of tribe and state formation through a critical discussion of a number of contributions by historians using anthropological materials. Finally, I examine some of the main processes of confederation and state formation among Middle Eastern tribal groups.

TRIBE AND STATE IN ANTHROPOLOGY

Anthropologists have followed their own varying epistemologies to emphasize differing criteria and thus have failed to agree on a general definition of what constitutes a tribe. It seems that, as with so many would-be general or universal concepts, it is impossible to find an analytic terminology that both takes account of indigenous categories and applies widely enough to be useful for comparison and classification.

There is more agreement on the basic nature of the state as a territorially bounded polity with a centralized government and a monopoly of legitimate force, usually including within its bounds different social classes and ethnic-cultural groups. Some scholars have declared modern concepts of the state to be inapplicable to Islamic polities in the premodern Middle East in terms of the degree of central control and the forms, functions, and ideology of government. For our immediate purposes, however, the state is sufficiently defined by the existence of territorial frontiers (however vaguely defined), a central government (however weak and limited in its aims), and a heterogeneous population; in the absence of the last of these factors the term "chiefdom" is more appropriate.

Three fundamentally distinct conceptions of tribe have had currency among anthropologists. Perhaps the closest to popular English-language usage is the loose equation of tribe with *primitive society*, applied to the precolonial populations of many parts of the world. In this classificatory usage the population of a country or a continent is divided into "tribes" in the sense of objectively apprehended *cultural-linguistic groups*. Such "tribes" are, usually by implication, counterposed to "states," the "rational" political structures of the modern world. State formation among such "tribes" is, again usually by implication, conceived as the result of outside influences. However, the political structure and ideology, and usually scale, of such "tribes" are discounted, so that what are called "the tribes of Africa" range in size from a few hundred people to millions and in complexity from a scattering of hunter-gatherer bands to what are in effect states. More appropriate (but still unsatisfactory) modern terms are "ethnic group," "people," and "nation" or "nationality."

More precisely formulated is the second notion of tribe as a particular type of society, usually in some kind of *evolutionary* scheme, in which "tribes" (with their neolithic production techniques and egalitarian, clan-based political organization) develop in certain conditions from the bands of hunters and then evolve into more complex chiefdoms and states. A basic characteristic of such tribes is the pervasiveness of *kinship and descent* as principles of social and political organization, which are superseded by territory and hierarchical authority in the process of state formation.

A third usage, common in British social anthropology, follows E. E. Evans-Pritchard's classic analysis of the Nuer of the Sudan as a collection of tribes, that is, *political groups defined by territory* and by accepted mechanisms for settlement of disputes. Each such tribe segments into subsections at different structural levels down to that of the local community, and each such section has a dominant descent group. Descent groups in turn segment from the level of the clan dominant in a given tribe to that of the minimal lineage; but frequently the majority of members of the descent group reside elsewhere than in the territory of the section where it is dominant, and Evans-Pritchard carefully distinguished the descent framework from the politicoterritorial structure of tribes and their sections.[4] Such tribes differ from chiefdoms and states in having no central authority, and the development or imposition of such authority marks their transformation or integration into these more complex political forms.

Many ethnographers have defined "tribe"—or used the term without definition—as best fits their own analysis of a particular society, often attempting to translate a specific indigenous term. Unfortunately, for comparative purposes, one cannot expect groups labeled "tribes" to be identical in scale or function or expect such a usage to yield terms for an objective classification and comparison. Indeed, we have yet to take seriously the implications of E. R. Leach's warning of thirty years ago:

> I would claim that it is largely an academic fiction to suppose that in a "normal" ethnographic situation one ordinarily finds distinct "tribes" distributed about the map in orderly fashion with clear-cut boundaries between them. . . . My own view is that the ethnographer has often only managed to discern the existence of *a* tribe because he took it as axiomatic that this kind of cultural entity must exist.

Many such tribes are, in a sense, ethnographic fictions.[5] Other writers have since pointed out that many of the "tribes" of Africa and elsewhere were the creations of colonial administrators as well as of ethnographers.[6]

TRIBE AND STATE IN THE MIDDLE EAST

In the Middle East, groups referred to as tribes have never, in historical times, been isolated groups of "primitives," remote from contact with states or their agents; rather, tribes and states have created and maintained each other in a single system, though one of inherent instability. A. K. S. Lambton's remarks on Iran apply generally to much of the Middle East:

Control of the tribal element has been and is one of the perennial problems of government. . . . All except the strongest governments have delegated responsibility in the tribal areas to the tribal chiefs. One aspect
of Persian history is that of a struggle between the tribal elements and
the non-tribal element, a struggle which has continued in a modified
form down to the present day. Various Persian dynasties have come to
power on tribal support. In almost all cases the tribes have proved an
unstable basis on which to build the future of the country.[7]

The "tribal problem" and the role of tribes and their leaders as actors and agents in Middle Eastern political history have been the
subject of various detailed studies. If the rulers of the Middle East
have been preoccupied by a tribal problem, however, the tribes could
be said to have had a perennial "state problem." No tribe was ever, at
least in recent centuries, totally unaffected by any state; and an important theme in the literature is this state problem, that is, the role
of states in creating, transforming, or destroying tribal institutions
and structures. A focus on the role of tribes in state formation in the
Middle East needs to be complemented by awareness of the role of
states in "tribe formation"—and deformation.

"Tribe" in the Middle Eastern literature specifies little, if anything, about system of production, scale, culture, or political structure. Dale F. Eickelman has identified four different notions of tribe
in the Middle East: anthropological analytical concepts, state administrative concepts, indigenous explicit ideologies, and indigenous
practical notions.[8]

The first of the anthropological concepts outlined above—tribe as
a culturally and linguistically bounded "primitive society"—is particularly inappropriate for the major cultural-linguistic groupings in
the Middle East, such as Arabs, Berbers, Turks, Persians, Kurds,
Pashtuns, and Baluches, which can hardly be termed either tribes or
primitive societies, if only on grounds of scale, complexity, and lack
of unity. Although these ethnic groups, peoples, or nationalities cannot be called tribes, the term is commonly used for their major subdivisions. Criteria for identifying such groups as tribes vary. Many
anthropologists of the Middle East adopt the notion of tribe as descent group, the classical model of tribal society among Arabs and in
the Middle East generally, conforming with Ibn Khaldun's conception as well as with Emile Durkheim's notion of mechanical solidarity. Such a group may or may not be territorially distinct and
politically united under a chief, but many modern proponents of this
notion of tribe would deny the term to any group without a descent
ideology. The criterion best fits Arab tribal society, where tribal
genealogies are particularly extensive. A well-known example is the

Ruwala, a "tribe" of some two hundred fifty thousand people, though some even larger non-Arab groups such as the Bakhtiyari Lurs (five hundred thousand) or Durrani Pashtuns (two million) have been called tribes on the same grounds. Other scholars—but few anthropologists—apply the term to almost equally large groups such as the Qashqa'i, the Khamseh, the Shahsevan, or various Qizilbash groups on the criterion of politicoterritorial unity and chiefship, though they lack comprehensive descent ideologies and are heterogeneous in origins and composition.

At this level of major cultural-political groups of one hundred thousand or more people, there is a radical disagreement as to whether tribes should be identified culturally (a descent ideology) or structurally (chiefship and/or politicoterritorial unity). Other writers, however, not wishing to take either extreme position, have located tribes at a lower level of political structure, referring to the larger groups (whatever their apparent basis) as tribal confederacies (though their centralized and hierarchical administration would also qualify them as "chiefdoms" or even "secondary states"). Thus, when discussing such confederacies in Iran, Fredrik Barth (on the Khamseh), Gene R. Garthwaite (on the Bakhtiyari), Lois Beck (on the Qashqa'i), Reinhold Loeffler (on the Boir Ahmad), and Richard Tapper (on the Shahsevan) all use the term "tribe" for first- or second-order components numbering at most a few thousand individuals.[9] Such groups usually (but still not always) combine territorial and political unity under a chief with an ideology of common descent.

The general administrative view of tribal society is that it is inferior to settled urban society, the civilized Islamic ideal. Whereas the city was the source of government, order, and productivity, the tribes had a natural tendency to rebellion, rapine, and destruction, a tendency that might be related to the starkness of their habitat and its remoteness from the sources of civilization as well as to the underemployment inherent in their way of life. Such a view has some justification from a government perspective but is superficial and overgeneralized.

Beyond this, conventional images of tribes differ radically. Different writers—historians, anthropologists, administrators, political agents, travelers—have, according to their previous experiences, their personalities, and their objectives, constructed, maintained, and only occasionally confronted widely varying images of the tribes they have encountered.[10] In some areas tribespeople are renowned as hardy mountain villagers; in others they are supposedly desert-dwelling pastoral nomads. Some tribes are renowned for their independent spirit and their democratic institutions; elsewhere the stereotype is of strong centralized confederacies under powerful and aristocratic chiefs. Tribespeople in some parts of the Middle East are notorious for their ignorance of, and indifference to, religion; in others they have a reputation for rigorous, if not fanatical, devotion to Islam. There is some truth in these stereotypes, at least as a basis for drawing a contrast between tribes in different regions, but they are nevertheless exaggerated, and exceptions abound.

Strongly entrenched in academic and administrative thinking about tribes in many parts of the Middle East is the notion of tribe as the political dimension of pastoral nomadism, such that the category "the tribes" is conventionally synonymous with "the nomads."[11] Numerous observers have noted how the geography and ecology of most Middle Eastern countries favor pastoral nomadism. The terrain and climate make large areas uncultivable under preindustrial conditions and suitable only for seasonal grazing; and as only a small proportion of such pasture can be used by village-based livestock, vast ranges of steppe, semidesert, and mountain are left to be exploited by nomads—mobile, tent-dwelling pastoralists. Such nomads until very recently numbered tens of millions, and almost all were organized politically under chiefs. Moreover, in the history of the Middle East it is true that tribes (defined in political terms) have commonly also had a pastoral economic base and led a nomadic way of life.

Yet in many countries (such as Yemen, Afghanistan, and Algeria) major tribal groups (whether basically egalitarian, chiefless descent groups, or highly centralized and stratified chiefdoms) were settled cultivators with little or no leaning toward pastoralism or nomadism. In other words, as has been argued by Barth and others, tribalism is more necessary to nomadism than nomadism to tribalism.[12] Any coincidence is not so much a causal relation as it is a function of relations of both nomadism and tribalism with the central state, and there is little in either pastoralism as a production system or nomadism as a way of living that necessarily leads to organization in "tribes," whether defined politically in terms of territory and chiefship or culturally in terms of descent. Instead, nomads, by virtue of their shifting residence, and tribespeople, by virtue of their personal allegiances to each other or to chiefs, have always posed problems of control to officials of sedentary states, who have thus tended to classify them together and indeed to administer them similarly, in some cases creating tribal groups and appointing chiefs among nomadic (and settled) populations that previously did not have them.

Administrators—and many academics—still take a highly positivist view of tribes in the Middle East. They expect them to be mappable, bounded groups with little membership change, and they want an exact terminology for classificatory and comparative purposes. (Leach's warnings on this score were quoted earlier.) The resultant problems for the investigator—historian or anthropologist—were summed up by Basile Nikitine many years ago:

> Les notions d'unité ethnique et d'organisme politique ne sont plus les mêmes dès qu'on pénètre sur le terrain d'ethnologie asiatique. A un certain moment on y constate en effet des molécules qui tantôt se réunissent sous une forme de vague confédération, tantôt, avec la même facilité, se désagrègent. Les noms mêmes n'offrent aucune constance ni certitude. . . . Ce sera le nom du chef de la période de prospérité auquel pourra avec le temps se substituer un autre. Ajoutons à ceci des scissions et des regroupements constants à travers l'histoire et nous nous apercevrons de tout ce qu'il y a de délicat dans la tâche du chercheur.[13]

From the perspective of state rulers, according to which even the most autonomous inhabitants of the territory over which sovereignty is claimed should have representatives and identifiable patterns of organization, the allegiance of rural groups and minorities to a set of comparable political groups and leaders is often assumed. There is perhaps a longer history in the Middle East than elsewhere of governments creating tribes and chiefs for both political and administrative purposes. The Shahsevan of Iran, often cited as an example of an artificial tribe created by the shah with personal loyalty to himself, are in fact just one of the well-documented cases in the Middle East of a tribal or ethnic identity created through the writings of historians and ethnographers.[14] As for administrative creations, tribes and chiefs sometimes appear in the records as such, whereas they may not exist except on paper. Further, tribal names found in the sources imply a uniformity of structure that may be entirely due to administrative action and may disguise fundamental disparities of culture and society.

The nature of indigenous concepts of tribe, whether explicit ideologies or implicit practical notions, has too often been obscured by the apparent desire of investigators (anthropologists, historians, and administrators) to establish a consistent and stable terminology for political groups. Such investigators seem to believe that tribes are necessarily ordered in a hierarchical or segmentary system—with distinct terms referring to groups at separate levels—that can be translated, for example, as confederacy, tribe, clan, lineage, section, or whatever.

Unfortunately, Middle Eastern indigenous categories (of which perhaps the commonest to have been translated as tribe are *qabila*, *ta'ifa*, *quam*, and *il*) are no more specific than are English terms such as "family" or "group." Even in the most apparently consistent segmentary terminology, individual terms are ambiguous, not merely about level, but also in their connotations of functions or facets of identity—economic, political, kinship, and cultural. As with equivalents in English practice, the ambiguity of the terms and the flexibility of the system are of the essence in everyday negotiations of meaning and significance.[15]

Most of the terms that have been translated as "tribe" contain such ambiguities, and attempts to give them—or tribe—precision as to either level, function, or essence are misdirected. Tribe, I suggest, is rather a state of mind, a construction of reality, a model for organization and action. To describe any named group as a tribe is to mention only one facet of its nature and to deny that facet to other groups in the same system, at larger and smaller levels. A precise terminology may aid comparison but is unlikely to explain behavior or provide an adequate translation of local categories and perceptions.

A better understanding of the nature of tribal political organizations, of relations between tribal and nontribal societies, and of the role of tribes in state formation must be sought in a closer historical examination of the social and economic basis of tribal systems. Unfortunately, research on this topic is in its infancy. The sources for it are mostly written from a distance by outsiders viewing the tribes with hostility or some other bias. These sources usually concern such matters as taxation, military contingents, disturbances and measures taken to quell them, and inaccurate lists of major tribal groups, numbers, and leaders. They rarely deal specifically or in reliable detail with the basic social and economic organization of tribal communities; and they mention individual tribes only when prominent in supporting or opposing government, when involved in intertribal disorders, or when transported from one region to another. We still have only the vaguest notions of tribal economics in premodern times—what the relations of production were and how they have changed; who controlled land and how access was acquired; what proportion of producers controlled their own production; how many were tenants or dependents of wealthier tribesmen or city-based merchants; and whether control of production was exercised directly or through taxation or price fixing. The sparse information in the sources must be supplemented and interpreted by tentative and possibly misleading extrapolations from modern ethnographic studies. Otherwise, however welcome the shift of perspective from that of the state to that of minorities, the nature of the sources continues to dictate a history of politics and dynasties; tribal economic and social history remains nearly as obscure, and the tribespeople as faceless and voiceless, as before.

SOME HISTORIANS ON TRIBES AND STATE FORMATION IN THE MIDDLE EAST

The diversity of understandings of the notion of tribe among writers on the Middle East is reflected in a number of recent historical studies of social and political organization among early Islamic Arabs, Mongols, Ottomans, Turkmen dynasties of Anatolia and Iran, and the Qizilbash and their successors in Iran. For example, the pages of *Iranian Studies* have carried a debate on this subject, mainly involving Leonard Helfgott, whose main study has been of the rise of the Qajars, and James Reid, who has published a book on the Qizilbash.[16]

Helfgott argues that the Iranian state between the twelfth and the nineteenth centuries was composed of two or more separate but linked socioeconomic formations. Extrapolating from Barth's study of the Basseri of the modern era, he characterizes Iranian tribes as pastoral nomadic kinship-based chiefdoms that form closed economic systems: grazing rights are collective; rights in animals are individual; and production is predominantly for use, not for exchange. Such nomadic socioeconomic formations are distinct from, but in constant relation with, the settled agricultural and urban formations. Unfortunately, he produces little evidence for his argument, overstresses the roles of pastoral nomadism, kinship, and chiefship in Iranian tribal society, and underestimates the will and capacity of Iranian pastoral nomads to produce surplus.

Reid accuses Helfgott of theoreticism. In his version, to which he is led mainly by data on administration and the perspective of the state, the essence of tribal organization in Iran was the highly complex, centralized *uymaq* system of the Qizilbash that flourished under the Safavids. *Uymaq*s were not simply pastoral nomads; they combined three economic forms (pastoral, agricultural, and commercial) under separate administrative systems controlled by a city-dwelling chief. Nor were they based on kinship (though their subdivisions, including the dominant chiefly dynasty, may have been). They were in effect states, but they were also tribes (says Reid) because their leadership was hereditary.

In his reply to Reid, Helfgott admits that tribes are not necessarily only pastoral and that the state has a much greater and deeper impact on tribal economic and political structure than he had allowed;

but he asks what is tribal about the agricultural and urban elements controlled by tribal chiefs. The *uymaq*s were perhaps some kind of tribal state, but such a classification avoids the necessity for analyzing the component elements, especially the nomadic tribes. Helfgott might have added that the *uymaq*s could not be called tribes according to most accepted criteria but were rather chiefdoms or confederacies; and they are not comparable with the nomadic tribal groups to which he directed his original argument. Further, on Reid's own admission, the *uymaq* system disintegrated during late Safavid times and hence is of no direct relevance to tribalism or pastoralism in the period since.

Various reviews of Reid's book have thrown doubt on the credibility of his whole argument, but in a comment on Reid's 1978 article R. D. McChesney demolishes his construction of the *uymaq* system. The information in the best accounts indicates that little is known about the *uymaq* and that Reid's speculations are based on partial, cavalier, or mistaken use of the sources.[17]

Two other scholars, in historical studies published in the 1980s, take diametrically opposed views of the tribes and their roles in state formation: Rudi Lindner, writing of the Huns and the early Ottomans, and Patricia Crone, whose main interest is in early Arab tribalism.[18] Lindner sets out explicitly to "test the utility of anthropological models in reconstructing a fairer history of medieval nomadic tribes in Eurasia." He first upbraids anthropologists for their continuing fascination with "genealogy and kinship structure" and the use of models such as the conical clan and the segmentary lineage "to reveal the real structure of tribes." He quotes two anthropologists with approval, however: Emrys Peters, who showed the segmentary lineage model to be a tribal ideology but a poor depiction of behavior, and Philip Salzman, who questioned why tribes should maintain such an inadequate model and found it to be a reserve or alternative ideology. Yet he dismisses the relevance of ideologies in the constitution of tribes. Referring to studies of the Basseri in southern Iran and the Marri in Baluchistan, he declares that clans and tribes are essentially political groups, concerned about shared interests as much as blood ties: "Turkish tribes in the Near East and in Inner Asia were pragmatic, often temporary political groupings around a successful chief. . . . The idiom of tribal ideology was one of kinship, but the tribal reality was formed of shared interest, advantage, and service." On this basis Lindner shows the organization of the Huns and the early Ottomans to have been tribal, an argument he develops for the latter in some detail in his book.

Apart from a persistent equation of nomadism, pastoralism, and tribalism (an error I discussed earlier), there are two problems with Lindner's conception of tribe in terms of only common interest and allegiance to a leader. First, it fails to specify in what way such a group differs from a chiefdom, a faction, or a party. The same could be said, however, of the definitions, explicit or implicit, adopted by several ethnographers of tribal groups in the Turco-Iranian world, including those referred to by Lindner.

Second, Lindner goes to some lengths to show that the subjugation of tribes to states in the twentieth century has led ethnographers to overemphasize kinship and ascribe to modern tribal organization a political and territorial stability and a kinship dominance that did not exist among nomadic tribes of the past. He acknowledges the way "genealogy may serve as an idiom or charter that nomads [sc. tribespeople] use to explain their history and politics," but this element receives no weight in his interpretation of the evidence for the Huns and early Ottomans. We hear nothing of the families of these warriors and the degree to which they were linked, for example, by marriage and ties of affinity. In the study of tribal groups in the nineteenth- and twentieth-century Middle East, both before and after subjugation to the power of modern states, historians and anthropologists (including several of those mentioned by Lindner) have found kinship ties, particularly those created by marriage, to be central elements in determining political strategies.

Lindner surely overstresses the role of shared interest in recruitment to tribal groups and underestimates the part played by kinship morality—ties of trust and preference. In my interpretation, the tribal character of the Ottomans and the Huns begins with, and rests on, links of kinship and marriage, even if the ideology did not become pervasive for some generations. Such early Eurasian groups, like more-recent Qizilbash, Shahsevan, or Qashqa'i, were formed through a complex blend of political allegiance and cultural ideologies and owed their success and their continuity as much to the ambiguity and flexibility inherent in this blend as to the military prowess of their leaders.

A further theme of Lindner's book is the analysis of nomadic society under the Ottomans, for which he constructs a model on the basis of extensive extrapolation from a selection of modern ethnographies, notably Barth on the Basseri of Iran and Bates on the Yürük of southern Turkey. Unfortunately, apart from a number of misreadings and misunderstandings of complex analytical issues, he is led to suggest as necessary to nomadic society several economic, social, and political characteristics that are in fact highly contingent. He would have avoided these errors if he had used a wider selection of available ethnographic accounts of nomadic societies such as the Bakhtiyari, the Qashqa'i, the Shahsevan, or the Turkmen, which on grounds of scale and culture at least might be expected to be far more comparable with the Ottomans than either the Basseri or the Yürük.

I would argue that Basseri ethnography is totally inappropriate for extrapolation onto earlier nomadic tribes, for various reasons. First, Barth's economic, social, and political data and analysis derive (mainly) from the camp of the Basseri khan's personal entourage, the Darbar, which must invalidate them as representative of ordinary Basseri nomadic society.[19]

Second, comparison with other contemporary nomadic societies, whether in Iran or elsewhere in the Middle East, shows Basseri data to constitute just one pattern among many in respect to household size and organization, herd size and productivity, human and herd demography, herding unit and camp structure, grazing rights, the organization of migration, the position of camp leader, the hierarchy of power and authority in the tribe, and the segmentary structure of tribal subdivisions.[20] This is not surprising, given that the Basseri pattern is an adaptation to specific natural, economic, political, and historical circumstances quite different from those of other tribal and nomadic societies, whether Ottoman, Qizilbash, or Shahsevan.

Third, what evidence there is for social, economic, and political organization among tribal groups elsewhere or at other times suggests that the Basseri model is highly unusual. A rather different typical model is suggested by the remarkable similarities, for example, between the confederate clans of the fifteenth-century Aqquyunlu, the *uymaqs* of the sixteenth-century Qizilbash, and nineteenth-century tribal confederacies such as the Boir Ahmad and the Shahsevan.[21]

Patricia Crone examines various definitions of the tribe and theories of the relation of the tribe to the state. First she declares that "few would disagree that a tribe is a species of that genus of societies which create all or most of their social roles by ascribing social importance to biological characteristics, or in other words societies ordered with reference to kinship, sex and age"—as opposed, presumably, to territory, occupation, or class. "A tribe is thus a primitive society." In a general sense "all stateless societies above the level of the band" are tribal, whereas in the specific sense a tribe is "a descent group which constitutes a political community." Tribal societies are "composed of identical and interchangeable units" and are characterized by an unspecialized economy and a low degree of wealth-status differentiation. Moreover, "whatever else a tribe may be, it is a stateless society . . . a tribal state is a state superimposed on a society which is designed to cope without it and which may accordingly revert to statelessness at any time."

Such a concept of tribe Crone finds "well entrenched in the anthropological literature," though not supreme, and she castigates the lobby for tribe as a "socio-cultural-ethnic entity"—that is, "people"—for two reasons. According to Crone, "cultural units," identified by "neutral observers" through objective criteria such as morpheme distribution, have little to do with "political units," which exist only if members think they do. (It should be noted that these definitions of the cultural and the political run counter to modern anthropological usage, in which culture is a system of symbols and meanings, and politics has more to do with objective power relations.) She maintains that tribe in her sense "stands for a certain type of political organization" and declares that "objective criteria do not on their own regulate behaviour." She protests that, like zoologists who distinguish tribe (phylum) from actual social groups of animals, anthropologists too should have different terms for "classificatory and ethological use," though "the term 'tribe' in a human context has been preempted for the study of behaviour," that is, for "political" as opposed to "cultural" units. She asserts, moreover, that "if tribes are political units they are unlikely ever to be cultural ones . . . conversely if they are cultural units they are unlikely ever to be political ones."

Her other objection to a "socio-cultural-ethnic" definition is the same point about scale I made earlier: in the Middle East it would make tribes of peoples like Jews and Arabs. Indeed, most African "tribes" are better termed "peoples" (a cultural classification), with component political "tribes." If East African peoples such as Nuer, Dinka, Turkana, Karimojong, Samburu, and Masai are comparable in scale to Arab tribes such as Ruwala, this, says Crone, is a result of the fact that the former herd cattle and the latter camels.

She goes on to discuss the place of tribes in evolution and state formation. Contrary to anthropologists like Marshall D. Sahlins and Elman R. Service, she argues that tribes do not evolve into states as they become more complex. Tribes and states are diametrically opposed, "alternative forms of organization evolved in response to similar problems," so much so that "tribes have to be destroyed in order to make way for states." Tribes have no evolutionary potential; "chiefs were the outcome of the transition to statehood, not its initiators." The first civilization (state?), she argues, was the product of religion. She declares, "There can hardly be much dispute about the fact that the superiority of state structures over tribal ones has caused tribal societies to retreat to the point where they have practically disappeared today," and hence she doubts Morton Fried's proposition that tribes *result* from state formation: "The state has undermined tribal organizations rather than created them."

Crone thinks it likely that "tribe in the specific sense of the word is an overwhelmingly or exclusively pastoral phenomenon (or so at least if we add the criterion of segmentary organization)." The tribe, moreover, "is that descent group within which control of pasture land is vested" and blood-money rules apply and which has a chief and forms a community. She considers nomads to be "pitiful creatures," doomed to tribalism by their environment, marginal, and hence inclined to avoid states; and she finds it "surprising" when they are converted to conquerors on a gigantic scale.

Finally, "tribalism" becomes equated with "egalitarian traditions." Crone argues that there is a strong element of such tribalism in Arab society and that the *shari'a* is a "tribal code." Islam highlights "an affinity between the tribe and the modern state: both are avowedly egalitarian, both espouse mass participation"; but "their affinity notwithstanding, the tribe and the modern state represent two opposite ends of an organizational spectrum."

There are serious flaws in all these arguments, resulting partly from a rampantly positivist approach and partly from mistaken underlying assumptions. Take Crone's definition of a tribe as a species of society, a political unit organized on biological principles, not as a people or "socio-cultural-ethnic unit." The assumptions involved here go counter to recent anthropological thinking. Thus, although she realizes that peoples cannot be precisely demarcated, she seems to think that "tribes" and "societies" can be classified into "types" (even genera or species), an assumption long ago invalidated by writers such as Leach.

Crone regards kinship as "facts" among which tribal societies choose a set for the purposes of social organization. The tribe, she says, is the most "obvious" (that is, "primitive") solution to the problem of social organization above the family level, being based like "race" on "plainly visible" features that people naturally take as a social signal. Such a view is nowadays only associated with (anthropologically discredited) extreme forms of sociobiology. The statement that "no discrepancy is supposed to occur [between] biological and social facts" is simply untrue for most cultures: here Crone goes even further than Ernest Gellner (in his twenty-five-year-old debate with Beattie and others) in denying that "physical and social kinship simply happen to coincide."[22] Surely we have now learned to view kinship systems, race, and indeed theories of biology, as socially constructed models of reality? They may or may not be "true," but this "truth" is of no relevance to the understanding of social organization. Crone's insistence that tribes in the Middle East and Central Asia are pastoral descent groups excludes most tribal groups in Anatolia, Iran, and Afghanistan (including the Marri Baluch, Basseri, and Ottomans discussed by Lindner), groups that are complex and heterogeneous chiefdoms, often the creation of states or colonial governments, and often settled cultivators.

On the question of scale Crone is wrong in the contrast she draws between Middle Eastern and East African tribes. First, she ignores the existence of substantial cattle-herding Arab groups in East Africa as well as small camel-herding non-Arab groups. Second, her main Arab example, the Ruwala, is exceptionally large for a "tribe." More common are tribes like the Al-Murra (fifteen thousand people), which are similar in scale to tribes (by her and Evans-Pritchard's definition) among the Nuer, which range from five thousand to forty-five thousand people. Other tribes in the Middle East, defined in Crone's terms, sometimes number only a few thousand or even a few hundred.

Crone assumes that any society must be organized on one principle or kind of principle alone: biology *or* (for example) religion, culture *or* politics. It may be that she is thinking of "society" in analytical terms as that aspect of culture or population that results from a given "principle"; but there is no indication of this. She does shift ground continually in the article, however, at times insisting that a tribe is a descent group, at others that it is "political."

Crone's opinion of the superiority of states to tribes in evolutionary terms is based on poor reasoning and a failure to distinguish either nomads from tribes or modern from premodern states. First, what is the evidence that kinship ideologies or ideas of race were evolutionarily prior to the religious ideas that Crone contends have given rise to the state? In what way can the former be regarded as internal and the latter external? Second, how are state structures superior to tribal ones: militarily, economically, or morally? A page of unconvincing assertions about the potential of nomadic organization is peppered with phrases like "it is obvious," "it is clear," "it stands to reason."[23]

It seems that Crone is imbued with the prejudice of the modern state against nomadic/tribal society. Her assertion that "in the long run tribes always proved inferior to states," and that the latter must destroy the former, is a modern notion and surely a perversion of the history of premodern Middle Eastern states, so often marked by the reverse—conquest of states by tribes, punctuating periods when states coexisted with, depended on, or at least merely claimed control of the tribes.

When Crone declares tribes and states to be irreconcilable opposites, she is clearly thinking of them in concrete terms and ascribes to them a purity of organization that is never found. Further, to call the *shari'a* a tribal code on the basis of its "egalitarianism" is to fall prey to a classic confusion: the equality prescribed in the *shari'a* is not the social and economic equality of tribalism but legal and religious equality before God. Yet in her recognition of tribe and state as "alternative forms of organization" and her identification of "egalitarian" and "populist" ideals in both the tribe and the modern state, Crone verges on the notion of modes or models that I propose as the most useful way of looking at both tribe and state.

CONFEDERATION AND STATE FORMATION AMONG MIDDLE EASTERN TRIBES

Attempts to explain variation in tribal forms and the emergence of confederacies and central leadership commonly posit a single, ideal-type tribal system, whose features typically include (apart from pastoral nomadism, which we have already had to reject) a simple division of labor, a segmentary lineage system, egalitarian ideals of organization, and political autonomy. This sort of approach has a long-established pedigree in studies of the Middle East. Very similar are theories of a tribal (pastoral nomadic) mode of production or socioeconomic formation. There is little agreement, however, on which features are essential to the ideal mode of production or socioeconomic formation; for some, the segmentary lineage is the minimal criterion for distinguishing tribal from nontribal societies; for others, it is political autonomy and cultural distinctiveness, or chiefship and a hierarchy of authority; yet others argue, whether from economic or logical a priori grounds, that egalitarianism is inherent to nomadism and tribalism.

Whatever the nature of the ideal type proposed, deviations from it are attributed to a series of differentiating variables commonly grouped into internal (such as culture, demography, ecology, and economy) and external (such as the role of the state and neighboring tribes and the proximity of frontiers, cities, and trade routes). Internal factors have been examined in detail elsewhere.[24] Most important is the nature of access to land for farming or grazing or wealth accumulation, whether individualized or communal. This in turn is the basis for the formation and nature of communities or corporations at determinate levels of tribal society as well as rivalries and factions between them, all of which contradict a segmentary ideology and inhibit unity in the face of an outside threat. In the absence of effective superior authority, relations between autonomous political units within a region take on the familiar chessboard pattern: neighbors maintain relations of hostility on the boundaries but ally themselves (often by marriage) with their neighbors' neighbors, forming a larger pattern of two coalitions or blocs throughout, or even beyond, the region. Such patterns have been recorded at various levels, sometimes several at once.[25]

Factional oppositions in a region mainly involve the leaders of the political units, and subordinate leaders may upset a balanced relation by defecting with their own followers to the other side. Sometimes regional alignments of tribal groups extend into cities, where they relate to institutionalized urban rivalries.[26] Out of this tendency arises the notorious reluctance of tribal groups to combine on a regional, let alone a national, basis.

When a strong leader seeks to control a whole region, he usually gains support first from one bloc and forms it into a coalition or confederacy to overcome the other. Such tactics have been employed by conquerors, established rulers, and imperial agents. In some areas, especially among predominantly segmentary Sunni groups, factional rivalries were mediated by locally based religious leaders: sayyids, sometimes from lineages merged in the tribal system; charismatic imams or mullas; or Sufi shaykhs or *pirs*. On occasion such religious leaders could move beyond their role of mediation and unite large groups into at least an ephemeral confederacy for specific politicoreligious purposes. It should be stressed that the ability to unite usually rested on the hope of material gain and the absence of material cause for conflict as much as, if not more than, on any tribal *'asabiyya*—notions of common descent or religious or other ideology of unity.

At the local level, effective leadership can be sustained as a nonproductive role only if a surplus is produced, whether from a pastoral or agricultural economy or from raiding, and whether traded or consumed within the tribal group. The ability to produce surplus also attracts attempts at control and extraction but does not necessarily lead to meaningful inequalities in the form of leaders or a ruling elite; tribespeople may deliberately underproduce or suppress potential leaders to frustrate attempts at control. Large-scale political coordination and the control of conflict certainly call for leaders—but they do not necessitate them.

Such internal factors and processes in tribal organization may be treated as systematically interconnected and to a degree culturally autonomous, that is, controlled by the perceptions and strategies of tribespeople themselves. However, the main variables determining the emergence of central leadership are generally agreed to be external, particularly the history and nature of relations with states and other tribes. Some scholars argue that tribes are naturally segmentary and egalitarian and that all central authority, indeed the very existence of tribes as defined cultural or political units, is an imposition by, or a reaction to, outside forces. For others, the potential for chiefship exists as a tendency that may be activated or suppressed by an external power. Still others argue that some (if not all) tribal systems are intrinsically centralized.

In historical Middle Eastern states, government control at any one time extends over only some tribal areas, and any one tribal area comes under control only part of the time. The extent of control depends partly on the strength of government and partly on the accessibility of the tribal group concerned, in terms of both terrain—for example, the proximity of mountain or desert refuges—and the distance from cities and roads to the main organs of government. It also depends on the will and attitude of both government and tribes, their motives for seeking or avoiding control.

Rulers' notions of "control," and indeed of "tribe," may be very different from the perceptions of tribespeople themselves. Tribespeople commonly contrast "tribal" with "governmental" periods in their history, whereas both governments and tribespeople refer to "government" and "tribal" areas. Pathans, for example, distinguish *hokumat* from *yaghistan*, Moroccans *bled el-makhzen* from *bled essiba*. These terms do not denote objective conditions but are cultural categories indicating perceptions of particular places at particular times, which we might call "situations."

Government control is clearly an important determinant of tribal political organization, but it is not simply an external force; its impact depends on how it is internalized by the tribespeople and how they react to it. Tribespeople normally have a number of choices. When a government is serious about administering tribal groups within its frontiers, the groups can react by submission or resistance—that is, they can seek a government or a tribal situation. Voluntary submission is usually conditional: the government continues to tolerate tribal patterns of organization and rules indirectly through chiefs responsible to them.

If the rulers are intent on unconditional submission and the more drastic measures of the total destruction of tribal structures and integration of the people into the wider population, resistance is likely and can take various forms. Tribespeople may organize for military confrontation as a confederacy. Another strategy is to avoid engagement, for example, by refusing to recognize any leader, indigenous or imposed, and by maintaining a diffuse form of organization—Gellner's "divide that ye be not ruled," or Malcolm Yapp's "jellyfish tribes." In some cases the avoidance strategy even leads to the abandonment of "tribal" forms of organization such as segmentary lineages, or tribespeople may choose to flee rather than fight.[27] All such avoidance strategies, whose most successful practitioners have managed not to attract government attention at all, are more feasible in frontier, desert, and mountain locations and under marginal conditions where surplus is not produced and strong indigenous leadership is unlikely; but they commonly go together with an institutional inability to unite in extremis to resist determined military aggression.

Strategies of particular tribal groups may alternate over time between acceptance of indirect rule, military resistance, and avoidance, depending on variations in the abilities and ambitions of both their own leaders and government. The most successful tribal groups are probably those that maintain a set of alternative political institutions (for example, leadership roles, institutionalized councils, and segmentary lineages) and ideologies (both religious and materialist) by which they can adapt to conditions of autonomy as well as to the different and changing aggressive policies of outsiders. Tribespeople are often reported to refer wistfully to an earlier golden age when, supposedly, there were "real chiefs we could willingly have followed, not like these charlatans of today." Such sentiments could be interpreted as evidence of alternative ideologies, an acceptance of the idea of central leadership under certain conditions.[28]

Historically, tribal groups in the Middle East have shown evidence of processes of both evolutionary and cyclical or alternating change. Political evolution in scale and complexity—from tribe to state or statelike confederacy, involving the unification of disparate groups, centralization of authority, and stratification—has occurred again and again, as have evolution from kinship and descent to territorial allegiance and control of means of production as principles of organization. The reverse process is also seen, however, whether in terms of "devolution" or retribalization from powerful confederacies into more diffuse organization and simpler groups or indeed in terms of the abandonment, by a tribal group resisting external control, of territorial principles and chiefship in favor of segmentary lineage ideology and avoidance tactics.

None of these cases of apparent evolution or devolution, however, can be interpreted as clear-cut evidence in support of any particular theory of tribe or state formation. In all cases the role of the state and tribal reactions to government policies are the central factors in change. I have argued elsewhere that tribe and state are best thought of as two opposed modes of thought or models of organization that form a single system. As a basis for identity, political allegiance, and behavior, tribe gives primacy to ties of kinship and patrilineal descent, whereas state insists on the loyalty of all persons to a central authority, whatever their relation to each other. Tribe stresses personal, moral, and ascriptive factors in status; state is impersonal and recognizes contract, transaction, and achievement. The tribal mode is socially homogeneous, egalitarian, and segmentary; the state is heterogeneous, stratified, and hierarchical. Tribe is within the individual; state is external.

This tribe-state system involves a constant tension, the dynamics of which are the concern of other theories and models. One of these is the well-known cyclical theory of early Islamic history developed by Ibn Khaldun in the fourteenth century, largely on the basis of his own observations of Northwest Africa but applicable with minor modifications to much of Middle Eastern history since.[29]

The tension also exists at the level of ideas, so that there are elements of state within every tribe and of tribe within every state. Few states, if any, deny the relevance of kinship or descent as criteria for citizenship. At the same time, the egalitarianism and democracy of certain Middle Eastern tribal groups in the twentieth century are not evidence of a pure, untouched condition of tribal society, unaffected by any state or empire, but may be the privileged and precarious result of insulation or encapsulation, possible only in certain frontier conditions and as a direct reflection of ideological, if not military, confrontation with states.

Most empirical tribes and states are some form of hybrid—chiefdoms, confederacies, or tribal states. A chiefdom is a territorially bounded collectivity of groups (usually tribal groups) with coordinated and possibly dynastic leadership but with little elaboration of government or stratification of society. "Confederacy" is a term used for a union of tribal groups for political purposes, sometimes an alliance on the basis of imputed common descent (like the Bakhtiyari), usually with central leadership but sometimes without (as among the Yamut Turkmen)—though some would term such an uncentralized alliance a coalition. Other confederacies are more heterogeneous in composition, unified under a leader either by state action (like the Shahsevan) or electively as an indigenous response to state or other external pressure (like the Qashqa'i). Centralized tribal unions (which may be tribal only in the sense of being composed of tribes) often approximate states, being territorially defined and stratified under a ruling dynasty and elite; by origin they are secondary states, but many independent Muslim dynasties had such origins.

Tribal states may be of three forms. Perhaps the commonest among premodern states has been where one tribal (descent-based) elite or dynasty rules a conquered territory and its heterogeneous population: examples surviving into the present century include the Ottomans, the Qajars, the Durrani, and a number of Arab states. Another form is where a nontribal dynasty is brought to power by, and continues to depend on, tribal support. The best known premodern example is the Safavids in Iran, but some modern Arab states are similar in that central administration is no longer tribal, yet tribalism continues to be important in much of society. In all these cases the state resembles an empire in conceding a certain recognition to semiautonomous tribal groups and minorities. Rulers of other modern states (such as Kemalist Turkey or Pahlavi Iran), while attempting to eradicate tribalism completely from the country—claiming common descent or origins for all citizens and denying or eliminating differences—have promoted a nationalist ideology of integration that resembles a tribal ideology.

How are tribe and state conceptualized by tribespeople? Numerous studies have shown how both modes exist not merely in the structure of the system but as opposed cultural categories within the experience of individuals. The terms in which they are articulated represent alternative models used both for explaining social organization and as guides for practical action in crises and disputes.[30]

Similar opposed categories are reported from many other contexts. One of the best known in anthropology is the *gumsa-gumlao* system of the Kachin of Highland Burma. Leach analyzed three "types" of community as part of a single system: the egalitarian *gumlao*, the hierarchical Shan kingdom, and the intermediate and unstable *gumsa* chiefdom. These types were ideal patterns, set out for Kachin in ritual and myth, but by means of ambiguous symbols allowing alternative interpretations, which individuals could exploit. The whole system was full of inconsistencies, and Leach showed evidence that individual communities in the long term oscillated between the extremes, each of which was inherently structurally unstable.[31]

Leach's model of oscillation, derived from Vilifredo Pareto's discussion of the alternating dominance of "lions" and "foxes," has often been compared with Ibn Khaldun's theory of the circulation of tribal elites in Northwest Africa and its development by Montagne and Gellner, in terms of relations between *siba* (peripheral, dissident, segmentary, and egalitarian tribes) and *makhzen* (areas administered by the state).[32] This model has recently been subject to debate. A too-literal application of terms such as "segmentary" and "egalitarian" to North African places and peoples has been criticized as part of a general reconsideration of classical anthropological segmentary theory. These terms, the critics insist, as well as *siba* and *makhzen*, are not descriptive but cultural categories, idioms that are inadequate to explain the fluid and complex workings of actual tribal societies, let alone the relations of tribe and state. Account must be taken of the antisegmentary communities that form at certain levels of organization; of the patterns of rivalries, alliances, and blocs among them; and of increasing centralization involving networks of dyadic ties of patronage, channeling communication to and from the powerful center.[33]

I would argue that varying articulations of all three processes (segmentarity; communities, rivalries, and bloc alliances; and patronage and centralization) produce the empirical transformations of tribal society. The major variable is the influence of the state both as an external force and as an idea in opposition to the idea of tribe. The essence of the latter is indeed kinship and egalitarian democracy (the basis of a segmentary lineage system), whereas that of the former is territoriality (the basis of communities, rivalries, and alliances) and central authority (the basis of patronage networks). The most purely segmentary tribal groups are, as argued earlier, not those completely independent of states but rather those in a position—and with the motivation—to maximize their segmentarity, practically and ideologically, in opposition to either a real state or the idea of state. Diffuseness of organization, where segmentarity is also weakly developed, occurs either in tribal groups beyond the influence of (real or ideal) states or as a strategy by a weak tribal group to resist an encroaching state. As an alternative ideology or reserve structure, segmentarity persists in many modern tribal societies in spite of bearing little relation to political groups and behavior. When state control strengthens, state principles (territoriality, hierarchy of authority) grow in influence, and so then do the roles of factionalism and patronage.

It is in these terms that we can understand both variation in actual tribal forms and changes that occur, whether we adopt a cyclical (oscillation) model of change or acknowledge the apparently irreversible (evolutionary) changes that have now taken place in the transition from tribe to state.

NOTES

1. This is a revised version of the paper presented at the Harvard-MIT Conference on Tribes and State Formation and also at a seminar at the Center for Near Eastern Studies, UCLA; I am grateful for comments received on both occasions, as well as from the editors of this volume.

2. See, for example, Morton Fried, *The Notion of Tribe* (Menlo Park, Calif., 1975), and "The State, the Chicken, and the Egg: Or, What Came First?" in Ronald Cohen and Elman R. Service, eds., *Origins of the State* (Philadelphia, 1978).

3. Fried, *Notion*, and Cohen and Service, *Origins*.

4. E. E. Evans-Pritchard, *The Nuer* (Oxford, 1940).

5. E. R. Leach, *Political Systems of Highland Burma* (London, 1954).

6. See, for example, June Helm, ed., *Essays on the Problem of Tribe* (Seattle, 1968).

7. A. K. S. Lambton, *Islamic Society in Persia* (London, 1954), p. 6.

8. Dale F. Eickelman, *The Middle East: An Anthropological Approach*, 1st ed. (Englewood Cliffs, N.J., 1981), pp. 88–89; he discusses the notions in a different order.

9. Fredrik Barth, *Nomads of South Persia* (London, 1961); Gene R. Garthwaite, *Khans and Shahs: A Documentary Analysis of the Bukhtiyari in Iran* (Cambridge, 1983); Lois Beck, *The Qashqa'i of Iran* (New Haven, 1986); Reinhold Loeffler, "Tribal Order and the State: The Political Organization of Boir Ahmad," *Iranian Studies* 11 (1978): 145–171; Richard Tapper, *Pasture and Politics* (London, 1979).

10. For the mistaken stereotypes with which British Indian agents approached the Pathans of the Northwest Frontier, see Malcolm Yapp, "Tribes and States in the Khyber, 1838–1842," in Richard Tapper, ed., *The Conflict of Tribe and State in Iran and Afghanistan* (London, 1983); for Russian attitudes to the tribes in the southeastern Caucasus, see Richard Tapper, "Nomads and Commissars in the Mughan Steppe," in Tapper, *Tribe and State*, and also Richard Tapper, *The King's Friends* (forthcoming).

11. See several of the historians discussed later in the text. For an economic and ecological approach to tribe, see Emanuel Marx, "The Tribe as a Unit of Subsistence," *American Anthropologist* 79 (1977): 343–363.

12. Fredrik Barth, "Nomadism in the Mountain and Plateau Areas of South West Asia," in *The Problems of the Arid Zone: Proceedings of the Paris Symposium* (Paris, 1962).

13. Basile Nikitine, "Les afshars d'Urumiyeh," *Journal Asiatique* 214 (1929): 122–123.

14. Richard Tapper, "Shahsevan in Safavid Persia," *Bulletin of the School of Oriental and African Studies* 37 (1974): 321–354, and "Ethnicity, Order and Meaning in the Anthropology of Iran and Afghanistan," in Jean-Pierre Digard, ed., *Le fait ethnique en Iran et en Afghanistan* (Paris, 1988); see also Jan Ovesen, "The Construction of Ethnic Identities," in Anita Jacobsen-Widding, ed., *Identity: Personal and Socio-Cultural*, Uppsala Studies in Cultural Anthropology (Uppsala, 1983); and Yapp, "Khyber."

15. I have elsewhere analyzed the ambiguity between *tira* (tribal section, political-administrative grouping under an elder), *göbek* (patrilineage), and *jamahat* (community, congregation) among the Shahsevan (Tapper, *Pasture and Politics*); and the ambiguities of *qaum* (family, nation, endogamous groups), *wolus* (political community), *aulad* (patrilineage), and *tayfa* (local tribal section) among the Durrani in Afghanistan (Nancy Tapper and Richard Tapper, "Marriage Preferences and Ethnic Relations," *Folk* 24 [1982]:

157–177). See also Martin van Bruinessen's discussion of Leach's and Barth's difficulties with the terms *ashiret, tira,* and *tayfa* among the Kurds, *Agha, Shaikh and State* (Utrecht, 1978), pp 52–53.

16. Leonard M. Helfgott, "Tribalism as a Socioeconomic Formation in Iranian History," *Iranian Studies* 10 (1977): 36–61; Helfgott, "The Structural Foundations of the National Minority Problem in Revolutionary Iran," *Iranian Studies* 13 (1980): 195–214; Helfgott, "Tribe and Uymaq in Iran: A Reply," *Iranian Studies* 16 (1983): 73–78; James J. Reid, "The Qajar Uymaq in the Safavid Period, 1500–1722," *Iranian Studies* 11 (1978): 117–143; Reid "Comments on 'Tribalism as a Socioeconomic Formation in Iranian History,'" *Iranian Studies* 12 (1979): 275–281; Reid, *Tribalism and Society in Islamic Iran, 1500–1629* (Malibu, Calif., 1983); Reid, "Studying Clans in Iranian History: A Response," *Iranian Studies* 17 (1984): 85–92.

17. R. D. McChesney, "Comments on 'The Qajar Uymaq in the Safavid Period,'" *Iranian Studies* 14 (1981): 87–105. See reviews of Reid, *Tribalism and Society,* by John E. Woods, *International Journal of Middle East Studies* 18 (1986): 529–532; A. H. Morton, *Journal of the Royal Asiatic Society,* 1986: 281–282; D. O. Morgan, *Bulletin of the School of Oriental and African Studies* 49 (1986): 342. Reid's response ("Studying Clans") to McChesney is abusive and fails to answer his detailed criticisms; in the words of another critic, it is "game, set and match to McChesney" (Morgan). In his important book on the Aqquyunlu, Woods does not make analytical use of the notion of tribe but concentrates on the structure of the dominant tribal groups in fifteenth-century Anatolia and Iran, composite political confederacies of nomadic "clans" with a dynastic paramount clan. *The Aqquyunlu: Clan, Confederation, Empire* (Minneapolis, 1976).

18. Rudi Paul Lindner, "What Was a Nomad Tribe?" *Comparative Studies in Society and History* 24 (1982): 689–711; Lindner, *Nomads and Ottomans in Medieval Anatolia* (Bloomington, Ind., 1983); Patricia Crone, "The Tribe and the State," in J. A. Hall, ed., *States in History* (Oxford, 1986).

19. See Tapper, *Pasture and Politics,* p. 252.

20. For some contrasts between Basseri, Yürük, Turkmen, and Shahsevan nomadic social organization, see Tapper, *Pasture and Politics,* pp. 240f. John Masson Smith, Jr., "Turanian Nomadism and Iranian Politics," *Iranian Studies* 11 (1978): 57–81, much used by Lindner, also extrapolates inappropriately from the Basseri and the Yürük (minimum and average herd sizes, production values, etc.) in his account of Mongol nomadic society; he also misunderstands Barth's analysis of the Basseri as a tribe.

21. Woods, *Aqquyunlu;* McChesney, "Comments"; Loeffler, "Tribal Order," pp. 154f.; Tapper, "Nomads and Commissars."

22. See, for example, Ernest Gellner, *Cause and Meaning in the Social Sciences* (London, 1973).

23. Crone, "The Tribe and the State," pp. 72–73.

24. Tapper, Introduction to *Tribe and State,* where much of the argument in this section is further developed.

25. Opposed blocs are pervasive among Swat Pathans (Fredrik Barth, *Political Leadership among Swat Pathans* [London, 1954], and "Segmentary Op-

position and the Theory of Games," *Journal of the Royal Anthropological Institute* 81 [1959]: 5–21]; among Cyrenaican Bedouin (Emrys Peters, "Some Structural Aspects of the Feud among the Camel-Raising Bedouin of Cyrenaica," *Africa* 37 [1967], and Foreword to Jacob Black-Michaud, *Cohesive Force: Feud in the Mediterranean and the Middle East* [Oxford, 1975]); among Yamut Turkmen (William Irons, *The Yomut Turkmen* [Ann Arbor, Mich., 1975]); among Shahsevan nomad camps (Tapper, *Pasture and Politics*); and among Shahsevan tribal coalitions (Richard Tapper, "Raiding, Reaction and Rivalry," *Bulletin of the School of Oriental and African Studies* 49 [1986]: 508–531. See also *leff* and *soff* in the Maghreb, the division of the Qajars into upper and lower branches, the Kurds into left and right, the Bakhtiyari into Chahar and Haft Lang, various Pathan groups into Zirak and Panjpay, Spin and Tor, Gar and Samil, and so on.

26. See, for example, Tapper, "Raiding."

27. Ernest Gellner, *Muslim Society* (Cambridge, 1981); Yapp, "Khyber"; see also Bernt Glatzer, "Pashtun Nomads and the State," in Tapper, *Tribe and State.*

28. See Gellner, *Muslim Society*, chap. 4; Philip C. Salzman, "Does Complementary Opposition Exist?" *American Anthropologist* 80 (1978): 53–70, and "Ideology and Change in Tribal Society," *Man* (n.s.) 13 (1978): 618–637; F. G. Bailey, *Stratagems and Spoils: A Social Anthropology of Politics* (Oxford, 1969), pp 15–16.

29. Ibn Khaldun, *The Muqaddimah*, trans. F. Rosenthal (London, 1967); see Gellner, *Muslim Society*, esp. chap. 1; Tapper, Introduction, pp. 62f.

30. For examples, see Tapper, *Tribe and State.*

31. Leach, *Political Systems*. His analysis has received—and survived—a good deal of criticism and revaluation, notably that of Jonathan Friedman, "Tribes, States and Transformations," in Maurice Bloch, ed., *Marxist Analyses and Social Anthropology* (London, 1975).

32. Vilifredo Pareto, *The Mind and Society* (New York, 1963); Robert Montagne, *The Berbers*, trans. J. D. Seddon (London, 1972); Ernest Gellner, *Saints of the Atlas* (London, 1969). See also Owen Lattimore, *Inner Asian Frontiers of China* (New York, 1941).

33. See, for example, C. Geertz, H. Geertz, and L. Rosen, *Meaning and Order in Moroccan Society* (Cambridge, 1979), pp. 106, 264, 377; Michael Meeker, *Literature and Violence in North Arabia* (Cambridge, 1979), pp. llf., 220; Eickelman, *The Middle East*, esp. p. 104; Peters, "Structural Aspects"; E. L. Peters, "Aspects of Affinity in a Lebanese Maronite Village," in J. G. Peristiany, ed., *Mediterranean Family Structures* (Cambridge, 1976). For Gellner's response to some of these critics of segmentary theory and its applications, see his *Muslim Society* and "The Tribal Society and Its Enemies," in Tapper, *Tribe and State*. More recent contributions to the debate include M. Eliane Combs-Schilling, "Family and Friend in a Moroccan Boom Town," *American Ethnologist* 12 (1985): 659–675; Paul Dresch, "The Significance of the Course Events Take in Segmentary Systems," *American Ethnologist* 13, no. 2 (1986): 309–324; and Steven C. Caton, "Power, Persuasion and Language," *International Journal of Middle East Studies* 19 (1987): 77–102.

Anthropological Theories of Tribe and State Formation in the Middle East: Ideology and the Semiotics of Power

Steven C. Caton

The aims of this essentially theoretical and comparative essay are twofold. The first is to provide a fairly detailed comparative investigation of the ideas contained in various anthropological models bearing on tribe-state relations. I have limited myself to an examination of four models, though probably several more deserve careful scrutiny.[1] I begin with the Marxist model (excluding Karl Wittfogel's hydraulic thesis, which I consider to be a special and rather idiosyncratic case in Marxist literature and therefore will not treat here), not necessarily because it has been the most successful in Middle Eastern ethnography, but because it spells out some of the basic issues that dominate the discussion of tribe and state, particularly the issue of ideology. An exposition of Ibn Khaldun immediately follows. There are interesting parallels between the two, which I do not intend to make explicit but which the readers no doubt will catch on their own by virtue of the juxtaposition of the two sections. Ibn Khaldun is important not only because he represents a distinctly Muslim point of view on the origin of the state but also because his point of view has been incorporated in late functionalist theory, especially in the work of Ernest Gellner. It thus behooves us to examine functionalism in connection with Ibn Khaldun's theories and our concerns with tribe and state in the third section, which focuses on the segmentary lineage system. I leave for the end a discussion of a theory that comes not out of political economy, theoretical anthropology, or Muslim political philosophy but rather has emerged from the research of historians and anthropologists on tribal elites.

My second aim is to give a particular critical "reading" of the four models, which will, I hope, stimulate thinking on the question of tribe and state in a particular direction. The basic point recapitulated in the analysis of all four models, a point that I believe has been neglected in theoretical models to date, has to do with the importance of ideology in the process of state formation. I will argue, however, that to understand the role of ideology in that process, one must study sign use in social acts of communication, something that has yet to be done by any student of political action in the Middle East.

That argument is worked out in detail in the first section of this essay. Subsequent sections allude to it again but also refine it by suggesting that the analytical concept of the charismatic personality (in the figure of either the tribal chieftain or the religious/prophetic saint) is a key component in these concrete contexts of sign use. It is this system of ideas—production of ideology through the use of signs in concrete, social acts of communication by charismatic personalities—that I will refer to as the *semiotics of power*.

MARXIST APPROACHES

Marx and Engels on the Tribe and State

To understand Marx's theory of precapitalist economic formations, it is essential first to clarify his concept of humankind.[2] Marx and Engels write in *The German Ideology*, "Men can be distinguished from animals . . . as soon as they begin to *produce* their means of subsistence." Production is here understood not simply as maintaining individuals' physical existence but as "a definite form of expressing their life, a definite *mode* of life on their part."[3] Natural factors, such as the physical form of the body as well as ecological conditions under which production takes place, deeply affect the outcome of human labor; but most significant of all is the factor of society, for humans are social animals who produce not only for their own subsistence but also for that of the family. The family in turn enters into essential relationships with other families in a larger social group, and so forth. According to Marx, society is not formed by some sort of social contract or convention; it is the product of "spontaneous evolution." He speaks on the same page of "the spontaneously evolved tribal community or, if you will, the herd."[4]

Humans are also reflective animals, possessed of a powerful faculty for thought and language, but to Marx it was essential "to realize that neither thoughts nor language in themselves form a realm of their own, that they are only *manifestations* of actual life."[5] This statement should not be read as a crude form of determinism of mental life by the material conditions of existence, however. Rather, thought is always directed to the solution of real, objective problems of existence, problems created by the division of labor and class structure.

Certain deductions flow from these initial axioms. To be a producer, the individual must wrest control over a part of nature, appropriating it for his or her own use. Furthermore, the individual must prevent others from stealing his or her appropriation. True, a particularly strong person might wrest control by brute force, but to Marx this is hardly a plausible evolutionary solution to the problem of appropriation. Therefore, the individual can only appropriate if society has already determined the conditions of his or her property ownership. In other words, the modes of property ownership are prior to the individual's appropriation of land.

The individual at the beginning of human history is only "a generic being, a tribal being, a herd animal" who gradually "individualizes" himself.[6] By what process does this individualization occur? To answer that question, we must first examine more closely Marx's concept of society and the division of labor within it.

In the earliest stage of human history, society is constituted of the family and the tribe. In the family is to be found a "natural" division of labor between man and woman, parents and offspring. A division of labor also naturally exists in the rest of the tribe. Some persons hunt, some fish, and others cultivate, but all must exchange the surplus of their goods and services to obtain a fully rounded subsistence. It is in the division of labor that the "generic being" first begins to "individualize" himself or herself; he or she is one kind of producer in contrast with other kinds within the society: "The division of labor implies the contradiction between the interest of the separate individual or the individual family and the communal interest of all individuals." Individualism is thus tied in large part to the material conditions of existence. With the division of labor in society is also introduced human alienation, one of Marx's most profoundly tragic concepts: "For as soon as the distribution of labor comes into being, each man has a particular, exclusive sphere of activity, which is forced upon him and from which he cannot escape. He is a hunter, a fisherman, a shepherd, or a critical critic, and must remain so if he does not want to lose his means of livelihood."[7] What Marx laments in the passing of the earliest human society and promises to restore in the communist one is an idyllic wholeness of life and activity, such that people do not have to feel alienated in their labor. What is also important is the fact that for Marx the exchange of surplus goods and services is never equal, so that even with respect to the early human family he hints darkly of a "latent slavery." It stands to reason that power is based on the individual's favorable control over the system of exchange and that conflict over power is endemic to the division of labor.

These fundamental axioms are the building blocks out of which Marx constructs his logical models of precapitalist economic formations. These formations, in turn, tell us something of the way in which Marx envisioned the relationship of the individual to the (tribal) community and to the state, the basic concerns of the present book.[8]

In the first form of property (variously called ancient or tribal) to emerge out of the pastoral, herd-animal existence of early man, the tribe, which is a union of families identified by "the common ties of blood, language, custom, etc.," is the owner of the land. The individual may "possess" land—that is, may have rights to use it—but only insofar as he or she is a member of the tribal community. "We take it for granted that pastoralism or more generally a migratory life, is the first form of maintaining existence, the tribe not settling in a fixed place but using up what it finds locally and then passing on."[9] Eventually people settle in villages and, depending on ecological circumstances, may even found cities at crossroads in trading networks. The social structure is still fairly simple, merely an extension of the family with some slaves acquired in conquest and a rudimentary division of labor. Two alternative forms of production are possible at this stage of property ownership. One such form entails each village being allotted land on which the individual labors to produce goods for the family's needs along with a small surplus to be used for the common welfare. The other form of production may involve villages uniting and cooperating to build large-scale irrigation systems or communication networks (Mexico, Peru, the ancient Celts, and some tribes of India are cited as examples), and Marx adds that it is the latter form that is "very important among the Asian peoples."[10]

The second form of ownership, which Marx variously called Oriental, communal, Roman, or Asiatic, is also founded, as in the first case, on the community, but individual ownership or private property now begins to emerge alongside communal land. "To be a member of the community remains the precondition for the appropriation of land, but in his capacity as member of the community the individual is a private proprietor."[11] Also prominent at this stage is the more widespread existence of cities that arose through the union of several tribes "by agreement or by conquest."[12] In fact, in this economic mode it is the city that is the seat of the community, not the land (as in the "tribal" formation), which is now merely an appendage of the city. Slavery becomes more evident; there now emerges a distinct class structure composed of the free citizens of the city at one end and the slave class at the other. Even within the free citizenry there develops an incipient conflict between the small peasantry and the more powerful landowners. This class conflict notwithstanding, Marx views the major antagonisms as arising between the city and the rural hinterland and resulting from the division of labor, that is, the antagonism between town and country. "War is therefore the great all-embracing task, the great communal labor" for which the city-states require armies. The community, consisting of kinship groups, is therefore in the first instance organized on military lines, as a war-like, military force, and this is one of the conditions of its existence as a "proprietor." It is no wonder that under such conditions of war the state now becomes the means by which the citizens can unite "against the outside world" and be "their safeguard."[13] In this phase the state is still serving and protecting the interests of the community at large against the interests of the individuals; but as class structure becomes more pronounced, it increasingly becomes the instrument by which the dominant class can oppress the non-owning class (the slaves and the lesser landowners, who gradually become dispossessed, move to the cities, and lease their labor to the land-owning class while competing with the slaves).

The third precapitalist formation, which Marx calls Germanic, marks the period of the early Middle Ages. Here the land is not owned by the community. Only a part of it remains common land; the rest belongs to individual households, which form independent centers of production scattered across the land. In other words, private property becomes the basis of ownership. A gradual "individualization" of man has led to his becoming an individual proprietor. The community, such as it is, is defined by "the common element in language, blood, etc., which is the premise of the individual proprietor" and "has real being only in its *actual assembly* for communal purposes" such as ritual, war, and dispute mediations. Cities do not exist, only the settlements of the individual households, and for that reason Marx declares that "the community has no existence as a *state, a political entity.*"[14]

Tribe and State in the Marxist Model

According to Marx, then, the state first emerges in the tribal formation as a structure that "represents" the interests of the community as a whole. It may be created by internal consensus or imposed by external conquest; it may either be despotic or democratic in form, but it is closely tied to the existence of the city.

The reason that the state emerged in the first place has to do with the contradictions inherent in the division of labor. This division, as we have seen, pits the interests of the individual against the interests of the family, and those of the family against those of the tribe. "And out of this contradiction," explains Marx, "between the interest of the individual and that of the community, the latter takes an independent form as the State."[15] At first the state represents the general interest of the community, or tribe, which must practically control the conflict of individual interests threatening its unity. In the beginning the state safeguards the general interest. In the "Oriental" mode, however, this conflict inherent to the division of labor is exacerbated by a more highly developed economic class structure. Indeed, the owners of the modes of production now dominate the rest of society, with the result that the state is no longer the guardian of the public interest but rather the instrument by which the dominant class attempts to realize its individual interests: "Every class which is struggling for mastery, even when its domination, as is the case with the proletariat, postulates the abolition of the old form of society in its entirety and of domination itself, must first conquer for itself political power in order to represent its interest in turn as the general interest."[16] In time the state becomes increasingly the "tool" of the oppressor, the property-owning class, serving its individual interests. This development logically corresponds to Marx's concept of the gradual individualization of man in historical time as a consequence of the division of labor. My point, however, is that the state first emerged as a solution, or attempted solution, to the problem of order created by the contradictions apparent in the tribal division of labor; then, with the completion of an economic class structure, it became an institution by which the property-owning class could exploit the class of non-owners.

What are the means by which the dominant class gains and maintains control of the state apparatus? An obvious means is the military, which, we have seen, arose to safeguard the general interest of the community from the contradictions created by the division of labor. The military can also be used by the property-owning class to coerce the propertyless class. Another, more interesting means is what Marx called ideology. In fact, the increasing division of labor creates a class of people whose main occupation is to produce ideas and fashion new styles to mold the consciousness of the citizens. In keeping with his axiom that mental life is never self-contained but always tied to the material conditions of existence, Marx sees ideology as serving the interests of the state. Ideology represents the state as serving the "general interest"; but with the completion of an economic class structure, this representation of reality becomes illusory or mystifying because it hides the actualities of the class struggle and the domination of the property-owning class. Ideologists then become the tool of the dominant class.

Whatever one may think of the correctness of these views on ideology, they still beg the question of what precisely an ideology is. It cannot be any pure Hegelian spirit or consciousness if it is tied to the material conditions of existence. Yet it cannot be a reflection of material reality either, for ideology is a mystifying or distorting representation of it. The latter leads to the conclusion that ideology entails a semiotic mediation of reality, a point most forcefully made by the Marxist theoreticians V. N. Vološinov and M. M. Bakhtin: "The reality of ideological phenomena is the objective reality of social signs."[17] In effect, their book *Marxism and the Philosophy of Language* (1929) is an attempt to redress one of the oversights in classical Marxist thinking on ideology.

Vološinov and Bakhtin point out that pure idea cannot exist because "understanding is a response to a sign with signs," and "nowhere is there a break in the chain, nowhere does the chain plunge into inner being, nonmaterial in nature and unembodied in signs." However, that idea must be communicated (even in "inner speech" or thought) by signs; and these signs cannot exist except in social action:

> Signs can arise only on *interindividual territory*. It is territory that cannot be called "natural" in the direct sense of the word: signs do not arise between any two members of the species Homo sapiens. It is essential that the two individuals be organized socially, that they compose a group (a social unit); only then can the medium of signs take shape between them.[18]

To analyze ideology, then, one must examine its mediation through signs in concrete social acts of communication. In terms of modern developments in the study of language in its social context, this view anticipates what today is called the ethnography of communication,[19] though it is infused with a dose of social psychology in the vein of G. H. Mead. "Each period and each social group has had and has its own repertoire of speech forms for ideological communication in human behavior," and Vološinov and Bakhtin assert that "a typology of these forms is one of the urgent tasks of Marxism."[20]

It is impossible in the space of this essay to develop the richness of their argument any further, but the basic point Vološinov and Bakhtin make regarding the semiotic mediation of ideas in social acts of communication is the one that needs to be stressed as a corrective to the underdeveloped notion of ideology in the writings of Marx and Engels. Moreover, it is rarely heeded in the use of the Marxist model for the study of tribe and state in the Middle East.

The Marxist Model of Tribe-State Relations in Middle Eastern Ethnography

The ethnographic literature on the Middle East is still relatively lacking in Marxist analyses of tribal societies.[21] The research of Jean-Pierre Digard on the Bakhtiyar of Iran is a good example.[22] Like most studies of nomadic societies, Digard's work emphasizes ecological factors to which Bakhtiyari society is closely adapted.[23] Digard also notes that the division of labor within the tribe, as well as among tribesmen, other ethnic groups, and sedentary populations, creates unequal access to material resources. In addition, he does not believe that the various levels or segments within the levels are equal to each other in political power but rather asserts that a pyramidal power structure exists with the *il-khan* at the top, followed by the *kalantar*, the *katkhoda*, and so forth.[24] The explanation for this so-called centralized system of power is complex. It has partly to do with ecology, that is, the scarcity of usable land and its demand by an expanding population. This demand potentially creates conflict, which may throw the whole delicately balanced social system into disarray. The khans are the effective peacekeepers who, supposedly, can impose settlements on recalcitrant parties and mobilize troops in case of massive conflict, with (or without) the consent of the collective will. With this kind of power goes private ownership by the khans of considerable tracts of land both inside and outside the tribe; such ownership turns them into overlords of the tribe and potentially puts them in conflict with it. In other words, a division of labor between leaders and followers is marked also by a duality in the modes of production and an unequal ownership of the fruits of that production, leading in turn to an incipient class conflict.

At this point in the argument Digard connects the problem of a rising class structure within the tribe to the tribe's relationship with the central nation-state. He does not deny the fact that there may have been a need for brokers or middlemen to mediate between the tribe and the state bureaucracy—a role for which the khans may have been eminently suited during the course of their rise to prominence in the eighteenth century—but only that they were already in place within the tribal power structure before they played this role and in place as a result of economic forces, not political ones. This is an important theoretical point, which distinguishes the Marxist explanation for the rise of tribal political elites from the model that is currently being developed by a number of investigators (see below). Talal Asad realizes and articulates the point most lucidly:

> The political elite may indeed act in the capacity of entrepreneur, middleman or representative, but it does so as a middleman who has a privileged monopoly in relation to his tribal "clients." As with all holders of crucial monopolies this gives the elite-middlemen dominant power over others: the middleman is able to define the conditions for the fulfillment of his clients' interests, and even to determine their essential priorities.[25]

True, Asad is alluding to Fredrik Barth's description of the Basseri nomad chief rather than the analysis of the political elite by G. R. Garthwaite, Lois Beck, and others, but the essential point applies to both.[26] Within the Marxist model the emergence of the elite is to be explained by changing patterns in the division of labor and their attendant consequences for the unequal distribution of the fruits of this labor. With their dominance in the tribal hierarchy bolstered by the state, the elites of the Kababish and Bakhtiyar then attempt to monopolize the forces of production, becoming the exploiters of the tribal "commoners."[27]

What Digard had done for the Bakhtiyar material in the way of a Marxist analysis Asad had already attempted for the Kababish Arabs of the Sudan and in a provocative reanalysis of Barth's data from Swat.[28] But from our perspective Asad's Marxist framework is more interesting in that it also addresses the neglected role of ideology in the maintenance of power by the ruling class: "We cannot understand the historical structure of political domination unless we also undertake a critical investigation of ideologies in order to uncover the partial, distorted conceptions of reality built into them, and which being thus built, constitute an indispensable part of such structures."[29]

The term *Kababish* refers to a loose confederation of pastoral tribes located in northwestern Sudan. Asad views the tribe as composed of unequal "segments"—the Awlad Fadlallah rulers, who are descendants of a powerful nineteenth-century shaykh, and their subjects—and characterizes the relationship between them as exploitive both materially (the appropriation of surplus from the collective process of pastoral production to which the elite does not directly contribute) and politically (only the rulers can make decisions affecting the lives of the rest of the Kababish).[30] Asad denies that the elite is necessarily given its authority by consent of the tribe in exchange for its peacekeeping services or for its role as middleman with the central state; he asserts that the tribe could in actual fact find other alternatives to solve these problems:

> Much more important...is...the perpetuation of a particular structure of inequality which is part of its definition of the Kababish tribe. This is the essential mode in which the Kababish population is brought together. And in order to carry out this function effectively, the rulers must impose a distinctive ideological order on their experience of political life. They must convince not only their subjects but also themselves of the legitimacy of their distinctive position and privilege.[31]

What is interesting is Asad's contention that the primary basis for authority among the Kababish is neither coercion nor consent but rather a historically created process in which an unequal structure is *legitimated* by ideology. "The significance of 'legitimation' goes beyond the process of justification in the sense of mere endorsement of a political order to include the conceptualization of what the order 'really' is."[32]

In other words, what is needed to complete the Marxist analysis of tribe is an elucidation of the way in which a culture defines political reality. Although Asad does give a fairly detailed and coherent account of that ideology, he does not show how political beliefs held by members of the tribe are enacted in everyday social relations. That is, it is not enough to lay bare the ideology, as Vološinov and Bakhtin have made clear; it is also necessary to relate it to key contexts of social action in which the elite does in fact persuade or compel the Kababish to accept its authority by manipulating efficacious political symbols.[33]

Problems with the Marxist Analyses

Except for Asad's, there have been no detailed Marxist ethnographies of tribal societies in the Middle East, though Marxist historical analyses have been given of Central Asian nomadic states.[34] Such analyses will have to confront and resolve certain empirical dilemmas. It is obviously not enough to say that economic inequalities exist, for surely they do regardless of the society or historical period. Rather, at what point does it make sense to argue that these inequalities are indicative of class structure? In part, the answer to this question depends on the answer to others. To what extent does the economically advantaged group own or control the means of production without necessarily being directly involved in the process of production? Does the economically advantaged group really exploit the economically less dominant one? And by what ideology is the dominant group able to legitimate its political authority within the system?

Several studies of Middle Eastern tribal societies have suggested that the governance of the tribal polity can be divided into roughly two tiers—the subtribal level, which usually includes the pastoral camp led by headmen and the extended households of several, usually related families; and a hierarchy of tribal leaders above them.[35] Beck, for example, described in detail for the Qashqa'i (a nomadic pastoralist society of southwestern Iran) a sociopolitical organization composed of subtribal camps led by elders whose source of power comes from within the local group, which was, at least until recently, independent of the central state.[36] Above them rose a pyramid composed at the top by the *ilkhani*, who dealt directly with the state, and below him a middle echelon of khans who mediated between the pastoral camps and the *ilkhani*. It is also recognized that these two levels within tribal society are based on distinct modes of production. In the pastoral camp, ownership of the land is collective, whereas herds are privately owned by the individual households. The elites may also own large herds, but they derive their income mainly from their ownership of the means of agricultural production and from rents collected from urban properties. Although real economic and political inequalities exist, it is not at all clear from the ethnographic data that the relationship of the elites to their tribal followers can be said to be "exploitive."

P. C. Salzman has raised doubts about Asad's assertion to that effect for the Kababish.[37] The basic point of the article seems to be to advise caution in the use of the terms *egalitarian* and *oppressive* as overarching categories to describe sociopolitical organization among pastoral nomads. Salzman argues that Asad has underplayed the significance of the state's relation to the tribal elite as a source of political inequality. At the same time, this elite has not managed to gain control over the means of pastoral production that still is collectively held by the tribespeople. Because of their mobility (and possibly other means of resistance such as violence), such economic exploitation by the elite would be difficult unless, of course, the national government were willing to heavily support them.[38] In the Kababish case, then, Salzman argues that though economic inequality exists, it would be wrong to suppose that the tribespeople feel "oppressed" by their tribal elite: "This is not to argue that there is consent in the tribe for the elite monopoly, but to suggest that the elite monopoly per se is not a matter of great concern for the tribesmen."[39]

In short, ethnographic studies have not convincingly demonstrated the application of the Marxist model to an understanding of pastoral or sedentary tribal societies and state formation in the Middle East. Nevertheless, let me restate the main theoretical themes of the model that will be contrasted with other theories to be considered subsequently. The concept of tribe, it is argued, is based essentially on modes of production. Where a division of labor occurs, an unequal distribution of wealth follows leading to economic and social inequalities among segments or between the elite and the rest of the tribe. In cases where the economically advantaged group can exploit the less advantaged one, a class system develops with attendant political conflicts. At first, to contain these conflicts, a state apparatus is formed, but it eventually becomes an instrument for further exploitation by the elite. Critical to the means of this exploitation, at least in the theories of Marx and Asad, is a group's ideology. In Marx the elite's ideology "mystifies" the objective reality of the elite's exploitation of society. In Asad the problem of ideology is linked to Weber's concept of the legitimation of authority. My point has been that to understand the nature of ideology in either sense, we must delve into its semiotic mediation in concrete acts of communication, a neglected, though crucial, area of research.

IBN KHALDUN'S THEORY OF THE TRIBE AND STATE

It seems appropriate to include the fourteenth-century Maghrebi philosopher Ibn Khaldun (1332–1406) in our theoretical overview because, as Muhsin S. Mahdi has observed, "the problems of the creation of the state, the stages through which it passes, its various forms, and the causes of its decline, are the central problems of Ibn Khaldun's science of culture."[40] Like Marx, Ibn Khaldun builds his model deductively from what he takes to be certain axioms of human nature. Accordingly, it is essential for us to understand his concept of humanity before tracing in detail his intricate model of the state.

Humans are distinguished from the animals by their reason: "God distinguished man from all other animals by an ability to think, which He made the beginning of human perfection and the end of man's noble superiority over things."[41] But he is still cursed with enough aggressive animality to want to seek domination over his fellow men. Indeed, a contradiction exists between this aggressive nature and man's need for social cooperation, for without the latter he is unable to obtain the food resources his existence requires or to defend himself against more powerful predators (pp. 45–46). Thus, man is also a profoundly solitary creature by dint of natural circumstances and his psychological constitution.

Ibn Khaldun argues that once social organization has begun, people need someone to exercise a restraining influence, someone to curb animal aggressiveness. "The person who exercises a restraining influence, therefore, must be one of themselves. He must dominate them and have power and authority over them, so that no one of them will be able to attack another. This is the meaning of royal authority" (p. 47). He concedes the possibility that obedience to authority also exists "among certain dumb animals" (such as bees) but insists that in humans, to the contrary, this obedience is founded on the ability to reason and in the exercise of free will. Humans voluntarily agree to submit to a higher authority because their (practical) reason convinces them of the wisdom of the choice.

Almost all commentators have noted that Ibn Khaldun's "god term," to repeat a phrase of Kenneth Burke's, is 'asabiyya, "solidarity." We are told that "group feeling produces the ability to defend oneself, to offer opposition, to protect oneself, and to press one's claims" (p. 111). To only a limited extent does reason determine social solidarity among men, as in, for example, the realization of the mutual need for defense against other hostile groups. More important is "[respect for] blood ties...[as] something natural in men.... It leads to affection for one's relations and blood relatives, [the feeling that] no harm ought to befall them nor any destruction come upon them.... This is a natural urge in man, for as long as there have been human beings" (p. 98). This passage captures the basic assumption that can be traced to at least L. H. Morgan at the beginning of anthropology, namely, that kinship, understood as descent, creates "natural" bonds among people. Blood descent in Ibn Khaldun's model is not the only factor in maintaining solidarity, however. There is also the closeness of the shared space, for he contends that when kinsmen live relatively far apart, their feeling of solidarity may need prodding. Shame also reinforces the bond of descent and impels kinsmen to come to the defense of their blood brothers. If that is the case, then obviously solidarity can work only within a specific ideological system.

The exposition of Ibn Khaldun's basic notions of humanity is now more or less complete. What we need to examine next is the political model that he constructs out of them.

It stands to reason that if solidarity is based on blood ties, then the group with the "purest lineage" is also the most cohesive. Which group might that be? The answer is the Bedouins. So arduous, painful, and impoverished is their life in the desert that no sensible being would want anything to do with them; hence "their pedigree can be trusted not to have been mixed up and corrupted" (p. 99). In contrast to "hill Arabs," who occupy lusher pasturage that attracts people of different races, they have not lost their purity and, by extension, their solidarity.

In spite of their solidarity, however, the Bedouins cannot escape the predicament of man's naturally aggressive nature, as the logic of the model would predict; so the state must already exist within the tribal order if that order is to survive. This is an important point to bear in mind when comparing Ibn Khaldun's theory of the state with those of others, such as the segmentary-lineage system. Even though the state may assume different "forms" among pastoral tribes and sedentary ones, it is, according to Ibn Khaldun, essentially the same phenomenon: that is, it is the instrument, fashioned by reason, through which man's natural propensity for aggression can be muted.

What would a tribal state look like? "The restraining influence among Bedouin tribes comes from their shaykhs and leaders. It results from the great respect and veneration they generally enjoy among the people" (p. 97). (Implicit here is an ideology of honor to which I will return in a moment.) Note that Ibn Khaldun is distinguishing two kinds of rule: chieftaincy and kingship. "Leadership," he says, "means being a chieftain, and the leader is obeyed, but he has no power to force others to accept his rulings. Royal authority means superiority and the power to rule by force" (p. 108). Of the same distinction Ibn Khaldun remarks elsewhere:

> It is difficult for them [the Bedouins] to subordinate themselves to each other because they are not used to [any control] and because they are in a state of savagery. Their leader needs them mostly for the group spirit that is necessary for purposes of defence. He is, therefore, forced to rule them kindly and to avoid antagonizing them. Otherwise, he would have trouble with the group spirit, resulting in his undoing and theirs. Royal leadership and government, on the other hand, require the leader to exercise a restraining influence by force. If not, his leadership would not last. (p. 120)

If the basis of power for the Bedouin chieftain cannot be coercion, what is it? Again, Ibn Khaldun invokes 'asabiyya: "Leadership over people, therefore, must, of necessity, derive from group feeling that is superior to each individual group feeling" (p. 101). Yet he had said in a previous passage that the shaykh's restraining influence, hence his power, derived from the "great respect and veneration" he enjoyed among the people. This would suggest that the shaykh possesses authority because his conduct is deemed legitimate in the light of some ideology or system of values. The system of values is expounded in only the briefest of terms, basically one long paragraph in the *Muqaddimah* (p. 112). That there has to be something else at work here to ensure restraint, something other than solidarity, follows from Ibn Khaldun's assumption that if man is a naturally aggressive creature, then he will turn against his leader unless either force (coercion) intervenes or a cultural belief system persuades men to obey their ruler, or both. The question is, how can ideology have an effect on sociopolitical action?

With the rise of the strong man, a dynastic cycle begins, the analysis of which is certainly Ibn Khaldun's best-known, though not his sole, contribution to the theory of the state. This cycle is so familiar to anthropologists and political scientists that it is unnecessary to describe it in detail here, except for the lesser-known aspect concerning the nature and role of prophecy in state formation. The problem of the royal tribal state is that it founders on its own political contradictions—an urban civilization that ultimately tears apart the sturdy Bedouin solidarity created in the close blood ties of the desert, a burgeoning bureaucracy that alienates the ruler from his own house, and so forth.[42] The way to transcend these contradictions is to establish the state on some firmer footing than common blood. For Ibn Khaldun, the new state must be founded on prophecy and the religious law that prophecy reveals. By being constructed on the model of an Islamic, as opposed to a merely tribal, state, the society is seen by Ibn Khaldun as advancing toward a higher stage of civilization.

In the *Muqaddimah* Ibn Khaldun develops a complex theory of consciousness, which is related to ideology and the problem of state formation. The Sixth Prefatory Discussion of chapter 1 outlines the three kinds of "human souls." The first of these is confined to "thinking in the body," that is, knowledge acquired through sensory perception and imagination. The lowest form of knowledge, it nevertheless is the one commonly possessed by the scholars of the community. More elevated in spirituality is the soul that does not depend on the body for its knowledge but is moved by "inward observations, which are all intuitive." Generally speaking, only the saints, the mystics of Islam, are privy to the workings of this soul. The highest soul to which men may aspire is of the third kind, which "is by nature suited to exchange humanity altogether, both corporeal and spiritual humanity, for angelicality of the highest stage, so that it may actually become an angel in the flash of a moment, glimpse the highest group within [its] own stage, and listen to essential speech and divine address during that moment" (p. 76). Possession of this knowledge is unique to prophets and is apparent in their miraculous performances, though Mahdi makes it clear that it is the prophet's knowledge of how "to guide the nation on the path of righteousness" that is the essential sign. Like many other Muslim philosophers, Ibn Khaldun emphasizes the *political* nature of prophecy: "The true prophet, therefore, is not merely an inspired man or a man who has the unusual power of performing miracles. He is primarily a statesman and a legislator."[43]

How does the prophet obtain the allegiance of his followers? He cannot rely on 'asabiyya alone, though the support of his kinspeople may be crucial in the beginning of his career; nor would he necessarily want to rely on them, for, as we have seen, they are the source of countless conflicts in the tribal community. According to Mahdi, "he needs the power of persuasion through which he can induce his fellow men to believe his assertions about what he had seen and what he considers the best principles of action." Since "the many are by far the overwhelming majority for whom the Law has been revealed, and rhetorical persuasion is the common denominator through which the prophet can address the many and the few," it is no coincidence that "the Law, therefore, has for the most part employed rhetoric and the simple ways of demonstration, i.e., arguments whose premises are few and self-evident, and whose conclusions can be easily deduced from these premises."[44] A new solidarity emerges, one based on religious belief or a compelling vision of the good and pious life as rendered in revelation and deed by the prophet-leader and as communicated to the urban masses and desert tribes by the educated elite. In essence, the message of this prophecy is that rewards come not in this life but in the life to come, a message that, if accepted, leads to the transcendance of those contradictions plaguing the kingly state. Men will no longer envy the ruler for his wealth and power because they will no longer covet worldly possessions and glory. The spiritual leader will spurn the luxury that had sapped the king's vigor in the tribal state. Having transformed itself from kingship based on blood ties to prophetic rule based on Islamic law, the state has reached its apogee.

Ibn Khaldun's logicodeductive model is holistic in conception, complex, rich, and subtle, embracing human psychology, social organization, the state, religion, and economy in accounting for human reality. True, some of his generalizations may strike us as empirically untenable—particularly his folk views on the human psyche—but the very fact that he realized the importance of including human personality in his explanation for the state is laudable and, as we shall see, not without justification. Not enough has been made of the point that Ibn Khaldun's model hinges crucially on a Weberian notion of the charismatic personality, in the guise of either the desert chieftain or the prophet.[45] For an understanding of Ibn Khaldun's model, a semiotic account is needed of the way in which revelation, a form of ideology, is used to persuade various kinds of audiences as to the rightness of prophetic doctrine in the Islamic state. Akbar S. Ahmed's study of a particular case of tribal prophecy from Northwest Pakistan, to be examined shortly, will illustrate this point. Undoubtedly, because the model is so rich, other avenues of fruitful research could be explored, but it is precisely at the junction of ideology and sign use in concrete communicative acts that problems of analysis arise. As we found to be true of Marxist approaches, ideology ultimately becomes critical in the explanation of the state's operation in the Khaldunian model as well, and yet neither one explores deeply the social use of signs through which ideology affects action.

THE MODEL OF THE SEGMENTARY-LINEAGE SYSTEM

Functionalist theory in sociology has, of course, a long, eminent tradition that is impossible to summarize adequately here. Within anthropology, and specifically in the study of Middle Eastern tribal societies, it is most immediately identifiable with the work of E. E. Evans-Pritchard.[46] His theory of social organization has produced a model most commonly known as the segmentary-lineage system, which stands in marked contrast to the Marxist model we have delineated. To the Ibn Khaldunian viewpoint, however, it has a more ambiguous relationship, primarily because of Ernest Gellner, who has attempted to incorporate it within a lineage-segmentary model of tribal society.[47]

According to Evans-Pritchard, in tribal society the state—at least in our sense of a political entity with a bureaucracy, a territory that it defends, and policies enforced by coercion—does not exist. Tribes do have rulers, of course (the Nuer leopard-skin chief or the Cyrenaican shaykh, for example),[48] but their power, if understood as coercion, is minimal, perhaps even nonexistent. Given the absence of such a state, how can order be maintained? In Marx's theory, the state, though in a highly attenuated form, already exists in the tribal mode of production, for the contradictions engendered by this division of labor must somehow be contained, either by a democratic representative of the communal interest or by a more despotic form of government. In the *Muqaddimah* the state exists at the inception of tribal solidarity in the guise of the desert chieftain and later the urban ruler, not because of economics but because of social psychology—that is, the naturally aggressive tendencies of man must be checked. In Evans-Pritchard's functionalism, however, tribal society can exist outside of the state, and it is precisely by setting the terms of the problem in this fashion (which will be seen to be problematical) and by proposing a *sociological* solution to it that his political theory is original.

In the absence of the state a tribesman whose (culturally defined) rights have been violated by another has no recourse to a sovereign, the courts, or an assembly from whom to seek justice. He must, therefore, rely on someone else or something else. To some anthropologists this may seem like a strained way to pose the problem; rather than "someone else or something else" why not just say "his kinsmen" straight off, for in the theory it is the lineage that gives support to one of its own members. This assumption, namely, that blood descent serves as a basis of social solidarity, Evans-Pritchard and Ibn Khaldun hold in common along with scores of other anthropologists since at least the time of Lewis Henry Morgan. Certain theoretical developments in cultural anthropology, particularly in the United States, however, suggest that kinship is not necessarily the adhesive that keeps the group together. Dissenting voices in Middle Eastern ethnography have also been raised to challenge this assumption, most notably that of Michael Meeker, a student of David Schneider, who has for some time argued against it in general kinship studies.[49]

Specifically, segmentary-lineage theory contends that a tribal society will split into smaller groups, usually as a result of scarce water resources or sparse vegetation cover, and only unite for ritual occasions or more likely in the event of the threat of external aggression. Furthermore, the groups separate along lineage lines, the branches of the genealogical tree allowing for divergence at the crown and convergence at the trunk. However, to paraphrase Meeker, why not overturn the generally accepted logic by maintaining that kinship ties form the basis on which people are allowed to disagree and even to fight each other.[50] To make sense of this argument, one has to add that Meeker interprets blood descent in terms of a prevailing Bedouin idea—system of honor. To be an honorable man means, according to Meeker, acquiring prestige in gloriously aggressive deeds such as hospitality, warfare, and political oratory (shades again of Ibn Khaldun); but it is only honorable to aggress against an equal, and the most equal of opponents are one's immediate kinsmen. Hence, there is a certain logic inherent in a cultural system of blood descent leading to bloody dissent. If taken to its extreme, this view of kinship in the Middle Eastern context also has its problems, for it invokes a sinister, even a terrifying, prospect of human motives that is no less problematical.[51]

That the concept of honor and the value of individual human dignity are close to the Nuer experience is a fact to which Evans-Pritchard repeatedly draws the reader's attention throughout his famous ethnography. The trouble arises when one tries to account for it in his model. The feud, for example, is the means by which a wronged individual and, by lineal extension, his group try to recover, say, their stolen cattle; we are led to believe that raids, fisticuffs, or just threatened violence are the unavoidable outcome—unavoidable because of the absence of the state. A close reading of the text reveals an alternative interpretation, one that suggests that the Nuer are quick to come to blows because of their cultural concept of honor. Children are socialized into believing in their own autonomy and trained to defend it belligerently. Does the belief system mechanically serve the modus operandi of the feud? That is, does honor fuel the fires of conflict, which in turn keep the group solidified? Does it instead engender within itself the social oppositions that are symbolically enacted in the feud (i.e., a Dumontian analysis that begins with the dominant system of ideas and moves outward toward the structures of social action)?

To return to Evans-Pritchard's model, the feud unifies the social group that is fighting an opponent; hence social conflict may be conducive to social order, a paradox artfully explored in Max Gluckman's functionalist writings. In line with a mechanical model that is invoked for understanding this kind of political order, we must assume that the two forces opposed to each other in a conflict are equal, much as the outward stresses of walls bearing a huge cathedral vault must be matched by the inward support of buttresses, or collapse is inevitable. The principle of the balanced opposition of lineage segments was supposed to combat these social stresses. If segments are more or less equivalent in population and military strength, their confrontation will not lead to liquidation or flight of the weaker opponent. Should one party in the dispute seek an ally on the next-higher level of the lineage system in hopes of defeating the adversary, the opponent too can immediately call on its kinsmen on the next-higher level to mobilize an equally effective counterforce, resulting once again in a balanced opposition of higher-order segments. To continue the mechanical analogy, the feud has a ceiling, an upper limit to the lineage system beyond which the dispute cannot be carried if it is still to be contained within the tribe, and a basement, a lower limit of the domestic household in which confrontation between father and son cannot be allowed to become murderous lest it destroy the reproductive unit. That this is not always the case, particularly that a feud, once launched, seems to tear through the upper levels of the system threatening it with collapse, is a problem for the model whose solution I will return to shortly when examining Gellner's work.

For now, let me mention a side to the feud that Evans-Pritchard also emphasized, namely, mediation. Aggression and mediation are two sides of the same coin, which is yet another paradox in the principle of balanced opposition. Conflict cannot be resolved by force, for the outcome in a balanced opposition is necessarily indeterminate; yet as the feud begins to encompass higher and higher levels of the system, the hazard of murderous violence increases. Mediation, therefore, is a mechanism whereby the bloodier consequences of the feud may be avoided or at least attenuated. Note that the model does not make mediation the means by which a conflict is resolved. A conflict never is completely resolved, though it may lie dormant for a time, perhaps even for years, before it flares up again, often as a result of a new threat invading the body politic. In response to the new attack, mediators again spring into action to bring the system back to some kind of equilibrium, though the cycle is endless and indeed vicious. As E. Peters once expressed it, "The feud has no beginning and no end."

This model is both simple and elegant, with roots in segmentation theory of Durkheimian sociology (mechanical solidarity or the idea that groups cohere because they are "like" each other) and W. Robertson Smith's reconstruction of pre-Islamic Arabia. But as Peters and, later, Gellner were to point out, the system does not work as neatly as the model predicts. Peters was probably the first to show that the principle of balanced opposition rarely, if ever, is found in practice, for reasons having to do with the complexity of demographic, ecological, and economic variables that rarely allow segments to be equal.[52] I have already anticipated this criticism above and need not dwell on it. Peters also complained that the segmentary-lineage system was a native model and not a scientifically objective, sociological one, finding enough reason in this objection to jettison the model altogether, a move that some might find equivalent to throwing out the baby with the bath water. One of the positive effects of Peters's second criticism, however, is that it drew attention to the distinction between the subject's belief system and the observer's view and raised the question of what is to be done with the former in the latter model of reality. In the light of Peters's criticism we are confronted with the irony that Evans-Pritchard had actually been doing a symbolic analysis without realizing it. Indeed, there is a growing tendency to interpret Evans-Pritchard's mechanical principle of balanced opposition as a self-conscious strategy on the part of tribesmen to realize their symbolic (and not utilitarian) motives, such as individual autonomy and freedom of action, a consensual process of decision making, and so forth.

After Peters abandoned the very model in which he was trained to make sense of tribal society, he did not, as far as I can determine, replace it with another one. Ernest Gellner has taken a very different tack. For one thing, he has clung to the conviction that a theoretical model that attempts to explain reality is always better than no model at all. Second, the model he adopts as a corrective to the segmentary-lineage system comes out of the tradition of Muslim political philosophy, more specifically the work of Ibn Khaldun. Indeed, it is owing largely to Gellner's influence that Middle Eastern anthropology is paying attention to Ibn Khaldun's model and showing us how it might be relevant.

Gellner too observes that the system is not in balanced equilibrium, and he deliberately invokes another paradox: "So as to work at all, the system also must not work too well." He elaborates on this point in the following passage:

> The driving force behind the cohesion of the groups is fear, fear of aggression by others in an anarchic environment. If the balancing system really worked perfectly, producing a kind of perpetual peaceful balance of power at all levels, the society would cease to be anarchic, and fear would cease to be a powerful spring of action. . . . The persistence of a segmentary society requires, paradoxically, that its mechanisms should be sufficiently inefficient to keep fear in being as the sanction of the system.[53]

In other words, as the model predicts, feuding must exist between segments on all levels of the system, feuding that, as Peters has shown, increases in violence as the conflict escalates and broadens.

Part of the problem is that one does not always know in these writings whether the view of the tribes as being violent, feud-addicted, or anarchic is one espoused by the village religious elite, the tribespeople, or the anthropologist. It is certainly the case, for example, that during my time in North Yemen the *sada*, who saw and sometimes still see themselves as the rightful overlords of the tribes, rarely missed an opportunity to tell me that nothing except *fawda*, "chaos," prevails in the tribal hinterlands. But when I did actually experience a violent confrontation among Yemeni tribes, I was struck by how ritualistic and almost theatrical it was in comparison to what my initial apprehensions had led me to expect; then by slow degrees, and after several months, the violence became bloody as the economic and political stakes were raised, generating for the first time a true

anxiety among its participants. Thus, the feud may not be anticipated by the actors in the same fearful way at all levels on which it
erupts, particularly at the lower levels of the system, where it may
become more like a symbolic act than like a deadly pursuit of material gain. In response to this observation one might argue, again entirely within the segmentary-lineage model, that actors would fear
even the apparently harmless, almost ritualistic contests of honor
because of the potential they have of becoming explosive and that
such potential is always present because the system is inefficient in
curbing conflict either by an outside mediator or by a tyrant who can
impose peace by force. However, the tribes of Yemen, who until 1962
had for centuries been ruled by a fairly strong imamate, were no
strangers to the apparent pax Islamica, but they also feared tyranny
(or, to put it differently, the loss of their political autonomy) more
than the (apparent) anarchy of their political system. When weighing
one fear against another, the tribes may not choose in the direction
of state intervention at all; they may simply be choosing to live with a
lesser evil.

At this point in the argument Gellner proposes that the role of the
saints is a kind of working compromise between the potential anarchy of tribal violence and the encroaching tyranny of the state.[54] The
saints' authority, legitimated by their descent, their literacy, their er-
udition, their piety, and above all their peaceful demeanor, is a moral
counterpoint to the tribal shaykh, whose authority is legitimated by
his socially aggressive behavior as enjoined by the honor code. The
saint and his descendants are thus welcomed into the tribal fold in
their capacity as peacekeepers. Their primary, though not sole, function is to keep the system going when it threatens to grind to a halt
after mediation has been exhausted at the highest levels.[55]

What has been deliberately grafted onto the model of the
segmentary-lineage system, then, is an Ibn Khaldunian concept of
the state, which is in an important sense Gellner's own contribution
to the development of segmentary theory. Section 26 of chapter 2 in
the *Muqaddimah* begins:

> Because of their savagery, the Bedouins are the least willing of nations
> to subordinate themselves to each other, as they are rude, proud, ambi-
> tious, and eager to be leaders. Their individual aspirations rarely coin-
> cide. But when there is religion (among them) through prophethood or
> sainthood, then they have some restraining influence in themselves.
> The qualities of haughtiness and jealousy leave them. It is, then, easy
> for them to subordinate themselves and unite (as a social organiza-
> tion). (p. 120)

Bearing in mind Ibn Khaldun's political theory, we can better understand, as Gellner makes perfectly clear, the extent to which saintly lineages are part of a theory of the state *in* tribal society.

But what happens, asks Gellner, when a crisis occurs, an emergency of such magnitude that the very foundations of the society seem to be on the verge of buckling? We must recognize the assumption that the tribes, according to this theory, need the urban state far more than it needs the tribes, and when the state is threatened, the tribes will necessarily come to its defense. In this situation the mundane sacredness of the "petty" holy man cannot inspire the tribes to action. What is required, says Gellner, is "an unusual, outstanding, more general and demanding leadership," which Ibn Khaldun identified with the prophet who usually emerges in the town.[56] Thus enters the Weberian charismatic personality. Moreover, what is required is not simply a cultural-belief system but an *ideology* of puritan unitarianism—the difference between the two, of course, is not unproblematic[57]—that renews the faith of men, purifies their ritual, and spurs them on to righteousness. Recall Ibn Khaldun's formula: by displacing men's desires from the profane and the mundane to the transcendent world of the hereafter, the prophet is able to weld the community into a psychologically cohesive group. In other words, the theory explains how it is that a charismatic leader *negates* or transcends the segmentary tendency of tribal society.

Gellner, following Hume, thus views religion, or more specifically Islam, as an oscillation between idolatry and fundamentalist monotheism. He situates this oscillation in religion within a particular political context that purports to explain it. In the everyday tribal world of segmentary politics, heterodox Islam, as symbolized by the saints and which supposedly suits the "psychology" of the tribes, functions to maintain a political order whose violence, the model asserts, is constantly threatening to rend the tribal fabric. Yet in the extraordinary world into which the whole society—tribal and urban—is occasionally plunged, a potent ideology ideally emerges in the town as a response to a more general problematic situation. Two different aspects of Islam are thus systematically related to each other and together are related dynamically to a changing political arena.

A discussion of an extended case study, the rise and fall of the mulla of Waziristan in northwest Pakistan, analyzed by Akbar S. Ahmed, may help draw out the strengths and weaknesses of this model. The area is controlled by two opposed tribes, the Wazirs and the Mahsuds. Ahmed remarks that "in the ideal, the tribal structure does not admit hereditary rights of leadership and sociopolitical division according to superior and inferior status, nor does the poor ecological base allow the growth of powerful chiefs."[58] Political decisions are arrived at through consensus in the *jirga* assembly, which is composed of land-owning elders. Social behavior such as cousin rivalry (*tarboorwali*) and the upholding of female honor (*tor*) is interpreted in terms of the honor code, or *pukhtunwali*, which Ahmed summarizes thus: "courage (*tora*), revenge (*badal*), hospitality (*melmastia*), generosity to a defeated adversary supplicating for peace (*nanwatee*), and heeding the voice of the *jirga*."[59] Both tribes keep fairly elaborate genealogies. Ahmed asserts that the opposition between the Wazir and Mahsud is played out in *tarboorwali*, that is, in the local cultural categories of what the model refers to as feud. Islamic ideals are also incorporated in the code of Pakhtun behavior, an important point too often overlooked in anthropological investigations stressing the honor system above everything else in the definition of the tribesman: "To the tribesman Islam provides specified political and socioreligious formations within which his Pukhtunness operates." So far, so good: as Ahmed observes, "The degree of segmentation and segmentary consciousness is high in Waziristan and locally is so perceived."[60]

What about the religious figures in Waziristan society? Three types may be distinguished. First, there are the *'ulama' (maulvi)*, who represent the legalistic, scriptural, and bureaucratic tradition of Islam and advise the central state. Next, the Sufi saints (sayyid, sharif, or *mian*) "command a vague and generalized respect, especially if they live up to idealized behavior, which is pacific, dignified, and neutral between warring groups and clans."[61] Ahmed, unfortunately, does not say whether they play any important role as mediators in tribal disputes, though confirmation to that effect may be obtained from Barth.[62] Finally, there is a religious figure called mulla who is neither scholar-judge nor Sufi mystic and occupies the most junior grade in the religious hierarchy. The following remarks by Ahmed recall Gellner's thesis that a charismatic religious figure arises in a crisis to weld the tribes into a greater collectivity: "The mullah restricts himself largely to the village level of social and political life except in extraordinary circumstances. He appears to thrive in crisis. . . . The mullah may rise to power in extraordinary times, rallying Muslims against invading non-Muslims."[63] Such religious persuasion is not like an appeal to a puritanical fundamentalist faith, however. The mullas have been known to utilize various tricks—some of them nefarious, others harmless and hilarious—by which they hoped to convince their more gullible followers of their miraculous and superhuman powers. Ibn Khaldun observed that a prophet must utilize miracles as signs. It is precisely this utilization of miracles as signs, which amounts to a semiotic theory of religious persuasion, that Ahmed is superb in revealing to us when he examines the extraordinary career of the mulla Noor Muhammad.

In 1963 Noor Muhammad succeeded his father as the mulla of a local mosque in Wana, Waziristan. One of his first acts was to build a magnificent new mosque through donations he managed to obtain by "his powers of oratory and persuasion." A thriving nearby market, which was dominated by the Wazirs, became the source of funds for the mulla's later political activities. The mulla also demonstrated considerable skill in mediating a land dispute between two different Wazir clans, a dispute that had become ugly after two men on each side were killed. Eventually he managed to impose a general cessation of conflict among Wazir clans in the area by fining and punishing those who quarreled. He also acquired a reputation as a healer.

The crisis brewing in Pakistan in the early 1970s illuminates the story. Bangladesh had been created in 1971 by a charismatic leader pitting himself against the central government, an example that must have inspired other ethnic causes within Pakistan. Furthermore, the nation was still reeling from the effects of its war with India, particularly the capture of more than one hundred thousand troops, who continued to languish in Indian prisons. "Many Pakistani Muslims considered this fact, along with the ignominy of defeat, unique in the annals of Islamic history."[64] A mood of pessimism and despair prevailed.

According to Ahmed, the mulla apparently tried to engineer crises in Waziristan in order to challenge various authorities—the local political leadership of the Wazirs, the Mahsuds, and ultimately the Pakistani state represented by the political agent—in an effort to win power for himself. Instead of transcending segmentary tribal anarchy, he encouraged it to the point where the president of Pakistan had to order air strikes against the Wazirs and arrest the mulla to avert what the state perceived as potential insurrection.

Ahmed maintains that the mulla's motives were largely ambiguous. They were a complex mixture of personal ambition, ethnic assertion against the state, and prophetic yearnings.[65] What is interesting is that the parochial view he espoused as well as his somewhat reproachful moral behavior were the antithesis of the universalistic and puritanical spirit that we would associate with fundamentalist Islam and that the model predicts. Ultimately it is not the power of monotheistic ideology that explains the mulla's success in the segmentary tribal world but his charisma. Indeed, some notion of the person or "personality" shown in this case is crucial to understanding the Waziristan case (in addition to the "district paradigm" Ahmed argues has more general relevance to Muslim tribal societies).[66] It is important to emphasize the fact that this personality builds power not only through the manipulation of political blocs, the utilization of economic resources, or terrorist acts against his opponents but also through *symbolic interaction* with the followers he wants to win and the enemies he hopes to vanquish. To understand this symbolic interaction, we must not only take the subjective view, or, as Ahmed states, "examine events through the eyes of the actors."[67] We must also focus on key actors like the mulla—in other words, we must focus on the significant individual and not just segmentary groups—using culturally laden signs in concrete acts of communication.

TRIBAL CONFEDERATION AND STATE CENTRALIZATION

All the theories we have so far examined have viewed the state in response to conditions from within tribal organization.[68] The Marxist paradigm, for example, explains the state in terms of the tribal mode of production, which creates stratified groups whose conflict must be contained by either a representative assembly or a despot, a political agency that subsequently becomes the means of oppression by the economically dominant class. According to Ibn Khaldun, the state in the form of either a desert chieftain or a king must exist within society at its inception, for there has to be some way of curbing man's naturally aggressive impulses in order to ensure social cooperation. Perhaps only the segmentary model appears to contrast with the previous theories in this regard, for, as we have noted, the segmentary tribe is by definition stateless, if the state is defined essentially in Western terms. According to later developments of that theory in the writings of Gellner, the tribe appears to be unable to govern itself without the intervention of an outside "statelike" agency such as the saints.

In the model under consideration in this section, the problem is understood somewhat differently. Certain tribal personnel, the great khans who possess large herds, agricultural lands, and rentable properties in the towns and cities, act as mediators between the central state and the ordinary tribesman. Though this is something of an oversimplification, the model contends that these tribal leaders are in a certain sense the creation of the outside state. The state uses them as a means to govern a remote, mobile population located in a difficult or nearly inaccessible terrain, making direct rule virtually impossible. Certain ethnically, linguistically, and historically related tribes become organized into an ad hoc confederation led by a khan, usually chosen from within the ranks of the tribal aristocracy, who "governs" with his hierarchy of personnel. He is in charge of gathering the state's taxes, mobilizing fighting men to defend the state in the event of a military emergency, and at the same time representing the interests of the tribe and individual tribesmen in the maze of the state bureaucracy. That the state's strategy of bringing the tribal population indirectly under its control is a double-edged sword is apparent when khans, who become heads of extremely powerful confederacies, then challenge the state's power during periods when it is weak. There is thus contained within the model a dialectical relationship between the power of the state and the power of the tribal elites. That is, when the state is powerful, it will tend toward direct tribal rule by circumventing, or perhaps even eliminating, the tribal elites. When it is vulnerable to external aggression and internal strife, the state, through the power of the tribal elites, and in spite of the future threat they may pose to its own absolute power, will, *faute de mieux*, rule indirectly through them.

Perhaps a convenient starting point for a more thorough examination of the model is G. R. Garthwaite. His 1983 article "Khans and Kings" is important in the debate on state-tribe processes within the Iranian context. It begins with a key hypothesis: "Within an organized state the potential for tribal confederation is inversely proportional to the degree of bureaucratic centralization."[69] He contrasts, for example, Pahlavi centralization with nineteenth-century Qajar decentralization.

The Qajar state depended on indirect rule of the tribes by the khans and great confederations (which are defined essentially as a structure above the level of the tribe or *tayafeh*). Garthwaite distinguishes three kinds of indirect rule. First, the state may appoint a leader, not necessarily from within the group, to maintain order, collect taxes, and provide conscripts for the army. Alternatively, a tribal leader may manage to amalgamate power from within, successfully uniting larger and larger groups under his control in the confederation (the Qashqa'i are said to provide an example of this process, though Garthwaite contends that it is rare in Iranian history because of the "difficulty of obtaining outside support without threatening the central government").[70] Finally, in a process combining amalgamation and designation, a tribal leader may start to build a confederation through his own efforts, then offer his services to the state, which then tries to co-opt him. The celebrated Hosain Qoli Khan Ilkhani (1862–1892) is said to be an example of the third process. This *ilkhani* (tribal leader) garnered a considerable income from landholdings outside the tribe and from government posts and thus did not depend significantly on tribal economic resources. His case contrasts, however, with that of the other powerful khans of the nineteenth century.

The specific example under consideration is the Bakhtiyari confederacy. What emerges from Garthwaite's description is a two-tiered political structure. At the base is the tribe and at the top the confederation, which shifts with the vicissitudes of the state's fortunes. Within the tribe the family unit forms the basis of everyday life: "From the tayafeh to the whole of the Bakhtiyari confederation, groups function within an essentially negative framework and align and define themselves through interaction with external factors—neighboring tribes, the state, or the broader ambitions of the khans." What one gets is the typical conception of tribal society as being a primary group organized along kinship lines, "the basis for loyalty and identification." Everything above this level is much more ephemeral and contingent on historical circumstances. "The confederation . . . seldom furnished more than a vague, administrative identity."[71] As a result of its confrontation with the state, the Bakhtiyari confederacy—in other words, the upper tier of the political structure—was more or less destroyed, but the lower level or tribe has managed to maintain its integrity and autonomy. The reason for its survival has probably to do with the fact that it is peripheral to the nation-state and economy. Again this case contrasts with that of the Qashqa'i, who have not been isolated and have fared less well.

Garthwaite makes some attempt to explain the reasons for the khans' inability to rally the Bakhtiyari tribes against the Pahlavi state. One, if not the most important, of the reasons is that "they could not articulate a viable alternate ideology without threatening their position either with the state or the tribes." Furthermore, in his discussion of the failure of a mid-eighteenth-century Bakhtiyari to rally the tribes in overthrowing Nader Shah, Garthwaite remarks that there was "no appeal to a Bakhtiyari identity and nothing particularly tribal or nomadic about either the concepts expressed or the language in which they are couched."[72] Here we see articulated a crucial link between ideology and power, which is, as I have repeatedly stressed, one of the neglected problems of research.

Beck's ethnography *The Qashqa'i of Iran* (1986), on the nomadic pastoralists of southwestern Iran (the Zagros Mountains), represents the best analysis to date of a tribal elite. She divides Qashqa'i sociopolitical organization into three levels: subtribal camps led by their own headmen, whose elders' power came from within the local group and was, until only recently, independent of the central state;

middle-level tribal khans who mediated between the nomads and the *ilkhani* and *ilbegi*; and the paramount leaders of the confederacy (the *ilkhani* and his *ilbegi*) whose support came from the khans and the central state. The power of the khans and *ilkhani* depended largely on wealth, their contacts with outside powers (either the Iranian state or Western powers), and their ability to symbolically manipulate the image of Qashqa'i indomitableness before potential allies and enemies.

The basic argument of Beck's book is that political organization on the tribal and confederacy levels arose in symbiotic relationship to the emergence of a centralized state, an argument that is related to Garthwaite's claims. Elites were in a certain sense created by the state in order that it may rule a difficult and remote population more efficiently. This elite was responsible for collecting taxes, conscripting young men into the state's army, and implementing policies; in short, it was the state's indirect ruler. However, the elite also acted to safeguard the interests of its constituents in the face of encroaching state power; and having been elevated to power by the state, elites could become its potential enemies, a fact that motivated the Iranian state from time to time to wage a campaign against them (especially brutal during the reign of Muhammad Reza Shah and Khomeini). The argument must be viewed in the light of the larger theoretical effort to rethink the categories of tribe and state in the Middle East, which suggests that tribes and the state have never lived in isolation from each other but have always been interdependent, and that tribal formation (at least on the second or upper tier of the political structure), which has traditionally been viewed as a product of forces working from the bottom up, is also a product of forces working from the top down.

Chapter 9, "Qashqa'i Leadership," is perhaps the most intriguing one of the book. Beck writes that "no leader exercised absolute power" because "tribespeople who were discontented could effectively deny support to leaders, ultimately by severing ties and joining other units or forming their own."[73] It never happened that the leaders at any level tried to coerce their followers by using governmental troops. To explain power in such a system, one must begin, as Beck does, by acknowledging the importance of the cultural system: "An essential unifying factor of the Qashqa'i political system has been its association with the cultural system of the Qashqa'i people. Qashqa'i leaders, drawing legitimacy and identity from this cultural system and contributing to its maintenance and perpetuation, also helped to create certain key Qashqa'i symbols and utilized them in their leadership." Beck goes on to give a detailed excursus on Qashqa'i identity and how it is communicated in political signs: "For example, when Naser Khan resumed active leadership as the new *ilkhani*...he introduced a distinctive hat...which in a few years was worn by practically all Qashqa'i men....The hat symbolized political autonomy and ethnic distinctiveness at a historical period immediately following state-directed attempts to erase the Qashqa'i as a unique people in Iran." In fact, we are explicitly told that the *ilkhani*'s camp, his supporters, his acts of hospitality, his life-style, and his political contacts are all "symbols of paramount leadership."[74] In the context of this symbolic analysis the description of the *ilkhani*'s reception of people eager to discuss their problems with him, often asking him to mediate their disputes, takes on special significance.[75] These discussions, which the *ilkhani* never dominate but try to direct toward a consensus, both symbolize the leader's role in the political process and enact or embody it. By analyzing how the individual, charismatic personality in face-to-face interactions uses the signs of authority in communicative acts, we may better understand how power is exercised.

CONCLUSION

I suppose that by now the direction in which I would prefer future research on the question of tribe and state to tend is obvious. Each of the four models under investigation has stressed the importance of belief systems or ideologies in the understanding of tribe, state, and the relations between them. Asad—to his credit, I believe—deepens Marxist analysis of the problem by his insistence that the power of the Fadlallah is not only based on their control over the means of production but also on their use of what he calls ideology to create a hierarchical view of the social world. In the segmentary-lineage model, with Gellner's grafting onto it of Ibn Khaldun's political philosophy, cultural systems and ideologies naturally play a critical role. What now needs to be articulated in richer ethnographic detail is the kind of material that Richard Tapper has admirably presented in his study of Shahsevan nomadic life: face-to-face interactions of significant individuals and their audiences, who are communicating their culturally constituted aims through the use of politically laden signs.[76] That such research can more than compensate for the theoretical investigations undertaken in tribe-state relations is evident in the studies by Ahmed and Beck, among others.

If the direction of study is clear, at least to me, the path is perhaps less so. Do we go the route of "semiotics"? Or is Geertzian "interpretation" what we want? The "pragmatics of discourse"? The "ethnog-

raphy of communication"? A Meadian "social psychology"? A
Burkean "dramatism"? Habermas's theory of "communicative acts
in society"? We all sense, I think, that symbols, signs, their meanings, and their use by personalities to communicate key ideas and attitudes of the culture in concrete acts are important to our problems
of analysis and are worthy of attention. Just how we study these notoriously difficult facts so as to illuminate their salience may not, of
course, be an easy matter. Nevertheless, it ought not prevent us from
trying.

NOTES

1. Conspicuously absent in this list are Fredrik Barth's analyses of political leadership among the Basseri nomads and Swat Pathans. It is a serious
omission not only because his work has been so extremely influential in
both Middle Eastern tribal research and general theoretical anthropology
but also because of the way in which his ideas, directly or indirectly, will be
referred to in my discussion of the above models. However, four models in
one essay are probably already three too many, and I chose to omit his from
the overview. A longer work should accommodate it.

2. It is impossible in this paper to discuss the theories of all the major
Marxist anthropologists. See E. Terray, *Marxism and 'Primitive' Societies*
(New York, 1972); M. Godelier, "The Concept of 'Tribe': A Crisis Involving
Merely a Concept or the Empirical Foundations of Anthropology?" in Jack
Goody, ed. *Perspectives in Marxist Anthropology*, trans. R. Brain, Cambridge
Studies in Social Anthropology, vol. 18 (Cambridge, 1973), pp. 70–96; M. Go-
delier, *The Making of Great Men*, trans. R. Swyer (Cambridge, 1986); M.
Fried, *The Evolution of Political Society* (New York, 1967); and R. Firth, "The
Skeptical Anthropologist? Social Anthropology and Marxist Views on Soci-
ety," in M. Bloch, ed., *Marxist Analyses and Social Anthropology* (London,
1975), pp. 29–60.

3. Karl Marx and Friedrich Engels, *The German Ideology* (1846; New
York, 1970), p. 46.

4. Karl Marx, *Pre-Capitalist Economic Formations* (1857–1858; New
York, 1965), p. 68.

5. Marx and Engels, *German Ideology*, p. 118.

6. Marx, *Pre-Capitalist Economic Formations*, p. 96.

7. Marx and Engels, *German Ideology*, p. 53.

8. A remark is in order, however, in regard to the analytical status of
these economic forms. Marx appears to have intended them in the Preface to
the *Critique of Political Economy* to be successive states in an evolutionary
sequence, yet in *Pre-Capitalist Economic Formations* it is not clear that he
conceptualized them in precisely this way. I will follow E. J. Hobsbawm, Introduction to *Pre-Capitalist Economic Formations*, p. 36, in maintaining that

the three types to be discussed below—that is, the "tribal" or "ancient," the "Oriental," and the "Germanic"—were *alternative* evolutionary outgrowths of a preceding "herd-animal" stage, where each formation represents a greater degree of individualization of property ownership than the logically preceding one.

9. Marx, *Pre-Capitalist Economic Formations*, p. 68.

10. Marx, *Pre-Capitalist Economic Formations*, pp. 70–71. This key passage obviously brings to mind Wittfogel's hydraulic hypothesis to account for the rise of the "Oriental-despotism" thesis. Such a conclusion seems bolstered by the remark appearing immediately after this section, namely, that these public constructions "will then appear as the work of the higher unity—the despotic government which is poised above the lesser communities" (p. 71).

11. Marx, *Pre-Capitalist Economic Formations*, p. 73. Presumably, the Germanic system (or either of the preceding two systems) evolves into the feudal mode, though Marx says curiously little about feudalism in *Pre-Capitalist Economic Formations*. Of course, capitalism in turn supposedly evolves out of the contradictions of the feudal society, though apparently again Marx has shed little light on the nature of these contradictions in his works. See Hobsbawm, Introduction to Marx, *Pre-Capitalist Economic Formations*, p. 45.

12. Marx and Engels, *German Ideology*, p. 44.

13. Marx, *Pre-Capitalist Economic Formations*, pp. 71–72, 75.

14. Marx, *Pre-Capitalist Economic Formations*, pp. 75, 80, 78.

15. Marx and Engels, *German Ideology*, p. 53.

16. Marx and Engels, *German Ideology*, p. 54. See also Friedrich Engels, *The Origin of the Family, Private Property and the State* (1884; New York, 1942), pp. 96–97.

17. V. N. Vološinov, *Marxism and the Philosophy of Language* (1929; Cambridge, Mass., 1973), p. 13. M. M. Bakhtin is thought to be the coauthor of this work and for this reason I sometimes refer to the authors as Vološinov and Bakhtin.

18. Vološinov, *Marxism*, pp. 11, 12.

19. D. Hymes, *Foundations in Sociolinguistics* (Philadelphia, 1974).

20. Vološinov, *Marxism*, pp. 19–20.

21. Even among Marxist anthropologists there is disagreement over the reality of tribal social relations. This disagreement is perhaps best articulated by Godelier in his essay "The Concept of the 'Tribe,'" in which he critiques Sahlins's analysis of tribal society (Marshall D. Sahlins, *Tribesmen* [Englewood Cliffs, N.J., 1968]).

22. Jean-Pierre Digard, "Histoire et anthropologie des sociétés nomades: Le cas d'une tribu d'Iran," *Annales: Economies, sociétés, civilisations* 28, no. 6 (1973): 1423–1435; "On the Bakhtiari: Comments on 'Tribes, Confederation and the State,'" in Richard Tapper, ed., *The Conflict of Tribe and State in Iran and Afghanistan* (New York, 1983), pp. 331–336.

23. Digard, "Histoire et anthropologie," p. 1425.

24. Digard, "Histoire et anthropologie," p. 1427.

25. Talal Asad, "Political Inequality in the Kababish Tribe," in Ian Cunnison and Wendy James, eds., *Essays in Sudan Ethnography* (New York, 1972), p. 137.

26. Fredrik Barth, *Political Leadership among Swat Pathans* (London, 1959), pp. 77–79; G. R. Garthwaite, *Khans and Shahs: A Documentary Analysis of the Bakhtiyari in Iran* (Cambridge, 1983); Lois Beck, *The Qashqa'i of Iran* (New Haven, 1986).

27. In his 1983 critique of Garthwaite's analysis of the Bakhtiyari, Digard ("On the Bakhtiyari") more or less repeats his earlier interpretation of Bakhtiyari social organization in terms of class structure, namely, that it is founded on two distinct modes of production. Whereas other models would view the hegemonic acts of Reza and Muhammad Shah as a sort of centralizing drive of the modern state, Digard's model accounts for it in terms of a "monopolizing drive" of a dominant economic class. See also Talal Asad, "Equality in Nomadic Systems? Notes towards the Dissolution of an Anthropological Category," in Centre Nationale de la Recherche Scientifique (CNRS), *Pastoral Production and Society* (Paris, 1979), for a reanalysis of Digard, "Histoire et anthropologie."

28. Talal Asad, *The Kababish Arabs* (New York, 1970); "Market Model, Class Structure and Consent: A Reconsideration of Swat Political Organization," *Man* 7, no. 1 (1972): 74–94.

29. Asad, "Political Inequality," p. 146.

30. Asad, *Kababish Arabs*.

31. Asad, "Political Inequality," pp. 135–138, at p. 137.

32. Asad, *Kababish Arabs*, p. 240.

33. Clifford Geertz, "Centers, Kings, and Charisma: Reflections on the Symbolics of Power," in Geertz, *Local Knowledge: Further Essays in Interpretive Anthropology* (New York, 1983), pp. 121–146.

34. A. M. Khazanov, *Nomads and the Outside World*, trans. Julia Crookenden (Cambridge, 1984). See also Lawrence Krader, *Social Organization of the Mongul-Turkic Pastoral Nomads* (The Hague, 1963); *Formation of the State* (Englewood Cliffs, N.J., 1968); and "The Origin of the State among the Nomads of Asia," in CNRS, *Pastoral Production and Society*, pp. 221–234.

35. Richard L. Tapper, "The Organization of Nomadic Communities in Pastoral Societies of the Middle East," in CNRS, *Pastoral Production and Society*, pp. 43–65.

36. Beck, *The Qashqa'i*.

37. P. C. Salzman, "Tribal Chiefs as Middlemen: The Politics of Encapsulation in the Middle East," *Anthropological Quarterly* 2 (1979): 203–210.

38. William Irons, "Nomadism as a Political Adaptation: The Case of the Yomut Turkmen," *American Ethnologist* 1:1 (1974): 635–658; P. Burnham, "Spatial Mobility and Political Centralization in Pastoral Societies" in CNRS, *Pastoral Production and Society*, pp. 349–360.

39. Salzman, "Tribal Chiefs as Middlemen," p. 433.

40. Muhsin S. Mahdi, *Ibn Khaldun's Philosophy of History* (Chicago, 1957).

41. Ibn Khaldun, *The Muqaddimah*, trans. F. Rosenthal (Princeton, 1967), p. 333. All citations in the following discussion are from this edition.

42. For a summary, see Mahdi, *Ibn Khaldun's Philosophy*.

43. Mahdi, *Ibn Khaldun's Philosophy*, pp. 89, 91.

44. Mahdi, *Ibn Khaldun's Philosophy*, pp. 91, 93.

45. The model has been assimilated by anthropology in several ways. See Ernest Gellner, *Saints of the Atlas* (Chicago, 1969), on the social system of Atlas Berbers, which investigates the relationship of Islam to the problem of political order in tribal society. See also "Flux and Reflux in the Faith of Men" in Ernest Gellner, *Muslim Society: Essays* (Cambridge, 1981), pp. 1–85.

46. E. E. Evans-Pritchard, *The Nuer* (Oxford, 1940); *The Sanusi of Cyrenaica* (Oxford, 1949).

47. Gellner, "Flux and Reflux."

48. Evans-Pritchard, *The Nuer; The Sanusi*.

49. David Schneider, *A Critique of the Study of Kinship* (Ann Arbor, 1984).

50. Michael Meeker, "Meaning and Society in the Near East: Examples from the Black Sea Turks and the Levantine Arabs," *International Journal of Middle East Studies* 7 (1976): 243–270, 383–422.

51. Michael Meeker, "The Twilight of a South Asian Heroic Age," *Man* n.s. 15:4, pp. 682–701.

52. E. Peters, "The Proliferation of Segments in the Lineage of the Bedouin of Cyrenaica," *Journal of the Royal Anthropological Institute* 40: 29–53; "Some Structural Aspects of the Feud among the Camel-Herding Bedouin of Cyrenaica," *Africa* 37, no. 3 (1967): 262–282.

53. Gellner, *Saints*, p. 53.

54. Gellner, "Flux and Reflux," p. 41.

55. What is not often noted in the literature is the extent to which a solution to such a problem may engender other problems, as in, for example, the potential competition for power between shaykh and sayyid. R. B. Serjeant somewhere reports having heard a Yemeni tribesman say to his comrades within earshot of a sayyid, "we all know what a shaykh is, but what is a sayyid?"

56. Gellner, "Flux and Reflux," p. 53.

57. See, however, Gellner, "Notes Towards a Theory of Ideology," in Ernest Gellner, *Spectacles and Predicaments* (Cambridge, 1979), pp. 117–134.

58. Akbar S. Ahmed, *Religion and Politics in Muslim Society* (Cambridge, 1983), p. 23.

59. Ahmed, *Religion and Politics*, p. 24.

60. Ahmed, *Religion and Politics*, pp. 141, 145.

61. Ahmed, *Religion and Politics*, p. 93.

62. Barth, *Political Leadership*, p. 10.

63. Ahmed, *Religion and Politics*, pp. 93–94.

64. Ahmed, *Religion and Politics*, p. 55.

65. Ahmed, *Religion and Politics*, pp. 86–88.

66. To avoid misunderstanding, it should be pointed out that this notion is not the same as the *cultural* construct of the person as espoused by Dale F. Eickelman, *Moroccan Islam* (Austin, Tex., 1976), and Lawrence Rosen, *Bargaining for Reality: The Construction of Social Relations in a Muslim Community* (Chicago, 1984), for Ahmed clearly has in mind a social-psychological entity.

67. Ahmed, *Religion and Politics*, p. 146.

68. M. H. Fried, *The Evolution of Political Society* (New York, 1967).

69. G. R. Garthwaite, "Khans and Kings: The Dialectics of Power in Bakhtiyari History," in M. E. Bonine and N. R. Keddie, eds., *Modern Iran: The Dialectics of Continuity and Change* (Albany, 1981), pp. 159–172, at p. 160. See also *Khans and Shahs: A Documentary Analysis of the Bakhtiyari in Iran* (Cambridge, 1983).

70. Garthwaite, "Khans and Kings," p. 169.

71. Garthwaite, "Khans and Kings," p. 163.

72. Garthwaite, "Khans and Kings," pp. 164, 165.

73. Beck, *The Qashqa'i*, p. 200.

74. Beck, *The Qashqa'i*, pp. 203, 206, 213.

75. Beck, *The Qashqa'i*, p. 218.

76. Richard Tapper, *Pasture and Politics: Economics, Conflict and Ritual among Shahsevan Nomads of Northwestern Iran* (London, 1979).

Tribalism and the State in
the Middle East

Ernest Gellner

The typical Middle Eastern tribal quasi-state is based on a combination of the following elements:

1. *Segmentary-lineage organization.* This means in effect the existence of cohesive social groups that ensure order by joint effort. They have a high military participation ratio, to use S. Andreski's phrase[1]; in practice all adult males take part in organized violence and share the risks involved.

The most characteristic institution of such a society is the feud. An offense perpetrated by a member of group A against a member of group B is followed by retaliation by *any* member of B against *any* member of A. If peace is made and compensation paid, members of A all make a contribution, and the members of the receiving group B all share it. The consequence of this kind of institutionalization of collective responsibility is that each group has a strong incentive to police its own members. No one else can do it for them, and they will suffer if they fail to do it.

The corresponding negative strait of this kind of society is that there is little or no external or superimposed policing by some specialized order-enforcing agency, ideally neutral. The circular, self-perpetuating, and self-reinforcing mechanism inherent in this situation is obvious: strong self-policing and self-administering groups result in a weak or absent central agency; a weak central agency results in the need for strong, self-protecting mutual-ensurance groups.

A vital aspect of segmentary society is *nesting*. Groups contain subgroups, which in turn contain other subgroups, whose relationship to each other is once again similar. There is no preeminent or crucial level of social organization. The balance of power operates *inside* groups as much as it does between them. The groups that appear in the literature as tribal confederations, tribes, clans, or segments all function in roughly the same way. Conflicts are likely to arise at any level and then to activate the relevant groups. Otherwise, they remain relatively latent, though they come together for festivals, pasture migrations, and other occasions.

The self-image and self-definition of these groups in the Middle East is usually, but not always, genealogical and patrilineal. If group membership is a function of descent, and descent is counted in one line only, this automatically engenders a neat and unambiguous system of nested groups such as is required by this kind of social order. When carrying out fieldwork in the central High Atlas of Morocco, I found that ordinary lay tribesmen, as distinct from holy lineages, possessed Occamist genealogies; that is, they did not multiply ancestors beyond necessity. The number of ancestors remembered (or invented) corresponded closely to the number of actually existing social groups, each of them requiring an apical ancestor for their definition.

The fact that these groups are not merely unilineal but also patrilineal may be held to be a consequence of the pervasive Middle Eastern and Mediterranean agnatic ethos or of the requirements of pastoral social organization. One interesting exception does exist in an area otherwise continuous with, and similar to, the Middle East— the Saharan Tuareg, who have a matrilineal ideology and had, in some measure that has never been properly explored, a matrilineal social organization. (They are also atypical in possessing a highly developed hierarchical ranking among tribal groups. This feature is also occasionally encountered elsewhere, though in less extreme form.)

Contrary to popular belief, these groups are not always self-defined genealogically. Among mountain peasants the definition of groups, at any rate above the microlevel of extended families, is often territorial rather than genealogical. Moreover, even when the definition is genealogical, recognized procedures exist for the reallocation of groups and individuals in defiance of what would be the commands of "blood" (or of "flesh" or "bone").

What this kind of system of collective responsibility does require is unambiguous membership. When blood is rectified by a recognized public ritual, the resulting situation still satisfies the needs of the system. So in a supposedly kin-defined unit it is common to find subgroups that have become effective kin by ritual rather than by blood.

2. *Weak, quasi-elective, or even fully elective leadership*. The commonest pattern is the existence of a chiefly segment or lineage, which is traditionally empowered to provide the leader for a wider

group also comprising other lineages and segments. It is characteristic of this system that there is no clear and unambiguous rule of succession.

The consequence is that at the demise of a given chief, the selection of the successor depends on the balance of power and prestige rather than on the simple application of a rule. The succession can go to son, brother, nephew, or paternal uncle, and the terms for paternal uncle and son of paternal uncle are used in a classificatory way, embracing a wider category than would be implied in the English usage of these terms. Hence the succession may be determined either by an informal vote—it may go to the man whose potential for leadership is demonstrated by the support he receives from other segments—or by conflict, in which case the leadership potential is demonstrated by what one might call bloody praxis.

These societies are caught in a dilemma: they need leadership for the purpose of indulging in, and resisting, raids and for external relations. At the same time, their internal organization is based more on a balance of power than on its concentration. A rough generalization is tempting: the more important the group's external relations, the more centralized and effective is its leadership likely to be.[2]

3. *Symbiosis of pastoral and agricultural populations.* This type of organization is especially appropriate for pastoralists and even more so for *mobile* pastoralists. The latter's mobility, and the fact that their wealth is on the hoof, makes them both inclined and able to resist or evade centralized government. Such organization is also frequently found, however, among sedentary peasants in inaccessible terrain. The political implications of such a location are similar to those of nomadic or seminomadic pastoralism. This kind of organization has much smaller prospects of survival among vulnerably located agriculturalists constrained by the limits of an oasis or dependent on irrigation.

Vulnerable agriculturalists and aggressive pastoralists are complementary and economically symbiotic.[3] In a barely governed, or ungoverned, condition, grain or dates are exchanged for meat or milk products, but the rates of exchange are unlikely to be determined exclusively by the principles of the market. The rate at which products are exchanged or handed over can be interpreted as some kind of cross between price, tribute, protection money, and insurance premium against failure of production. The pastoralists have an interest in not allowing their oasis clients to starve when the harvest happens to fail.

The setting up of a stable relationship between the two parties is politically delicate and may favor the emergence of a stable leadership, a strong chieftaincy, or a tribal quasi-state. The agriculturalists have an interest in dealing with a single authority, which in turn has an interest in their own survival and in their taxable prosperity. They prefer this arrangement to being exposed to simultaneous and unpredictable harassment from a number of uncoordinated would-be exploiters, some of whom may be tempted by a onetime, destructive seizure of large booty, even if it diminishes the prospect of future and repeated tribute. After all, future tribute may go to someone else.

Both agriculturalists and pastoralists also have an interest in the availability and proximity of craftsmen and traders. From the viewpoint of an oasis protobourgeoisie the attractions of a relatively strong and stable protector are similar to those that it possesses for the agriculturalists. The pastoralists, by contrast, have an interest in access to a well-supplied, reasonably priced, and safely accessible market.

4. *Complementarity with holy lineages.* An institution common, though not universal, in the region is the presence of status-differentiated holy lineages dispersed among the segmentary tribes. These usually claim descent from the Prophet. Their elevated status—especially if combined with abstention in principle from involvement in the feuds of lay tribes, exemplifying a kind of limited, role-specific pacifism—qualifies their groups, or at least their more prominent members, to act as arbitrators for the ordinary tribal citizenry. They also provide a kind of loose leadership, which, however, is dependent on the optional support of the led.

5. *External trade and pilgrimage routes.* A strong chieftaincy or tribal protostate is likely to be located on trade routes, pilgrimage routes (the two are often combined), or, indeed, on a possible route for the hajj, or pilgrimage to Mecca. Traders and pilgrims on the move need transport, accommodation, and protection. Like locally settled artisans and traders, they prefer to deal with a single and effective patron rather than with a number of competitive ones probably both unreliable and rapacious. Trade is often a necessity rather than a luxury. The general ecology and the extremities of climate and aridity impel social groups toward specialization. This in turn obliges them to trade; but the requirements of trade push the society toward some measure of political order.

6. *External ideological input.* For reasons not easy to grasp for an organizationally oriented social scientist, the Muslim world is pervaded by a reverence for the high-culture variant of Islam—egalitarian, scripturalist, puritan, and nomocratic. This ethos seems to have a life and authority of its own, not visibly dependent on any institutional incarnation. In normal conditions this ideal is imple-

mented, at most, in a relatively small part of Muslim society by the urban scholars and by their socially well-placed clientele. The ideal presupposes literacy and an ethic of abiding by rules rather than of personal loyalty. Its often emphatic reprobation of claims to special mediation with the divine (the sin of *shirk*) makes it inappropriate for illiterate tribal groups. Those units have a great need for mediators practicing arbitration between men in the name of mediation with God. Nonetheless, the authority of the exclusive and unitarian ideal is widely respected, even by those who do not and cannot at most times implement it. From time to time this ideal is activated and becomes a powerful and effective sentiment; it then plays an important part in state-building.

7. *The wider political game.* The tribal territories of the Middle East are peripheral and yet internationally important. Before the appearance of oil wealth they were seldom important for what they produced or contained, but they did possess strategic, and sometimes symbolic, significance. This led outside powers to take an active interest in controlling them or denying such control to others. These powers were in rivalry with each other, and they fostered rivalries within the tribal regions. In the nineteenth century the nominally centralized Ottoman Empire, for instance, operated in the tribal regions of the Arabian Peninsula from two mutually independent bases, one in Egypt and the other in Iraq.

8. *The mercenary or* mamluk *option.* Tribal chieftains proper did not possess the resource base for creating professional armies and bureaucracies. Their armed forces were the tribe, activated by conflict or prospect of loot or by inspired leadership. This characteristic was both their strength and their weakness. The tribal military unit was a preexisting social group, endowed with cohesion by its shared experience and concerns and habituated by the normal conditions of its life to mobility, violence, and frugality. The continuity between the social and military existences of the tribal armed forces often made them formidable; they did not need, like ordinary recruits, to be specially trained and endowed with an artificial esprit de corps. They arrived, fully trained and *encadré*, with recognized leaders and a familiarity with the terrain in which they were to be deployed.

Their weakness lay in the very same attributes. Their social organization predisposed them to fissiparousness as well as cohesion. The lack of a separation between their civil and military roles made them exceedingly responsive to pressures other than the long-term plans of the supreme command. Notoriously, they went home when it suited them, oblivious to strategic considerations. Seasonal obligations and customs meant at least as much to them as long-term strategy. Hence, any tribal chief whose domain came to exceed a purely tribal base naturally attempted to supplement and balance his tribal following by a professional, individually recruited armed force composed of mercenaries and slaves. To do so required no social inventiveness on his part; the model of such organization was highly developed in the Middle East ever since the decline of the caliphate.[4] The *mamluk* system worked, and on occasion it worked exceedingly well.

DISCUSSION OF THE COMBINATION OF THE ELEMENTS

It is unlikely that the original inventors of the system were careful students of Plato's *Republic*. Nevertheless, in a Muslim idiom the underlying ideas constituted a remarkable implementation of Platonism. Social corruption and decline were to be avoided: members of the ruling elite were to be systematically trained from early youth in military and administrative skills and, at the same time, were to be profoundly imbued with a pervasive ethos intimately linked to the legitimacy of the state they served. They were to be cut off from the temptations of kin and wealth, which otherwise distract men from the performance of their political duty.

The fact that these elites were to be called slaves rather than guardians was relatively unimportant. The state owned them, but they owned the state. A meritocratic career pattern reinforced their commitment to the state and its service; their recruitment from geographically, ethnically, even religiously and pigmentationally alien zones strengthened their loyalty or at any rate reduced their temptations. Like the tribesmen who made up the original power base of an expanding chieftaincy, they came from a rough background and were not habituated to the softening snares that weaken urban rulers; but unlike the tribesmen who came collectively, they were also severed from the seductions of kin links.

If the system did not last forever, its eventual decline was due to precisely the reasons Plato foresaw: this ruling guild, its cohesion originally forged not by the shared perils of the desert but by subjection to the common rigors of deliberately severe training, in the end succumbed to the temptations of honor, kinship, and wealth. This was the order in which Plato expected the temptations to operate, as was to be reflected in successive degenerative shifts of the body politic. The actual decline need not be quite so neat. Hinduism is another remarkable kind of implementation of Platonism, though one that wholly surrenders to the principle of kinship while retaining the rigid hierarchy of wisdom, coercion, and production. So the *mamluk* system is but one variant of Platonism. It fully deploys certain elements in the Platonic recipe: education, insulation, propertylessness, and kinlessness.

From another viewpoint the *mamluk* system appears as an extraordinary attempt to produce bureaucrats ahead of their time. The traditional state is hampered in its centralizing tendency by the inveterate inclination of men to forge local and kin links, which lead them away from duty and obedience and cause the state to break up into autonomous regional units. It is only in the modern world that a number of factors—a general atomization of society, a widespread orientation toward work and vocation, the pervasive socialization of men by formal education rather than local community—have jointly turned virtually everyone into a potential bureaucrat. Men can now be trusted, on the whole, to perform their tasks in bureaucratic organizations without constantly yielding to the temptation to bend the rules so as to favor their own kin. We are all *mamluk*s now. Traditional society did not have this advantage; for reliable bureaucratic performance it had to rely on slaves, eunuchs, priests, or aliens.[5]

We may well ask whether, when the *mamluk* principle and its modification are brilliantly successful on a large scale, we can still talk about a tribal state. There would indeed be something preposterous about referring to the Ottoman Empire in its fully developed form in such terms; that was how it started, but it did not retain that form. The *mamluk* principle is an alternative to a tribal base, and pure versions of either one constitute the two endpoints of a spectrum; societies located at the extreme ends are rare, and many Middle Eastern polities were located somewhere along the middle of this range.

We can put the question in another way. Given the emergence of the Ottoman state, is Ibn Khaldun's theory of Middle Eastern society, on which I have been relying heavily, still defensible as an overall theory of the Muslim world of the arid zone? My own inclination is to say yes and to offer the following argument: no doubt the two elements, the paradigmatically Ibn Khaldunian use of a tribal base and the rival one of a slave bureaucracy, could and did mix in diverse proportions in various Middle Eastern state formations.

The Ottoman Empire began as a cluster of typical tribal polities in Anatolia. It was only when one of them achieved outstanding success that two things happened: it acquired an atypical base, in the Balkans and western Anatolia and eventually in the Nile valley, of docile sedentary peasants; and the *mamluk* element came to display a kind of hypertrophy, eliminating the rival element. The two changes were no doubt connected. An extensive and taxable peasant base made it possible to sustain a nontribal state apparatus, and the new base was ill suited for governance by tribesmen. The system then reproduced itself in an autonomous form in Tunis and Algiers and perhaps elsewhere.

In extensive areas, however, the Ibn Khaldunian formula, using the old elements, persisted alive and well. It constituted the normal political condition of a large proportion of Middle Easterners despite the nominal Ottoman overlordship. It was signaling—perhaps not always wildly—to be let out. In due course it made its public reappearance, with 'Abd al-Qadir in Algeria, the Mahdiyya in the Sudan, the Wahhabis in the Peninsula, the Sanusiyya in Cyrenaica, the Rashidis in Ha'il, petty tribal chieftaincies in Eastern Anatolia, the Ibadi imamate in Oman, and the Zaydi one in Yemen. In extensive areas it had never really been hidden.

The way in which all these various elements combine in state formation varies a great deal. One can think of a number of possible scenarios. Tribesmen who herd their flocks in an arid hill range that also shelters an oasis, and who are governed, in as far as the term is appropriate at all, by a loose chieftaincy, may secure control of the oasis. They thereby provide the chiefly lineage with a dual base. Henceforth the chief divides his time between an oasis town base, whose prosperity he may enhance further by inviting craftsmen and traders to settle, and a seasonal chiefly progress among those of his kinsmen who have remained on the pastures. His more privileged wives remain in the town house while he fortifies his links with his tribal kinsmen by marriages, possibly short-lived, with daughters of segment chiefs. He balances the concerns of the diverse constituents of his chieftaincy, and he encourages the pastoralists to practice their depradations, not on his own subjects, but preferably outside. He has to balance the advantages of allowing his old supporters and kinsmen the benefits of both kinds of pillage against the advantages of receiving protection money by proscribing pillage. The optimal solution is to allow just enough pillage to retain the loyalty of the tribal segments and provide maximum encouragement for the payment of protection. Marginal pillage should equal marginal tribute in a finely tuned tribal chiefdom.

The chief has to guard against defections among the tribal segments by giving subsidies that can rival those promised by other similar chieftaincies, ever ready to seduce some of his following by offering better terms. All this takes money; so he himself is in the market for the reception of subsidies and arms from outside powers, which in turn are eager to use his strategic position either to ensure their own communications or to undermine the communications and claims of their rivals. Each outside power has its own local clients, but the alignments inevitably are unstable. Treachery is endemic.

Trade and pilgrimage routes are also tricky. Insistence on excessive security may antagonize tribal dependents and diminish revenue. The game is played out within the chiefly lineage as well; rival cousins, brothers, and nephews enlist, and are enlisted by, external participants in this complex, never-ending game. New entrants appear with changes in the international scene, and some old ones are eliminated. Nothing, certainly not death, ever terminates the game; leadership in a segmentary society has a dragon's-teeth quality. I heard this complaint in Pahlavi Tehran: however many tribal leaders you kill, new ones always emerge from the chief's lineage. The killed or assassinated chief or claimant cannot return to compete some other day, but his brother, son, or nephew will.[6]

There is another possible scenario. Consider an alternative story in which all these elements are indeed present, but with one further participant: religious fundamentalism and revivalism. Islam is ever reformation-prone; it might even be described as the permanent reformation. The faithful are frequently willing to respond to a preacher calling for return to a purer version of the faith (assuming that they or their ancestors had ever really known it), a form unblemished by questionable and quasi-pagan practices. The community-polity equation impels the preacher to become a political figure as well.

Shi'is consciously reenact the founding martyrdom of their special faith, but other Muslims are likely to reenact or refeel the original conflict between the establishment of the faith and the preceding—yet ever-present and menacing—age of ignorance. The enthusiasm evoked by such an appeal to purification may give the purifying chief the advantage of an extra element of cohesion among his followers and a special capacity to organize units far larger than those supplied by their own kin-based political language. This action may confer on him some of the advantages that are painfully, and much more expensively, acquired by larger states through the revenue produced from their control of extensive agricultural territory and through the recruitment of mercenaries and *mamluks* with the help of that revenue. This special formula of tribe plus religious revival can lead to political fortune, particularly when combined with the good fortune of an alignment with outside powers victorious in a world war. The faith-linked chieftaincy can then triumph over its main rival, whom in other respects it resembles. This is in effect the story of the Saudi victory over the Rashidis.

A different kind of tribal state can also arise, one based on the mutual complementarity of lay tribal leaders and holy lineages. In such a case the wider society is divided into a majority of lay tribesmen and a minority of hereditary saints. The saints are settled around one or more shrines, which are revered by all. The lay tribesmen comport themselves in accordance with the well-known rules governing a segmentary society: collective responsibility, diffusion of power, weak leadership (elective or quasi-elective), and wide participation by male heads of household in all political and other responsibilities.

The conflicts that inevitably arise between groups of all sizes are arbitrated or mediated at the shrines by the hereditary saints, who are determined by birth rather than chosen in any kind of human election. The shrines are strategically located close to the points of maximal conflict—at the border of major tribal segments or near pastures, which require seasonal reoccupation and periodic reallocation. The number of men of saintly birth is much smaller than those of lay birth but at the same time much larger than the number of saints required to preside over shrines and act as effective arbitrators. The real, so to speak operational, saints are selected from the wider pool of latent saints-by-birth.

According to the locally accepted theory, this selection is made by God. In reality, *vox Dei vox populi*. The choice of the possessor of *baraka* is made by a drawn-out and tacit process, stretching over generations, in which the attribution of divine grace works through the bestowal of support on this or that saint by the lay tribesmen. It is this support that effectively endows some saints with charisma. He who is treated as a saint becomes one. The respect he is shown enables him to arbitrate effectively and thereby display and prove his sanctity. The donations he receives enable him to entertain generously without seeming to count the cost and thereby, once again, to demonstrate his saintly status.

The lay tribesmen are obliged to feud, and the saints are obliged by the very definition of their role to abstain both from violence and from litigation, the latter being but the continuation of the feud by other means. By their comportment some saints attract special reverence. The respect they inspire in some of their clientele then makes them attractive to other potential parishioners; an arbitrator who is widely respected, and whose judgment is heeded, is of more use than one whose verdict may be spurned by the other party to the conflict. In this way a kind of quasi-state crystallizes. Violent lay elective chiefs and pacific hereditary saints complement each other in the system. An elegant, stable, and satisfactory system of internal balance of power can develop. In the central High Atlas a system of this kind persisted and provided cheap and satisfactory quasi-government for about three centuries.[7]

Two things deserve note in connection with the saints of Ahansal: the stability of their local power and their abstention at most times from wider political ambition. They did not in general intervene in wider Moroccan history. On only a single occasion did one of their number display a wider ambition. He paid for it by a horrible death, the occurrence of which, however, is denied by local tradition, which credits him with an occultation, to be followed by an eventual return in the hour of greatest need. So far, this prognostication has not been borne out. By an accident, most fortunate for the historian, his real death was witnessed by Thomas Pellow, an English renegade-captive in the service of the then sultan, who in the end managed to return to England and publish an account of his adventures. The local faith in an occultation, faith that persisted into modern times, can on this occasion be corrected by independent external documentation.

This kind of scenario, which might be called the Ahansal version, differs from the preceding variant, which could be called the Saudi pattern. A different type of Islam is involved in each of the two models. We are dealing with a tribal state in each case, but the religious cement is quite different. The social incarnation of Islam stretches out along a kind of spectrum, ranging from a scholarly, puritanical, egalitarian theology at one end to an anthropolatrous, ecstatic, hierarchical folk religion at the other. Either form can make a significant contribution to tribal-state or quasi-state formation. Hereditary saints, based on the principle of *shirk* (mediation or refraction of the deity) and vehemently reprobated by the orthodox high theology, can provide that minimal centralizing agency, which, however, deals very satisfactorily with the political problems of extensive populations. It can do so without much in the way of coercive centralizations, that is, what we would call a real state. It can help regulate the complex patterns of seasonal pasture use in a complex ecology, requiring seasonal migrations of large flocks and human populations from the Sahara to high mountains, and it can help keep the peace between the transhumants and the sedentaries.

By contrast, puritan unitarian Islam can endow one leader with sufficient legitimacy to overcome tribal fissiparousness and help him set up a more effective state, in which the written requirements of the faith receive a more stringent implementation. Here the men of religion become bureaucratic, ideological, and judicial servants of the state, rather than being equal, or more-than-equal, partners of the petty practitioners of coercion. The revered marabout arbitrates between segment leaders and helps fuse the segments into a kind of polity; the scribe-judge helps a shaykh to become an amir by providing him with the appropriate legitimacy and with a rudimentary bureaucracy.

The available forms of religious political cement are by no means exhausted by these two versions, the Saudi and the Ahansal types. Intermediate forms combining political centralization with the use of hereditary religious arbitrators are available. The traditional Yemeni state, for instance, fused the central authority of an imam—legitimated by the Zaidi version of Shi'ism—with local arbitration by Sadah families, dividing their authority (based on a hereditary-religious standing outside the tribal segmentary system) with tribal shaykhs whose authority was based on leadership *within* the tribes and also with legal families.[8] An interesting and well-documented mixed form of this kind emerged in Cyrenaica under the impact of Italian colonial aggression.[9] The Sanusiyya combined the organizational form of a Sufi (mediationist, religious order, or *tariqa*) with doctrinal commitment to a relatively reformist ideology, that is, to supplying a purer version of the faith to the ignorant and illiterate Bedouin. Reformist Islam is normally hostile to religious orders, but in tribal areas, devoid of an urban infrastructure, Sufi organizational principles provide the only available institutional tool capable of sustaining missionary work. The doctrine must compromise if it is to be endowed with the minimum of social underpinning. The preconditions of the only possible form of political organization at the time, given the ecological milieu, eventually impelled the Sanusi toward the Ahansal version, the insertion of saintly lodges at the crucial interstices of the segmentary system. There they could provide mediation and arbitration. The need, by contrast, to unite a wide area and invoke a religious legitimation more potent than that of the traditional preexisting *marabtin-bil-baraka* (petty saints attached to small segments) also impelled them toward a more unitarian and scripturalist version of the faith.

There is a permanent tension between the two principles of legitimacy, the egalitarian-scripturalist and the kin-based mediationist. The former is incarnated in the theologian-scholars who, on their own, have little potential for state-formation. They are neither well organized nor skilled in coercion. They can, however, provide a monarch, or a chief aspiring to become monarch, with both legitimation and a bureaucracy. The tribal segments, the social base of the second and rival principle of state formation, are inherently well trained in the exercise of violence; but they normally lack legitimacy in the eyes of the wider Muslim society. In fact, their normal life constitutes a kind of paradigm of moral illegitimacy. They are seen as licentious and ignorant, neither willing nor able to live the good Muslim life. This, given the socially pervasive intensity of commitment to Islam, is no trivial matter. Only those who succeed in combining into large and powerful units in the name of orthodoxy can then spoliate those remaining sinners who remain fragmented and who failed to join the snowballing movement of revival.

The *mamluk* system can be seen as an extreme version, one that endeavors to dispense with the kin or tribal element altogether and stand it on its head. Individuals are recruited into the state service in an atomized manner and are torn out of their kin background by being technically slaves and/or of non-Muslim origin. Sustained religious and military training, which is *not* tribal, becomes a means of inducing an esprit de corps. One can look at the *mamluks* either as an artificial, education-produced tribe, or one can see them as the result of turning a religious elite, normally ineffectual politically, into a for-once coercively and politically effective body. There are *mamluks de robe* as well as *mamluks d'epée*. When the system works well, individuals within it can successfully perform each of these rules at various stages of their career—they can be soldiers in their youth and cleric-administrators later. Thus, they really live up to Plato's ideal of the guardians.

What in general are the prospects of building a social and political order, a framework within which men may work creatively and enjoy the fruits of their labor with some degree of security and where both civilization and stability are present? In these respects, how does the Muslim Middle East compare with Europe?

Consider the pair of the most celebrated commentators on the two systems, Ibn Khaldun and Niccolo Machiavelli. What the two share, apart from their greatness, is a marked inclination toward dispassionate analysis instead of pious moralizing. Ironically, it is Machiavelli, whose notoriety comes from an alleged cynicism, rather than his Muslim counterpart, who more frequently abandons *Wertfreiheit* and slips into moral concern and expressions of regret. Ibn Khaldun's detachment was far more complete.

Their accounts of the problems of social cohesion and of order deserve juxtaposition. They were not quite contemporaries; Ibn Khaldun died in 1406, and Machiavelli was born a whole generation, or to be precise, sixty-six years, later. The lifetime that separates the death of one from the birth of the other contains at least one momentous event, namely, the fall of Constantinople and hence the definitive emergence of the Ottoman Empire. This event makes a considerable difference, one that is reflected in their thought; Machiavelli ponders on the Ottoman state, and Ibn Khaldun could not yet do so.

Nevertheless, their two worlds were not so very distant and can usefully be compared. Machiavelli, much impressed by the Ottoman Empire, considered its strength, like that of the empire of Alexander, to be due to the weakness of civil society in the East. Once you defeated the center, society could no longer oppose you, and the rest fell into your lap. How different from Europe, where barons might initially help you by betraying their overlord, but they would cause you perpetual trouble even if you succeeded in defeating their king. This argument has of late earned Machiavelli the rebuke of being the initiator of the "Orientalist" heresy of Western denigration of the East. It is true that Machiavelli did not notice that in the Middle East, tribes will also cause you trouble, even after you have defeated and replaced the sultan. The distinctively Middle Eastern path to political fragmentation eluded him.

An extraterrestrial observer, investigating the political life of man at that time and using the works of these two thinkers as his main texts, would probably come to the conclusion that the political prospects of the Middle East were far better than those of Europe. The sadness and pessimism that intermittently and irresistibly burst through the otherwise cool prose of Machiavelli's accounts were only too well founded.

In Ibn Khaldun's world, sketched out in the earlier part of this essay, there were three effective principles of political order: the natural cohesion of tribal life; the principle of military-administrative slavery; and religion. No single one of these was perfect or exempt from eventual decay; but, in various forms of combination with each other, they held out some hope of at least a measure of political stability, temporary place, and effective government. A tribal coalition, endowed with unity by religion, could set up a state; a state that was guided and served by the religious scholars could function, upholding right and suppressing evil, and both observing and enforcing that fundamental entrenched political constitution already contained, even legally prefabricated, in the faith itself.

Logically, Muslim states need no constitution because religion already constitutes, and provides the entrenched clauses of, moral and political order. Religiously trained slaves of the state could endow the state with strength and operate the famous circle of equity, in which civil society, though disenfranchised, could produce sufficient wealth to sustain the state and so receive the required protection in return.[10] Thus, some degree of fusion of both civilization and cohesion was possible, even if the basic human dilemma—the conditions of cohesion and of civilization are mutually incompatible—could not be overcome altogether. Urban and tribal virtues cannot come together, one being born of the city and the other of the tribe; but carriers of each set of virtues, tribesmen and scholars, can occasionally combine and jointly set up and run a state.

These elements are present in a far lesser degree in the Italy and Europe observed by Machiavelli. Let us take each of them in turn:

Tribalism. Machiavelli notes that the only people in Europe who still live as the ancients did are the Swiss. By this he means that a society with an exceedingly high military and political participation ratio, and one that is firmly committed to a religion sustaining civic virtue, is consequently free from outside interference and is fairly egalitarian internally: "The Swiss are strongly armed and completely free" (*The Prince*); "The Swiss . . . are the only people who today, with respect both to religion and to military institutions, live as the ancients did" (*The Discourses*). This clearly corresponds to what Ibn Khaldun means by tribal *'asabiyya*; natural cohesion emerges when a group is bound to administer and defend itself. The military implications of this situation, the joint presence in one international system both of *'asabiyya*-endowed participatory units and of urban ones, are precisely those Ibn Khaldun had postulated for all mankind. In war the Swiss beat everyone, and no one, not even the French monarchy, could win without their help: "The French are no match for the Swiss, and without Swiss help feel no match for anyone else" (*The Prince*). The armies recruited from urban civil societies, such as the Italian, are useless; Machiavelli notes that they only win if for some reason the rival army runs away.

Machiavelli was mistaken in supposing that the Swiss were the only armed, participatory self-governing communities left in Europe. He was close enough to the truth, however, for though some are also found elsewhere, they are marginal. Montenegro or the Scottish highlands escaped his attention. But in early modern Europe, barbarians, whether as a threat or as a salvation, were indeed in short supply. As late as the eighteenth century, Edward Gibbon, wondering whether the fate of Rome might also befall Augustan Europe, noted this with a touch of surprise: Europe had run out of savages.

Slaves on horseback. For some reason or other, Europe had lost the institution of slavery. Especially in Italy, the regrettable principle of a free labor market developed and flourished in a sphere of activity for which it is especially unsuitable—the market for military service. The consequences were disastrous, and Machiavelli comments on them at length and with feeling. Mercenaries are useless, he says. In danger they desert you; in victory they become your mas-

ters. It is in fact hard to say whether it is their success or their failure that spells the greater danger for their employer. How about
auxiliaries, the armed forces supplied by an ally? The disadvantages
that attend their use are at least as great. What is to be done? Civic
societies supply armies that only win when the enemy happens to
flee; mercenaries and allies turn against you when they prevail. In
despair, the only advice Machiavelli is able to give is that of deploy-
ing *mixed* forces. Presumably, the hope is that not all of them will be-
tray you at the same time.

The Muslim world was better endowed: on the one hand, a kind of
generalized and pervasive Switzerland without cuckoo clocks, full of
free rural communities, surrounded virtually all states. It provided
an ever-present reservoir of natural political and military talent; the
future, Ibn Khaldun predicted in his autobiography, belonged to the
Turks and the Arabs because of their populousness and cohesion.[11]
The relatively small territory of the central Alps could hardly match
the expanses of Central Asia and all the mountains and savannah of
the Middle East. The future may belong to Turks and Arabs, but it
does not belong to the Swiss. The *mamluk*s, drawn in large measure
from the Caucasian and Central Asian reservoirs, and later from the
Balkans, were the Switzers of the Muslim courts. "Where are my
Switzers? Let them guard the door," cries the king in *Hamlet*. But
soon he announces, "The doors are broke." Claudius would have
been much safer with janissaries. The *mamluk*s, produced according
to the Platonic recipe of sustained training, deep indoctrination, and
meritocratic promotion, were clearly superior to the opportunistic,
treacherous, and volatile mercenaries, whose suspect motivation
was bound to turn them into unreliable supporters.

Religion. The contrast is just as unfavorable to Europe if we turn
to religion. Ibn Khaldun was clear about the great political potential
of faith. Religious enthusiasm, when superimposed on the natural
cohesion of participatory groups, engenders large units and a more
effective discipline. Ibn Khaldun did not greatly discuss the micro-
structural services provided by petty saints, though he was familiar
with them; but he was explicit about the services religion could provide in helping to enlarge the political unit.

By contrast, the role of religion in Europe, according to Machiavelli, is dismal. In *The Prince* he first declares that there is no
point in discussing ecclesiastical principalities: "I shall not argue
about them; they are exalted and maintained by God, and only a rash
and presumptuous man would take it on himself to discuss them."
But the temptations of rashness and presumption quickly become
too strong for him, and he goes on to describe how the political as-

tuteness of three successive popes for a time made the Papal States great. In *The Discourses* he is more explicit and damning: "Owing to the bad example set by the Court of Rome, Italy has lost all devotion and all religion. It is the Church that has kept, and keeps, Italy divided.... Italy...has now become the prey...of anyone who attacks it. For which our Italians have to thank the Church, and nobody else." The Swiss, says Machiavelli, are the only European people to maintain the ancient virtues; but if the court of Rome were to move to Switzerland, the Swiss would soon be brought down in utter disorder. This ingenious experiment has never actually been tried.

So there are no tribes (but for the blessed Swiss), no corps of well-trained servants of the state, no socially effective and inspiring faith. What hope, then, can there be for Italy or Europe? In the tribal-urban complex of the Muslim Middle East, by contrast, the blend of tribal cohesion and urban civilization is at least periodically revived. Faith and virtue are committed to an eternal return. One could hope for some peace during the stable periods before the wheel of political fortune turned once again. To the north of the Mediterranean, however, there seems to be no hope at all.

On the evidence available at the time, such a conclusion would have been entirely reasonable. History has turned out rather differently. It is not part of this essay to speculate about how Europe, and in the end even Italy, broke out of the impasse. The manner in which a new centralized bureaucratic state came about, one in which everyone was turned into soldier and bureaucrat and became a *mamluk*; the way in which the relationship between state and civil society was transformed, so that civil society took part in politics and the state took part in the economy; the manner in which religion recovered its social potential in a new form—all this is another theme.

But it is appropriate to look, at least briefly, at the subsequent fate of the world of tribal politics in the Middle East. There are many who hold that the Ottoman Empire makes Ibn Khaldun's account inapplicable to recent centuries. I do not believe this to be so. Under the surface the world of Ibn Khaldun continued to function; it re-emerged as the empire declined. It only came to an end when new military and administrative technologies were imported and tilted the balance of power in favor of the state. The subsequent new order has a number of conspicuous features: civil society continues to be weak in face of the state; political conflict within the state apparatus, even when nominally ideological, is generally a matter of the rivalry of patronage networks, often with a regional or quasi-communal base. This is a kind of tribalism in a new milieu and idiom. In marked contrast to other parts of the world, in the Middle East religion has retained or enhanced its capacity to act as a political catalyst. Secularization is conspicuous by its absence. Politics is frequently fundamentalist. Strong religion, strong state, weak civil society, and the fragile 'asabiyya of quasi-kin, quasi-territorial patronage—that seems to be the heritage.

NOTES

1. See S. Andreski, *Military Organisation and Society* (London, 1968).

2. See A. M. Khazanov, *Nomads and the Outside World* (Cambridge, 1984).

3. See also Ross Dunn, *Resistance in the Desert* (Madison, Wisc., 1977).

4. See Patricia Crone, *Slaves on Horses: The Evolution of the Islamic Polity* (Cambridge, 1980).

5. See K. Hopkins, *Conquerors and Slaves* (Cambridge, 1978).

6. Madawi Al Rasheed, "The Political System of a North Arabian Chiefdom" (Ph.D. diss., Cambridge University, 1988).

7. See Ernest Gellner, *Saints of the Atlas* (Chicago, 1969).

8. On this topic I am much indebted to research students who have not yet published their findings, notably Shelagh Weir and Gabriella von Bruck.

9. See E. E. Evans-Pritchard, *The Sanusi of Cyrenaica* (Oxford, 1949), and the posthumous collections of papers by Emrys Peters, to be published.

10. See Lucette Valensi, *Venise et la Sublime Porte: La naissance du despote* (Paris, 1987).

11. See Ibn Khaldun, *Le voyage d'Occident et d'Orient*, trans. Abdesseiain Cheddadi (Paris, 1980).

The Simultaneity of the Unsimultaneous: Old Tribes and Imposed Nation-States in the Modern Middle East

Bassam Tibi

Before the dissolution of the Ottoman Empire two types of state formation were known in the Middle East: the imperial and the territorial. The collapse of the last Islamic imperial state, the Ottoman Empire, resulted in the emergence of a multitude of nation-states via a period of colonial rule. This new pattern of state formation, which first evolved in Europe, is not only new but also foreign to the civilizational area known as the Muslim world. Since its forceful integration into the new world system, this "world of Islam" is no longer a world of its own.[1] Its Arab core has become a subordinate system for which the Eurocentric term *Near East* ("near" in terms of the proximity to Europe) has been coined. The Near East, or Middle East, is a regional subsystem of nation-states that has been integrated into the international system. The nation-state is in two ways a novelty to Arab-Islamic history. In the first place, it is based on the concept of internal sovereignty. A basic component of this internal sovereignty is the idea of citizenship, which presupposes transforming tribal and, in general, prenational ties into a national identity and loyalty. Second, the modern nation-state is based on the concept of external sovereignty, which refers to the mutual recognition of boundaries by a set of states that form a systemic framework of interaction, a concept that has no counterpart in Arab-Islamic history. Neither in the imperial nor in the territorial state were tribes transformed into a homogeneous polity; tribal ties have always been the basic element of group reference, despite the fact that they were suppressed and rhetorically renounced. This happened in the past within the framework of a universal Islamic *umma* and in the present with reference to the secular idea of the nation.[2] Thus, the modern nation-state, like the classical Islamic state, is expected to achieve the transition from tribe to nation.

It is true that the Middle East has been undergoing vast socioeconomic and political changes. These processes are related to the forceful integration of the former Ottoman provinces into the world economy and later into the international system of nation-states. They have contributed to large demographic transformations. Hence, we may ask whether we can still justify talking about tribes in the Middle East. Today only small portions of the populations of the Middle East can be viewed as tribal segments. However, the structural changes alluded to here have not contributed to the transition from tribal ties to patterns of national identity and loyalty. Though the tribe as an actual social structure has declined in significance, the tribe as a referent for social identity and loyalty has persisted. Only in this sense do I refer to the German philosophical concept of *Gleichzeitigkeit vom Ungleichzeitigen* (simultaneity of the unsimultaneous) for conceptualizing the parallel existence of two social and political patterns with their social origins in crucially different historical periods: the old tribes and the modern nation-state.

TRIBES AND THE STATE:
THE ISSUES, CONCEPT, AND SCOPE OF THE INQUIRY

The current crisis of the nation-state in the Middle East—its weak internal sovereignty—has been examined within the framework of Islamic revivalism,[3] whose exponents contest the nation-state and also reject it as *hal mustawrad* (an imported solution).[4] In this article I suggest that the crisis of nation-state not only promotes the revival of universal Islamic claims but also gives rise to the resurgence of local commitments that are referred to in the literature on the Middle East as tribal, ethnic, and sectarian. This rise has contributed to the revival of Ibn Khaldun's classical theme: the tribes and the state.

Recent events in the Sudan, Libya, Iraq, Syria, and elsewhere in the Middle East render this theme topical. In the social science literature of the 1960s, national integration as related to nation-building strategies was the prevailing issue, and it appeared to be a promising prospect.[5] Those hopes faded, however. Scholars are now confronted with the need to examine what caused the disintegration of the nominally existing sovereign nation-states. Western authors are not the only ones reexamining the concept of nation building to reformulate their hypotheses; Arab scholars, who were formerly obsessed with national unity, are also rethinking their earlier assumptions, but without rejecting the idea of Arab unity. For instance, Ghassan Salamé recalls Ibn Khaldun's formula that "in the lands which are inhabited by a multitude of tribes it is difficult to establish a state."[6]

Salamé's major idea revolves around the hypothesis that Arab urban elites have failed to cope with the post-Ottoman developments, thus unwittingly smoothing the way for the ascendance of tribal-rural groups to power: "While most parts of the urban body politic have lost ground...some rural groups, hitherto denied political participation, have been able to intrude into the modern state and to step up in the social hierarchy and also to enforce their political positions. Finally, they were able to capture the state." Salamé adds that the "armies have been the swords in the hand of the rural population.... Rural elements gradually became urban and reversely the state power became rural. The development of the modern state and its institutions were overladen with the herefrom emerging *asabiyyas*." A salient feature of this Middle Eastern variety of the simultaneity of the unsimultaneous is the reemergence of tribal *'asabiyya* in the guise of national sovereignty and national legitimacy, which are obviously not related to tribes but to the modern nation-state. As Salamé puts it, "These *asabiyyas* hate to sign their political practices with their own name. Instead, they present their state as if it were the exemplary instrument in the service of the entire society, a feature that characterizes modern Arab discourse....The ruling Arab authorities are imprisoned in the ideology of modern state which compels them to obscure their origin." Thus, tribal power, for which the Alawite tribes of Syria provide a clear example, is presented and legitimized as a national power of the modern nation-state.[7]

Does this statement suggest that Ibn Khaldun's concept of the tribe and the state is still valid for the study of Arab-Islamic history even now that the Middle East has become a part of the world system and is constrained by it? From a comparative vantage the classical Islamic state and the modern nation-state, in spite of their essential differences, seem to share the feature of opposing the tribes, be they the structurally based ones of the past or the communal solidarity groups of the present. This assumption justifies a comparative inquiry into the achievements of the two state patterns in the past and in the present, that is, an inquiry aimed at establishing a conceptual framework for understanding the interplay between tribes and states in different processes of state formation. Let us, then, define the scope and the underlying concepts of this inquiry.

To begin with, does the reference to Ibn Khaldun and to the classical dichotomy between the tribes and the state impute the historical vision that history is cyclical? Does it support the view that Arab-Islamic history takes place in cycles in which a circulation of tribes prevails? Unfamiliar with Ibn Khaldun's dichotomy of the state and the tribes, as well as with the historical cycles of rise and decay of states, Friedrich Engels believed that Arab history lacked the dynamic of progress inasmuch as it is circular and static. In his view Arab history manifested itself in "a periodically recurring collision" between nomads and city dwellers. The first are the tribes, and the latter are the holders of state power who have transformed themselves from Bedouins into urban residents. "After a hundred years, of course, they are exactly at the point where those apostates stood [and] a new purification of the faith is necessary."[8] In this circulation of tribes that became urban and then were overthrown by other tribes, there is no progress; the world does not move forward. Edward Said may qualify such views as attitudes reflecting the spirit of Orientalism. It should be made clear here that it is not my concern in this article to follow such a line of argument. Rather, I aim to present a historically oriented framework for understanding and explaining the dichotomy of the state (centralized monopoly of power) and tribes (segmentary groups either fully or partly autonomous).

The German philosopher Ernst Bloch warns us in his study on Hegel, "Feeble, insignificant thinking is seldom concise. It is wordy . . . [and] endlessly circles around a subject because it cannot seem to touch, perhaps does not really want to touch, the subject it has condemned itself to express. The more protracted the babble, the thinner the meaning and the more treacherous its condensation."[9] Thus, we have the major hypothesis of this inquiry: any state structure, being a centralized monopoly of power, runs counter to all kinds of segmentary tribal social organization insofar as a distinctiveness and a certain degree of autonomy are basic features of any tribe.

This hypothesis leads to the question about the ways in which the traditional Islamic state coped with the dichotomy of the state and the tribes. It is true that the Qur'an acknowledges the existence of the tribes in stating, "We have formed you into peoples [*shu'ub*] and tribes [*qaba'il*] that you get to know each other" (49:13). However, the notion that the believers constitute a homogeneous community (*umma*) prevails. In going beyond the scriptural approach, Islam can be viewed in sociological terms as an organized religion that historically was a state religion. An examination of the formative period of Islam later in this essay should elucidate whether it provides a model for understanding the conflict between stateness and tribal segmentation and whether this model is relevant to the present.

Having stated the central problem and the importance of examining it over the *longue durée*, we still need to specify the terms to be employed and to elucidate the grounds on which we are operating. To do so we need to elaborate on the concept of tribe and its location in the current social-science debate. Whereas historians and anthropologists mostly refer to prenational groups as tribes, social scientists seem to have replaced the concept of tribe with the concept of *ethnie*.[10] The Middle Eastern context does not support the equation of tribes and ethnies, that is, ethnic communities. Without anticipating this debate, it must suffice in these introductory remarks to note that the ideal type of tribe, in the Weberian sense, is a stateless, segmentary social group characterized by a (myth of) common lineage and bound together by linear loyalties. Historically, no such pure tribe has ever existed; there has always been interaction among tribes on all levels (including intermarriage). Furthermore, tribal autonomy was regularly diminished by the subjection of tribes to state power. When tribes became holders of state power, they changed in many ways. Today Middle Eastern tribes, whether in Syria, Iraq, Sudan, or Libya, constitute a part of the nominally national population. The internal sovereignty of the state is thus a nominal sovereignty. This argument does not imply that Middle Eastern populations are still organized into tribes. In the course of the last two centuries the Middle East has undergone rapid social change as a consequence of its integration into the modern world system. Tribes were not left untouched by these processes. With some exceptions, the social reproduction of tribal life exists hardly anywhere in the contemporary Middle East. This does not imply, however, that Middle Eastern tribes have been integrated into national communities. Despite the effects of rapid, disruptive social change (what some theorists call modernization), there has been little national integration along the lines of the nation-building model. Tribal and other varieties of prenational loyalties and identities still persist. Thus, the dichotomy of tribes and states is not a purely academic issue; nor is it an issue exclusively related to the past. Rather, this dichotomy is addressed in the social-science literature in terms of ethnicity and is viewed as a source of ethnopolitics.[11] This concept needs to be treated cautiously with regard to the Middle East, however. Although it may be valid in the case of Africa to apply the concept of ethnicity to the description of segmentary groups, it may not be in the Middle East because Arabs are not as ethnically divergent (in terms of language, religion, and so forth) as Africans are. Nevertheless, there are tribally related lineages for which we can employ the concept of ethnicity.

The reference to the modern state as a nation-state and to culturally homogeneous social groups as nations compels me to outline the historical scope of this inquiry. It is related to the major characteristics of the modern age for which Theda Skocpol has coined the term *world time*.[12] From the end of the nineteenth century the rapid spread of modern communication and transportation systems contributed to the mapping of the world as one entity. World time is the result of both the globalized international system of nation-states and the transnational structures of world economy. Before the integration of the Middle East into these global structures and worldwide interactive processes that characterize world time, the Middle East was a "Muslim world." Under the prevailing world-historical setup there no longer exists such a thing. The Middle East can no longer be seen as a world of its own, if it ever was one. Rather, the Middle East is a regional subsystem of the international world order.[13] On the one hand, this subsystem has its own regional dynamic, to which the dichotomy of the state and tribes belong. On the other hand, it is greatly affected by its international environment. These regional and global levels of the analysis are inexorably interrelated, and they may, only for heuristic needs, be separated. The subsystem is composed of nation-states. Elsewhere in this volume Albert Hourani defines the state as "an entity that has a recognized authority claiming legitimate and exclusive power." Insofar as this definition focuses on the monopoly of power by a central authority, it seems to apply to all states in history, its modern connotation (the issue of legitimacy) notwithstanding. However, an effort at historicizing this concept of the state in relating it to modern times will impel us to specify the term as a *nation-state and not a state in general.*[14] In addition, we have to add to the definition the elements related to the principles of (internal and external) sovereignty. Both sovereignty and nation-state are definitely modern phenomena that originated in Europe and then were made global. Thus, both are modern accretions in the Middle East. It is obvious that an implementation of the concept of nation-state in a heterogeneous tribal society contributes to a greater intensification of the dichotomy of the state and the tribes than does the imposition of a traditional state. A nation-state requires more than the submission of tribes to a central authority; it also requires national integration, which affects not only the autonomy of a tribe but its uniqueness as well. Nations are based on the concept of citizenship, which presupposes a national loyalty in contrast to tribal loyalties and identities. A tribal segmentary grouping may coexist with a traditional state formation but not with a real national state. We shall see that the formation of nation-states in the Middle East did not contribute to the transformation of prenational and especially tribal loyalties and identities into national ones. Thus, the Middle Eastern nation-state failed to integrate the tribes into a citizenship-centered national structure.

In the modern Middle East the dichotomy between the state and the tribes can no longer be explained by a reference to Ibn Khaldun's theme, which can be interpreted as a circulation of tribes. I am not talking about state formation in general but rather about the transition from nominal sovereignty to a real stateness under the conditions of world time.

In the following section I shall discuss the Arab-Islamic background of the conflict between stateness and tribal segmentation and on that basis pose two questions: How did Islam, as a state religion, cope with this major conflict in its formative period? Does Islam provide a model for the transition from tribe to state that is relevant to the present?

STATE FORMATION AND THE PERSISTENCE OF TRIBES

In pre-Islamic Arabia, as in other regions with similar standards of development, local religions were the expression of local sentiments and attitudes that enforced the unity of local tribal segmentary communities. In terms of cultural anthropology, religion can be viewed as a cultural system that affects the worldview of its believers. In terms of the sociology of religion, belief systems constitute a symbolic code of communication and provide a focus for social organization. As the scope of a religion widens from a local to a universal creed, a change in the worldview of the given community normally occurs. In this sense the shift in Arabia from local religions to a universal Islam was the vehicle for much greater change. As Anthony Smith has suggested, "the rise of monotheistic salvation religions ...tended to override ethnic and political boundaries."[15] The result of this overriding of tribal boundaries was the creation of an Islamic state, which manifested a centralized public authority with control over the means of violence first in the city of Medina and then in Arabia. In fact, this centralization was the basic achievement of early Islam. The Constitution of Medina declared in its first article that the believers constituted a single community (*umma*), and Medina served as a symbol for overriding tribal commitments and boundaries in Arabia. After Muhammad captured Mecca in 630, he defeated a concentration of opposing tribes in Hunayn and thus imposed the new order.

The commitment to the Islamic *umma* ranked above tribal affiliations and smoothed the way for the establishment of the new state structure. The question that arises here is whether an integrated community developed out of this new setup. Was it expected only to override tribal affiliations or also to transform them into new affiliations? W. Montgomery Watt concedes a growing complexity in the changeover from the tribal system to a new state structure based on an organized religion, Islam. He adds, however, that the body politic Muhammad directed "did not make pre-Islamic concepts irrelevant. . . . The result . . . was to create a federation of tribes in alliance with Muhammad. . . . Such an alliance meant that the tribe in question became a part of the Islamic state or body politic."[16] The new order, for which Watt coins the term *pax Islamica*, was based on Muhammad's tribal policy and was designed to come to grips with the "bewildering multiplicity of groups within groups"[17] called tribes. To achieve this, Muhammad combined the virtues of religious preacher, military leader, and statesman.[18] He succeeded in establishing a state among and against the tribes. In Watt's assessment, Muhammad's accomplishment "may be regarded as the building on religious foundations of a political, social, and economic system. . . . His tribal policy was merely an aspect of this."[19] However, the unity brought about by the new state did not overcome the tribal element. Rather, it subordinated it to the new polity; as Watt states, "The quarrels and rivalries of the tribes had not been removed, but they had been subdued."[20] If we accept this interpretation and at the same time draw on the dual function of religion, as unification and division, we must reach the conclusion that the Islamic state from its inception had a fragile structure. It failed to dissolve tribes; instead, it adapted to them the structure of the new state. Viewed from this angle, the Islamic *umma* can be seen as a supertribe that evolved from a tribal federation. It was not a homogeneous community. This federation was susceptible to fragmentation when its underpinnings were weakened. As Smith argues, "Organized religions, particularly after the first enthusiastic phase, have had to come to terms with existing economic and cultural divisions, especially if they have received political expression; and as a result, we find religions often reinforcing, if not igniting, ethnic sentiments with which they have coalesced to form distinctive religio-ethnic communities."[21] With regard to our topic and with specific reference to early Islamic history, we must recall the difference between tribal and ethnic divisions. The divisive forces of the body politic in early Islam were both tribal (intra-Arab rivalries) and ethnic (the conflict between Arabs and *mawali*, or non-Arab converts). The equation of ethnicity and tribalism, which may be valid for other cultural areas, cannot be supported in the historical context of the Arab-Islamic Middle East.

In sum, Watt's interpretation suggests that Islam failed to transmute the tribal structure of Arabia into a homogeneous entity, inasmuch as the pax Islamica did not assimilate the numerous tribes to the standard of a single, homogenous Islamic community. On the contrary, the tribes left their imprint on the new order. Despite the fact that Watt's interpretation reflects the historical record of Islam, it requires refinement.[22]

In the first place, Islam is an organized religion. In the debate among scholars on the origins of state and civilization, there is general agreement that religious change precedes the rise of central state institutions when organized religions are involved. As this institutionalized center is being generated, "it creates a religious overlay above the familistic and local segmental cult levels that is society-wide, encompassing all activities. This religion worships true gods, not just vaguely defined spirits. The public monuments and temples where the ceremonies take place pertain to the society as a whole, and are built by society-wide corvée labor,"[23] as the anthropologist Elman Service stresses. In the second place, Islam is a monotheistic religion. Service's argument applies to organized religions in general. In the case of monotheistic religions a special emphasis is needed. For sociologists of religion, monotheism signifies the proclamation of a comprehensive and unique source of authority. This monotheistic claim must leave its imprint on the political order established within this context. Marshall Hodgson's assessment of the political achievement of Islam is especially supportive of this line of interpretation: "The political structure which Muhammad built was by now clearly a state structure like the states in the nations round about Arabia with an increasingly authoritative government, which could no longer be ignored with impunity. Muhammad sent out envoys who taught the Qur'an and the principles of Islam, collected the *zakat,* and presumably arbitrated disputes so as to keep the peace and prevent feuding."[24]

Hodgson puts the new Islamic state on equal footing with the central states of that historical period. However, this early Islamic model of a state-organized and integrated Islamic community was not a lasting one. Division (not unity) has been the salient feature of Islamic history. In Arabia, as well as in the Arabized and Islamized provinces of the new imperial state, the tribes remained the basic social units despite the existing state order. This remark is not meant to imply that the tribes did not change. The dilemma of Arab-Islamic history was, and still is, that the structural dissolution of the tribes was not consequential to tribal solidarity. Thus, although the economic basis of the social reproduction of tribes had been undermined by change, the sense of tribal identity continued to thrive.

One important group of Arab social scientists concedes the persistence and predominance of tribal organization—for instance, in the Maghreb (the Makhzan state notwithstanding)—while calling attention to the socioeconomic, cultural, and transtribal constraints that have altered the social reproduction of tribes in the Middle East. These scholars argue that Ibn Khaldun's cycles may have applied in some historical periods, but have no application beyond the sixteenth century.[25]

Despite the propositions in Ibn Khaldun's philosophy of history, historical developments cannot be interpreted as if they were subject to historical laws of change. In this sense the general hypothesis that the social establishment of organized, monotheistic religions accompanies the grounding of a strong central state has to be modified with regard to Islamic history. The new sociopolitical and economic order introduced by Islam created structural changes that superseded the pre-Islamic tribal order. It failed, however, to relate these achieved structural changes to the powerful preexisting tribal commitments.

Watt's assessment regarding the dichotomy of the state and the tribes in Arabia and the historical balance of Islam is acceptable provided the refinements suggested above are introduced. Watt fails to distinguish between tribal attitudes, as a variety of self-awareness, and the tribal organization of society. Michael Hudson modifies Watt's interpretation that Islam failed to preserve stability and unity among the tribes by suggesting that "the failure is not obviously attributable to Islam but rather to the fragmented kinship society, poor communication, and quality of leadership of the time."[26] Islam remains an urban culture directed against the tribes. The process of recurrent Islamization in West Africa provides a more recent but similar experiment. Islam spread there from the urban centers and consequently encouraged an urban orientation for the peasants in nineteenth-century West Africa. As the ethnosociologist Gerd Spittler puts it, "The Muslim is expected to have supralocal orientation. . . . A Muslim belongs to a universe which transcends the tribe."[27]

The integration of the Middle East into the modern world economy and into the modern international system of nation-states contributed to a vast mobilization of societies and to crucial interactional and structural changes. Today there exist very few nomadic tribes in the Middle East, yet Middle Eastern societies still display the features of tribal entities, especially tribal loyalty and self-awareness. As Hudson notes, "The tribes are not but a small fraction of Arab society. . . . The tribal way of life has been waning in the Arab world as modern transportation, communications, and the oil economy have taken root. Today perhaps less than five percent of the Arab world's population is actually nomadic. . . . A far larger portion, however, retains a degree of tribal identity."[28]

In response to contemporary societal crises, ideologies of salvation have arisen that mainly preach universal outlooks, such as those associated with Islamic neofundamentalism. They may prove to be less effective if compared with deeply rooted local commitments. Both varieties, the universal and the local, contribute to the current disintegration of the nation-state in the Middle East. We are concerned here with the latter and whether the current revival of local commitments and loyalties can be explained in terms of a revival of tribal attitudes or in terms of ethnicity, the preferred approach of contemporary social science.

SUBSOCIETAL DIVISIONS IN THE MIDDLE EAST: TRIBAL, ETHNIC, OR SECTARIAN?

One major contention of this essay is that most societies in the Middle East lack a homogeneous national population, the basic requirement of the externally imposed nation-state.[29] Despite the structural dissolution of the tribe as a premodern social organization, tribal identity and solidarity are still salient features of Middle Eastern societies. This section focuses on the tribal element and its relationship to current social-science debates on ethnicity.[30] The tribal fragmentation of many Middle Eastern societies has obstructed the establishment of a homogeneous population that undergirds the national community with national symbols and loyalties. Indeed, most of the Middle Eastern states, in varying degrees, accommodate diverse communities characterized by their own local symbols and loyalties. Pan-national ideologies (e.g., Arab nationalism) or local-national ideologies (e.g., Algerian or Syrian nationalism) have been mostly the concern of intellectuals and have failed to strike deep roots in the fragmented communities of many Arab states.[31] The question remains: how do we explain this fragmentation in individual states? Is it tribal, ethnic, or just sectarian?

Social scientists concerned with the Middle East have adopted the concept of ethnicity as an analytical tool for depicting the subsocietal divisions in nation-states without a national (i.e., homogeneous) community. Is the term *ethnie* (see note 10) simply another word for tribe, thus indicating a change in the nomenclature, or does ethnicity introduce a new analytical concept for dealing with our topic? Louis Snyder suggests "the term [ethnicity] has assumed so many diverse meanings that it would be best to reject it."[32] Before reaching such a definitive judgment we would do well to ask why scholars talk of ethnies instead of tribes. European historians usually refer to social groupings in premodern periods of their own history as ethnies but refer to similar entities in non-European history disparagingly as tribes. Thus, tribalism is seen as an Arab or African social phenomenon but not as something European. Social scientists in general, and students of the Middle East in particular, now avoid the term *tribe*, referring instead to prenational social groupings as ethnies, since they want to be free of the Eurocentric connotations of tribe.

Whereas contemporary Arab intellectuals make disparaging reference to *qabaliyya* (tribalism), in contrast to their praise of *qawmiyya* (nationalism), we cannot overlook the fact that those who claim descent from the prophet Muhammad (*ashraf*) are proud of their tribal (Qurayshite) origin. Meanwhile, anthropologists who work on the Middle East are familiar with avowed tribal descent of common local people who cannot claim *ashraf* descent. Furthermore, in the Arab context the adjective *tribal* does not bear the negative connotation that it does in the African context. More important, unlike in Africa, the terms *tribe* and *ethnie*, as employed by Smith, cannot be used synonymously when dealing with the Middle East. Thus, it makes sense to continue to use the term *tribe* as a subdivision of the ethnie, or ethnic community, in the Middle Eastern context. Let us turn to the example of the Alawites of Syria, who are ethnically Arabs and are organized into four different tribes. In terms of their interrelation with the rest of the Syrian community, the Alawites can be viewed as an ethnie. Even though they are Arabs, they distinguish themselves from other Arabs by embracing a myth of common descent and a common belief. A closer look at relationships within the Alawite community compels us, however, to employ the concept of the tribe. On this level we cannot equate tribe with ethnie since the Alawites are subdivided into four tribes: Matawira, Haddadin, Khayyatin, and Kalbiyya. The current ruling elite in Syria is recruited from the Matawira tribe and more specifically from the Numailatiyya clan.[33] It is obvious that we cannot refer to these tribes as separate ethnic communities, nor can we simply view them as an Alawite sect since they are not only split into four tribes but also religiously subdivided into Shamsis, Qamaris, and Murshidin.

At this juncture it is difficult to concur with Milton Esman and Itamar Rabinovich, who employ the concept of ethnicity as a general framework and impose it on the Syrian context without a single reference to tribes. Esman and Rabinovich subscribe to the concept of ethnicity in explaining the existing subdivisions within contemporary Middle Eastern nation-states. They define ethnicity as "collective identity and solidarity based on such ascriptive factors as imputed common descent, language, customs, belief systems and practices (religion), and in some cases race or color."[34] Basically, Esman and Rabinovich, and the contributors to their volume, are interested in what repercussions have followed from the adoption or imposition of the European model of the sovereign nation-state on the Middle East. They correctly hold to the view that the rise of "ethnic" (or tribal) politics in the Middle East is related to "(1) control by the modern state of political and economic resources that are vital to the security and well-being of its inhabitants, and (2) tensions between the pluralism of society and claims of the state to regulate the lives of all who live in its territorial boundaries. . . . The [adopted] European model of sovereign state. . . was the threat to minorities, and in some cases to majorities, that exacerbated tensions among the various ethnic group communities in the Middle East and between those communities and the new states."[35] Hence, these new states are only nominally nation-states based on the concept of nationalism, which suggests the preexistence of a national community that in fact never existed. Reaching beyond Esman and Rabinovich, it might be fruitful to differentiate between ethnies (as subnational divisions in the communities of the modern nation-states of the Middle East) and tribes. Thus, we can refer to the Berbers of Morocco, the Alawites of Syria, the Dinka of Sudan, and the Kurds of Iran, Iraq, Turkey, and Syria as ethnies without overlooking that they are subdivided and organized along tribal lines. This reasoning leads us to infer that the concept of ethnicity cannot be substituted for that of tribe. Ethnicity can be referred to as a supercategory that helps delineate differences in a prenational community. It reveals the ethnic origin of existing nations, on the one hand, and the subsocietal divisions of communities in the process of developing themselves into nations, on the other. Nevertheless, it fails to provide insights into the inner structures of ethnies and to provide tools needed for analyzing them. Thus, the concept of ethnicity continues to be useful, but not as an outmoded definition of tribe.

We can no longer equate tribes with nomads and rural populations. In Syria, for instance, the Alawites are prominently represented in the populations of major towns such as Damascus, Aleppo, and Hama as well as in Latakia. They also constitute major segments of the ruling military and civilian elites in the current Syrian regime whose members, according to Hanna Batatu, are "chosen with extreme care and it seems unlikely that preference in selection would not have been given to men with close *tribal* links to Hafiz al-Asad. Many of them are even said to be from his birth place, the village of Qardaha."[36] In the case of the Alawite tribe of al-Matawira we are dealing with a tribal community whose kinsmen have advanced to the ruling political elite. There are other cases in which tribespeople have ended up in towns, but on the lower end of the socioeconomic scale, without losing their tribal identity. This is true of the southern Sudanese Dinka people, who now live in the slums of Khartoum. In short, tribal affiliations are subethnic societal divisions in the nation-states of the Middle East. Tribal affiliations continue to exist despite the fact that Middle Eastern societies have undergone essential transformations.

A similar problem raised by the equation of tribes and ethnies is the equation of ethnic entities with sectarian groups, as in the case of the Shi'a of Iraq. As in Syria, where the Sunni-Alawite conflicts are not simply sectarian, in Iraq the tensions between the Sunni establishment represented by the kinsmen of Saddam Husayn (the clientele of Takrit) and the underground Shi'a are not solely sectarian either. Batatu has shown that this element among the Shi'a is of a rural origin. He brings to our attention the fact that

> for very long and well into the first decades of this century vast segments of the countryside were the home of semi-tribal groups. . . . At the same time it is necessary to remember that many of the rural Shi'is were of relatively bedouin origin and the bedouin have not been known for the vigor of their religion. . . . One other relevant factor, which needs to be stressed, is that not a few of the tribes, to which the rural Shi'is belong, were relatively recently converted to Shi'ism. For example, the important tribes of Rabi'ah, Zubayd, and Bani Tamim turned to Shi'ism only within the last 180 years or so.[37]

Moreover, it is the tribal element that explains this conversion to Shi'ism and not vice versa.

Earlier I emphasized autonomy, or at least a certain degree of it, as a major trait of a tribe. This helps explain why tribes stand in opposition to the state as a central monopolizer of power and why they resist being subdued by it. As Batatu argues, "Shi'ism's antigovernmental motif, its preoccupation with oppression . . . and its miracle play representing Husayn's passion accorded with the instincts and suffering of tribesmen-turned-peasants and must have eased the tasks of the traveling Shi'a mu'mins," who helped convert the Bedouins to Shi'ism.[38] Thus, to reduce Shi'i hostility directed against the Iraqi state to a sectarian explanation completely ignores the tribe-state dimension of the conflict.

In the final analysis, to understand the complexity of the existing societal subdivisions in Middle Eastern nation-states, we must recognize how intertwined ethnicity and sectarianism are with tribalism. In this sense the tribe, not as a social organization but rather as a referent of identity and group solidarity, is the most important element of what we may call ethnopolitics.[39] It is a central element in the current crisis of the Middle Eastern nation-state, and it has contributed in certain cases (such as Lebanon and Sudan) to the nation-state's disintegration. We must keep in mind that to date there exists no alternative to the nation-state since all units of the international system have to be structured along nation-state lines.

To view any ethnic community as a variety of a nation is as wrong as viewing tribes as ethnies. Ethnic communities have existed throughout history, whereas the emergence of nations is an entirely modern phenomenon that dates from the second half of the eighteenth century. Consequently, the collective cultural units and sentiments related to ethnicity are different from those of the nation. Ethnic bonds did not simply disappear when nations emerged. Anthony Smith does not subscribe to the analyses of the modernists who assert the utter novelty of the nation by insisting that there had been a radical break between premodern units and the modern, collective unit of the nation.[40] Nor does he accept the analyses of the primordialists who, in contrast, question the novelty of the nation and regard it as simply an updated version of older large collective units. Rather, Smith subscribes to the view that there has been a greater measure of continuity between the prenational ethnic ties and the new national ones. It is within this context that he looks to the concept of ethnie as an ethnic community and to its symbolism.[41] Smith's analysis seems helpful to the *problématique* of this essay insofar as it highlights the historical conditions under which ethnies were transformed into nations. It helps us understand why in the Middle East ethnic groupings of tribes like the Alawites, Druzes, Berbers, and Kurds were not transformed into nations encompassing other ethnic-tribal segments as well. In conceding the ethnic origins of nations, Smith points out that "important changes within collective units and sentiments...have occurred within a preexisting framework of collective loyalties and identities, which has conditioned the changes as much as they have influenced the framework." From this conclusion, he infers the need "for a type of analysis that will bring out the differences and similarities between modern national units and sentiments and the collective cultural units and sentiments of previous eras, those that I shall term ethnie." In Smith's view, the core of ethnicity "resides in this quartet of myth, memoirs, values, and symbols and in characteristic forms or styles and genres of certain historical configurations of populations."[42] This concept promises to be more useful than Esman and Rabinovich's for conceptualizing the status of tribes as subethnic entities in the course of state formation. Esman and Rabinovich, among others, indicate common language and ethnic descent as major characteristics of ethnicity without taking into consideration that the tribes of the Alawites, the Druzes, and even the Palestinians (whom they qualify as an ethnie) not only share Arabic as a common language but also claim a common Arab ethnic origin.[43] Even a narrower concept of ethnicity, one confined to drawing distinctions between Arabs and non-Arabs, does not provide a way out of the impasse. Neither approach helps us integrate the inquiry about the tribes and the state into the concept of ethnicity.

At this juncture we may conclude that ethnies are best characterized by the quartet of *myths, memories, values,* and *symbols* in their respective historical configurations. In this sense ethnicity also encompasses Arab tribes whom we have defined as a subethnic unit since an ethnic grouping (for example, the Druzes or Alawites) is composed of many tribes, however interrelated.

There remain the questions of why modern European industrial societies not only required but also attained cultural homogeneity by melding various ethnies into single nations and why Middle Eastern societies have so far failed to do the same. Industrialization and modernization in Europe were comparatively organic; moreover, they were indigenous processes of social change that accommodated the various ethnic origins of the nation. In the Middle East, as in other parts of the Third World, processes of modernization have been rapidly and externally induced and thus have proceeded unevenly. These processes, notes Smith, "necessarily uproot villages and entire regions, eroding traditional structures and cultures and throwing many people out of their environments into the one dominated by anonymity and conflicts of modern urban centres. . . . The urban melting pot fails to assimilate the newcomers into the dominant literate culture through the education system."[44] Those who under such conditions cannot be absorbed rely on their ethnic-tribal kin groups as reference groups; they can survive only through maintaining the network of prenational tribal loyalties and ties. Social conflicts over scarce resources assume an ethnic or, in an even narrower sense, tribal character. The cities of Khartoum and Casablanca provide ample evidence of this process. When subethnic tribes like the Alawite Matawira in Syria are capable of obtaining control of the state, not only do underdogs become topdogs but they also instrumentalize their prenational tribal ties to maintain their control.[45] Ironically, the national ideology of Arabism serves as a legitimizing formula in this tribal setup in Syria. This leads us to inquire into the quality of the modern state in the Middle East and also to ask why the institutional transplant of the nation-state has failed to take root in the Middle East and engender the needed national community. Why does tribal identity persist when the structural framework for the social reproduction of tribal life no longer exists? A closer discussion of the emergence of the nation-state in Europe and its extension to the Middle East, owing to the spread of the European international economy and the globalization of the European system of nation-states, may produce some preliminary answers.

THE INTERNATIONAL SYSTEM OF NATION-STATES AND ITS
MIDDLE EASTERN SUBSYSTEM

This conceptually oriented inquiry into the debate on tribes and the state in the Middle East can be contrasted with two other approaches: the world system approach and the regional studies approach. The world system approach is insensitive to regional conditions, whereas the regional studies approach is narrow and rarely more than descriptive. In the first place, modern states are not necessarily nation-states; moreover, the latter are new to the Middle East and are an imposition on it. In this regard the general and unspecific concept of the world system unpardonably ignores local factors and domestic developments. Its leading proponent, Immanuel Wallerstein, holds that "the states are...created institutions reflecting the needs of class forces operating in world-economy...within the framework of an interstate system....The ideology of this system is sovereign equality, but the states are in fact neither sovereign nor equal states."[46] This combination of economic reductionism and globalism must be deemed useless for an inquiry into the interplay of tribes and states under conditions of world time. As for advocates of the regional studies approach, they have tried to understand the regionally specific elements of the phenomenon under consideration by examining the Middle East as a world of its own, be it an Arab or Muslim world, rather than viewing it as a regional subsystem, that is, as a part of the larger, world-encompassing international system of nation-states (see note 13).

To be sure, there are definitions of nations as cultural, homogeneous communities that divorce the nation from the state. Such definitions compel us to draw a distinction between cultural homogeneity, which some authors allege is based on culturally immutable traits, and the specific variety of societal homogeneity that is intrinsically related to a nation-state. In other words, not every culturally homogeneous group is a nation, and cultural homogeneity is not always national. The nation cannot be defined in static terms such as by language, religion, and the like. To make this point more concrete, let us turn to the Middle East as a case in point.

Despite the existence in the Arab Middle East of "minorities," the bulk of the population in the Arab states is composed of Muslim Arabs. Michael Hudson appropriately warns against premature conclusions resulting from this observation. It is true "that the Arab world is fundamentally homogeneous in terms of widely shared national and religious values." However, "in a political culture noted for effectivity and the persisting salience of . . . primordial identifications, Arabism must coexist or compete with certain other parochial but intensely held corporate identifications. . . . It is too easy to assume that modernization is performing an assimilationist melting pot function in the area."[47] Moreover, Arabism in the sense of pan-Arab unity is a modern issue that is not yet deeply rooted in Middle Eastern societies. "Primordial" or prenational identifications like the tribal ones discussed above still prove to be more effective than the modern national ones in terms of affecting existing patterns of identity and loyalty.

Given that the cultural affinity among Arabs is not the equivalent of the specifically national homogeneity found in the nation-state, nation-states in the Middle East are often referred to by scholars matter-of-factly. James Piscatori, for instance, warns his reader to be "conscious of the debate over the proper terminology" and suggests, as a way to avoid confusion, that he "will use the terms state, territorial state, sovereign state, and nation-state interchangeably."[48] He then proceeds to confuse the state in general with the traditional territorial state, the sovereign absolutist state of the early modern period, and the modern nation-state. He rejects the view "that the nation-state is either impossible in theory, or . . . inherently contradictory to Islamic values" and prefers to posit "that the nation-state is, or can be an Islamic institution."[49] According to Piscatori, not only the terms of historically different patterns of the state can be used interchangeably but also "sovereignty" can be equated with "territoriality" and "exclusivity."[50] Piscatori's analysis runs against my contention that the nation-state is a modern political structure much different from earlier state formations and that it was first established in Europe and then imposed on the rest of the world. Anthony Giddens, by contrast, asserts that

> a nation-state . . . only exists when a state has a unified administrative reach over the territory over which its sovereignty is claimed. . . . A nation-state is . . . a bordered power-container. . . . All traditional states have laid claim to the formalized monopoly over means of vio-

lence within their territories. But [it is] only within the nation-states that this claim characteristically becomes more or less success-ful. . . . The nation-state which exists in a complex of other nation-states is a set of institutional forms of governance maintaining an administrative monopoly over a territory with demarcated boundaries (borders), its rule being sanctioned by law and direct control of means of internal and external violence.[51]

One of the basic requirements of this new institution is a nationally homogeneous population.

The historical precursor of the nation-state is the sovereign state that was formed in the aftermath of the Peace of Westphalia (1648). By contrast, a concept of political sovereignty never developed in Islam. This is understandable since in the Islamic faith human beings have no sovereignty; the only sovereign is God. Jean Bodin was the first to elaborate such a concept before it found its historical expression in the European system of states formed after the peace.[52] Following the French Revolution, sovereignty became national sovereignty, and the hitherto-prevailing sovereign states developed into nation-states.

The European sovereign state after Westphalia was not only the precursor of the modern nation-state but also the nucleus of the first international system of states in world history.[53] Charles Tilly tells us that "[over] the next three hundred years the Europeans and their descendants managed to impose that system on the entire world. The recent wave of decolonization has almost completed the mapping of the globe into that system."[54] Thus we have my contention that nation-states in the Middle East are externally imposed. There can be no adequate historical analysis of the dissolution of the Ottoman Empire and, via a period of colonial rule, the formation of nation-states without taking into account this historical process. It is for this reason that, unlike Piscatori, we must draw clear distinctions between different patterns of state formation, in particular between the traditional territorial state and the modern sovereign state as well as the ensuing nation-state. Historically, these patterns cannot be equated, nor can they be used interchangeably.[55] Sovereignty is not exclusivity, nor does it simply refer to territoriality.

Giddens's historical reconstruction of what sovereignty has meant for the establishment of a nation-state underscores the importance of defining the meaning of a homogeneous population in other than culturally static terms. As he points out:

The development of state sovereignty expresses and further stimulates a new form of administrative order, signaled by the formation of the absolutist state, but maximized in the nation-state. A state can only be sovereign . . . if large segments of the population of that state have mastered an array of concepts connected with sovereignty. . . . The development of notions of citizenship . . . are intimately bound up with this. In many cases the mass of the population of traditional states did not know of themselves to be citizens of those states, nor did it matter particularly to the continuity of power with them. . . . The expansion of state sovereignty means that those subject to it are in some sense aware of their membership in a political community.[56]

In the nominally sovereign nation-states of the Middle East this basic infrastructure is still lacking. To understand state sovereignty contextually, it is important to recognize that more is required than a change in the political culture of the polity. Structural change is equally important, and it is related to what Giddens calls the "nature and scope of discursive articulation of information available in the public domain."[57] The development of printing and the extension of literacy belong in this process. The new forms of group symbolism, of which the national ones are the most potent, are structurally reinforced by the exigencies of industrial society, which "demand the diffusion of common modes of thought and belief throughout the whole population. Nationalism is precisely the attachment of such modes of thought and belief to the state, which provides the means of their coordination."[58] In contrast to modern European nationalisms, Arab nationalism posited a utopia but not the requisite structural and societal needs to support that utopia. We can conclude that sovereignty and nation are not simply concepts but also are related to a corresponding structural reality.

The nation-states in the Middle East, as elsewhere in the Third World, did not develop out of similar or comparable processes of social change, as they did in Europe. The simultaneity of old tribes and externally imposed nation-states can only be understood within this historical context.

CONCLUSION

This inquiry into the parallelism of modern nation-states and old tribes as an expression of the simultaneity of the unsimultaneous is intended to be a contribution to understanding state-society relations in the Middle East under the conditions of world time. The questions we have been grappling with are familiar to scholars studying the state elsewhere in the Third World: how to explain the weak character of the state, and why the modern Middle Eastern state, as Joel Migdal says, has "such difficulties in becoming *the* organization in society that effectively establishes [society's] rules and behavior."[59] Migdal has coined the term *strong societies / weak states*. For the purposes of our inquiry, we can restate this duality as *segmentary fragmented societies / artificial imposed states*. At this conjuncture we know why Middle Eastern societies are fragmented. With the exception of the few relatively homogeneous societies such as Egypt and Tunisia, most Middle Eastern societies are still characterized by the persistence of tribal, ethnic, and sectarian ties as sources of identity and loyalty. But why are Middle Eastern states weak? Can this weakness be formulated in general terms or with reference to the model of nation-states?

Unlike the imperial and the territorial-dynastic states that were familiar in Middle Eastern history, the externally imposed new pattern of nation-state is defined as a national, not as a communal, polity. Its underlying concept is sovereignty, which not only presupposes the capability of the central power to establish itself over the entire territory but also requires established citizenship and a corresponding national identity and loyalty. In varying degrees all states of the Middle East lack this infrastructure. With the exception of the Arab lands that were not subjected to Ottoman or colonial rule, all Arab states have to cope with the dual legacy of the Ottoman Empire and colonialism, which has exacerbated the process of underpinning the new state formation.

The Ottoman legacy lies in the existence of prenational identities and loyalties, which have survived the appearance of the modern nation-state. In the Ottoman Empire the major distinction was between Muslims and non-Muslims. Non-Muslims were divided along religious and ethnic lines into separate millets. Kemal Karpat writes that "the establishment of religion as the chief identifying characteristic of both Muslims and non-Muslims . . . did not destroy the ethnic sense but in fact strengthened it."[60] The Ottoman Empire, as an imperial state, did not deny local communities their particular ties and did not have sovereignty in the sense outlined in the preceding pages. Only under external pressures did the Ottomans start to change their imperial structure. They failed to achieve this end, however, and finally vanished. Karpat adds, "While the Ottoman government took its legitimacy from Islam and enforced, to the extent possible, Islamic legislation, it did not identify itself politically and ideologically with the Muslim community until the nineteenth century." Thus, "the Muslim community encompassed a great number of ethnic and linguistic groups. . . . The early Ottoman state recognized these ethnic divisions."[61] To specify this statement, we have to draw on the debate pursued in the third section of this essay about whether some ethnic groups, like the Druzes and the Alawites of Syria, were organized and subdivided into tribes.

The second legacy, that of European colonialism, generated two opposing sociopolitical movements. On the one hand, the colonial rulers instrumentalized existing tribal-ethnic and religious divisions in society through a policy of *divide et impera*. French colonialists played the minorities—in Morocco the Berber tribes and in Syria the Alawite and Druze tribes—against the majority to help establish their rule. On the other hand, their colonial methods unwittingly gave rise to anticolonial nationalist movements. Thus, historically, colonial rule simultaneously mobilized two kinds of forces: a unifying nationalism and divisive tribalism. The appropriate and legitimate framework for decolonization was nationalism, which emanated from the "imported" idea of the nation-state. The old dichotomy of the city and the countryside, as expressed in the conflict between city dwellers and tribes, received under these colonial conditions a new cover. In Syria under the French mandate, for example, the problem can be stated in terms of nationalism and separatism. The center of nationalism was the town and of separatism the tribal countryside. For Syria, Philip Khoury describes the "birth of the nationalist movement within a relatively unified and integrated political culture" that was maintained by a "cohesive Sunni upper class in four towns."[62] By contrast, Alawite and Druze political cultures were "divided along tribal or clan lines," which enabled the French to promote their "separatism." It is for this reason that the "French promoted certain Alawite leaders" to counterbalance the national urban center.[63] The Syrian nationalist leadership of that center "embodied and articulated its beliefs and enforced its code of moral behavior";[64] but though it succeeded in obtaining national independence, it failed to translate those beliefs and urban code into a strong sovereign state. In postcolonial Syria the Alawite tribes managed to seize state power by establishing their rule on a weak state structure. To be sure, *weak state* is not contrasted with *strong state* in terms of coercion. Institutionally, a state can only become strong when it can furnish its sovereignty with an accepted pattern of shared citizenship, thus becoming the organization that establishes rules and behavior. A coercive Alawite state structured along the lines of patron-client relations is not a strong state, the sustained political stability of the regime notwithstanding.

In most of the states of the Arab Middle East sovereignty is fairly nominal. The tribal-ethnic and sectarian conflicts that the colonial powers exacerbated did not end with the attainment of independence. The newly established nation-states have failed to cope with the social and economic problems created by rapid development because they cannot provide the proper institutions to alleviate these problems. Because the nominal nation-state has not met the challenge, society has resorted to its prenational ties as a solution, thereby preserving the framework of the patron-client relationships (see note 45). The patron may have state power at its disposal, as in the case of the Alawites in Syria, or its power may be within the society, as in the case of the Berbers of Casablanca or the Dinkas of Khartoum.

In the Middle East, as in much of the Third World, postcolonial conflicts cannot accurately be addressed as a struggle for political power. They are essentially struggles for resources. The "ethnicization of conflict" suggests that tribalism has been revived under a new cover and that it obstructs the process of state formation in the contemporary Middle East.

NOTES

1. It should be made clear at the outset that I do not subscribe to Immanuel Wallerstein's concept of the world system. Moreover, I consider Wallerstein's concept to be economistic as well as reductionist and thus a crude simplification of the complexity of the global structure I allude to here as a world system (see note 46 below).

2. It is confusing that in Arabic both the Islamic concept of a universal community (*al-umma al-islamiyya*) and the secular idea of nation (Arab nation, *umma 'arabiyya*) are conveyed by the same term, *umma*. For more details see Bassam Tibi, "Islam and Arab Nationalism," in Barbara Stowasser, ed., *The Islamic Impulse* (London, 1987), pp. 59–74.

3. See the illuminating article by Philip S. Khoury, "Islamic Revival and the Crisis of the Secular State in the Arab World," in I. Ibrahim, ed., *Arab Resources: The Transformation of Society* (London, 1983), pp. 213–236.

4. Yusuf al-Qurdawi, *Al-Hulul al-mustawrada wa kayf janat 'ala ummatina*, vol. 1 of *Hatmiyyat al-Hall al-Islami*, 2 vols. (Beirut, 1980).

5. For more details see Bassam Tibi, *Arab Nationalism: A Critical Inquiry* (New York, 1981), part 1.

6. Ghassan Salamé quotes the Muthana Press edition of *Al-Muqaddimah* (Baghdad, n.d.), p. 164, in his remarkable volume, *Al-Mujtama' wa al-Dawla fi al-Mashriq al-'Arabi* (Beirut, 1987), p. 11.

7. Salamé, *Al-Muqaddimah*, pp. 23–24.

8. Friedrich Engels, in Karl Marx and Friedrich Engels, *Über Religion* (East Berlin, 1958), p. 256.

9. Ernst Bloch, *Subjekt Objekt: Erlaeuterungen zu Hegel*, 2d ed. (Frankfurt-am-Main, 1972), p. 32.

10. Anthony D. Smith introduces the term *ethnie* into the English language, meaning ethnic community in contrast to nation. See Smith's path-

finding analysis in his book *The Ethnic Origins of Nations* (Oxford, 1986), esp. pp. 13–16. In an important recent work on ethnicity edited by John Rex and David Mason, *Theories of Race and Ethnic Relations* (Cambridge, 1988), we find phrases like "ethnic or tribal sentiments" (p. 158) and "tribal" or "ethnic conflicts" (p. 159). These phrases suggest an equation of ethnic with tribal that I contest in this essay.

11. With regard to the Middle East, see Milton J. Esman and Itamar Rabinovich, eds., *Ethnicity, Pluralism, and the State in the Middle East* (Ithaca, 1988), in particular the introduction by the editors and the contribution of Gabriel Ben-Dor, "Ethnopolitics and the Middle Eastern State," pp. 71–92.

12. Theda Skocpol, *States and Social Revolutions* (Cambridge, 1987), p. 23.

13. For more details about this concept with regard to the Middle East, see Bassam Tibi, *Konfliktregion Naher Osten. Regionale Eigendynamik und Grossmachtinteressen* (Munich, 1989), part 1. See also Bassam Tibi, "Structural and Ideological Change in the Arab Subsystem since the Six Day War," in Y. Lukacs and A. Battah, eds., *The Arab-Israeli Conflict* (Boulder, Colo., 1988).

14. The standard book on this subject is Anthony Giddens, *The Nation-State and Violence* (Berkeley and Los Angeles, 1987).

15. Smith, *Ethnic Origins of Nations*, p. 35.

16. W. Montgomery Watt, *Islamic Political Thought* (Edinburgh, 1968), p. 13.

17. W. Montgomery Watt, *Muhammad at Medina* (Oxford, 1977), p. 78.

18. For more details about this combination, see Maxime Rodinson, *Mohammed*, trans. Anne Carter (New York, 1971).

19. Watt, *Muhammad at Medina*, p. 144.

20. Watt, *Muhammad at Medina*, p. 149.

21. Smith, *Ethnic Origins of Nations*, p. 35.

22. Bassam Tibi, *The Crisis of Modern Islam: A Pre-Industrial Culture in the Scientific-Technological Age*, trans. Judith von Sivers (Salt Lake City, 1988), chap. 4.

23. Elman R. Service, *Origins of the State and Civilization* (New York, 1975), p. 297.

24. Marshall G. S. Hodgson, *The Venture of Islam*, vol. 1, *The Classical Age of Islam* (Chicago, 1974), p. 193.

25. Ghassan Salamé, Elbaki Hermassi, and Khaldun al-Naqib, *Al-Mujtama' wa al-Dawla fi al-Watan al-'Arabi*, ed. S. E. Ibrahim (Beirut, 1988), esp. pp. 103–118.

26. Michael C. Hudson, *Arab Politics: The Search for Legitimacy* (New Haven, 1977), p. 99.

27. Gert Spittler, *Herrschaft über Bauern: Die Ausbreitung staatlicher Herrschaft und einer islamisch-urbanen Kultur in Gabir/Niger* (Frankfurt-am-Main, 1978), p. 103.

28. Hudson, *Arab Politics*, pp. 88–89.

29. On this topic, and also with reference to the Middle East, see Hugh Seton-Watson, *Nations and States: An Enquiry into the Origins of Nations*

and the Politics of Nationalism (London, 1977), esp. pp. 239–271; and John Breuilly, *Nationalism and the State* (Manchester, 1982).

30. In addition to Smith, *Ethnic Origins of Nations*, see Joane Nagel, "The Ethnic Revolution: The Emergence of Ethnic Nationalism in Modern States," *Sociology and Social Research* 68, no. 4 (1983–1984): 417–434.

31. See Tibi, *Arab Nationalism*.

32. Louis Snyder, "Nationalism and the Flawed Concept of Ethnicity," *Canadian Review of Studies in Nationalism* 10, no. 2 (1983): 263.

33. Hanna Batatu, "Some Observations on the Social Roots of Syria's Ruling, Military Group and the Causes of Its Dominance," *Middle East Journal* 35, no. 3 (1981): 331–332. See also Patrick Seale, *Asad: The Struggle of the Middle East* (Berkeley, 1989), pp. 8–11.

34. See Esman and Rabinovich, eds., *Ethnicity*, p. 3. Rabinovich (pp. 155–172) refers to the Alawites of Syria and points out that the "community's modernization and politicization during the past two decades" has been the structural background of the Alawite's "spectacular rise from the fringes of Syrian public life to a position of power and dominance." For Rabinovich, the explanation of this phenomenon "remains a mystery" (p. 162). The concept of ethnicity does not lead us out of this impasse.

35. Esman and Rabinovich, *Ethnicity*, pp. 3–4.

36. Batatu, "Some Observations," p. 332; see also Seale, *Asad*.

37. Hanna Batatu, "Iraq's Underground Shi'a Movements: Characteristics, Causes and Prospects," *Middle East Journal* 35, no. 4 (1981): 583–584.

38. Batatu, "Iraq's Underground Shi'a Movements," p. 585.

39. Gabriel Ben-Dor, "Ethnopolitics and the Middle Eastern State," pp. 71–92.

40. Smith, *Ethnic Origins of Nations*, pp. 7–13.

41. Smith, *Ethnic Origins of Nations*, pp. 13–16.

42. Smith, *Ethnic Origins of Nations*, pp. 13, 15.

43. See Esman and Rabinovich, *Ethnicity*, pp. 3–24.

44. Smith, *Ethnic Origins of Nations*, p. 10.

45. To this phenomenon Ghassan Salamé's formula *tamaddun al-sukkan wa tarayuf al-sulta* (the urbanization of the population and the ruralization of political power) applies. See Salamé, *Al-Mujtama'*, pp. 215–218. Sociologically, the links between holders of state power, as a center of resource allocation, and their prenational tribal community can be characterized as a patron-client relationship. For an effort at grappling with this complicated issue, see John Waterbury, "An Effort to Put Patrons and Clients in Their Place," in Ernest Gellner and John Waterbury, eds., *Patrons and Clients* (London, 1977), pp. 329–342.

46. Immanuel Wallerstein, *The Politics of the World Economy: The States, the Movements and the Civilizations* (Cambridge, 1984), p. 33.

47. Hudson, *Arab Politics*, pp. 56–57.

48. James P. Piscatori, *Islam in a World of Nation-States* (Cambridge, 1986), p. 168 n. 8.

49. Piscatori, *Islam*, pp. 149, 150.

50. Piscatori, *Islam*, p. 74.

51. Giddens, *Nation-State and Violence*, pp. 119–121.

52. For an analytical survey of the history and development of the concept of sovereignty, with a comparative view to non-Western cultures (including Islam), see F. H. Hinsley, *Sovereignty*, 2d ed. (Cambridge, 1986). See also Hinsley, *Nationalism and the International System* (London, 1973).

53. A closer elaboration of the argument that ancient state systems were not international systems, in this sense, can be found in the first part of the ground-breaking book by the late Hedley Bull, *The Anarchical Society: A Study of Order in World Politics* (New York, 1977). See also the valuable contributions in Hedley Bull and Adam Watson, eds., *Expansion of International Society* (Oxford, 1988).

54. Charles Tilly, ed., *The Formation of National States in Western Europe* (Princeton, 1975), p. 45.

55. In his review of Piscatori's book in *MESA Bulletin* 21, no. 2 (1987): 245–247, John Voll points out that Piscatori "seems to assume that 'state' in the medieval context was basically similar to what is meant by 'state' in the modern world."

56. Giddens, *Nation-State and Violence*, p. 210.

57. Giddens, *Nation-State and Violence*, p. 211.

58. Giddens, *Nation-State and Violence*, p. 214.

59. Joel S. Migdal, *Strong Societies and Weak States* (Princeton, 1988), p. xx.

60. Kemal Karpat, "The Ottoman Ethnic and Confessional Legacy in the Middle East," in Esman and Rabinovich, eds., *Ethnicity*, p. 43.

61. Karpat, "Ottoman Ethnic and Confessional Legacy," pp. 44, 45.

62. Philip S. Khoury, *Syria and the French Mandate: The Politics of Arab Nationalism, 1920–1945* (Princeton, 1987), p. 13.

63. Khoury, *Syria and the French Mandate*, p. 515.

64. Khoury, *Syria and the French Mandate*, p. 521.

Tribe and State Relations: The Inner Asian Perspective

Thomas J. Barfield

The relationship between tribes and states in the Middle East is still a focus of debate for anthropologists, historians, and political scientists because tribal peoples have never disappeared from the region's political scene. Beginning with the early Islamic conquest itself, any list of the important empires and dynasties appears to be a roll call of tribes turned imperial conquerors: Saljuqs, Ghaznavids, *mamluk*s (at one remove), Mongols, Timurids, Ottomans, Mughals, Qizilbash, and Qajars, to name just some of the more prominent. Of equal importance were the larger number of tribal groups that maintained continual social and political cohesion in opposition to state rule, such as the Berbers of Morocco, the Bedouin tribes of Arabia and the Libyan desert, the Kurds of the Zagros Mountains, the Pashtuns of Afghanistan, or the tribal confederacies of Iran (Bakhtiyari, Shahsevan, Qashqa'i, etc.). Middle Eastern governments have never ignored the tribal peoples within their borders, for they were peoples with an influence out of proportion to their numbers, to be suppressed or placated as policy dictated.

Although scholars of the Middle East have taken this situation for granted, elsewhere it was unusual for states and tribes to coexist within a common territory over the long term or for tribal peoples to be the founders of so many ruling dynasties. Only in the Middle East did tribal peoples remain a permanent presence, both on the frontiers of the region and within the boundaries of every state. In other areas of sedentary civilization tribalism was long on the wane, limited to marginal areas of little significance. In western Europe the powerful German, Celtic, and Gothic tribes that overran the Mediterranean world following the collapse of Rome in the fifth century lost their political organization and identity soon thereafter. By 1000 all of Europe, even beyond the old Roman frontiers, had witnessed the disappearance of tribal organization, except in the far reaches of Scotland and Ireland or on the marches of the south Russian steppe.[1] Similarly, even under the most powerful of foreign dynasties the Mongolian and Manchurian tribes of northeastern Asia were unable to retain their cohesiveness once they moved south of the Great Wall into China.[2] By contrast, from 1000 to 1500 Iran and Anatolia experienced a series of invasions by Turco-Mongolian peoples that resulted in the establishment of powerful empires led by elites with tribal origins, and tribal groups remained intact within these states. Elsewhere in the region indigenous tribal groups in mountain and desert areas maintained a distinct identity in opposition to neighboring states.

As early as the fourteenth century the North African social historian Ibn Khaldun analyzed the cycles of relationships between tribal peoples and sedentary states of the Middle East.[3] Weak dynasties in sedentary states, he argued, were vulnerable to attack and replacement by tribes possessing superior military ability and 'asabiyya, or group solidarity. 'Asabiyya was the product of close kinship ties or patron-client relationships that developed most strongly among tribal peoples. In times of warfare such bonds better ensured mutual aid and cooperation than did the weaker political or economic interests motivating the mercenary armies employed by states. Nevertheless, those dynasties of tribal origin that succeeded in establishing themselves in sedentary areas invariably lost their 'asabiyya as they became more acculturated to urban civilization; such dynasties had a normal lifespan of only three or four generations. In addition, although tribal peoples were a periodic military threat to their neighbors, they were generally at an economic disadvantage in dealing with states because of their dependence on urban areas as markets for trading surplus animals, buying grain, and obtaining agricultural tools, weapons, or other handicrafts, without which they could not survive. Ibn Khaldun describes this situation with regard to the Bedouins: "While [the Bedouins] need the cities for their necessities of life, the urban population needs [the Bedouins] for conveniences and luxuries. . . . They must be active on the behalf of their interests and obey them whenever [the cities] ask and demand obedience from them."[4]

The modern ethnographic literature on tribal peoples in the Middle East resonates with many of these same themes, so much so that many models of tribal organization and leadership follow, implicitly or explicitly, Ibn Khaldun's formulations.[5] However, he drew most of his examples from the tribes of North Africa and Arabia, which were politically egalitarian and unable to organize large groups of people without resorting to nontribal leadership. Although such tribes were tenacious in maintaining their autonomy against outsiders, they rarely formed great empires. By contrast, the tribes that arrived in the Middle East from Inner Asia often played a major role in empire formation. In social structure and political organization they were quite unlike the tribes familiar to Ibn Khaldun, for the new arrivals brought a tradition of hierarchical leadership capable of incorporating many different tribal groups into large and powerful confederations. Motivated by more than localized 'asabiyya, they established most of the region's great empires, and their dynasties long outlived the four-generation cycle of political decline and replacement Ibn Khaldun had observed in dynasties of North African and Arabian origin. Therefore, to understand the relations between tribes and states, we must first ask two related questions: what type of tribe, dealing with what type of state?

DEFINITIONS

States in the Middle East fell into two major categories with very different dynamics: large empires and small regional states. Empires were centralized states that encompassed a wide variety of peoples and places whose resources could be mobilized against tribal peoples within the state and on its borders. Their political structures were remarkably stable, with long-lived dynasties and large standing armies. Regional states, by contrast, were organized around a far more limited set of resources that could support only relatively weak military forces incapable of controlling even their own hinterland with any permanent degree of success. Their political structures were inherently unstable and subject to regular collapse. In late pre-Islamic times the area we now refer to as the Middle East was divided between the Roman Empire in the west and the Parthian-Sasanian Empire in the east. For a short time in the early Islamic period much of the region was united under Arab rule, but that empire quickly devolved into many independent regional states. From that time forward the imperial states were centered almost exclusively on the Iranian and Anatolian plateaus under dynasties of Turco-Mongolian origin, reaching their most stable form under the Ottoman (in Anatolia) and Safavid (in Iran) dynasties. North Africa, Egypt, and Arabia were never united again after the Islamic conquest except for a short time as peripheral parts of the Ottoman Empire.

In contrast to states, tribal political structures employed, in theory, a model of kinship to build groups that acted in concert to organize economic production, preserve internal political order, and defend the group against outsiders. Relationships among people and groups in such systems were mapped through social space rather than geographic territory. Political units and the territories they occupied existed primarily as products of social relations: rights to use land and exclude outsiders were based on tribal affiliation. Nontribal groups were generally organized in a converse fashion, with social groups defining themselves in terms of a common residence, system of cultural beliefs, or political affiliation. Although tribal organization in the Middle East was generally associated with nomadic pastoralists, sedentary tribes located in marginal mountain and desert regions, such as the Berbers, Kurds, and Pashtuns, probably constituted an equally large population.

The concept of tribe itself, however, is by no means easy to define precisely once we move away from generalities to specific cases, as other essays in this volume amply demonstrate. Of particular importance is the need to distinguish between a tribe, which is the largest unit of incorporation based on a genealogical model, and a tribal chieftaincy or confederation, which combines tribes to create a supratribal political entity. Because tribal systems are segmentary, with successively larger units of incorporation, it is often assumed that each level is simply the product of the same principles applied to an ever-expanding population. That is not the case.

Often what are perceived of as "actual" kinship relations (based on principles of descent and on affiliations by marriage or adoption) are empirically evident only within the smaller units of the tribe: nuclear families, extended households, and local lineages. At higher levels of incorporation clans and tribes often maintain relationships of a more political origin: client or slave descent groups that have no proper genealogical connections but are nevertheless an accepted part of the tribe; alliances or rivalries between descent groups that appear to violate their genealogical charters; cooperation among networks of people that crosscut kinship relations; or the blatant rewriting (or re-reciting) of genealogies. But it is at the confederacy level where these anomalies are most stark. Confederations need not be composed of genealogically related tribes because here the segmentary principle is applied in a reverse hierarchical order; the imposition of a new political order is the product of reorganization enforced by division from the top rather than alliance from the bottom.

The question of whether tribes were ever truly genealogical has led to a particularly sharp debate among historians about how best to interpret their development.[6] From an anthropological point of view there is less to this problem than meets the eye. The closer we get to the bottom ranks of any tribal system, the more the system relies on actual descent and affinal ties; the higher we go in the same structure, the more political its relationships become. The focus of debate, therefore, needs to be shifted to the larger question of why some tribal organizations appeared to be capable of much more expansion than others.

In an important article comparing the tribal cultures of the Middle East and Inner Asia, Charles Lindholm has pointed out the marked structural differences between the hierarchical Turco-Mongolian cultural tradition of Inner Asia and the egalitarian cultural tradition of tribes indigenous to the Middle East.[7] Although he focuses largely on the nature of kinship organization and its relationship to ideologies of political belief, his analysis has important implications for understanding tribe-state relations. Indeed, it may be possible to extend his analysis further to show that in the Middle East both tribes and states fall into distinct hierarchical Turco-Mongolian and egalitarian Arabian types, each with very different policies and historical development.

If we look closely at the course of medieval and modern Middle Eastern history, we find that the Turco-Mongolian and Arabian patterns of interaction developed in two largely discrete areas with different tribal cultural traditions and state organizations: (1) the deserts of North Africa and greater Arabia and the mountain zones throughout the whole region, generally divided into small regional states, which were inhabited both by Bedouin nomads and sedentary tribes such as the Berbers, Kurds, and Pashtuns with egalitarian lineage structures long indigenous to the region; (2) the Iranian and Anatolian plateau zones, generally under the control of great empires, which were inhabited by tribes organized into large confederations of Turco-Mongolian descent.

Among tribes in the Middle East, success in maintaining large-scale political organizations was restricted by narrow cultural limitations on political legitimacy. Where tribes were composed of egalitarian lineages whose leaders ruled by means of consensus or mediation and could unite rival groups only through use of segmentary opposition, the maintenance of a broad confederation for longer than a single lifetime was extremely difficult. For example, tribes such as the Bedouins, who defined themselves through localized lineages and drew the upper boundaries of the tribe quite tightly, resisted cooperation at the supratribal level.[8] By contrast, in Turco-Mongolian tribal systems, where a hierarchical kinship organization was accepted as culturally legitimate, local lineages, clans, and tribes became the building blocks of political-military coalitions created by hereditary leaders whose authority was rarely challenged from below. Large tribal confederacies, such as those in Iran, could not have incorporated hundreds of thousands of people without employing such a "top-down" definition that made no excuses for the variety of tribes it brought together.[9]

Within large empires tribal peoples faced the possibility of losing their autonomy, and even their identity, if directly administered by officials of sedentary governments. Rebellious tribes that could not be controlled in their own territory were often deported to alien frontiers. Even at their margins empires could mobilize resources against frontier tribes, and the tribal conquests in border areas were likely to last only as long as it took the empire to raise an expeditionary force. But since such control of marginal places and peoples could be had only at great financial cost, an equally popular imperial strategy was to co-opt the tribal leaders and employ them as tools for indirect rule through the use of official appointments and subsidies. (Just who was manipulating whom in such relationships is often difficult to tell.) Compared with state policies in Europe or China, such compromises allowed a higher degree of cultural and political autonomy within Middle Eastern empires. Because the virtues of 'asabiyya were more effectively displayed as a means of defense rather than aggression, the autonomy granted to egalitarian tribes rarely threatened imperial stability except during periods of anarchy resulting from decay at the center.

Tribes were on more even terms when dealing with regional states. Such small states generally controlled only limited territories and were surrounded by rival states with similar problems. Lacking the manpower and financial resources to control effectively the territories on their margins, they were always vulnerable to attacks both by neighboring tribes and by other states. Indeed, as Ibn Khaldun wrote, tribal leaders were the main source of new ruling dynasties for such regional states, although he argued that such dynasties rarely lasted more than three or four generations before falling victim themselves to new tribal conquest.[10] Tribes also posed an indirect threat to the stability of small regional states when they raided one state and then avoided retaliation by escaping across a neighboring frontier. It was the vulnerability of small states to disruption and conquest that gave Ibn Khaldun's model its explanatory power, but it is a model that best describes only the relationship between egalitarian tribes and small regional states.

The creation of large tribal confederations and the establishment of great dynasties of tribal origin were the products of Turco-

Mongolian peoples who moved from Inner Asia into the neighboring Iranian and Anatolian plateaus. These Turco-Mongolian confederacies had hierarchical political structures that often incorporated hundreds of thousands of people under the authority of powerful khans. Some of these khans conquered large empires and created long-lived states. Characteristically, the founders of such empires had little experience with the administration of sedentary governments, but they were highly receptive to the hierarchical models of a centralized administration proposed by their local advisers because the models provided a means to control their tribal followers as well as extract revenue from their conquered subjects. Although the imperial traditions of Iran and Byzantium may have been foreign to the nomads of Inner Asia, the acceptance of hierarchical authority and hereditary right to leadership was already deeply embedded in their culture and was reflected in the organization of tribal confederacies.

However successful this style of organization was for the Turco-Mongolian peoples, it was culturally alien to the peoples outside the northern plateau areas. In the rest of the Middle East there was a very different pattern of tribal organization, which consisted of relatively egalitarian segmentary lineages with weak chiefs who acted more as mediators than autocratic leaders. These tribal groups were relatively small, with the maximal effective units numbering in the tens of thousands of people. Even this maximal group was largely theoretical and was rarely united for any length of time. Its potential for expansion was poor because tribes within the system refused to accept the authority of leaders outside their own tribes. Most successful large-scale organizations, therefore, depended on using nontribal models of political organization, most often created by religious figures. Leaders of these movements had a keen understanding of their urban neighbors because of their close economic ties with them.

States dealing with tribes organized along the egalitarian Arabian lines had quite a different experience from that of those that encountered the Turco-Mongolian peoples. The Iranian and Anatolian plateaus, which were the zones of interaction with Inner Asian peoples, produced the most powerful tribes and empires. North Africa and Arabia, which were the locus of the egalitarian Arabian pattern, historically produced weak tribes that confronted either small regional states or marginal parts of empires. This geographic division, and the persistence of the Arabian model throughout most of the Middle East, was probably due to the high cost of maintaining large tribal confederacies. The Turco-Mongolian confederacy was a voracious consumer of resources and could not survive where these were lacking. Leaders of subordinate tribes within these confederacies expected large subsidies of luxury goods, which they then redistributed to their own followers. Only through military expansion or by acting as a mediator between the tribes and the large states could such a confederacy provide its followers with the necessary benefits. The better-watered plateau areas of Anatolia and Iran best met these conditions. By contrast, the Arabian tribal model could survive on the limited local resources found on the margins of the deserts or in the highland mountain zones. Tribal leaders there provided their kinsmen and clients only with relatively small gifts, and even their highly vaunted hospitality consisted mainly of feasting a few hundred people on special occasions. Cheaper to run because it demanded little from its leadership, the Arabian model was also more parochial in its interests. This characteristic was a liability in terms of expansion but a strength in resisting outsiders.

THE EGALITARIAN (ARABIAN) TRIBAL MODEL

The survival of tribal peoples in the Middle East was a product of both the ecology and the economy of the region. The centers of sedentary civilization were located in the major river valleys and oases, where irrigated agriculture flourished. They were bordered by desert and mountain areas occupied by subsistence farmers and nomads, areas that remained centers of opposition to state rule. This opposition between center and periphery (*bled el-makhzen* and *bled es-siba* in North Africa or *hokumat* and *yaghistan* in Afghanistan) was reflected throughout the region. Even so, these highly marked divisions were geographically scattered and never produced a linear polar frontier such as the Great Wall, which divided China from its northern tribal neighbors. This fragmentation was also reflected in the "mosaic" distribution pattern of ethnic groups in the Middle East.[11] But in spite of the political differences between core and periphery, all tribal peoples in the Middle East traditionally maintained close economic and cultural ties with their urban neighbors.

The Arabian model of tribal organization was based on nested groups of egalitarian lineages assumed to descend from a common ancestor. The relationship between each lineage rested on segmentary opposition, that is, lineages were supported by, or opposed to, one another based on their degrees of relatedness. This ideal, though often more honored in the breach, gave rise to the ethnographic cliché often cited by anthropologists and tribesmen alike: Me against my brothers; my brothers and me against our cousins; my brothers, cousins, and me against the world. The tribe was the largest group of

effective kinship and marked the outer limits of both ordinary identification and political leadership. The populations of such tribes normally hovered in the tens of thousands, but collective action was not
common at this level. Even in extremely large tribes, such as the Ruwala Bedouins, who number as many as a quarter of a million, political cooperation is restricted to much smaller lineages. Similarly, the
detailed Pashtun genealogies, which in theory could incorporate millions of people, have never defined corporate groups of that size. Although in theory segmentary systems of genealogy extended beyond
the tribal level, and a chart could be produced to relate all the Bedouin or Pashtun tribes to a primordial ancestor, such extensions
were largely symbolic because these relationships had no organizational potential.

Leadership in egalitarian tribal systems displayed little hierarchy.
Although some lineages demonstrated a greater capacity than others
to assume political leadership, each lineage considered itself to be
the equal of any other. There has been much debate, however, about
the extent to which this accepted ideal of structural equality ever really existed, except as mystified folk belief, because ruling lineages
periodically emerged to dominate their neighbors.[12] However, even
where such lineages gained control over their rivals, the strong egalitarian ideology that identified such power with oppression (*zulm*)
undermined its growth and eventually brought about its collapse. If
set against the example of the acephalous segmentary organization
of the Nuer, a Middle Eastern tribal shaykh and his lineage does appear despotic and permanent; but (as we will see below) when compared with an Inner Asian tribal khan whose political role is much
stronger and whose lineage rules for centuries, status differences
among lineages within an Arabian-style tribe seem minor and only
temporary. Ibn Khaldun's own account of cycles of tribal-leadership
rule, in which power changed hands every few generations, showed
that these were an old feature in the region.

The social structure of egalitarian lineages in the Middle East
also emphasized the fracture lines that made their supratribal organizations so weak. The practice of parallel cousin marriage of a man
to his father's brother's daughter (FBD) turned the local kin group on
itself at the cost of sacrificing ties with other tribal groups. Even
when marriage took place outside the patriline, it usually stayed
within the tribe. This marriage pattern produced lineages with deep
time depth but a very narrow set of affinal or matrilineal connections. The belief that such marriages maintained the honor and purity of the lineage (by men's refusing to marry women outside the
patriline) and limited the dispersion of property also restricted the

ability of kin groups to enter alliances through reciprocal marriage ties, which was a key element of tribal relations in other parts of the world.[13]

Leaders in such egalitarian tribal organizations gained their positions by displaying special skills in mediating problems within the tribe or successfully organizing raids and wars. It was an achieved status not automatically inherited by a man's sons, for there were always potential rivals ready to seize any opportunity to replace an incumbent or his heir. Leadership rarely remained for long in a single lineage. Such a role had little inherent power because the ability to command without consent was severely limited.

The necessity to prove leadership by building a social consensus is seen most clearly in the negotiations of Bedouin tribal shaykhs. They must persuade disputing parties in a blood feud, for example, to accept a settlement although they lack the authority either to impose a punishment on the murderers or to force the murder victim's kin to accept blood money. Convincing rival parties, usually over an extended period of time, to come to terms brings prestige and more followers. In dealing with states, shaykhs act on behalf of their tribes because they are men of influence and are expected to mediate disputes on behalf of their fellow tribesmen; but their ability to negotiate is limited by the knowledge they can impose nothing on their followers.[14] Similarly, among the Pashtuns of Afghanistan and Pakistan the importance of the tribal assembly, or *jirga*, forces effective leaders to build a consensus in support of their decisions. As Akbar Ahmed reports, "The prejudice against ranks and titles and the hierarchy they imply is strong in [Pashtun] tribal society and is summed up by the choice the Mahsud *mahshar*, speaking on behalf of the clan elders, gave the British, 'Blow us all up with cannons or make all eighteen thousand of us Nawabs.' "[15]

Without a strong group of retainers, who stood outside the kinship network, to do their bidding, leaders of egalitarian tribes were always potentially at the mercy of their followers no matter how great their past achievements. Thus, even effective leaders were rarely able to organize their own tribes, let alone other tribes, into political units for extending their influence. Warfare conducted by such tribes in Arabia, for example, was traditionally limited to camel raiding or extorting local oases.[16] Among the Berbers the distribution of rival tribes in a checkerboard pattern across the landscape meant that geographically contiguous leaders were the least likely to cooperate.[17]

This focus on maintaining internal order by consensus, without the ability to command, affected political relations with the outside world. Tribes could not challenge the authority of neighboring states unless those states were very weak. In part, this inability was due to the structural problems of raising a powerful military force for anything other than short-term raids. However, it was also true that the indigenous tribal peoples accepted the structure of the regional political system in the Middle East and worked within it. They needed access to the urban markets where they could dispose of livestock and purchase manufactured goods, and exclusion from such centers was a greater threat than the prospect of an armed attack. Even when tribal leaders did conquer a local sedentary state, this simply produced another dynasty of tribal origin and not a new set of relationships. Arabian-style tribes were therefore not perceived as major threats to the stability of neighboring states. In sharp contrast to Inner Asia, the tribal peoples of the Middle East did not inhabit a world of their own. They were marginal only in terms of political control, for there was constant interaction between tribes and states in trade, and they shared similar cultural and religious traditions.

The virtue of small, tightly defined tribes lay in their 'asabiyya, or group solidarity, yet this very strength made it difficult to organize groups of tribes where group feeling was absent and where leaders refused to subordinate themselves to someone else's command. Like the inverse square rule for diffusion of light, the strength of tribal 'asabiyya fell off rapidly as it grew beyond the local lineage. Leaders could only become powerful political players by overcoming these inherent divisions. One way out of this dilemma was to organize tribes around a common nontribal principle. As Ibn Khaldun observed, in the Middle East this principle was traditionally Islam:

> Bedouins can acquire royal authority only by making use of religious coloring, such as prophethood or sainthood, or some great religious event in general. The reason is because of their savagery, the Bedouins are the least willing of all nations to subordinate themselves to each other, as they are rude, proud, ambitious, and eager to be leaders. Their individual aspirations rarely coincide. But when there is religion (among them) through prophethood or sainthood, then they have some restraining influence upon themselves. The qualities of haughtiness and jealousy leave them. It is easy then to unite (as a social organization). . . . This is illustrated by the Arab dynasty of Islam. Religion cemented their leadership with religious law and its ordinances, which, explicitly and implicitly, are concerned with what is good for civilization.[18]

The growth and spread of early Islam was strongly associated with the movement of tribal peoples out of the Arabian Peninsula in the seventh century. Much has been written about why the desert tribes, which had been weak and divided in Roman times, suddenly became powerful enough to create an empire. From a tribal perspective Islam provided a new style of organization and leadership, which, although composed at least in part by tribesmen, was not dependent on tribal principles. The concept of *umma*, the community of egalitarian believers, was congruent with the traditional rejection of social hierarchy, whereas *jihad*, holy war against the unbelievers, provided the ideological base for a new type of segmentary opposition for expansion in vulnerable sedentary territories.[19] On a smaller scale, religious orders such as the Sanusi in Libya or the Wahhabi in Arabia provided this framework for uniting the tribes in political dealings with the outside world, and among the Berbers strategic disputed territory was often occupied by saintly lineages standing outside the tribal system of competition.[20]

Scholars take the critical importance of Islam as a given, so deeply has it permeated every aspect of life in the Middle East. Yet Islam, like much else, was a development specific to the region, for in other parts of the world, religions, including Islam, did not always take root as an organizing principle among tribal peoples. The brilliance of the early Islamic conquests should not blind us to their exceptional nature. Both before and after this time neither the Arab tribes of the desert nor the mountain tribes of North Africa and the Iranian plateau ever again established hegemony over the region. The tribes that did so were Turco-Mongolian in origin, and their conversion to Islam disguised their continued fundamental differences with the indigenous tribes of the Middle East.

INNER ASIAN HIERARCHICAL (TURCO-MONGOLIAN) TRIBAL CONFEDERATIONS

The Inner Asian pattern of tribal organization was much more hierarchical than that of the Middle East. This difference was reflected in both its social structure and its political organization. Kinship terms made distinctions between elder and younger brothers, junior and senior generations, and noble and common clans. These created a structure of nested kinship groups, called a conical clan, in which all patrilineally related members of a common descent group were ranked and segmented hierarchically along genealogical lines.[21] However, because of their rules of exogamy these patrilineages and clans were more closely bound to neighboring nonpatrilineally related groups than their endogamous Middle Eastern counterparts. The emphasis placed on reciprocal marriage ties created patterns of alliances that crosscut the seemingly rigid set of patrilineal relationships within a conical clan. For this reason polygynous marriages by the tribal rulers were common and helped incorporate nonrelated tribes into regular relationships.

Although the relationships among local clans or lineages were closely tied to kinship roles and marriage alliances, higher levels of tribal or supratribal political organization were more political than genealogical in nature. Conquering tribes could wipe the slate clean by promoting themselves to power after they had eliminated their rivals or reduced them to marginal territories, and tribal chieftains often employed personal followers who renounced their own kinship ties by swearing exclusive loyalty to their patron. Confederations formed through alliance or conquest always contained unrelated tribes, and the leaders of such confederations held offices with the power to command their subordinates. However, the idiom of kinship, even when overtly manipulated or distorted for political purposes, remained the common currency of legitimacy within the ruling dynasties of large steppe empires. The cultural tradition among the Inner Asian tribes of drawing leadership from a single ruling lineage was strong and produced dynasties of unparalleled duration. The direct descendants of the Hsiung-nu founder, Mao-tun, ruled over the Mongolian steppe for six hundred years in greater and lesser capacities, as did the direct descendants of Chinggis Khan, for seven hundred years; and in the Middle East a single, unbroken Ottoman dynasty ruled in Turkey for more than six hundred years.

To explain both the power of Inner Asian tribal leaders and the stability of their political organizations, we must explore the roots of their authority. Obviously, the hierarchical ideology of Turco-Mongolian social structure made the cultural acceptance of status differences more natural, for no honor was lost in assuming a junior role in a larger group; but kinship organization alone cannot account for the rise of large empires or their success at dominating their neighbors.[22] Whereas tribes in the Middle East could muster political or military units only in the tens of thousands (and then only to control effectively their own territories), Inner Asian confederations proved capable of combining hundreds of thousands of people living over vast distances and of employing them militarily for faraway campaigns. Moreover, these confederations were politically centralized, with greater strength and stability than any other tribal organizations in the world. Their leaders were no mere chieftains, for from the beginning they possessed what Bedouin shaykhs rarely achieved, what Ibn Khaldun called royal authority: "It is more than leadership. Leadership means being a chieftain, and the leader is obeyed, but he has no power to force others to accept his rulings. Royal authority means superiority and the power to rule by force."[23]

The development of royal authority by Inner Asian leaders was not, however, the result of internal evolution within a tribal society. The vast majority of confederations was engaged in nomadic pastoralism with low population densities and relatively undifferentiated economies. Although the hierarchical clan structure legitimated status differences among tribes and clans, such tribal societies could not support large-scale political structures with their own resources; nor was there any pressing need for much supratribal cooperation to organize the nomadic pastoral economy itself or to handle internal political affairs beyond what could be provided by segmentary opposition. When large-scale organization did emerge, it arose to deal with surrounding sedentary states.

As William Irons has put it, "Among pastoral nomadic societies hierarchical political institutions are generated only by external relations with state societies and never develop purely as a result of the internal dynamics of such societies."[24] We might go further to include nonnomadic tribes and add that their size and complexity of political organization appear directly related to the power of the sedentary states they opposed and their ability to maintain independence from them. In gross terms we see an arc of growing centralization running from East Africa to the steppes of Mongolia with four increasingly complex types of tribal organization: (1) acephalous segmentary lineages in sub-Saharan Africa where tribal societies encountered few state societies until the colonial era; (2) lineages with permanent leaders but no supratribal organization in North Africa and Arabia where tribal societies faced regional states with which they had symbiotic relations; (3) supratribal confederations with powerful leaders who were part of a regional political network within large empires in Iran or Anatolia linking tribes to states as conquerors or subjects; (4) centralized tribal states ruling over vast distances on the steppes north of China or Iran supported by predatory relationships with neighboring sedentary civilizations.

Unlike in the Middle East, where tribal societies that were distributed in a mosaic fashion across the region shared close economic and cultural ties with neighboring sedentary states, in Inner Asia tribal societies were more isolated, inhabiting their own distinct territories in which they were completely dominant and separated by linear frontiers from neighbors whose societies and cultures were alien. These sedentary neighbors were far larger in population and more centralized than their tribal neighbors, often refusing to trade with them except under threat of force. To deal with these powerful sedentary states, tribal societies had to organize their own state structures of sufficient power to force their neighbors to treat them as equal.

The structural solution to this problem was the creation of imperial confederacies uniquely designed to maintain tribal social organization at the local level while providing centralized administration for organizing military affairs and foreign relations. From the outside an imperial confederacy appeared to be a state, with a centralized government and monopoly on the use of force. Internally, however, it retained tribal organization locally and allowed a great deal of autonomy. Although often established as the result of great military conquests by charismatic tribal leaders, the imperial administration owed its continued existence to its success in gaining resources from sedentary neighbors. Small tribes alone could never hope to breach the defenses of great empires or force them to open border markets, but the tribes together, united as a single state, could deal as an equal even with the most powerful native dynasties of China. Politically and financially, the imperial confederacy had its roots in foreign relations, not in the evolution of social organization on the steppe itself.[25]

The first example of an imperial confederacy was that of the Hsiung-nu nomads, established at the end of the third century B.C. when they conquered all the other tribes of Mongolia and united them into an empire. Contemporaneous with the unification of China under the Han dynasty, the Hsiung-nu Empire had a population of a million people and was ruled by an unbroken dynasty for the next three hundred years. Its model of organization (although not its specific terminology) was later adopted by the Turkish empires from the mid-sixth to mid-ninth centuries to deal with the T'ang dynasty and by the post-Yuan Mongol khanates in the Ming period.[26]

A closer look at the details of Hsiung-nu political organization provides an outline of how so many tribal groups could incorporate into a single structure. According to Chinese accounts, the Hsiung-nu administrative hierarchy had three levels: an imperial government and court bureaucracy, imperial appointees governing tribes throughout the empire, and indigenous tribal leaders running the local affairs of their own people. At its apex was a supreme ruler known as the *shan-yu*.

Under the Shan-yu are the Wise Kings of the Left and Right, the left and right Luli Kings, left and right generals, left and right commandants, left and right household administrators, and the left and right Ku-tu marquises.... The Left and Right Wise Kings and the Luli Kings are the most powerful, while the Ku-tu marquises assist the Shan-yu in the administration of the nation. Each of the twenty-four leaders in turn appoints his own "chiefs of ten," as well as his subordi-

nate Kings, prime ministers, chief commandants, household administrators, chu-ch'u officials, and so forth.[27]

The Hsiung-nu had two systems of ranking, each with a separate
function. The system of named, nondecimal ranks was used for the
political administration of tribes and territories, which included
groups of many different sizes. The system of decimal ranks was
used in time of war when large numbers of troops from many parts
of the steppe were brought together under a single military command structure. The twenty-four imperial leaders, each with the
rank of "Ten Thousand Horsemen," who acted as governors for the
major regions of the empire, were usually close relatives of the shan-
yu or members of the Hsiung-nu aristocracy. Their appointments
were not strictly hereditary because each shan-yu made his own
choices, and a person might hold a number of different ranks during
his lifetime. Such positions owed their power and authority to the
strength of the Hsiung-nu state. At the local level was a large class of
indigenous tribal leaders (subordinate kings, prime ministers, chief
commandants, household administrators, etc.) who were officially
under the command of the twenty-four imperial governors. In practice, however, they drew their support from their own tribal groups,
each of which had its own territory.

The shan-yu and his court were the indigenous leaders of the
Hsiung-nu core tribes; since in other respects the core tribes consisted of ordinary tribesmen, they therefore had double ties to the
shan-yu, who could rely on their consistent support. The indigenous
leaders of the tribes incorporated into the empire by conquest or alliance were linked to the imperial administration under the control
of one of the twenty-four Ten Thousand Horsemen, who acted as the
shan-yu's agents. Structurally, the weakest part of the system was
the link between the leaders of the incorporated tribes and the imperial commanders. Although the leader of an incorporated tribe held
a position within the Hsiung-nu imperial hierarchy, his power derived from the support of his own people. Such leaders retained a
great deal of local autonomy. Trouble within the empire usually
broke out at this level over the amount of independence granted to
the leaders of the incorporated tribes. The power of the shan-yu to
rule in absolute fashion, though unlimited in theory, was constrained in practice. In fact, force was a less effective tool for maintaining unity than for providing benefits to local tribal leaders that
they could not have obtained on their own.

The imperial confederacy owed its stability and continued existence to its ability to deliver luxury goods, border trade, and military

protection from the outside world to participating tribes. It was only by establishing a large source of outside revenue that such a complex system of political hierarchy could be maintained. The shan-yu kept his state intact by acting as the sole intermediary between the Chinese government and the tribes in the empire, both as a negotiator and as a war leader. Tribal foreign policy in Inner Asia was based on the principle of extortion.

The Hsiung-nu established a deliberately predatory policy in its relationship with China and cultivated a particularly violent reputation in order to maximize its bargaining position with the Han government. Raids provided loot directly to the tribes that participated in them, and the nomads always retreated back to the steppe before Chinese armies could retaliate. Raiding parties were always followed by nomad envoys, who assured the Chinese court that an end to hostilities could be obtained by providing subsidies and border trade on favorable terms. Over time the value of these treaties grew inexorably; this practice was later disguised under the rubric of the tributary system, in which the nomads made token gifts and appropriate gestures in return for massive payments. It is estimated that the cost of such payments to the Chinese in the eastern Han dynasty amounted to about one-third of the annual government payroll, or about $130 million.[28] Similarly, by the early ninth century the T'ang dynasty was delivering a half million bolts of silk annually to the Uighur Empire to maintain good relations with the nomads.[29]

These payments allowed the nomad ruler to act as the controller of an enormous system for the redistribution of luxury goods. Local tribal leaders were prohibited from establishing independent relationships with China, and the imperial government gained their support by showering them with gifts. Ordinary tribesmen were won over by providing them with opportunities to trade at the border. In principle China was opposed to border markets, but frontier trade was a key demand made by each nomadic empire as part of the treaty framework. Should China attempt to strangle the nomadic state by cutting off trade or aid, the imperial confederacy reverted to its original military function and maintained unity by organizing the nomads against invasion and by conducting plundering raids to make up for lost treaty revenue. Only the collapse of the Chinese economy struck a death blow to imperial order on the steppe, for without resources to extract, there could be no state structure there. When China suffered periods of economic collapse and fell into anarchy, the component tribes of the empire acted on their own.[30]

The relationship between the Inner Asian nomads and their sedentary neighbors was therefore indirect. They never attempted to rule sedentary areas directly when they could get what they wanted by extortion of an existing administration. This left them surprisingly ignorant about such basic concepts as regular taxation, governmental administration, and the organization of peasant production.[31] Although they appreciated the value of international trade, they had only a hazy idea of how the goods they acquired were produced, much as modern urban children assume milk comes from packages rather than cows.

The emphasis on an imperial government providing benefits overcame the normal pressures toward tribal fragmentation. Although Ibn Khaldun observed that in the Middle East only religious leaders had been able to unite a large number of tribes, in Inner Asia religion played no such role. Originally, all the tribes there shared a form of shamanism. Although shamans sometimes became personally influential, they did not become rulers of states; and the belief system itself had little organizational potential. Whenever confronted with a more sophisticated religious system, the Inner Asian nomads were quick to convert, adopting at various times Buddhism (Mongols, Oirats), Manichaeism (Uighurs), Nestorian Christianity (Keraits, Naimans), Judaism (Khazars), and Islam (western Turks, Mongols in Iran and southern Russia). Unlike the believers in most sedentary societies, they had little difficulty in tolerating religious pluralism among the tribes within a confederation or, indeed, within families.

The implication of this flexibility for Middle Eastern history is twofold. First, although most of the tribal peoples entering the Iranian and Anatolian plateau areas after A.D. 1000 had become Muslims before they arrived, they did not need to employ a religious philosophy or leadership to create tribal confederations. Second, their religious identity was subordinate to their cultural identity. The Qu'ran may have recommended patrilineal first-cousin marriage as ideal, but even after a millennium of Islamic belief the Turco-Mongolian peoples still considered it incestuous. Turco-Mongolian rulers acted as patrons of religious figures and were quick to adopt Islamic ideology in support of their dynasties, but almost none of them rose to power as leaders of religious movements.

ENTRY INTO THE MIDDLE EAST

The invasion of the Middle East by tribal peoples from Inner Asia had a long pre-Islamic history dating back at least to the Bronze Age when, during the middle of the second millennium B.C., cattle-keeping, Indo-European–speaking peoples overran Iran and Anatolia. Later the most important dynasties of the western Iranian world—Achaemenid, Parthian, and Sasanian—had their origins there, as did the Kushans and Sakas in the eastern Iranian world. Therefore, though the expansion of Turco-Mongolian peoples in the Islamic period marked the arrival of a new cultural-linguistic group in the area, it was the continuation of a very old pattern.

The constant influx of tribal people from Inner Asia affected the structures of states as well as their relationships to tribes. The Turco-Mongolian nomads brought with them the model of the imperial confederacy, the policies of extortion they had successfully employed in Inner Asia, and the military power to implement them. Of these, the concept of the imperial confederacy was the most easily transformed into a state structure. Its combination of imperial control over relatively autonomous tribes or provinces was similar to earlier Iranian states, and its hierarchical structure made the ideological transformation of tribal khan to shah or sultan easier. Less adaptable and more destructive was the tradition of raising revenue by raiding or extortion. This method worked well in Inner Asia because the tribal peoples were geographically separate from neighboring sedentary civilizations and never took responsibility for their administration. In the Middle East tribal peoples, peasants, and urban residents were more symbiotically linked together. The extortionary policies initially employed by Turco-Mongolian tribes profoundly disrupted regional economic life. For this reason tribal peoples were perceived as threats not just to the stability of weak dynasties but to the very fabric of government as well.

After the year 1000 the great Middle Eastern empires would all have Inner Asian roots: Ghaznavids, Saljuqs, Khwarazm Shahs, *mamluks*, Mongols, Timurids, Aqquyunlu, Safavids, and Ottomans. However, the first of these dynasties established between 1000 and 1500 were the products of recently arrived Turco-Mongolian elites from Inner Asia with little experience in administration and alien cultural values. Those dynasties established after 1500 still had Turco-Mongolian elites, but they were by then long resident in the region and brought to it more order and stability than did their predecessors. With the exception of the Mongols, the tribes that formed dynasties before 1500 first entered the Middle East as the defeated parties in struggles for control of the steppe. Perhaps the most extreme example of a change in fortune after entering the Middle East were the *mamluks*, Turkish slave soldiers who first displaced their masters in Egypt and then came to rule a large empire themselves.[32]

Conflict arose between these tribal elites and their subject peoples about basic concepts of state administration, dynastic succession practices, and military organization, conflict that often produced

chaos until the newly arrived Turco-Mongolian rulers adapted themselves to their economic and political environment. However, no
sooner did one dynasty begin to master the art of sedentary administration and adopt Middle Eastern cultural values than it was displaced by a new group from Inner Asia. Thus, it was not until the
tribal invasions-cum-emigrations from Inner Asia ended around
1500 that the Turco-Mongolian tribes from within the Middle East
were able to establish dynasties that proved both extremely powerful and long-lived. The best examples were the Safavids in Iran and
the Ottomans in Turkey. Both had Turco-Mongolian origins but were
familiar with sedentary administration and the virtues of centralized government. Although in the earlier dynasties religious ideology had played a subordinate role to tribal ideology, now the tables
were reversed. The Safavids took advantage of Shi'i ideology to move
away from the Turco-Mongolian emphasis on tribal descent, whereas
the Ottomans became defenders of Sunni orthodoxy by reviving the
caliphate.

The relationships described above were fully played out only in
Iran and Turkey, on the borderland with Inner Asia. Despite their political and military successes, neither the Turco-Mongolian dynasties
nor their tribal confederations took root elsewhere in the Middle
East. Even in Iraq and Syria, which were overrun on numerous occasions, no Turkish tribes ever successfully transplanted themselves to
become a permanent presence. The Turkish *mamluk* rulers of Egypt
maintained themselves only by the constant importation of slave recruits from the Inner Asian heartland. Thus, primarily for lack of examples, those scholars examining the history of Arabia, Egypt, or
North Africa rarely appreciate the level of complexity tribal organization could reach and its potential to create powerful, long-lived dynasties.

TRIBES THAT CREATED EMPIRES

Although Turco-Mongolian tribal leaders were skilled at building
tribal confederations, they lacked the basic understanding of sedentary administration, a knowledge that was second nature to the indigenous tribes of the region. They had to learn a whole new set of
skills and were forced to rely heavily on the assistance of sedentary
advisers to train them in the arts of government. The somewhat
slow-witted Turkish-speaking shah and his crafty Persian vizier became stock figures in the poetry of Sa'di, who wrote during the Mongol period, highlighting the cultural difficulties in adapting the
thinking of tribal imperial confederacies to the limits of sedentary

administration. Established imperial confederacies in Inner Asia were more interested in trade and extortion than conquest. Those nomads who left the steppe had to establish themselves in a new world with very different values. As rulers of new dynasties, they found that their interests and those of their tribal followers were at odds. The transformation of a tribal khan who gave generously to a Persian shah, or of a Turkish sultan who taxed heavily, could occur only if the tribal confederation was incorporated into the state administration.

One of the major problems was the different way of achieving and maintaining power on the Inner Asian steppe from that in Iran or Anatolia. In one of his stories (presumed to be apocryphal) about the nature of shahs, Sa'di satirized the concerns of a vizier who protested the ambitions of a ruler to gain everlasting fame by giving the entire treasury away as gifts to his subjects:

> If thou distributest a treasure to the multitude
> Each householder will receive but a grain of rice.
> Why takest thou not from each a barley-corn of silver
> That thou mayest accumulate everyday a treasure?[33]

However, this dispute was not a foolish one: an Inner Asian tribal leader owed his power to his ability to give lavishly, just as a sedentary ruler owed his power to his ability to concentrate wealth. A sure sign of cultural adaptation to urban sedentary values was a healthy respect for the value of money, a characteristic colorfully absent among rulers in the steppe tradition. In his biography of the Mongol khan Ogodei, Rashid al-Din devoted a whole chapter to the khan's seemingly irrational fits of generosity. For example, upon receiving a report that the storehouses of the capital were full to bursting with gold and silver ingots (*balish*), Ogodei ordered that they be given away: " 'What profit,' he said, 'do we obtain from storing all this, for it has to be constantly guarded? Proclaim that whoever wants some *balish* should come and take them.' The people of the town, noble and base, rich and poor, set out for the treasury, and everyone received his full share."[34]

One reason for this attitude was that Turco-Mongolian leaders were more adept at extorting wealth than producing it. Familiar with the intricacies of trade and the profits of raiding, they were surprisingly unsophisticated about the way in which this wealth was produced. This mismatch between military power and administrative ignorance in Turco-Mongolian dynasties was most apparent in the initial neglect of agriculture and urban life, the result of their skewed development in Inner Asia, where extortion was the key to political success. For example, when the Saljuqs first entered Khorasan and conquered Nishapur in 1038, their leader, Toghril, had difficulty in restraining his brothers from looting the city. He had to point out to them that as the conquerors and new rulers of the land, they were in fact now destroying their own property.[35]

Such examples could be cited for almost all newly arrived tribes. The worst case was that of the Mongols.[36] Forty years after conquering Iran, they were just beginning serious attempts at regular government during the reign of Ghazan Khan (1195–1204). His appeal to his fellow tribesmen underscores their severe incomprehension of even the simplest principles of governing a sedentary state:

> I am not on the side of the Tazik *ra'iyyat* [Persian peasant]. If there is any purpose in pillaging them all, there is no-one with more power to do this than I. Let us rob them together. But if you wish to be certain of collecting grain and food for your tables in the future, I must be harsh with you. You must be taught to reason. If you insult the *ra'iyyat*, take their oxen and seed, and trample their crops into the ground, what will you do in the future?... The obedient *ra'iyyat* must be distinguished from the *ra'iyyat* who are our enemies. How should we not protect the obedient, allowing them to suffer distress and torment at our hands.[37]

The concern for establishing a proper administration was only the first of many cleavages between Turco-Mongolian elites and ordinary tribal peoples in the Middle East. In a tribal system the spoils of war, including conquered land, were supposed to be distributed among the participants. Yet no dynasty could allow itself to be dismembered in such a manner and expect to survive. Hence arose the difficult game of providing benefits to the tribal supporters while at the same time building a separate standing army and administration outside of the tribal system. Strategies included the use of various sorts of military fiefs granted to supporters of the dynasty and the movement of tribal troops to the frontier of the empire where they could be kept busy fighting outsiders. The danger, of course, was that some of these groups could (and periodically did) turn on their erstwhile masters and displace them.

Even when these transformations of tribal confederations into state administration were successful, the Turco-Mongolian rulers still preserved the framework of the imperial confederacy as a model for large empires. Just as tribes maintained their own identity and local leadership subordinate to governors within the imperial confederacy on the steppe, so too did local elites maintain considerable authority and cultural identity within the various Persian and Turkish empires, as long as they accepted the ultimate authority of the shah or sultan. The rise of the Ottomans demonstrates the metamorphosis of a small tribal group into a great empire. First it combined with other small tribal groups into a confederation, and then it destroyed these same tribal groups that had aided in its rise, as it created a sedentary administration with the structural characteristics of an imperial confederacy.

TURCO-MONGOLIAN TRIBAL CONFEDERATION WITHIN STATE STRUCTURES

Tribes that formed dynasties were the easily visible consequence of the immigration of Turco-Mongolian peoples from Inner Asia, but most tribes soon found themselves in opposition to state authority. They attempted to maintain their autonomy either by inhabiting the frontier zones between states, allowing them to play one power off against another, or by forming confederations in opposition to existing state structures that surrounded them.

The strategy of border tribes was the most problematic because it depended on the existence of a political no-man's-land between two states beyond the control of either. The two most important Turco-Mongolian border zones were the Khorasan/central Asian frontier and the Iranian/Anatolian frontier, both occupied by Turkmens who arrived in the Middle East as the tribal followers of the Saljuqs in the eleventh century. Because these frontiers were more political than ecological, they could change over time as a consequence of state power. An expanding empire could encapsulate such an area by conquering the rival state, or both states could become powerful and turn what had been an ill-defined frontier into a garrisoned border. By contrast, the indigenous Middle Eastern tribes that inhabited ecological frontier zones in the mountains or the deserts were less affected by political changes because state power could rarely penetrate these areas in the best of times.

The organization of Turkmen tribal groups in both these border regions was decentralized. Tribes organized into confederations, and dynastic states were usually known by their founding ancestor or clan name (Saljuq, Aqquyunlu, Ottoman, Uzbek). Turkmen, therefore, appears to be a residual category for a type of Turco-Mongolian frontier tribe that lived independently just beyond the control of state power—as much a political category as an ethnic label. The Turkmens who straddled the borderland between northeastern Iran and central Asia took advantage of weak political control to raid neighboring sedentary areas but did not form states or confederations. In the nineteenth century they were infamous slave raiders, selling captive Iranians in the markets of central Asia. The expansion of czarist Russia into central Asia first cut off their slave market and then led to their conquest in 1884 with the capture of Merv.[38]

The more significant example is that of the Anatolian/Iranian frontier, although because it is not an important tribal frontier today, it is largely forgotten. From the time of the Saljuqs it was never securely controlled by a single power, and it maintained its autonomy even during the invasions by Mongol Il-khans and Tamerlane. It sat on the border between Mongol and Timurid Iran, *mamluk* Egypt, and Saljuq and Ottoman Anatolia. Nominally under Saljuq control, Turkmen tribes raided neighboring areas with little regard to government policy, grafting the concept of Islamic *ghazi*, or holy warrior, with their Inner Asian penchant for raiding and extortion. Many powerful dynasties had their roots in the area but formed states elsewhere. For example, the Ottoman dynasty began as a Turkmen raiding group that moved west to create an empire, and many of the tribes that put the rival Safavid dynasty in power in Iran were drawn from the same Turkmen tribal base. Ironically, the rise of these two rival empires squeezed the tribes from both sides, and after 1600 few escaped incorporation into one or the other.[39]

Tribes within an empire faced a very different set of problems than did border tribes. They could not adopt an ad hoc policy of flight when faced with trouble, nor could they rely on help from outside states. To be successful, they had to employ the more formal structure of a tribal confederation with permanent rulers to maintain autonomy. In Iran such confederations have survived in weakened form until the present day—the Bakhtiyari, Shahsevan, Qashqa'i, Khamseh, and others. In Turkey they have almost completely disappeared, in part because the Anatolian plateau provided fewer refuge areas to escape from government administration. Two striking aspects of these confederations were their mobility and their ability to politically transform themselves in the face of state opposition. Few confederations claim to have been permanently attached to a single region; rather, in their accounts of their origins they almost always cite specific military or political events that set them in the regions they now occupy.[40]

Just as the imperial-confederacy model was employed by tribal dynasties to create empires, at the tribal level the same organizational principles were employed to maintain autonomy within large states on the Iranian plateau and Anatolia. The Inner Asian imperial confederacy was centralized and statelike, with a supreme ruler whose major functions included foreign relations, warfare, trade, and maintenance of internal order. Yet internally the component tribes retained their own leadership and handled local affairs themselves. Tribes of diverse origin and even different languages became part of the same confederation, which protected them from outside attack and negotiated on their behalf with officials of surrounding states. The organization of tribal confederations in the Middle East followed a similar pattern on a smaller scale, with powerful khans handling the relationship between their tribes and the state.

The leadership of these confederations proved remarkably long-lasting. Although their histories are filled with often bloody disputes within ruling clans, confederacy leadership remained within these clans for centuries. Here we see the bias in Turco-Mongolian political culture toward limiting supreme leadership to the descendants of confederacy founders. In that tradition completely new leadership could come about only with the creation of a new confederacy. For example, in the confederacies we see today in Iran (Qashqa'i, Bakhtiyari, Khamseh, Shahsevan), the current leadership can be traced back to each confederation's founding. Yet most of these confederations do not date back to pre-Safavid times (and some only to the nineteenth century), when we find a whole host of other confederations occupying the same territory. Internal revolts against ruling khans or their destruction by external forces brought about new confederations with new names, not the reorganization of existing ones.

Ironically, the relationship between tribes and states was most problematic under dynasties of tribal origin. To the extent that they claimed kinship with the ruling dynasty, the tribes posed a threat to its stability by assuming an active role in politics. For example, tribes and clans played key roles in succession struggles and civil wars where members of the ruling family fought for supremacy—the practice of a steppe tradition known as bloody tanistry.[41] The periodic struggles of the Aqquyunlu elite (1350–1500) always involved rival leaders seeking support among the component tribes of the empire.[42] Yet tribes were also an auxiliary source of troops that could be used to fight frontier wars or put down rebellions. The Saljuq and Qajar dynasties in Iran depended almost exclusively on tribal levies. Yet in such situations tribal leaders often expected to be rewarded with military fiefs or administrative positions in return for their aid. To prevent such tribes from building a strong political base, dynasties such as the Mongol Il-khans, Safavids, and Ottomans often uprooted whole confederations and moved them to the edges of the empire, far removed from the court.[43]

Confederations whose leaders played a role linking them to the state hierarchy became the most common form of relationship between tribes and empires, especially after 1600, when the power of the border tribes entered a period of irreversible decline. Confederation leaders sought political autonomy, but their independence varied inversely with the power of the central state. When centralized rule was powerful, the leaders of tribal confederations still acted as the political links between tribes and states, and they often were co-opted by accepting subsidies for keeping their people under control. Particularly among nomadic peoples, this form of indirect rule was much more efficient than attempting to rule them through the regular bureaucracy. However, when states were able to undermine tribal leadership and rule directly, the tribe and the tribal confederation collapsed as political units.[44] When states were weak, confederation leaders were virtually autonomous and became important political actors in national politics, often ruling over nearby nontribal people as agents of the state.

In either case what distinguished these confederation leaders from other political actors was their role as legal authorities for the tribes they controlled. Inside the confederation the khans were equivalent to the government, regardless of whether they were perceived as oppressors acting as agents for a powerful dynasty or, more favorably, as protectors of local territorial and political integrity against outside demands. Such leaders ruling over hundreds of thousands of people met Ibn Khaldun's definition of royal authority, possessing the right to command obedience (by force if necessary), collect taxes, administer justice, and handle all external political relations.[45]

STATE AND EGALITARIAN LINEAGES

The appearance of such royal authority within a tribal society in Iran and Anatolia, as well as its failure to emerge elsewhere in the Middle East, was a product not simply of external pressure but also of the structural capacity of tribal leaders to create and maintain large-scale confederations. Although seemingly powerful, the Turco-Mongolian model of confederation could not easily be adopted outside of the Iranian and Anatolian areas. First, it required the mobilization of economic resources available only in the better-watered plateau area where abundant steppe and mountain pasture could support large numbers of tribal nomads. Second, it was specifically adapted to meet the political and economic needs of tribal people who were nomadic pastoralists. Indeed, for those familiar only with Turco-Mongolian tribes, tribalism is synonymous with pastoral nomadism. Finally, it presumed a political culture in which hierarchy was acceptable and ruling lineages or clans could enforce a monopoly over political affairs. These criteria did not fit a number of important tribal groups in the Middle East.

States, therefore, faced a different type of opposition when confronted by indigenous Middle Eastern tribes employing an egalitarian lineage structure. These tribal groups, such as the Kurds and Pashtuns, had an extremely long historical connection with the lands they occupied and successfully insulated themselves from both the cultural and the political hegemony of Turco-Mongolian dynasties and rival tribal confederations. Although they often lacked formal political structures, their ability to resist outside pressure was striking and has continued to this day.

Kurds and Pashtuns successfully maintained their autonomy against a wide range of threats in spite of their inability to unify. Composed of both sedentary and nomadic tribal units, they inhabited rugged mountainous terrain that offered little attraction to invaders seeking profitable conquests and gave the advantage to defensive warfare. They were known for both their military skills and their penchant for bloodfeud. Their lack of formal political organization made it difficult to use their leaders as efficient tools of indirect rule because they could only persuade their followers, not command them. Both the Mughals and their British successors found it impossible to maintain complete control over the northwest frontier of India.[46] Similarly, Iran, Iraq, and Turkey have shown no better success than their Ottoman, Safavid, or Qajar predecessors in subduing the Kurds.[47] Empires that dealt with these types of tribes tended to work around them—to control them in areas of vital interest and engage in punitive military campaigns periodically—but in general to leave them alone (a policy still considered wise today).

As noted above, the tribes described by Ibn Khaldun rejected political hierarchy, and sedentary tribes were of equal importance. to nomadic ones. Tribal leadership rarely stayed in the same lineage for more than a few generations, and supratribal political organization was normally the product of religious leadership. Although the lack of supratribal political or military organization was a distinct disadvantage in seeking to conquer other peoples, in the proper environment it was actually a strong defense against being conquered. Turco-Mongolian confederacies rose and fell around them, but the Kurds and Pashtuns persisted. They not only preserved their language and culture from rival Turco-Mongolian tribes, but they succeeded in preserving their autonomy against modern states as well. Even in the late twentieth century the Kurds and Pashtuns have proved to be potent military obstacles to even the armies of superpowers.

CONCLUSIONS

The debate about the nature of tribe-state relations in the Middle East has often generated dispute because it is assumed that all Islamic tribal peoples are fundamentally similar. I have argued in this essay that two types of tribal cultural traditions with different styles of political organization were present in the region: the egalitarian-lineage groups described by Ibn Khaldun, associated with regional states in Arabia and North Africa; and the Turco-Mongolian tribal confederation, associated with imperial states on the Iranian and Anatolian plateaus. The dynamic of tribe-state relations depended largely on what type of tribe and what type of state. Turco-Mongolian tribes founded dynasties and formed large confederations having predatory relationships with their neighbors. Arabian tribes established more-symbiotic relationships with regional states with whom they shared a common cultural background. Regional states rarely faced large tribal confederations, for if they were nearby, so was an empire that devoured regional states. Egalitarian tribes succeeded in maintaining their autonomy to the extent that their territory was defensible. The Turco-Mongolian confederation was restricted to the grassland plateau areas and so posed no threat to desert Bedouin tribes. Sedentary tribes successfully fended off attacks by both tribal confederations and imperial states when located in mountain regions.

NOTES

1. Marc Bloch, *Feudal Society* (Chicago, 1961) 1:1–58.
2. Owen Lattimore, *Inner Asian Frontiers of China* (New York, 1941).
3. Ibn Khaldun, *The Muqaddimah*, trans. Frans Rosenthal (Princeton, 1967) pp. 91–122.
4. Ibn Khaldun, *Muqaddimah*, p. 122.
5. Ernest Gellner, *Muslim Society* (Cambridge, 1981).
6. See Richard Tapper's essay in this volume.
7. Charles Lindholm, "Kinship Structure and Political Authority: The Middle East and Central Asia," *Journal of Comparative History and Society* 28 (1986): 334–355.
8. All recent Bedouin ethnographies stress the difficulties in maintaining political authority at this level: Donald Cole, *Nomads of the Nomads* (Arlington Heights, Ill., 1975), pp. 93–94; William Lancaster, *The Rwala Bedouin Today* (Cambridge, 1981), pp. 73–97. See also Emanuel Marx, *Bedouin of the Negev* (New York, 1967).
9. See Lois Beck's essay in this volume.

10. Ibn Khaldun, *Muqaddimah*, pp. 105–108, 136–139.

11. Carlton Coon, *Caravan: The Story of the Middle East* (New York, 1951), pp. 295–323.

12. E. Peters, "Some Structural Aspects of Feud among the Camel-Raising Bedouin of Cyrenaica," *Africa* 32, no. 3 (1967): 261–282. Also Talal Asad, "Political Inequality in the Kababish Tribe," in Ian Cunnison and Wendy James, eds., *Studies in Sudanese Ethnography* (New York, 1972).

13. Lindholm, "Kinship Structure," pp. 343–350.

14. Lancaster, *Rwala Bedouin Today* pp. 73–97.

15. Akbar S. Ahmed, *Pakhtun Economy and Society* (London, 1980), pp. 141–142.

16. Louise Sweet, "Camel Raiding of the North Arabian Bedouin," *American Anthropologist* 67 (1965): 1132–1150.

17. Ernest Gellner, *Saints of the Atlas* (Chicago, 1969).

18. Ibn Khaldun, *Muqaddimah*, pp. 120–121.

19. Bernard Lewis, *The Arabs in History* (New York, 1966).

20. E. E. Evans-Pritchard, *The Sanusi of Cyrenaica* (Oxford, 1949); Gellner, *Saints of the Atlas*.

21. Marshall D. Sahlins, *Tribesmen* (Englewood Cliffs, N.J., 1968), pp. 24–27.

22. Lindholm, "Kinship Structure."

23. Ibn Khaldun, *Muqaddimah*, p. 108.

24. William Irons, "Political Stratification among Pastoral Nomads," in *Pastoral Production and Society* (Cambridge, 1979), p. 362.

25. Thomas J. Barfield, "The Hsiung-nu Imperial Confederacy: Organization and Foreign Policy," *Journal of Asian Studies* 41 (1981): 45–62.

26. The pattern of interaction between China and the tribes to the north is actually more complex than this summary statement implies. Chinggis Khan's empire was not an imperial confederacy, and most of the foreign dynasties in China were of Manchurian, rather than Mongolian, origin (see Thomas J. Barfield, *The Perilous Frontier: Nomadic Empires and China* (Oxford, 1989).

27. Ssu-ma Ch'ien, *Shi Chi* (po-na ed.), chap. 110, pp. 9b–10b; Burton Watson, *Records of the Grand Historian of China* (New York, 1961) 2:163–164.

28. Ying-shih Yu, *Trade and Expansion in Han China* (Berkeley and Los Angeles, 1967), pp. 61–63.

29. V. Minorski, *Hudud al-'Alam, 'The Regions of the World': A Persian Geography* A.H. *372–A.D. 982* (London, 1948); Colin Mackerras, *The Uighur Empire* (Columbia, S.C., 1973).

30. Barfield, *Perilous Frontier*, pp. 10–11.

31. John Smith, "Mongol and Nomadic Taxation," *Harvard Journal of Asiatic Studies* 32 (1971).

32. Patricia Crone, *Slaves on Horses: The Evolution of the Islamic Polity* (Cambridge, 1980).

33. Sa'di, *The Gulistan*, trans. by Edward Rehatsek, p. 95.

34. Rashid al-Din, *The Successors of Genghis Khan*, trans. by John Boyle (New York, 1971), p. 82.

35. C. E. Bosworth, "The Political and Dynastic History of the Iranian World (A.D. 1000–1217)," in J. A. Boyle, ed., *The Cambridge History of Iran*, vol. 5, *The Seljuq and Mongol Period* (Cambridge, 1968), pp. 20–21.

36. Joseph Fletcher, "The Mongols: Ecological and Social Perspectives," *Harvard Journal of Asiatic Studies* 46 (1986): 11–50.

37. This speech is reproduced in I. P. Petrushevsky, "The Socio-economic Condition of Iran under the Il-khans," in Boyle, *Cambridge History of Iran*, 5:494.

38. William Irons, "Nomadism as Political Adaptation: The Case of the Yomut Turkmen," *American Ethnologist* 1, no. 1 (1974): 635–658; G. C. Napier, "Memorandum on the Condition and External Relations of the Turkomen Tribes of Merv," in *Collection of Journals and Reports from G. C. Napier on Special Duty in Persia 1874* (London, 1876).

39. H. Inalcik, "The Rise of the Ottoman Empire," in M. A. Cook, ed., *A History of the Ottoman Empire to 1730* (Cambridge, 1976); Rudi Paul Lindner, *Nomads and Ottomans in Medieval Anatolia* (Bloomington, Ind., 1983).

40. There are now a number of studies on these confederations: Richard L. Tapper, *Pasture and Politics: Economics, Conflict and Ritual among Shahsevan Nomads of Northwestern Iran* (London, 1979); Lois Beck, *The Qashqa'i of Iran* (New Haven, 1986); G. R. Garthwaite, *Khans and Shahs: A Documentary Analysis of the Bakhtiyari in Iran* (Cambridge, 1983); Fredrik Barth, *Nomads of South Persia: The Basseri Tribe of the Khamseh Confederacy* (London, 1961).

41. Joseph Fletcher, "Turco-Mongolian Monarchic Tradition in the Ottoman Empire," in Ihor Sevcenko and Frank Sysyn, eds., *Eucharisterion: Essays Presented to Omeljan Pritsak*, Harvard Ukranian Studies, vols. 3–4, pt. 1 (Cambridge, Mass., 1979–1980), pp. 236–251.

42. John Woods, *The Aqquyunlu: Clan, Tribe, Confederation* (Minneapolis, 1976).

43. John Perry, "Forced Migration in Iran during the 17th and 18th Centuries," *Iranian Studies* 8 (1975): 199–215.

44. Lawrence Krader, *Social Organization of the Mongol-Turkic Pastoral Nomads* (The Hague, 1963).

45. Ibn Khaldun, *Muqaddimah*, pp. 120–121.

46. Malcolm Yapp, "Tribes and States in the Khyber, 1838–1842," in Richard L. Tapper, ed., *The Conflict of Tribe and State in Iran and Afghanistan* (London, 1983); Ahmed, *Pakhtun Economy and Society*.

47. Martin M. van Bruinessen, "Agha, Shaikh, and State: On the Social and Political Organization of Kurdistan" (Ph.D. diss., Utrecht University, Netherlands, 1978).

PART TWO

Middle Eastern Case Studies

Tribes and the State in Nineteenth- and Twentieth-Century Iran

Lois Beck

The Qashqa'i of southwestern Iran were members of a tribal confederacy of Turkish-speaking nomadic pastoralists who had a long history of interaction with the Iranian state. When I began research among the Qashqa'i, I was not prepared by my anthropological training to deal adequately with this history or with the political situation in Iran in the 1960s and 1970s. The Qashqa'i were encountering grave difficulties, and I came to see that their situation was similar to that of other tribal, ethnic, and national-minority groups in Iran at the time.[1]

The Qashqa'i were living under harsh, government-imposed restrictions in the 1960s and 1970s. The secret police, the army, gendarmes, land-reform officials, forest rangers (who administered pastures), and other agents of the state kept the Qashqa'i under surveillance and control. Mohammad Reza Shah exiled from Iran or removed from office their major political leaders, and gendarmes disarmed the tribespeople. State agencies confiscated and controlled access to the land of Qashqa'i pastoralists through land reform and the nationalization of pastures. Non-Qashqa'i agriculturalists and livestock investors encroached on land on which the Qashqa'i depended. State authorities pressured Qashqa'i nomads to settle, but settlement on former tribal lands was forbidden. Military forces controlled and restricted their seasonal migrations; the Qashqa'i could no longer migrate according to ecological conditions and economic needs. Government manipulations of the national economy, through massive meat and dairy imports and subsidized prices, disrupted the economy of the Qashqa'i, who needed to sell their own meat and dairy products in Iranian markets. These and other pressures were forcing most Qashqa'i to abandon nomadic pastoralism, settle, and adopt low-paying wage labor and agricultural work.

Conflicting government policies adversely affected the Qashqa'i. One set of policies aimed to Persianize Iranian society; another set aimed to exploit what state agents came to perceive as the exotic, picturesque elements of Iranian society. Neither set of policies was developed in the interests of the people most directly affected.

Mohammad Reza Shah, like his father Reza Shah, intended to modernize and unify Iran by Persianizing the heterogeneous population through Persian chauvinistic policies. Persians—people whose first language is Persian—were "almost surely a slight minority" in twentieth-century Iran.[2] Fifty to fifty-five percent of the Iranian population was non-Persian. Both shahs viewed tribes and ethnic groups as threats to the state and attempted to destroy their political and military power. They perceived such groups as anachronisms in a modernizing Iran and obstacles to development, and they sought to eradicate non-Persian linguistic and cultural affiliations. Where formal education was made available, instruction in the Persian language was mandatory, and use of other languages in publishing and broadcasting as well as in education was forbidden. Officials, most of whom were Persian, were sent to govern non-Persian areas. Persians, in fact, controlled the state and economy.[3]

Once state officials perceived that the many diverse tribal and ethnic groups of Iran were pacified and depoliticized, they began to develop programs to exploit the fragmented remnants of such groups as exotic, picturesque elements of the Iranian landscape for the benefit of elite, middle-class, and foreign consumption. Only when officials believed that Iran was well on the road to "development" did they allow its "undeveloped" side to be exploited for public relations for the Pahlavi state and for commercial purposes. Believing that its policies of pacification and incorporation had been successful, the government sponsored a Festival of Popular Traditions in 1977 to highlight Iran's cultural and seemingly apolitical diversity. Officials promoted the development and increased commercialization of "traditional" arts and crafts and established government handicraft stores in Iranian cities. Through rapidly expanding media and new roads they encouraged the middle class to gain firsthand experience of Iran's cultural richness and suggested, for example, that urban families drive into the mountains to spend a day in a Qashqa'i tent.[4] (A few years earlier, government officials had warned citizens and foreigners about the dangers of "tribal unrest," which they explained as banditry and highway robbery, in Qashqa'i territory. The government actually intended to limit the political activities of

Qashqa'i leaders, prevent the outbreak of resistance to its policies, and capture elusive Qashqa'i guerrillas and outlaws. It hoped to accomplish these ends by restricting access to Qashqa'i territory.)

It was precisely at this historical point that the Iranian government facilitated the work of foreign researchers—especially Americans—who wished to gain access to tribal and ethnic groups. I and many other researchers entered this situation without much understanding of the broader circumstances, particularly the role of the United States in influencing government policy in Iran.

With the Iranian revolution of 1978–1979 and the early months of the new Islamic Republic of Iran, most of the pressures and restrictions under which the Qashqa'i had fallen were suddenly gone, and they found themselves to be in new circumstances over which they expected to gain some control. They were not so fortunate, for the new regime soon introduced its own restrictions and then set out to crush militarily an insurgency led by the Qashqa'i elite.

To understand the transformations these changing circumstances were causing among the Qashqa'i and to see patterns emerging over time, I needed to understand Qashqa'i history. The first encounter of the Qashqa'i with the state certainly did not come in the 1960s and 1970s. The small body of published information on the Qashqa'i, however, was limited in coverage and, with few exceptions, lacked a historical and political analytical framework. Most writers created an image of an exotic society isolated in time and space, without consideration of any wider context. They romanticized a past that could not have existed. The changes I saw occurring in Iran led me to undertake a historical and political study of the state and the place in it occupied by the Qashqa'i and other tribal groups.

CHARACTERISTICS OF TRIBES IN IRAN

Despite problems with broad as well as narrow definitions of *tribe*, I believe the term is still useful.[5] Alternative phrasing is difficult to achieve. Other possible terms, some of which are too general (coalition, association, political-interest group, faction, party), do not adequately represent the complex and heterogeneous nature of this component of Iranian society.

The notion of tribe is best understood as a cultural category that tribespeople and others apply in a variety of situations and contexts and define situationally and contextually. A tribe is an idea, a cultural construct involving a set of principles that vary with the circumstances. Ideas concerning tribes have political, social, and symbolic manifestations. The term can be employed with some precision, not in general, but in specific contexts and periods.

The term *tribe* is of course an English one that specialists and others have used confusingly to depict what they perceive as actual groups of people, forms of organization, structural types, modes of behavior, cultural systems, and ideologies. It is often, but not always, an attempted translation of indigenous terms. The translation is not always accurate. The Qashqa'i, for example, used a variety of terms to depict their social, territorial, and political groups (including *oba, bunku* or *bailai, tireh, tayefeh,* and *il*), all of which English-speaking scholars and others have translated as "tribe." These terms represent (among other things) the hierarchy of sociopolitical groups found among the Qashqa'i. Some of the terms were interchangeable in local usage, and they varied according to context, circumstance, speaker, and audience. The English *tribe* cannot possibly represent adequately the subtleties and ambiguities involved.

The term *tribe*, both in English and as represented by other languages, can have different uses. Tribal people, government officials, and outside analysts have held different notions of the concepts, constructs, and manifestations represented by the term and its local equivalents.[6] Views from within did not necessarily coincide with views from outside. Many urban Iranians viewed tribes, which they feared, as synonymous with bandits, thieves, and outlaws, whereas tribespeople, who feared the loss of their own autonomy, thought of themselves as independent and loyal to their own groups. People had different purposes in invoking the notion and acting in terms of what they perceived as its representations. We should not expect the analytical constructs of outsiders to duplicate indigenous concepts; nor should we expect popular discourse to be the same as official terminology used by state agents.[7] From an urban perspective, tribe as rendered in Persian often meant nomads or other rural people beyond the reach of the government. Governments tended to reify the concept of tribe to facilitate their own administration. Officials considered tribes to be actual corporate bodies with fixed memberships and territories. They produced detailed lists and charts of the tribes under their supposed authority and acted in terms of them. Such attitudes and resulting policies created and fortified social, political, and physical boundaries. For tribal people themselves, who held clearer, probably more accurate notions of tribe than outsiders, the issue was not as problematic. They lived within environments in which their own tribal identities and those of others were salient features and important ways of classifying people. The problem for social scientists is to understand what being tribal meant for people in different contexts and circumstances and to discern patterns and processes in the political, social, and symbolic expressions of people who proclaimed themselves to be members of tribes.

It is often more appropriate to speak of tribal or tribally organized society than of tribe, for the drawing of boundaries around a single group may often be difficult. Many Kurds, for example, were tribally organized and held tribal identities, but we cannot speak of the Kurds as a tribe or even a group of tribes. Rather, there were tribal components to Kurdish society. Moreover, finding common denominators relevant to the five hundred members of a small, localized, tribally organized group such as the Komachi of central Iran,[8] as well as to the millions of tribally organized Kurds of northwestern Iran, demonstrates the difficulties in using a single term for widely varying groups.

Tribal identities are neither exclusive nor fixed, for linguistic, ethnic, religious, regional, class, residential, and occupational categories and traits also identified tribal people. Crosscutting and overlapping composite identities make it impossible to speak of tribes as bounded, clear-cut entities. In what ways, for example, does the term *tribal* relate to Qashqa'i who were urban, middle-class, white-collar workers and Qashqa'i who were nomadic pastoralists?

Tribal identity, as with ethnic and national identity, is an imagined identity based on continually revised conceptions of history and tradition in the context of contemporary circumstances. Identity is constructed. Tribal people in Iran invented and reinvented traditions according to changing sociopolitical conditions. Each tribal group was composed of people of diverse ethnolinguistic origins, yet each group forged its own customs and created legends of origins. Outsiders often perceived such customs and legends as ancient, just as they perceived the groups themselves. The origin of the distinctive felt hat worn by Qashqa'i men illustrates how identity is forged and perceived. In 1941 Naser Khan, paramount Qashqa'i leader, explicitly created this symbol of Qashqa'i power and identity when he was able to resume tribal rule after Reza Shah's abdication. Since then outsiders have assumed that the hat and the group it represented were relics of the distant past.

Tribes in Iran were formed out of the intersection of dependence on resources (land for pastoralism and agriculture, water, migratory routes, trade routes, markets), external powers and pressures, and mediating agents (tribal leaders, government officials, regional elites, foreign agents, outside analysts including social scientists). Tribes were a useful way of organizing people, from the point of view of the people so organized, their leaders, and external powers, all of whom could benefit by the organization. Tribal society in Iran had both nomadic and settled components, and many nomadic and settled tribal people relied in various ways on both pastoralism and agriculture. Hunting, gathering, raiding, trading, weaving, and other specialized craft production were also important. The local ties of tribally organized people were created on a voluntary basis according to principles and processes of kinship, marriage, coresidence, economics, and political association.

Yet these local ties did not create tribes. Rather, tribes were formed through the political affiliation of individuals and groups to local and in some cases higher-level groups and leaders. The extent of supralocal, wider tribal ties is in large part explained by the geopolitical and strategic setting, the value placed internally and especially externally on local resources and labor, the extent of external pressures (especially state and government intervention and influence), the ability of groups to organize and act in terms of their own interests, and the level of military expertise and power. As each of these circumstances altered, so too did the characteristics of tribal groups, leadership systems, and identities. Tribal people in Iran in the nineteenth and twentieth centuries (and earlier)—often nomads wielding military power and perceived to be autonomous— associated with more complexly organized society, the state and the market in particular. No local group was isolated. The main stimulus for tribal formation related to this wider association, and tribal leaders and government officials were the principal mediating agents. Tribal leaders were representatives of state power for tribal members, but at the same time they were spokesmen of the interests of the tribal polity for the state.[9] They played a major role in tribal formation.

Some scholars identify tribes as socially egalitarian units, whereas others see greater complexity. Tribes were not static entities, however, but were historically and situationally dynamic and had decentralizing and egalitarian as well as centralizing, inegalitarian, and hierarchical tendencies. The task of the analyst is therefore not to define tribes rigidly but to discover the conditions under which a decentralizing or centralizing tendency was dominant within a society at any given time and then trace the transformations through time and in response to particular circumstances. The possibilities can cover the range from decentralized to centralized society (inegalitarian, hierarchical, and perhaps class-based). Groups at one end of the continuum lacked leaders other than local elders, whereas groups at the other end had powerful and wealthy leaders who formed part of the Iranian elite and participated in provincial and national politics.[10] Tribal organization involved dynamic processes and could be created and enhanced as well as weakened and abandoned. Tribal groups expanded and contracted. Small tribal groups joined larger ones when, for example, the state attempted to restrict access to resources or a foreign power sent troops to attack them. Large tribal groups divided into small groups to be less visible to the state and escape its reach. Intertribal mobility was a common pattern and was part of the process of tribal formation and dissolution.

By *state* I mean a political entity characterized by territorial borders (not necessarily secure or clearly delineated), a governmental and bureaucratic apparatus, some success at legitimately monopolizing physical coercion (especially for suppression), extraction of resources (especially taxes), maintenance of order identified with distribution of goods and services (such as roads), and a socioeconomically stratified population. State rulers had centralizing tendencies or intentions. They aimed to control the territories they claimed and to subordinate and subjugate or pacify autonomous groups. The rulers of Iran were not always successful; because of a general problem with legitimacy and rules of succession they were vulnerable to competitors, especially those with independent military resources, such as tribal leaders.

Many definitions of, and models for, the state do not apply to Iran. Few states in Iranian history could claim recognized, legitimized power, and claims to such achievements as territorial control, unless the ruler were himself present, were often limited. Modern states are legal and international entities to be defined as well in these terms. We need to distinguish between premodern (pre-Pahlavi, although so-called traditional or premodern elements continued under the Pahlavis) and modern (Pahlavi and post-Pahlavi) states in Iran. Pahlavi states can be compared with other modern states, whereas premodern states such as Safavid, Zand, and Qajar ones were each unique and were different as a group from modern ones. We also need to distinguish between states and nation-states. When Reza Khan became shah in 1926 and established the Pahlavi autocracy, he did so on the basis of a modern, Western-style military and bureaucracy. State centralization was to bring about key changes in government and society, which included a nationalist ideology, economic development and control, modernization, Westernization, and secularization.

Tribes and states need to be defined in relation to each other. At any given historical point up to 1925, what was tribe and what was state in Iran depended on prevailing political circumstances and could at times be hard to determine.[11] The incorporation of tribal leaders into state structures blurs the distinction between tribal and state political systems and makes the analysis of tribes and states complex. Examples of complex polities characterized by both tribal and state features include the Kalat khanate and Swat, located east of Iran.[12] Some scholars, including contributors to this volume, use the term *tribal state*. Such usage can add to the confusion, although Richard Tapper's discussion here is worthy of attention. The term *state* is best used to refer to a higher level of political, economic, and social complexity than usually found in tribes and tribal confederacies.

Tribes and states in Iran through history were interdependent and maintained each other as a single system; they did not function as two separate, opposing systems.[13] They represented alternative polities, each creating and solving political problems for the other. State rulers especially depended on tribes for military power, revenue, and regional security. They often found it useful to consider a group of people to be a tribe. They exploited and strengthened the structures and systems they encountered, action that required little effort on their part and provided order and security. Tribal people in turn sometimes depended on state intervention in the case of regional competition and conflict, and their leaders drew sources of power, authority, and wealth from their connections with states. In certain periods a weak state allowed and facilitated the emergence of strong tribes; strong tribes in turn helped ensure a weak state.[14] In other periods strong states and strong tribes coexisted and were tolerant or antagonistic. Many states in Iran began as tribal dynasties through the exercise of tribal power and organization. Out of tribal societies emerged statelike confederacies, empires, and states, such as the Aqquyunlu dynasty and empire in Anatolia and Iran, the Ottoman Empire, and the Qajars in Iran.[15]

People situated at the periphery—the margins and hinterlands of power—simultaneously adapted to, and resisted, domination from outside by developing competitive structures, organizations, and ideologies. These competitive systems, sometimes taking the form of centralized, hierarchical leadership, often mirrored external systems. The emergence of tribal organization (and nomadism) among Lurs and Persians in the central and southern Zagros Mountains, for example, was possibly the result of pressures forced upon agriculturalists by tribally organized nomadic groups moving into the region who posed a threat to local resources.[16] Sedentary Lurs and Persians needed a competitive strategy to survive. Tribes were authority structures capable of countering other authority structures. The forms that many people identify as primitive and traditional were often creations responding to, and sometimes mirroring, more complex systems. Such local systems adapted to and challenged, or distanced themselves from, the systems of those who sought to dominate.[17]

The movement of tribal people to the borders of Iran and the creation of tribal groups there affected the structure of regimes and states. State institutions and ideologies and the nature of state rule over tribal people reflected the contact, competition, and potential threat. Much has already been written about only one side of the equation, that of the state's impact on tribal people. An ongoing dialectical process existed, for states too manifested the presence and pressure of tribes.

Albert Hourani suggests in this volume two kinds of rural entities in the Muslim world. One was based on cooperative herding and agricultural groups in which people were bound by proximity, common activities, and cooperation and linked by the moral bonds of kinship (descent and intermarriage). The other, which he terms a tribe, was larger than a herding group or village and was characterized by a wider solidarity. These larger groups were held together not by genuine kinship but rather by names and often myths of common ancestry. They may also have had defined territories for pasture and cultivation. Both entities held concepts of shared honor and leadership. Hourani's discussion of three spheres of radiation from cities helps explain the emergence of different kinds of tribes. The first sphere, the city and its dependent hinterland, was an area of direct administration. The second, the intermediate areas where the city and its government could exercise control only through intermediate powers, contained organized and permanent tribes with effective leaders. The third, the mountains and deserts and distant agricultural lands where a city-based ruler may have had some influence but where administration was weak or nonexistent, contained a different kind of tribal entity. Here "tribalism" was a system of ideas, symbols, and rituals that was sometimes dormant and was only periodically activated. Tribal leaders in the third sphere had intermittent authority and no effective or permanent power.

Social scientists often define tribes in terms of kinship, by which they usually mean descent. Notions of kinship, one of a number of symbolic systems of classification (including tribe), were important in relationships among tribal people at the local level, but kinship ties alone did not form tribes or tribal polities. Hence a definition of a tribe as a kinship or kinship–based group is not sufficient or accurate, for it places too much weight on kinship and neglects other, more significant factors.[18] Kinship principles do not exhaust tribes-

people's understanding of a tribe. Such principles were often important in giving people a sense of solidarity, especially at the local
level, but they were also important in nontribal societies, both rural
and urban, for conceptualizing relations between people and organizing people for specific activities. Van Bruinessen notes, for example, that nontribal Kurds had no autonomous social organization
beyond shallow lineages.[19] If notions of descent were important for
all people in Iran, how were tribal people different from nontribal
people? In addition, all tribal polities contained people whose ties to
local and wider groups were not defined by actual or even fictive kinship ties. For the larger tribal polities, no kinship system was elaborate enough to encompass all members. If people stated their
attachments to a genealogy or common ancestor, they were making
political statements. Genealogies were charters of organization and
not maps of actual kinship ties. By using genealogies and claiming
attachments to ancestors, people aimed to create and operate within
a given political context, and these manipulations and strategies
should not be glossed simply as kinship.

For all the tribal people of Iran, it is important to distinguish
among their residential and socioterritorial groups (which recruited
members on a voluntary basis), kinship groups (which were defined
on the basis of descent—actual and fictive—and marriage), and sociopolitical or "tribal" groups (which recruited members on the basis of political allegiance). The principles and processes of kinship
were only one means by which tribal people formed groups and
should not take precedence in analytical constructions. Social scientists need to ask why political relationships within and between
tribal societies were sometimes conceptualized in terms of kinship
bonds and what impact this conceptualization had on political processes and tribal structures.

Most of Iran's tribal groups, particularly the larger ones, lacked
notions of common descent for their members. Among the Qashqa'i,
for example, kinship was invoked as a unifying principle only at the
level of a section of a subtribe, and even at this level other principles
combined with those of kinship to form residential, territorial, and
political-interest groups.[20] Members of Qashqa'i subtribes, tribes,
and the confederacy defined their ties to these three groups in terms
of political affiliation.

Tribal leaders in Iran emerged from local, regional, and governmental relationships and processes. High-level tribal leaders drew
sources of power and authority from their contacts with the state
and other external forces, but they also needed support and allegiance at the local level. Their legitimacy was often based on the ide-

ologies and systems of values they shared (or professed to share) with their political supporters. Various symbolic systems linked tribal leaders of all levels with supporters. Such symbolic systems included notions of shared history, genealogies (political charters), rituals, language, notions of territory, notions of the tribe, tribal names, sentiments of honor, and notions concerning modes of residence, migration, dwellings, apparel, and expressive arts (music, dancing, and weaving). These systems were more developed in some tribal groups and confederacies than in others for reasons yet to be fully analyzed. Tribal people recognized, accepted, and supported leaders more because of shared cultural beliefs than because of threats of physical coercion. Leaders were usually limited in their ability to apply force because tribespeople could "vote with their feet," deny allegiance to leaders, and form ties with other groups and leaders. Oral histories and legends of origin for many of Iran's tribal groups often begin with the man or men who fled from one tribal leader to another or who left a leader in order to form a new group. High-level tribal leaders played important economic roles in a regional, often nontribal context and developed a base of power there as well. The most successful leaders simultaneously cultivated ties with, and drew support from, their political followers and their regional and government contacts.

High-level leaders of the larger tribal polities in Iran were almost always somewhat distinct socially and symbolically (as well as economically) from the people they led. They were often said to originate from groups with whom the affiliated people traced no actual or fictive kinship ties. In fact, their status as leaders often derived in part from their distinctive, exclusive identity. Many leaders descended from people who were originally said to be outsiders or strangers, and they preserved the separation such an identity implied in order to exercise power and authority more effectively. They set themselves apart ideologically to legitimize their distinctive social position, material privilege, and political authority.[21] They invoked genealogies to define and maintain their exclusivity, and their lineages were often highly endogamous. Occasional marriage outside the lineage was also important, for it served to expand political contacts and create intratribal (between the ruling lineage and others in the tribe) and especially extratribal alliances. A tribal elite claiming Kurdish origin and ruling over Baluch in Baluchistan demonstrates these processes, and one finds similar histories and legends of origins for other high-level tribal leaders in Iran.[22]

Tribal leaders in Iran who wanted to expand their power and authority beyond immediate tribal boundaries often needed to invoke wider ethnic, Islamic, or state and national notions. Bakhtiyari khans in the eighteenth and nineteenth centuries appeared to share Irano-Shi'i values and notions of kingship with many urban Iranians.[23] Kurdish leaders, to transcend local tribal sources of authority, utilized the institutions and ideologies of Sunni Islam, particularly religious brotherhoods. And in the 1950s the paramount Qashqa'i khans were active members of the National Front, an Iranian political grouping with liberal, democratic, and nationalist goals.

Tribes in Iran are often assumed also to be ethnic groups. Ethnic identities, like tribal identities, involve cultural categories, symbolic systems of classification invoked for political reasons under changing circumstances. Members of tribes, therefore, may or may not also have been members of ethnic groups. People may have simultaneously formed tribes and ethnic groups; the process for each category of group was more likely to have occurred separately. Ethnicity is a wider, more inclusive construct than is tribe, and it can encompass different kinds of principles, structures, and organizations. Tribes were often ordered differently from ethnic groups, especially as regards their culturally defined boundaries. The term *tribe* emerges in reference to some form of sociopolitical organization, whereas the phrase *ethnic group* emphasizes a culturally defined self-consciousness. Large and often complexly organized tribal groups, such as the Turkmen, Baluch, and Qashqa'i, are often considered to be ethnic groups as well, whereas small, decentralized tribal groups are frequently not considered to be ethnic groups or parts of one. When key tribal (that is, sociopolitical) organizations and institutions were undermined or eliminated, usually under state pressure, people formerly encompassed by these systems may have adopted or enhanced other traits associated with ethnic groups, particularly a self-conscious sense of distinctiveness. Tribal groups are sometimes said to have been transformed into ethnic groups, especially when the people involved, if they continued to invoke commonly held ideologies, were increasingly drawn under state control. Most scholars of ethnicity readily recognize that ethnic groups occur within the framework of states, but until recently many scholars of tribal societies did not consider such a context or account for the presence of the state in their analytical frameworks. People who note that tribal identities are transformed into ethnic identities as part of the processes of socioeconomic change in the twentieth century often define tribes as kinship-based groups (rather than as sociopolitical entities), and they stress the supplanting of egalitarian kinship ties by the asymmetrical, hierarchical ties of patronage and class. Both kinds of ties, however, can be present simultaneously in tribal societies. Also, the egalitarian qualities assumed to be found in what are said to be kinship-based societies are often only found, if at all, in ideology, not in practice.[24]

The evidence indicates that in Iran people of diverse origins, cultural heritages, languages, and customs came together to form tribes and that cultural diversity continued to exist in well-established tribes. This process occurred throughout Iranian history, was ongoing, and still occurs in the late 1980s. Tribes were sociopolitical entities with a history of development, and their members over time often came to proclaim what they perceived to be unique cultural traits. Such perceived uniqueness, serving political functions, often masked, and did not necessarily erase, cultural diversity. Symbols of group identity, such as the rituals, dwellings, apparel, and notions of honor that group members considered to be distinctive, emerged out of a political context and served political ends. Sometimes these symbols were indeed distinctive to the groups in question. The felt hat with two flaps worn by virtually all Qashqa'i men since 1941 and the woven, black-and-white striped cloak worn by many Bakhtiyari men are two examples.[25] Members of tribes may also have believed that their notions of honor and hospitality and patterns of endogamy made them unique. Many diverse people held such notions and exhibited such patterns, however, and differences among them cannot be determined empirically. To ask if Jaf Kurds or Yomut Turkmen were actually more hospitable than others demonstrates the point. Tribal groups were imagined communities in much the same way as modern nation-states were and are.[26]

The following examples illustrate these points. The Shahsevan tribes of Iran descended from a collection of Turkish, Kurdish, Arab, and other elements formed into a confederacy in the mid-1700s, although popular legends of disparate origins told by the Shahsevan have recently been replaced by an invented tradition of common origin in a single historical event.[27] Even the small, predominantly Persian-speaking Basseri tribe of the now-dissolved Khamseh (or Arab) confederacy, which many scholars have viewed as epitomizing tribally organized nomads in Iran, was composed of diverse elements claiming origins from Persian nomads indigenous to the area, Turks from central Asia, Arabs from the Arabian Peninsula, Qarachahi Qashqa'i, Nafar Turks, and former villagers from Sarvistan.[28] And 36 percent of the Komachi, a tribe of five hundred people that emerged around 1900 in Kerman province in central Iran, is said by Daniel Bradburd to have had "external origins."[29] The Baluch, according to Brian Spooner, were "a congeries of tribal communities of various origins."[30] "Many tribes," writes Spooner, "though now ac-

cepted as Baluch, are of known recent alien origin," and had entered
Baluchistan from other parts of Iran and Afghanistan and from Mus-
cat and the Indus valley.[31] The label *baluch* initially could have simply meant nomads who were beyond the control and administration
of settled governments.[32] These nomads did not necessarily share
common tribal, ethnic, or linguistic features. In other parts of Iran,
as well, labels such as *turk*, *lur*, and *kurd* have identified tent-
dwelling nomads in the countryside without necessarily implying
other common traits. Ann Lambton's comment (derived from Ibn
Hawqal) that the Baluch were Kurds who claimed Arab origin is
somewhat less puzzling given our understanding of tribes as "fortui-
tous conglomerations" of people and groups claiming disparate origins.[33]

Members of the Qashqa'i tribes traced descent from Turks, Lurs,
Kurds, Arabs, Laks, Persians, Baluch, gypsies, and others. Their
claimed disparate origins played an important part in their telling of
Qashqa'i history and their recounting of their own unique role in it.
To add to the complexity, none of these labels implies a single
group or place of origin. The term Turk, for example, includes diverse peoples from different parts of central Asia, northeastern and
northwestern Iran, and Anatolia. Under certain circumstances members of this disparate group have stressed their common identity as
Qashqa'i and have marked this identity by special attire, by use of the
Qashqa'i Turkish language, music, and dance, and by rallying around
their paramount leaders.

Some of the tribally organized ethnic populations of Iran, such as
the Turkmen, Baluch, and some Kurds, can also be considered national minorities. (Tribally organized Kurds are part of a wider
Kurdish national minority.) National minorities are groups united by
a shared political consciousness—a sense of nation—and by an interest in achieving political and cultural self-expression.[34]

CATEGORIES OF TRIBES

For analytical purposes relating to issues raised in this chapter,
tribal groups in twentieth-century Iran can be placed into four categories. The great differences in size, structure, organization, and
leadership system among these groups are explained primarily by
geopolitical and strategic location, military potential, resources, and
interest and intervention of outside powers. These differences are
not explained by principles and processes of kinship or segmentary-
lineage systems—one more reason to jettison the notion that the
main defining feature of tribes is kinship. Tribal groups in the first

two categories listed below received more attention from the Iranian state and foreign powers than did groups in the last two categories, and their structures, organizations, and ideologies reflect the intensive contact.

1. Large tribal groups located along Iran's international borders, predominantly Sunni Muslim and non-Persian. They formed part of larger ethnic and national-minority groups in Iran, and similar groups were found across international borders. They played a major role in relationships between Iran and its neighbors. Sections of these groups formed tribal confederacies during different historical periods. They include Kurds, Baluch, Turkmen, and Arabs. (Iranian Arabs were—and are—predominantly Shi'i.)

2. Large confederacies of tribes contained within Iranian territory, Shi'i Muslim and non-Persian. These tribal enclaves were characterized at times by centralized, hierarchical leadership systems. They played important roles in Iranian history, and during certain periods their leaders were part of the Iranian national political elite. They include Bakhtiyari, Qashqa'i, Khamseh, and Shahsevan. (The Shahsevan were located along a border.)

3. Small tribal groups, predominantly Shi'i Muslim, non-Persian, both "indigenous" and relocated groups, and both border groups and enclaves. They usually played minor roles in Iranian history; they occasionally allied with larger tribes and confederacies; and their impact was regional rather than national. They include Boir Ahmad Lurs, Mamassani Lurs, Lurs of Luristan, Kurds (who were Sunni) in Khorasan in northeastern Iran and in Baluchistan in southeastern Iran, Baluch (who were Sunni) in Khorasan in northeastern Iran, Afshars, Buchaqchis, Hazaras, Timuris, groups along the Persian Gulf littoral (Tangistanis, Dashtistanis, and Dashtis, some of whom were Sunni), and small groups of Turks and Arabs scattered throughout Iran.

4. Smaller tribal groups, Shi'i and Sunni Muslim, non-Persian and Persian, scattered throughout Iran. They were loosely organized, lacked institutionalized leadership systems, and played little role in Iranian history.

The labels used for and by these groups represent political statements; a given name does not necessarily describe the language, cultural identity, or actual origin of all or some of the people included. For example, members of Lur tribes on the southeastern border of

Kurdistan who spoke Laki considered themselves to be Kurds.[35] Because of many centuries of forced and spontaneous movement of tribal and other peoples in and near Iran (especially along the borders), because of the constantly changing nature of tribal identities and affiliations, and because of linguistic and other cultural shifts, it is not possible to conclude that groups labeled in a certain way (such as Baluch or Kurd, for example) necessarily held similar cultures or origins. Some people in northeastern Iran who in the twentieth century called themselves Kurds were not necessarily descended (biologically, historically, or socially) from Kurdish groups in Kurdistan in northwestern Iran. In the late sixteenth and early seventeenth centuries Shah 'Abbas did relocate some Kurdish groups from northwestern to northeastern Iran, but some self-defined Kurds there in the twentieth century may have had other, non-Kurdish origins. As another example, ancestors of members of a small tribal group in southwestern Iran calling itself Aqquyunlu (white sheep) may or may not once have been part of the great Aqquyunlu confederacy and empire in eastern Anatolia and northwestern Iran in the fourteenth and fifteenth centuries.

Labels, in other words, can be deceptive and have misled many social scientists and others. In their use of labels scholars emphasize ethnicity, but their meanings fluctuate through time, and they have been elastic categories.[36] We cannot assume that notions of ethnicity were unchanging through the centuries. Some scholars note that we cannot apply to premodern times concepts derived from, and applicable to, modern times. People calling themselves Kurds in the sixteenth century and in the late twentieth century were certain to be invoking different kinds of meanings. We do not yet fully understand the interrelationships of change in language, identity, and social status.[37]

To complicate the issue further, individual groups often held multiple names and used them situationally and contextually. In southwestern Iran, on the border of Qashqa'i territory, small local groups of people called themselves at various times Kuruni, Kurd, Kashkuli, and Qashqa'i, depending on the circumstance and audience. Their ancestors, they stated, were Kuruni Kurds from the Kermanshah area of northwestern Iran who joined Karim Khan Zand's army in the mid-eighteenth century, settled in Fars when he established state rule there, and affiliated with the Kashkuli tribe of the burgeoning Qashqa'i tribal confederacy in the early nineteenth century. When the Iranian government inflicted harsh punishment on Qashqa'i people for harboring outlaws in the 1960s, nearby Kuruni asserted their Kuruni identity. When the government offered low-cost grain to Qashqa'i in 1971 because of the drought, Kuruni were quick to assert their Qashqa'i identity.

Names and labels known to outsiders were sometimes not used or even recognized by the people to whom they were supposed to refer. Foreign researchers searching in Kerman province in the 1970s for Afshars, for example, were told that no such group existed there and that Afshar was only the name of a region.[38]

A HISTORICAL OUTLINE

An outline of the history of tribes and the state in nineteenth- and twentieth-century Iran must be general in coverage. The borders of Iran were changing up to the early twentieth century. Even in 1989 Iran's important eastern and western borders were not secure owing to semiautonomous tribal, ethnic, and national-minority groups and to international circumstances, in particular the aftermath of the Iraq-Iran war and the Soviet withdrawal from Afghanistan. Tribal groups have occupied Iran's border regions for centuries because the peripheries of state power were where tribal formation flourished and tribal groups endured. Borders were a place of refuge. Moreover, the frontier policies of state rulers in Iran before the nineteenth century included the relocation of tribal groups.[39] The relationship between tribes and the Iranian state frontier has been an intimate one.

States in Iran were formed from complex processes occurring at different levels and were given definition by leaders, both tribal and nontribal, who played major roles in state formation. All ruling dynasties of Iran from the arrival of the Saljuqs in the A.D. 1000s until Reza Shah Pahlavi in the 1920s were tribal in origin except the Safavids.[40] State rulers were themselves originally tribal leaders or their descendants. All these dynasties, including the Safavids, relied heavily on tribal support and power. States in Iran until 1921 emerged from, and were both sustained and undermined by, tribal power. Tribes took much of their form, organization, and leadership from their relationship with states.

Tribal groups in Iranian history have ranged from small, loosely organized, diffuse, noncentralized groups to fragmented and ephemeral tribal confederacies and large statelike confederacies with centralized, hierarchical leadership systems.[41] During any given historical period the tribal polities of Iran represented points all along this continuum. States in Iranian history have ranged from fragmented polities lacking autonomous structures of authority to decentralized polities with rudimentary institutions and centralized states maintained by a bureaucracy and standing army and claiming a monopoly of the legitimate use of power (the modern state in the Weberian sense).[42] Challengers to state rule as well as founders of states from the 1000s until the 1920s required the military and technological prowess of tribal groups, whereas state rulers, to maintain their positions and defend their rule against rivals, required tribal support for levies, revenue, and regional security. Tribes in Iran were a constant in that they offered a continual reservoir of military force; states, by contrast, offered no constants and were often changing in form and function. In the nineteenth and early twentieth centuries tribal combinations were Iran's largest and most effective organized political groups.[43] State rulers in Iran often had to share power with tribes. Their ability to penetrate the countryside often depended on their ties to the landed elites, some of whom were tribal.

Islam was rarely a mechanism for integrating tribes into the state in Iran in the nineteenth and twentieth centuries up to 1979, unlike in some other parts of the Middle East. Islamic institutions and ideologies did of course integrate Iranian society, including some tribal components, under the Safavids (1501–1722). The extent to which the Islamic Republic was successful in the 1980s in influencing and standardizing the religious beliefs and practices of Iran's Shi'i tribal people and in converting some Sunni tribal people to Shi'i Islam is not yet well documented.[44]

The close connections seen elsewhere in the region, particularly in the Arabian Peninsula and North Africa, between tribal society and the formal institutions of Islam (and the less formal forms, often labeled Sufism and including religious orders and saintly lineages),[45] were rarely found in Iran during these two centuries. Exceptions include part of Kurdish, Baluch, and Arab society. Baluch, most Kurds, and some Arabs, however, were Sunni and not Shi'i Muslims, and the links between these three societies and the Shi'i-dominated Iranian state were scarcely facilitated by Islamic institutions. In the nineteenth and twentieth centuries until 1979 'ulama' (Muslim religious and legal scholars) in Iran, who served urban areas, rarely held authority over tribal groups, almost all of which were made up of non-Persians and residents of the hinterlands. Most 'ulama' were Shi'i Persians, and many of the rest were nontribal, Shi'i, Azeri Turks. Kurdish religious leaders in some Kurdish areas became influential political leaders, but primarily for their own communities.[46] Because most Kurdish religious leaders were Sunni, they did not serve to link Kurdish society with Shi'i Iranian religious institutions or with the Shi'i-dominated state. In fact, they sometimes served to polarize tribal society and the state. Urban-based 'ulama' in Iran often viewed Shi'i and especially Sunni tribal people as poor or ignorant Muslims, heretics, or infidels. In the twentieth century, at least until the 1978–1979 revolution, Shi'i *'ulama'* successfully converted some Sunni Arab tribal groups in Khuzistan along the Persian Gulf coast. The processes of Shi'ization (including conversion and greater standardization of Shi'i beliefs and practices) and Persianization went hand in hand as religious and political powers simultaneously penetrated these areas.[47]

The Qajar dynasty (1796–1925), which established state rule at the end of the eighteenth century and ruled until Reza Shah, attempted to administer the tribes within the territorial boundaries it claimed while at the same time remaining reliant on tribal support.[48] A third to a half of the population of Iran in the early nineteenth century may have been tribal.[49] Early Qajar policies, following those pursued by previous state rulers, centered on the forced relocation of tribal groups, particularly to the frontier, but these policies proved to be ineffective, often counterproductive, and a drain on scarce state resources.

Qajar rulers, following a long tradition of state rule in Iran, settled on a policy of indirect rule through indigenous and appointed tribal leaders. They recognized existing leadership positions or created them where they did not exist, and they assigned responsibilities to leaders for collecting taxes, raising military levies, and establishing security in their own and surrounding areas. By co-opting or creating tribal leaders in this way, they turned these figures into agents of the state. Such a policy was effective, especially given that the Qajars lacked a standing army (the army was the main instrument and institution of state formation in Iran until 1979), a monopoly on physical coercion, and anything approaching a centralizing bureaucracy. Lacking the independent apparatus of a state, they relied through indirect rule on existing and newly created or enhanced tribal formations. During much of Qajar rule the authority of shahs did not extend much beyond the capital of Tehran and some provincial capitals (which were extensions of the center) without the loyalty and service of provincial elites (princes, tribal leaders, and the clergy). If state rulers disapproved of the actions of recognized or appointed tribal leaders, they attempted to replace, kill, or relocate them and then recognize or assign new ones. In one case a Qajar shah appointed a member of a nontribal Jewish-turned-Muslim merchant family in Shiraz as governor of a tribal confederacy (Khamseh) he had created to rival an existing confederacy (Qashqa'i).[50] Officials and foreign powers soon saw the Khamseh governor as a tribal leader equivalent to tribal leaders whose ancestors had been in

power for generations. Because both Khamseh and Qashqa'i governors were urban-based and encountered state and foreign agents in
Shiraz and other cities where they functioned as mediators, they
were perceived in the same way. The similarity ended at the city
gates. In the Qashqa'i case the governor enjoyed extensive ties as well
in the tribal countryside.

An attribute of indirect rule was the divide-and-rule principle.
State rulers, to aid their own tenuous hold over the territory they
claimed, created rivalry and dissension among men to whom they
entrusted certain state functions. They aimed to reduce the power
and authority of others and enhance their own. They held tribal leaders responsible for specific areas and tasks, and each one vied with
others for control of territory and acquisition of supporters and was
less likely to form alliances against the state. The lack of clear-cut
rules of succession for tribal leaders added to the instability. State
rulers were able to play one tribal leader against another. Competition among tribal leaders for supporters and the resulting relocation
and reaffiliation of people helped form and dissolve tribes and
change their size and strength. With state support, particularly successful tribal leaders became powerful and came to form part of
Iran's ruling elite.

The process of indirect rule consolidated people, often of diverse
origins and linguistic and cultural backgrounds, and strengthened
as well as created tribal polities. The Qashqa'i are a particularly
good example, for no Qashqa'i polity seems to have existed until state
rulers, Karim Khan Zand (r. 1756–1779) and Qajar rulers who followed him, bestowed administrative duties and privileges on men of
the prominent Janikhani (var. Shahilu) family. They held these men
responsible for administering people inhabiting and migrating in a
large territory in the southern Zagros Mountains. Janikhani men
consolidated this heterogeneous population, established their own
links among its groups, and became representatives of, and identified with, the affiliated people. In this manner the Qashqa'i polity
emerged.[51] A sense of a specifically Qashqa'i identity did not emerge
until the late 1920s, when different circumstances were present.
Other key tribal policies pursued by the Qajars included holding as
hostages tribal leaders or their close relatives at court or in provincial capitals and making marriage alliances with tribal and other
elite families.

These strategies of the Qajars worked fairly well until the second
half of the nineteenth century, when European powers began to develop stronger commercial, strategic, and political interests in Iran.
After 1860 European powers, particularly Great Britain and Russia,

who competed for influence in Iran (and other domains), used Iran's tribal groups for their own purposes in some of the same ways as state rulers in Iran had attempted to exercise rule. Acting as state surrogates, they followed the same strategy of appointing and removing tribal leaders, usually by promising rewards and threatening sanctions to the nominal state and provincial rulers if their "requests" were not carried out. When this strategy proved unsatisfactory, they tried to undercut tribal military and political power. State rulers and foreign powers vied for the support of tribal leaders and groups. Tribal leaders could manipulate these external powers for their own ends as well. They could play one foreign power against another as well as a foreign power against the state or against competing tribal polities. Rival tribal leaders, even within the same group, supported rival foreign powers in the effort to enhance their own power, authority, and wealth.

By the 1860s tribal groups in Iran, taken as a unit (although they were never unified), were still more powerful than the Qajar state, and the state weakened and continued to lose legitimacy as foreign powers increased their own influence in Iran. The presence of foreign powers and their competition did serve, however, to sustain the Qajar dynasty, delay its overthrow, and prevent viable challenges to state rule. Foreign powers also strengthened and supported Qajar military forces. Qajar rulers, viewing tribes as a major source of military power both for and against the state, continued to co-opt tribal leaders, although their reliance on tribal support for their military diminished as the nineteenth century progressed and as foreign support increased. Foreign powers also co-opted tribal leaders, for these powers depended on local military support and needed to prevent attacks against them. They were particularly concerned that tribes would form alliances detrimental to their interests. These various processes strengthened and weakened existing tribes and confederacies, for competition among them and with other powers had increased. These processes also created new tribes and confederacies that rivaled existing ones.[52]

During the constitutional revolution in 1906–1911, tribal groups—the Bakhtiyari in particular—were major powers in the struggle over the Qajar state. Tribal groups and leaders were once again variously allied with, or opposed to, foreign powers, and internal tribal and confederational struggles often mirrored the wider conflicts. These struggles over power further weakened the Qajar state and yet simultaneously served to sustain it precariously. During World War I, when tribes in Iran became pawns in the international struggle, the British, Russians, and Germans each exploited tribal groups for their own national interests. From the latter part of the nineteenth century until the 1920s foreign powers were more of a presence for some of Iran's tribal groups than were the agents and agencies of the Iranian state.[53]

In his effort to create his image of a modern nation-state, Reza Shah Pahlavi (r. 1926–1941) strove to eliminate competing powers and political loyalties, and tribal groups and affiliations were a major focus. He saw the collusion of tribal groups and foreign powers, which had been detrimental to Qajar rule, as one of his greatest threats and strove to eliminate the influence of both. Reza Shah's own legitimacy was weak. He hoped to win urban support and did so by turning against the tribes and centralizing power. He was supported by influential Iranian intellectuals in viewing tribes (and ethnic groups) as anachronisms in a modernizing Iran, and he harbored hostile sentiments against them. Initially even Reza Shah depended on some tribal military power to defeat tribal groups (by using Qashqa'i forces against Mamassani Lur forces, for example), but he quickly created a different kind of military and set about to crush all tribes. Reza Shah successfully implemented severe policies against Iran's tribal groups. He killed, imprisoned, or exiled leaders, imposed military governors, disarmed groups, forcibly settled nomads, and embarked on wide-reaching policies of Persianization through education, bureaucratization, conscription, and changes in language and dress.[54] His dress reforms initially reflected his Europeanizing policies, and all Iranians including Persians were forced to wear versions of European dress. Non-Persians, however, saw these policies as Persian chauvinism, for Persian officials enforced them, and the models were ones non-Persians saw among (and identified with) urban Persians.

Some of Reza Shah's policies were vital to processes of state formation and to the creation of a common citizenry and were not necessarily intentionally or specifically antitribal or antiethnic, even though tribal and ethnic people experienced and perceived them this way. Turkmen tribespeople in Khorasan, for example, were not necessarily more disadvantaged economically under Reza Shah than were nontribal Persian peasants in the same area. The Turkmen did, however, suffer from cultural discrimination and were forced to alter practices and customs and adopt others demanded by administrators enforcing Persianizing policies.

Many victims of Reza Shah's severe policies came to have for the first time a politicized sense of ethnic and tribal identity. Notions of Iranian nationalism, which had a decidedly Persian cast, had been developing since the late nineteenth century, but they had little impact on non-Persians outside of Tehran until the regime of Reza Shah and his oppressions against them. His policies had shown them the interests they needed to defend, and national-minority consciousness emerged for the first time among many ethnic and tribal groups. National minorities were a product of the attempt to create a modern nation-state. Modern state formation in Iran began in the twentieth century and only developed significantly after World War I.[55]

Reza Shah was forced to abdicate in 1941 when the British and Soviets occupied Iran. Many tribal groups, no longer under state-imposed restrictions to remain sedentary, resumed nomadism. Some reorganized politically, particularly if tribal leaders were able to assume or reassume positions of power and authority. Reza Shah had executed, exiled, or relocated the paramount leaders of almost all of Iran's major tribal groups, and in some cases their sons, brothers, or other male relatives took over and revitalized leadership. Their legitimacy was enhanced, and their efforts facilitated, if they were the close kin and successors of martyrs killed or otherwise victimized by Reza Shah. With the collapse of the state and Reza Shah's departure, tribal leaders activated local-level ties to gain or regain positions of power and authority. Outside recognition and appointment, important for many previous leaders, were not crucial, given the state's weakness. Other tribal groups were not able to resume former patterns of mobility, leadership, and military power because Reza Shah's severe and debilitating policies had achieved their desired ends. During World War II and then in 1946, with a Soviet-influenced government in Tehran, foreign powers were again involved in Iran. State, tribal, and foreign powers colluded and competed with one another, to many of the same ends as had been achieved under similar circumstances earlier in the century.

With the CIA-supported ouster of Prime Minister Mohammad Mosaddeq (who led the movement to nationalize Iran's oil industry) in 1953 and the reassertion and bolstering of Pahlavi rule through enhanced foreign backing, Mohammad Reza Shah (r. 1941–1979) was able to consolidate power and work to eliminate tribal strength. His policies, outlined earlier for the Qashqa'i and applied throughout Iran, were successful, in part because of the military and economic backing of his new patron, the United States. He ordered military and political pacification, nationalization of pastures, land reform, sedentarization of nomads (not as strictly or as harshly enforced as under his father), economic integration, and Persianization. School instruction was allowed only in Persian; publishing and broadcasting in any language but Persian were forbidden.

Among some Iranian groups, including Kurds, Baluch, Turkmen, and Qashqa'i, these policies led to a further heightening of ethnic and national-minority consciousness and, for parts of these and

other groups, a heightening of tribal consciousness as they all became increasingly aware of the interests they needed to defend. In
some cases groups organized to confront repressive Pahlavi rule and
resist "modernizing" reforms. Dissident Baluch in Iran, for example,
received support from Iraq, whose rulers were eager to retaliate
against Mohammad Reza Shah who had supported dissident Kurds
in Iraq. Despite the aspirations to regional autonomy and freedom of
cultural expression held by members of Iran's ethnic and tribal
groups, trends indicated that they and their descendants would inevitably be forced to assimilate into a Persian-controlled state and society at the lowest socioeconomic levels. They did not welcome the
increasing number of Persian officials sent to administer what these
groups regarded as their own territory. They watched their resources being siphoned off to benefit not local communities but,
they believed, the shah, his grandiose projects, the elite, and Tehran.
State and government exploited their territory and neglected to provide essential services to indigenous inhabitants. The state did provide education to many areas, but the language used and models
offered were those of a Persian-controlled Iran. The lesson of education was to direct the attention of youth outside their tribal, ethnic,
and regional communities. Many educated young men sought jobs
away from home. Expanding literacy and contacts with a wider
world simultaneously served to enhance tribal and ethnic awareness.
Among many groups people with the highest levels of political consciousness were those who were formally educated and had traveled.

Other tribal groups, debilitated by Mohammad Reza Shah's policies (and often not having recovered from Reza Shah's own deleteri-
ous policies), did not emerge in this period with new or enhanced
notions of identity and were not as politicized, and their members
more rapidly assimilated into Iranian society, also at the lowest socioeconomic levels. Parts of some tribal groups did profit from the
shah's policies of modernization, and they too assimilated into the
wider society.[56]

During the revolution of 1978–1979 few Iranian tribespeople outside of Kurdistan activated tribal ties and sentiments to organize
against the shah. For nontribal Iranians and outsiders, the absence
of an active tribal component to the revolution turned out to be one
of the many unexpected and unpredicted aspects of the revolution
and its aftermath. They expected tribal groups to be revolutionary
participants, especially given the severity of fifty-five years of repression under two Pahlavi regimes and the hostility that this repression
engendered. Despite the efforts of two Pahlavi shahs to pacify militarily Iran's tribal groups, tribesmen were still more militarily

trained, prepared, and in some cases equipped than almost all other segments of Iranian society (the state's armed forces, of course, being excluded). In addition, Iranians and others were well aware that tribal people had played important roles in opposing state rulers and overthrowing regimes in the past. Just as other components of Iranian society sought revenge against the shah and hoped to change the government, so too, they thought, would Iran's tribal groups. Some tribal people in cities did join demonstrations there, but with few exceptions they were not organized as tribal groups, nor did they express sentiments particular to their groups' interests. Their reasons for supporting the revolution and the ouster of the shah were similar to those of nontribal urban Iranians. Middle-class, formally educated, and urban tribal people, for example, held many of the same goals as other Iranians of this background. Even Kurds, the most politicized of Iran's national minorities, articulated demands (the freeing of political prisoners, respect for basic civil liberties) that did not specifically address Kurdish issues.[57]

One main reason why rural tribespeople in Iran, especially Sunni Muslims, were marginal to the revolution is that revolutionary activities were organized primarily through Shi'i mosques and urban markets. More pertinent, perhaps, is the fact that many of Iran's tribespeople, urban and rural, were skeptical about political events relating to the center and did not consider participating. A Qashqa'i man said to me in Shiraz in 1979, "So what if the mullas and communists [students and leftists] forced the shah to flee. Another 'shah' will soon take his place, and nothing will change for us." Qashqa'i people in Iran joked then that only a tiny dot (in Arabic script) marked the difference between being "struck by the West" (that is, the shah's Iran) and "struck by Arabs" (that is, the regime of Khomeini and other clergy in Iran, who were instituting Islamizing and arabicizing reforms).

Shortly after the establishment of the Islamic Republic in 1979, and because of the efforts of the regime of the Ayatollah Khomeini to consolidate power and eliminate opposition, ethnic, tribal, and national-minority consciousness reemerged in many areas and gained in strength because of discriminatory policies. Kurds in particular began to articulate specifically Kurdish demands. Authorities of the Islamic regime opposed regional autonomy by claiming that no basis for it could be found in the Qu'ran. (Of course, other, less divinely inspired factors were involved in their opposition.) For Muslim Iranians who were not Shi'i (including Baluch, Turkmen, most Kurds, some Arabs), conflict with the Shi'i Islamic Republic heightened religion as a major aspect of their identity.[58] Sunni religious leaders in some of these communities, especially among Baluch, rose in importance and power. Resistance to the new regime in its first year occurred initially in Kurdistan, shortly thereafter among Baluch and Turkmen, and from 1980 to 1982 among Qashqa'i, as each group experienced in turn neglect, discrimination, hostility, and military aggression.[59]

Iranian nationalism under the Islamic Republic as well as under the two Pahlavi regimes addressed best the interests of the urban, Persian, Shi'i Muslim components of Iranian society. From the time of Reza Shah to the late 1980s the process of state formation and the development of Iranian nationalism were impeded by loyalties and affiliations to religious, ethnic, and tribal ideologies and structures. The Islamic Republic initially took a nonnationalist stance. Nationalism was soon officially debased, but the regime, as with its predecessors, continued to favor the interests of urban, Persian, Shi'i Muslims. In fact, from this perspective the revolution of 1978–1979 meant only that rule in Iran was transferred from one segment of urban, Persian, Shi'i Muslim society to another. The Iraq-Iran war of 1980–1988 contributed to a rekindling of notions of Iranian nationalism, not only because of the military confrontation of the two states and the many casualties, but also because it highlighted differences between the two states' dominant populations (Arabs versus Persians, Sunni Muslims versus Shi'i Muslims). Such linguistic (Persian language), ethnic (Persian culture and identity), and religious (Shi'i Islam) elements have been, and have continued to play, an important part in forming Iranian nationalism. In the 1980s Iranian nationalism grew most quickly within communities of exiled and expatriate Iranians, most of whom were middle-class Persians.

The only active, organized resistance by tribal and ethnic groups against the Khomeini regime within Iran between 1982 and 1990 was in Kurdistan and to a limited extent in Baluchistan. Open opposition was stifled elsewhere. Kurds were protected by borders with Iraq and Turkey and could and did seek sanctuary there, and they received aid and support from outside. Their situation was complicated by the Iraq-Iran war and, in 1988, by the presence of the National Liberation Army of Iran near the border. Iran and Iraq experienced some success in mobilizing each other's Kurds as tactical allies in their conflict.[60] Baluch also experienced the advantages and disadvantages offered by borders and an international conflict (the Soviet occupation of Afghanistan). Afghan refugees, as many as 1.8 million, sought refuge in Iran, and many of them shared tribal, linguistic, and cultural ties with Iranians near the Afghan border. Iran's Baluch took advantage of the situation to ally with Baluch in exile from Afghanistan and with Pakistan's Baluch. A border location, as Kurds well knew, could also lead to factionalism, and people were caught up in struggles between bordering states.

Power in Iran in 1989 was still decentralized. Strong regional and local control was exercised through the power, authority, and surveillance of Revolutionary Guards, Revolutionary Committees, *hizbollahi*s, and local clergy and their supporters.[61] The process of state formation under the Pahlavi shahs, in which the state imposed itself on society, was reversed under Khomeini. In a "popular reconstruction of the state" society imposed itself on the state.[62] The revolution of 1978–1979 was directed against Mohammad Reza Shah's centralized, bureaucratic state.[63]

In the 1980s officials of the Islamic Republic took an interest in Iran's tribes and nomads, and a special agency within the office of the prime minister was established to investigate their role. The stated rationale for such interest was to assess and correct the damage caused to them by Pahlavi rule. The new regime permitted and in some cases supported research and the publication of books, articles, and a journal on tribes and nomads.

In the first decade of the Islamic Republic oppositional forces both in Iran (leftists particularly) and outside Iran (especially in Iraq, Paris, and London) had hoped and expected that the tribal groups of Iran would provide some military and strategic support for their efforts to overthrow or change the regime's leadership. At the very least they expected moral support. With few exceptions, such alliances did not occur.[64] Shapur Bakhtiar, the last shah's last prime minister, in exile in Paris, curried favor among what he perceived to be representatives of Iran's major tribal groups. In some cases, however, the men with whom he interacted lacked support from members of their own groups in Iran. Yet Bakhtiar and others, including United States State Department and CIA officials, who were also seeking what they considered to be the leaders of the opposition, seemed unfamiliar with these men's positions and reputations among their own tribal groups. Such ignorance doomed any such attempts to involve Iran's tribal groups in ousting or altering the regime.

Leftists and others in opposition to the regime of the Islamic Republic experienced difficulty in forming productive alliances with Iran's tribal, ethnic, and national-minority groups except in Azerbaijan and Kurdistan. Factionalism was the pattern in Kurdistan, and alliances there were unstable and often changed. Few organized leftists were members of tribal, ethnic, and national-minority groups except among Kurds, Baluch, and Azeris. (Azeris, Turkish-speaking and nontribal, were better integrated into Iran than other non-Persian groups largely because of their location, economic resources and contributions, and vast numbers, and a few scholars choose not to consider them a national minority.) Leftists acting within tribal, ethnic, and national-minority groups were usually outsiders, urban Persian men and women. From 1979 through 1982 members of the Feda'iyan-e Khalq, a Marxist guerrilla group, and other smaller leftist groups organized, or attempted to organize, land redistributions for settled tribal people in Kurdistan, Khuzistan, Khorasan, and Turkmansahra.[65] Iran's Baluch were affected by leftist activity among Baluch in Pakistan, where leftists were more active than in Iran.[66]

Iran's tribal, ethnic, and other minority groups in 1989 were not united. They were almost as unconnected as they had been in the past, the difference being that because of modern communications they possessed more knowledge of other groups and understood better the broader national scene in which they were all disadvantaged. But these groups, isolated from one another, perceived no common goal or purpose other than the desire to see the regime removed or changed, and they did not ally to take common action.[67] Partly because of the different locations and circumstances of each group, they disagreed about the extent of regional autonomy desired. No minority group, with the exception of a minority of Kurds, demanded secession from Iran.

A small group calling itself the Tribal Alliance of Iran and consisting of members of six tribal groups formed in the United States in 1987 in an attempt to secure United States government and media attention. The group included a Baluch, a Lur from Luristan, a Boir Ahmad Lur, a Qashqa'i, two Bolvardi, and an Arab from Khuzistan. Most of these seven men were the sons, grandsons, and great-grandsons of major tribal leaders who played important roles in Iran in the nineteenth and twentieth centuries. They had been affiliated in Paris in the mid-1980s with Shapur Bakhtiar, Iran's former prime minister and himself the son and relative of major Bakhtiyari leaders at the tribal and national levels.

The identity of the two Bolvardi members of the Tribal Alliance of Iran demonstrates several key points in this essay. Bolvardi (Abivardi) has been, and remains, a small but important component of the Qashqa'i confederacy. Shortly after the two Bolvardi Qashqa'i men joined Bakhtiar in Paris, they felt a need to establish their own identity because a member of the Janikhani/Shahilu family of paramount Qashqa'i leaders was also in Paris. They perceived themselves to be in competition with him. The Bolvardi Qashqa'i men began to assert their own Bolvardi (versus Qashqa'i) identity and soon were proclaiming that they headed an independent Bolvardi tribe. Other Qashqa'i men, joking with them, asked, "If you're a tribe, then where are your pastures and where are your migratory routes?" The notion of a tribe held by these men was broader than pastures and migratory routes, but the phrase symbolized for them a wider set of factors. Bolvardi people were dispersed within Qashqa'i territory and Shiraz and, as a group, lacked specific winter and summer pastures and migratory routes. Bolvardi nomads depended on Qashqa'i leaders for pasture rights.[68]

The seven members of the Tribal Alliance of Iran shared the notion that they each represented the tribal groups from which they came and that together, allied and supported by their respective groups, they could influence developments in Iran. They each viewed their own tribes as interest groups, political associations potentially able to engage in specific tasks, but they each were also connected to their own tribes by a history, sentiments of unity and solidarity, and symbols. In other words, for them, a tribe was a collectivity that could be activated for a specific task, but it was also a source of identity, emotional attachment, and commitment and was symbolically important. Many of the features that I have come to see existing in tribes in Iran were represented in this contemporary group.

Also relevant to the discussion in this essay is that these seven men were brought together in part by two Americans who were attempting, as foreigners have long done in Iran, to meddle in the internal affairs of Iran. The two Americans, who identified themselves as members of the National Freedom Institute and were said to be affiliated with the CIA,[69] held certain specific (but incorrect) notions about tribes and their capabilities—clearer notions, it seemed, than the seven tribal persons themselves. The enthusiasm and driving motivation of the two Americans were a source of commitment for the seven. They all seemed to believe that through the alliance something could actually be done to alter the state of affairs in Iran. The formation of this group in 1987 was not the first time that non-Iranians and representatives of foreign powers have attempted to manipulate Iran's leading tribal figures. Neither was it the first time that such outside attention served to stimulate and fortify tribal identities, sentiments, and actions—in a sense, to create them anew. None of the seven enjoyed any actual support from members of the groups with which they identified themselves, an issue they chose to ignore. They could not have mobilized a response from their respective groups, a situation of which their American sponsors seemed unaware. The Tribal Alliance was unsuccessful in soliciting interest from nontribal Iranians in the United States.

Five patterns in the relationship between tribal polities and the state in Iran have frequently emerged and reemerged in the past two hundred years. These patterns appeared in no particular order or sequence; no cyclical relationship occurred between two or more of these patterns, and no evolutionary or processual development is indicated. The emergence of each of these patterns was, for the particular tribes and states involved, temporary.

First, tribal polities fulfilled necessary functions for the state and became part of the state apparatus. They were instruments of state administration. State rulers depended on tribal leaders for local administration and control and for collecting revenue and assembling levies. Second, tribal polities and the state were in opposition. State rulers, aiming at centralization and control and threatened by the political autonomy and military prowess of tribal polities, attempted to eliminate this threat. Some tribal polities were successful in resisting such efforts, often by becoming more centralized themselves or by dissolving the structures that state rulers perceived to be threatening. Third, tribal leaders competed, sometimes successfully, against existing state rulers for state hegemony. (This pattern was prevalent from A.D. 1000 until after the rise of the Qajars in 1796.) Fourth, tribal polities were fragmented and therefore hard to organize and administer from outside. For lack of military and financial means, and because of territorial distance and the frequent inaccessibility of tribal groups, state rulers were unable or unwilling to exert control or influence over them. Tribal leaders relied predominantly on local sources of legitimacy, power, and authority. Fifth, foreign powers intervened in Iran and substituted their influence for that of the state. The state, weak and decentralized, had little impact on tribal polities, whereas foreign powers, often professing to act on behalf of the state, exploited tribal polities in their own struggles and for their own interests. The presence of foreign powers served to impede the emergence of new, more powerful state rulers who might have threatened tribal autonomy.

Under each of these five patterns, states and tribes, bound intimately together, were transformed. It is clear that tribal polities were responsive to, and changed within, wider political circumstances. They took the form, among others, of small diffuse groups and large powerful confederacies. Tribal structures lent themselves to diverse circumstances. As dynamic structures, they often survived despite rapidly changing conditions.

Some scholars analyze the oscillations between, or the polar modalities of, "the land of dissidence" and "the land of government" or between a "tribal situation" and a "government situation." These models, even though they are sometimes recognized as cultural constructs and seen as representing idealized situations, are of limited analytical value in the case of Iran, for they do not adequately represent the complexity of the relationships between tribes and states in Iranian history. The five patterns I have noted are also generalizations, and the processes I have described are extracted from the contexts that give them meaning. Actual relationships between any given tribal group and the Iranian state, even over a short historical period, demonstrate greater complexity than I have indicated.

CONCLUDING REMARKS

Many social scientists and others have traditionally viewed tribes as bounded, self-contained, autonomous, often isolated entities created by autochthonous factors. Tribes, however, were formed and sustained within the context of broad external forces. The resulting tribal formations were ways of integrating people into state structures while at the same time preventing these peoples' subordination to, or assimilation into, the state. Tribal structures emerged as components of state rule while simultaneously enabling people to resist certain forms of state encroachment. A loosely organized noncentralized tribal group was as much a response to external pressures as was a complexly organized, centralized one. Each pattern demonstrated an adaptive strategy. A loosely organized group, protected by the diffuseness of its structure and organization, offered little to state agents to manipulate, whereas a centralized group was able to use its complex organization to resist state pressure as well as benefit from being an instrument of state control.[70]

Tribal people were protected through their membership in these politics and were advantaged over many others in the countryside, especially peasants, who lacked such organizations and leadership systems. Through tribal membership people could maintain political autonomy and defend and expand their economic and territorial interests. Tribes were independent concentrations of power. Tribespeople also received prestige and support from tribal membership. They were well aware of the benefits tribal membership often conferred, and their allegiance to, and support of, leaders were important elements in tribal formation. Tribal structures survived after the events and circumstances that created them and hence offered some stability to tribal people during periods unfavorable to the process of tribal formation. Tribal structures, organizations, and ideologies offered "long-term survival value" because of their highly adaptive and flexible nature.[71] State structures, organizations, and ideologies, for these same tribal people, did not come close to achieving this end. Tribal ties and identities were more permanent and enduring for tribal people than the affiliations and loyalties sought—sometimes demanded—by Iranian states. States came and went for tribespeople; tribes remained a constant.

Conflicting tendencies are found in the rule over tribal people by the state and by tribal leaders. The state was characterized by mechanisms for extracting wealth from people, but it also contained mechanisms for protecting these same people from other extractions. Tribal leaders were vehicles for extracting wealth, and in fact they owed their position in part to the state's bequeathing this privilege to them, but they also limited the state's extractions. The state presented tribal leaders with the opportunity to gain a source of wealth independent of their tribal base by entitling them to govern nontribal, usually agricultural people in rural areas. By solidifying the rule of tribal leaders over nontribal areas, the state freed tribal leaders from becoming too dependent economically on the tribal base on which they relied for military support. By not jeopardizing their ties with supporters, tribal leaders came to pose a more formidable threat to the state.

Tribespeople often viewed tribal leaders as necessary (although sometimes unwelcome) mediators against what they perceived as the illegitimate, exploitative rule of the state. They were apt to perceive their own leaders as legitimate (at least as more legitimate than state rulers) because of their shared history and various uniting sentiments and symbolic systems. But tribal leaders were extensions of the state, a position they themselves saw more clearly than the tribespeople because of the mediating position they occupied and the role they played. Tribal leaders, in their rule over tribespeople and so as to serve their own interests, could obscure the true character of the state, which may have been more or less powerful and exploitative at any given point than tribespeople assumed it was. Tribal people rarely "saw" the state directly; their perceptions of the state were usually mediated by their leaders.[72] Tribal leaders, many of whom attempted to achieve a balance in their relationship both with the state and with tribal people, came to serve the interests of all three parties, an outcome that helps explain the resiliency of these institutions and patterns over a long historical period.

From the late eighteenth century until Reza Shah consolidated power in the late 1920s, and then again from 1941 to the mid-1950s, when they were exiled, the paramount Qashqa'i khans precariously but successfully balanced their often conflicting responsibilities to the tribal confederacy and the state. In 1979, with the collapse of the Pahlavi dynasty, these khans once again seized the opportunity to resume rule, but they fell victim to political machinations within the new revolutionary Islamic state, within a regional context with its competing sources of power, and within their own confederacy. The component parts and members of the confederacy had been transformed during the khans' twenty-five years of exile, and their attempt to resume rule was unsuccessful. The paramount khans were defeated militarily in 1982 by Khomeini's Revolutionary Guards, and they are now dead or in foreign or internal exile. The survivors plan no imminent return.

Further ambiguities and dilemmas are found in state rule and tribal rule. The incorporation of tribal leaders into state structures blurs the distinction between tribal and state political systems (and makes the analysis of tribes and states complex and hence worthy of further attention). Do we consider tribal leaders who served state interests and became part of the state's ruling apparatus simply to be "tribal" leaders? Tribal leaders who held government rank in what is today the Yemen Arab Republic were considered part of the state; tribal leaders who dissented were recast as "tribal."[73] Few scholars have detailed and analyzed the transformations occurring when men who were tribal leaders became heads of tribal confederacies, challengers to state rulers, and state rulers themselves.[74] Some "tribal" leaders in Iran were initially state appointees, with no tribal background, who were sent to govern a given territory and people. The Khamseh governors, who were instruments of the state, differed from the Qashqa'i governors, who in addition were instruments of, and identified with, the Qashqa'i polity and the people it contained.

A state may have been unable to rule, whereas a nonstate polity—a tribe—may have performed many state functions. State rulers, to administer their territory and subjects, were often forced to rely on tribal leaders because they lacked other means of administration; but in so doing, state rulers created powerful forces—tribes—that might contribute to the collapse of the state. (And many states and regimes in Iran did fall to tribal power and pressure.) A state's reliance on tribal polities fortified and enhanced them at the expense of its own independent rule and the development of its own independent institutions.

By assisting the state in its rule, tribal leaders were able to control the state's access to the tribe and help defend the tribe against the state. But they also helped the state impose central order on the tribe and increase state power;[75] thus they facilitated the state's efforts to control or eliminate both tribal leaders and the tribe itself. Tribal leaders, to meet the increasing power of an expanding state, could form a competitive polity—a statelike confederacy or protostate. Alternatively, they could dissolve the structures that the state perceived as threatening. State rulers, to meet the threat posed by an expanding tribal polity yet lacking the means necessary to control or defeat it, could permit tribal leaders greater autonomy and could even appeal to such ideals as egalitarianism, autonomy, and loyalty to patrilineal kin to enhance their own indirect rule over tribal peoples. This strategy was especially effective when state rulers themselves claimed tribal origins. And tribal leaders, as agents of the state, were forced or enticed into practices that could undermine the indigenous bases of their rule. Bakhtiyari khans, for example, were unable to be "tribal" leaders after they had transformed themselves into state rulers in the early 1900s. For this and other reasons the Bakhtiyari tribal confederacy was never perceived as a single polity or as a major power again. The most effective tribal leaders were those who understood these ambiguities and dilemmas and balanced their conflicting aspects.

NOTES

1. Ali Banuazizi, Jane Bestor, John Bowen, David Edwards, Gene Garthwaite, and Leonard Helfgott offered helpful comments on previous drafts of this essay. Participants in the Conference on Tribes and State Formation in the Middle East, at Harvard University in November 1987, particularly Theda Skocpol, Albert Hourani, Edmund Burke III, and Paul Dresch, also provided insights. Information on southwestern Iran and the Qashqa'i in this chapter derives from my research among the Qashqa'i (1970–1971, 1977, and 1979), archival research in Iran and London, and ongoing oral-history research among Qashqa'i in exile.

2. Nikki R. Keddie, "The Minorities Question in Iran," in Shirin Tahir-Kheli and Shaheen Ayubi, eds., *The Iran-Iraq War: New Weapons, Old Conflicts* (New York, 1983), p. 91. The sociolinguist Donald Stilo, in a personal communication, has stated that Persian as a first language is not a majority language in Iran. Some Iranian scholars of Persian origin dispute this assertion and insist that the majority of the people of Iran speak Persian as a first language. No reliable statistics exist. The policy in 1989 of the editor of *Encyclopaedia Iranica* was to label as Persian *all* inhabitants of Iran. Such labeling makes for confusion, especially where non-Persians are concerned.

3. For a discussion of the complex issue of the development of the modern Iranian state and the Persian character of Iranian nationalism, see Leonard Helfgott, "The Structural Foundations of the National Minority Problem in Revolutionary Iran," *Iranian Studies* 13, nos. 1–4 (1980): 195–214.

4. For an account of these uninvited guests and involuntary hosts, see Lois Beck, "Nomads and Urbanites, Involuntary Hosts and Uninvited Guests," *Middle Eastern Studies* 18, no. 4 (1982): 426–444.

5. For details and additional references, see Lois Beck, *The Qashqa'i of Iran* (New Haven, 1986), pp. 5–21. Richard L. Tapper, Introduction to Tapper, ed., *The Conflict of Tribe and State in Iran and Afghanistan* (London, 1983), and G. R. Garthwaite, *Khans and Shahs: A Documentary Analysis of the Bakhtiyari in Iran* (Cambridge, 1983), discuss the concept of tribe in ways that are compatible with my statement here. Both scholars have influenced the development of my ideas. I use the past tense in this paper to conform to the historical discussion. There is no "ethnographic present" concerning these issues, and the only tense that is accurate is the past tense.

6. Dale Eickelman, *The Middle East: An Anthropological Approach*, 2d ed. (Englewood Cliffs, N.J., 1989), pp. 126–150; Talal Asad, "Political Inequality in the Kababish Tribe," in Ian Cunnison and Wendy James, eds., *Studies in Sudanese Ethnography* (New York, 1972), p. 128.

7. Richard L. Tapper, "Ethnicity, Order and Meaning in the Anthropology of Iran and Afghanistan," in Jean-Pierre Digard, ed., *Le fait ethnique en Iran et en Afghanistan* (Paris, 1988), p. 26.

8. Daniel Bradburd, "Kinship and Contract: The Social Organization of the Komachi of Kerman, Iran" (Ph.D. diss., City University of New York, 1979).

9. I. M. Khazanov, *Nomads and the Outside World* (Cambridge, 1984), p. 269.

10. Thomas Barfield, in his contribution to this volume, discusses two types of tribal cultural traditions having different styles of political organization: an egalitarian-lineage type associated with regional states in Arabia and North Africa and a Turco-Mongolian tribal confederacy associated with imperial states on the Iranian and Anatolian plateaus. Because both types (and many other forms as well) were found in both areas, the notion of a continuum appears more useful than attempts to establish a limited number of discrete types.

11. For example, the Zand period, c. 1750–1789. For the case of Yemen, see Paul Dresch's essay in this volume.

12. See Nina Swidler, "The Political Structure of a Tribal Federation: The Brahui of Baluchistan" (Ph.D. diss., Columbia University, 1969) and "The Development of the Kalat Khanate," in William Irons and Neville Dyson-Hudson, eds., *Perspectives on Nomadism* (Leiden, 1972); Fredrik Barth, *Political Leadership among Swat Pathans*, London School of Economics Monographs on Social Anthropology, no. 19 (London, 1959); and Miangul Jahanzeb, *The Last Wali of Swat: An Autobiography as Told to Fredrik Barth* (New York, 1985).

13. See Tapper, Introduction to *Conflict of Tribe and State*.

14. Ernest Gellner, "Tribalism and Social Change in North Africa," in William Lewis, ed., *French-Speaking Africa: The Search for Identity* (New York, 1965), p. 113.

15. The processes involved in two of these cases are illustrated in John Woods, *The Aqquyunlu: Clan, Confederation, Empire* (Minneapolis, 1976), and Rudi Paul Lindner, *Nomads and Ottomans in Medieval Anatolia* (Bloomington, Ind., 1983).

16. Khazanov, *Nomads and the Outside World,* p. 105.

17. Gerald Sider, "When Parrots Learn to Talk, and Why They Can't: Domination, Deception, and Self-Deception in Indian-White Relations," *Comparative Studies in Society and History* 29, no. 1 (1987): 20–21.

18. Lisa Anderson's otherwise exemplary study of state formation in Tunisia and Libya (*The State and Social Transformation in Tunisia and Libya, 1830–1980* [Princeton, 1986]) relies heavily on the notion of tribes as kin-ordered groups, whereas the evidence presented by other scholars (e.g., John Davis, *Libyan Politics: Tribe and Revolution* [Berkeley, 1987]) indicates that tribal groups in these two regions were more complex than she indicates. She does not explain how kinship created tribeṣ, nor does she indicate what tribes were other than "kinship." She also incorrectly identifies kin-ordered groups as acephalous and egalitarian, an issue I discuss in this essay.

19. Martin van Bruinessen, "Kurdish Tribes and the State of Iran: The Case of Simko's Revolt," in Richard Tapper, ed., *The Conflict of Tribe and State in Iran and Afghanistan* (London, 1983), p. 376.

20. For a detailed example of one Qashqa'i subtribe, see Lois Beck, *Borzu Beg: A Year in the Life of a Qashqa'i Tribal Headman* (Berkeley, forthcoming).

21. Asad, "Political Inequality," p. 137.

22. See Jane Bestor, "The Kurds of Iranian Baluchistan: A Regional Elite" (Master's thesis, McGill University, 1979) and *The Kurds of Iranian Baluchistan* (unpublished book manuscript); Garthwaite, *Khans and Shahs;* Martin van Bruinessen, "Agha, Shaikh and State: On the Social and Political Organization of Kurdistan" (Ph.D. diss., Utrecht University, 1978); Brian Spooner, "Baluchistan," *Encyclopaedia Iranica,* vol. 3, fascicle 6 (London, 1988), pp. 598–632; and Beck, *Qashqa'i of Iran.*

23. Garthwaite, *Khans and Shahs.*

24. See, for example, the case of tribal Lurs in Iran, in Jacob Black-Michaud, *Sheep and Land: The Economics of Power in a Tribal Society* (Cambridge, 1986).

25. Jean-Pierre Digard, *Techniques des nomades baxtyari d'Iran* (Cambridge, 1981), p. 213.

26. Benedict Anderson, *Imagined Communities: Reflections on the Origin and Spread of Nationalism* (London, 1983).

27. Tapper, "Ethnicity, Order and Meaning," p. 28; and "History and Identity among the Shahsevan," *Iranian Studies* 21, nos. 3–4 (1988): 84–108.

28. Fredrik Barth, *Nomads of South Persia: The Basseri Tribe of the Khamseh Confederacy* (London, 1961), pp. 52–53.

29. Bradburd, "Kinship and Contract," pp. 147, 221.

30. Spooner, "Baluchistan," p. 607.

31. Spooner, "Baluchistan," p. 623.

32. Spooner, "Baluchistan," p. 607.

33. Ann K. S. Lambton, "Ilat," in *Encyclopedia of Islam*, 2d ed., vol. 3 (Leiden, 1960), p. 1098; Ian Cunnison, *Baggara Arabs: Power and the Lineage in a Sudanese Nomad Tribe* (Oxford, 1966), p. 6.

34. A fourth set of minorities in Iran consists of the religious minorities (Sunni Muslims, Jews, Christians [Armenians and Nestorian Assyrians], Zoroastrians, Bahais, Ahl-i Haqq, and Sabeans). Members of religious minorities, with the exception of many Sunni Muslims, were scattered in cities and small rural communities and did not pose threats to the state in the way that some tribal and ethnic groups were seen as doing. Under Pahlavi rule (1926–1979) some members of religious minorities, excluding most Sunni Muslims, were fairly well integrated into the state, formed part of the dominant Persian component of society, and benefited from modernizing reforms.

35. Van Bruinessen, "Agha, Shaikh and State," p. 18.

36. Spooner, "Baluchistan," p. 624.

37. Spooner, "Baluchistan," p. 625. Spooner's attempts to unravel the nature of Baluch origins and identity demonstrate these complex issues. See Brian Spooner, "Who Are the Baluch? A Preliminary Investigation into the Dynamics of an Ethnic Identity from Qajar Iran," in Edmund Bosworth and Carole Hillenbrand, eds., *Qajar Iran: Political, Social and Cultural Change 1800–1925* (Edinburgh, 1983), and "Baluchistan." He states that the Baluch, of heterogeneous origins, have undergone continuous processes of identity formation and change.

38. Georg Stober discusses the problematic nature of an Afshar ethnic identity: "The Influence of Politics on the Formation and Reduction of 'Ethnic Boundaries' of Tribal Groups: The Cases of Sayad and Afshar in Eastern Iran," in Jean-Pierre Digard, ed., *Le fait ethnique en Iran et en Afghanistan* (Paris, 1988), pp. 131–138.

39. John Perry, "Forced Migration in Iran during the Seventeenth and Eighteenth Centuries," *Iranian Studies* 8, no. 4 (1975): 199–215.

40. Even the Safavid dynasty had a Turkmen tribal component.

41. Tapper, Introduction to *Conflict of Tribe and State*, p. 45.

42. Garthwaite, *Khans and Shahs*, p. 15.

43. Tapper, Introduction to *Conflict of Tribe and State*, p. 49, and "The Tribes in Eighteenth- and Nineteenth-Century Iran," in Peter Avery and G. Hambly, eds., *The Afshars, Zands, and Qajars*, vol. 7 of *The Cambridge History of Iran* (Cambridge, forthcoming), p. 36.

44. Reinhold Loeffler, *Islam in Practice: Religious Beliefs in a Persian Village* (Albany, 1988), discusses the impact of the Islamic Republic on tribally organized Shi'i Muslim villagers in southwestern Iran.

45. See Lapidus's discussion in this volume; Akbar Ahmed and David Hart, eds., *Islam in Tribal Societies: From the Atlas to the Indus* (London, 1984); and Lois Beck, "Islam in Tribal Societies," *Reviews in Anthropology* 18, no. 1 (1990): 65–82.

46. Van Bruinessen, "Agha, Shaikh and State."

47. Rostam Pourzal, "Ethnic Politics and Religious Change among Arab Iranians: A Case Study" (unpublished manuscript, 1981). He conducted re-

search among tribal Arabs in the coastal region of southeastern Khuzistan province. G. Reza Fazel ("Tribes and State in Iran: From Pahlavi to Islamic Republic," in Haleh Afshar, ed., *Iran: A Revolution in Turmoil* [Albany, 1985], p. 91) notes the important role of three Boir Ahmad religious leaders (*mojtahed*). They were well integrated into the Boir Ahmad political system, and from 1963 they, along with lower-level Boir Ahmad religious leaders, identified with national religious leaders in their opposition to the shah.

48. Sources on tribes during the Qajar period include Lambton, "Ilat"; F. Towfiq, "Ashayer," in *Encyclopaedia Iranica*, vol. 2, fascicle 7 (London, 1987), pp. 707–724; Richard L. Tapper, *The King's Friends: A Social and Political History of the Shahsevan Tribes of Iran* (unpublished manuscript), and "Tribes in Eighteenth- and Nineteenth-Century Iran"; Spooner, "Who Are the Baluch?" and "Baluchistan"; Garthwaite, *Khans and Shahs*; Pierre Oberling, "The Qashqa'i Nomads of Fars" (The Hague, 1974); and Beck, *Qashqa'i of Iran*.

49. Because sources usually equate tribes and nomads, they probably do not include settled tribal people, and the overall figure would be higher. By the beginning of the twentieth century the figure had dropped to a fourth of the population. See sources in Towfiq, "Ashayer," pp. 709–712.

50. Naser ed-Din Shah in 1861–1862. See Beck, *Qashqa'i of Iran*, pp. 79–83.

51. For details and references concerning this process, see Beck, *Qashqa'i of Iran*. The Qashqa'i name, associated with a locally prominent family, occurs in historical records well before Karim Khan Zand.

52. Foreign powers in other parts of the Middle East were similarly involved with tribal groups. For the case of the French in Syria, see Norman Lewis, *Nomads and Settlers in Syria and Jordan, 1800–1980* (Cambridge, 1987); and Philip S. Khoury, "The Tribal Shaykh, French Tribal Policy, and the Nationalist Movement in Syria between Two World Wars," *Middle Eastern Studies* 18, no. 2 (1982): 180–193. For the case of the Italians in Libya, see Anderson, *State and Social Transformation*.

53. The process described by Martin van Bruinessen ("The Kurds between Iran and Iraq," *MERIP, Middle East Report* 16, no. 4 [1986]: 26–27) concerning the role of Iran and Iraq in the 1980s in fortifying the main Kurdish political party in each other's territory, at the expense of smaller Kurdish political parties, is similar to the process by which foreign powers and state rulers in Iran fortified certain tribal polities and diminished or eliminated others.

54. In a move symbolic of these processes, Reza Shah changed the names of some rebellious tribal groups after their pacification. In Baluchistan the Yar Mohammadzai (Yarahmadzai) became the Shah Navazi (meaning "caressing the shah") and the Isma'ilzai became the Shah Bakhsh (meaning "pardoned by the shah").

55. Nikki Keddie, "Religion, Ethnic Minorities, and the State in Iran: An Overview," in Ali Banuazizi and Myron Weiner, eds., *The State, Religion, and Ethnic Politics: Afghanistan, Iran, and Pakistan* (Syracuse, 1986), p. 158.

56. Jane Bestor, who conducted research among Kurds in Baluchistan in 1976, notes that she sensed virtually no opposition to the shah in the region.

People in Sangan village perceived themselves as better off economically in the boom economy and used new income to enhance their position in their own rural areas. She remembers reading that Baluch tribesmen in Zahedan tried to prevent Shi'i urbanites from knocking down a statue of the shah in late 1978 (personal communication, 20 July 1989).

57. Van Bruinessen, "Kurds between Iran and Iraq," p. 20.

58. That the Kurds of Iran are predominantly Sunni has had little importance in their attitudes toward the Islamic Republic, according to van Bruinessen, "Kurds between Iran and Iraq," p. 19. Sunni-Shi'i differences were not the cause of the Kurds' opposition to the regime (p. 23). Yet for authorities of the Islamic Republic, and particularly for the Revolutionary Guards sent against Kurds, the fact that most Kurds were Sunni and not Shi'i did play a role in their readiness to defeat the Kurds militarily, subjugate them, and gain control of their territory.

59. For a brief discussion of activities among Turkmen in 1979–1982, see Haleh Afshar, "An Assessment of Agricultural Development Policies in Iran," in Haleh Afshar, ed., *Iran: A Revolution in Turmoil* (Albany, N.Y., 1985), pp. 75–76.

60. Van Bruinessen, "Kurds between Iran and Iraq," p. 26.

61. See the case of an Iranian village presented by an anonymous author, "Current Political Attitudes in an Iranian Village," *Iranian Studies* 16, nos. 1–2 (1983): 3–29. See also Loeffler, *Islam in Practice*, and Erika Friedl, *Women of Deh Koh: Lives in an Iranian Village* (Washington, D.C., 1989) for information about the impact of the Islamic regime on a tribal village in southwestern Iran.

62. Shahrough Akhavi, "State Formation and Consolidation in Twentieth-Century Iran: The Reza Shah Period and the Islamic Republic," in Ali Banuazizi and Myron Weiner, eds., *The State, Religion, and Ethnic Politics: Afghanistan, Iran, and Pakistan* (Syracuse, 1986), pp. 212, 221.

63. Akhavi, "State Formation," p. 212, also notes elitist tendencies in the Islamic Republic.

64. A few members of the former Bakhtiyari tribal elite were involved in the abortive coup in the summer of 1980. In 1982 the Kurdistan Democratic Party of Iran (KDPI), the major Kurdish political organization in Iran, joined the National Resistance Council (NRC) formed in 1981 in France by Abolhasan Bani Sadr and Mas'ud Rajavi of the People's Mojahedin. In 1984 the KDPI left the NRC over a dispute about negotiating with the Islamic Republic. Between 1979 and 1983, when Iranian military forces drove the KDPI across the border into Iraq, the KDPI functioned as a government in "liberated areas" in Kurdistan (van Bruinessen, "Kurds between Iran and Iraq," pp. 21–22).

65. Afshar, "Assessment of Agricultural Development Policies," p. 75.

66. Selig Harrison, *In Afghanistan's Shadow: Baluch Nationalism and Soviet Temptations* (New York, 1981).

67. Some short-term, limited alliances among leaders of tribal and ethnic groups have served the purpose of helping people leave Iran via unoffi-

cial channels and routes. Members of tribal and ethnic groups who felt the
need to exit Iran or were forced to do so sought out tribal and ethnic leaders,
particularly on the borders, for help in traveling secretly through territory
not under the regime's direct control and then across international borders.

68. In a review of *The Qashqa'i of Iran* Bahman Abdollahi (one of the two
Bolvardi/Abivardi members of the Tribal Alliance of Iran) notes that I erro-
neously identify the Turkish-speaking Abivardis of Shiraz as urban
Qashqa'i. He says, as did I in the book (pp. 185–186, 209), that they are actually "descended from a settled group that came to Fars from Abivard in
Khorasan in the eighteenth century to govern the province for Nader Shah"
(Bahman Abdollahi, Review of *The Qashqa'i of Iran, MERIP, Middle East Report* 17, no. 5 [1987]: p. 44). This history, whether factual or not, does not necessarily mean that Bolvardi did not become part of the Qashqa'i
confederacy. In fact, all Qashqa'i told similar kinds of histories and legends
about their origins. The issue of Bolvardi versus Qashqa'i identity appears
to be similar to that of Brahui versus Baluch identity. Under certain circumstances Brahui asserted an independent identity; under other circumstances they proclaimed their common Baluch identity.

69. Hooshang Amirahmadi, "Middle-Class Revolutions in the Third
World," in Hooshang Amirahmadi and Manoucher Parvin, eds., *Post-
Revolutionary Iran* (Boulder, Colo., 1988), p. 228.

70. For discussions of so-called jellyfish tribes, see Malcolm Yapp,
"Tribes and States in the Khyber, 1838–1842," in Richard Tapper, ed., *The
Conflict of Tribe and State in Iran and Afghanistan* (London, 1983), p. 186;
and Tapper, Introduction to *Conflict of Tribe and State.*

71. Tapper, "Introduction," p. 75.

72. Bakhtiyari tribespeople, according to David Brooks ("The Enemy
Within: Limitation on Leadership in the Bakhtiyari," in Richard Tapper, ed.,
The Conflict of Tribe and State in Iran and Afghanistan [London, 1983], p.
360), experienced the state and their own statelike leaders with ambivalence.
Under the French mandate in Syria, mediating tribal shaikhs often appeared to the tribespeople more like French agents than like their own leaders and defenders (Khoury, "Tribal Shaykh," p. 186). The government
appeared to Kababish tribespeople in the Sudan as deus ex machina, im-
pinging on their life only indirectly, impersonally, and arbitrarily, mainly
through the authority of tribal leaders, merchants, and rising prices (Asad,
"Political Inequality," p. 142). When government was able to intrude on the
position of tribal leaders, nothing any longer stood between tribespeople
and government to obscure the government's true character, which was less
powerful than it had once appeared to be (Asad, "Political Inequality," pp.
145–146). Some Iranian tribespeople, confronting the government directly
for the first time in the 1930s, became nostalgic for the days when that domain of activity was handled for them. For a detailed example of how one
group of tribal people regarded the state in which they lived, see Beck,
Borzu Beg: Year in the Life.

73. See Dresch's discussion in this volume.

74. John Perry, *Karim Khan Zand: A History of Iran, 1747–1779* (Chicago, 1979), is one notable exception. Confusion in the literature concerning the definition of tribal states relates to this problem. A person such as Karim Khan Zand, who was a tribal leader who went on to form a state, is no longer simply a tribal leader, nor is his state to be considered tribal.

75. Ernest Gellner, "Tribal Society and Its Enemies," in Richard Tapper, ed., *The Conflict of Tribe and State in Iran and Afghanistan* (London, 1983), p. 439.

Transforming Dualities:
Tribe and State Formation
in Saudi Arabia

Joseph Kostiner

The evolution of the Saudi state reflects an encounter between a traditional tribal society centered in Najd and the drastic changes in its environment. In coping with these changes, Saudi society underwent a process of state formation in governmental, territorial, and societal spheres.

In the early years of the twentieth century Saudi society was divided into large tribal groups that maintained a corporate life and inhabited different regions in the central and northern Arabian Peninsula. The majority of the population in the Saudi core areas—Najd, al-Qasim, and al-Ahsa'—was nomadic. The tribes were organized under a chieftaincy, which was the common Saudi political organization during the first (1744–1822) and second (1823–1891) Saudi states and was reestablished by 'Abd al-'Aziz Al Sa'ud (Ibn Sa'ud) in 1902. Built on power sharing among tribes, town dwellers, and an urban-based ruler, the Saudi chieftaincy maintained both the autonomy of its different segments and a cooperating coalition based on personal, ad hoc arrangements among their leaders and between them and the ruler.

Two tribal functions that had developed in the Saudi chieftaincy were particularly relevant to state formation. Tribes were important as military power; they were the main force that escorted trade convoys, and they formed the bulk of forces that fought the enemies of the Saudi chieftaincy and expanded its territories. They were therefore regarded as the executors of the religious Wahhabi cause and had a strong influence on the foreign relations of the Saudi chieftaincy. But the Saudi power structure remained dominated by the *umara'* (lay rulers) of the Sa'ud family and the *'ulama'* (those trained in the religious sciences), who had traditionally ruled the chieftaincy as political and spiritual leaders. Despite their assigned roles, the tribes and their chieftains were not incorporated into the Saudi power structure and held no administrative positions. Tribes were also important as a source of the Saudi values system, which stemmed from the tribal segmentary organization that dominated the chieftaincy. Political decentralization, minimal administration, kin-related political behavior, social solidarity and economic cooperation, and territoriality based on tribal grazing zones were values shared by both nomadic and sedentarized populations, whose loyalties and settling patterns were cut by segmentary lines. These values affected state formation in its different stages.

The Wahhabi unitarian creed provided the ideology of the chieftaincy. Wahhabi principles functioned as a supreme norm, a raison d'être for the chieftaincy, and a unifying creed against an external enemy rather than a temporal political doctrine, and they did not interfere with the regime of the chieftaincy.[1] The changing functions of both tribal power and values are therefore keys to understanding Saudi state formation.

The Saudi chieftaincy underwent two dialectical phases of state formation, each composed of a drastic period of change followed by a period of adjustment and adaptation to these changes. One period of drastic change began in the late 1910s and continued into the 1920s. It featured territorial expansion and incorporation of new populations, which led to centralization of the regime and to territorial delineation in the next decades. Another period of drastic change, in the late 1960s and the 1970s, was notable mostly for an infrastructural buildup and the improvement and entrenchment of the administration in society. The 1980s have again been characterized by adaptation to these changes. Saudi state formation thus evolved around periods of change and adjustment.

THE TURNING POINT IN STATE FORMATION

Many scholars date the beginning of state formation in modern Saudi Arabia from Ibn Sa'ud's birth in 1881 or his occupation of Rashidi-held Riyadh in early 1902.[2] These assessments seem inadequate; in the 1880s an internal war in the second Saudi state between rival tribal factions precipitated its downfall, and it was occupied by the Rashidis in 1891.[3] Even the occupation of Riyadh and the growth of the Saudi state in the next years did not mark a departure from the chieftaincy patterns. During those years Ibn Sa'ud apparently developed a growing sophistication in his handling of foreign relations, notably by reaching a rapprochement with the British in the region, an act that in itself attested to his prospects for the future.[4] However, the Saudi state that emerged was a renewed version of a traditional chieftaincy. This change is evident from the tentative and fragile cooperation among its tribal groups and the personalized, noninstitutionalized rule that Ibn Sa'ud exercised.[5]

The process of state formation in this case denotes a departure from that chieftaincy phase and the assumption of more state attributes. Growth in the horse, camel, and transit trade of the al-Ahsa' and al-Qasim regions (along the Gulf littoral and the south of Jabal Shammar, respectively) enabled the local population to seek improved government (1906–1909) and Ibn Sa'ud to expand into al-Ahsa' (1913).[6] State formation, however, evolved more explicitly in response to strategic and economic changes that occurred during World War I.

Ottoman and particularly British influences affected the region decisively. Their war efforts were manifested in alliances with local chieftains—the Ottomans with Ibn Rashid and the British with Kuwait's ruler, Mubarak, and with Ibn Sa'ud, Sharif Husayn of the Hijaz, and al-Idrisi of 'Asir. These alliances led to an influx of economic assistance from the Great Powers to their local allies; the formation of the Hashimite-led but British-financed Arab revolt (during its first year the British contributed about £125,000 a month, in gold) was the main evidence of this effort. In addition, the British intervened more directly in imposing blockades of Red Sea ports and of Kuwait in the Persian Gulf; their aim was to prevent supplies from reaching Ottoman forces in the Hijaz and Mesopotamia.[7] The Red Sea blockade and the Rashidi cooperation with the Ottomans virtually shut down the traditional overland caravan route from Najd to Syria via Jabal Shammar. But at the same time new trade centers arose, and new caravan routes, such as the smuggling route from Kuwait to Ha'il at Jabal Shammar, were established.

The new situation posed unprecedented challenges to the Saudi chieftaincy. Its rudimentary structure was inept in coping with them and hence prone to change. Under the new conditions tribal groups increased their autonomy from the Saudi chieftaincy and sought to align with new economic beneficiaries and dwell near new trade routes. The Hashimites, leaders of the Arab revolt, were a main attraction for tribes. Moreover, rivalry for control of new commercial centers grew among rulers of chieftaincies. The diversification of Ottoman policies and those of various British agencies also encouraged chieftains to compete with one another. In fact, British officials of the Arab Bureau in Cairo and of the India Office in the Persian Gulf, Mesopotamia, and Aden all supported different local Arabian rulers. Thus, the Hashimite-led Arab revolt alienated the leaders of Kuwait, 'Asir, and Najd, who cemented their rivalry with the Hijaz. The Saudis had to cope with intensified rivalries in different arenas. Above all, there was the challenge of adaptation to new rules in the future strategic and economic game: postwar British dominance in the Arabian Peninsula, intensified integration of the region into European global strategies, the evolution of a market economy, and the breakdown of the limited, common superstructure hitherto provided by the Ottoman Empire.[8]

The new challenges to the Saudi chieftaincy also set in motion the avenues of its change. To surmount the aforementioned difficulties the Saudi chieftaincy engaged in two processes: territorial expansion to conquer new commercial and strategic areas and overpower other chieftaincies militarily; and internal consolidation to avoid the traditional unreliability of tribes, allow for integration of new conquered territories, and prepare for the postwar era. The interaction of these processes was sometimes harmonious but more often contradictory and asymmetrical. It produced a convoluted process of state formation.

EXPANSION AND CONSOLIDATION

Saudi state formation resembled empire building in the early Islamic period. Saudi society functioned, in the words of Ira Lapidus elsewhere in this volume, as a conquest movement, namely, a chieftaincy engaged in territorial expansion. The rudiments of the chieftaincy were not abolished, and its segments were intact, but they were channeled into a unifying movement for conquest. In fact, under these circumstances tribal power and the tribal value system were unprecedentedly salient in the Saudi state.

Tribes shaped the dynamics of expansion. First, tribal skirmishes were catalysts of Saudi occupation campaigns and pulled Saudi leaders into the fighting arenas. Tribal skirmishes between segments of the Saudi-controlled 'Utayba and Subay' tribes and the Hashimites in the vicinity of Khurma, or between the Saudi-controlled Mutayr tribe and the Rashidi-led Shammar, who were allied with the gulf-based 'Ujman tribe, generated the initial Saudi struggle against the Kuwaiti, Rashidi, and Hijazi chieftaincies in 1918–1919. These skirmishes, in turn, encouraged gradual intervention by the Saudi government. In 1920 a change took place. Following the discovery of an incipient anti-Saudi alliance, led by the Hashimites and the Rashidis, Ibn Sa'ud embarked on an orderly strategy of war and occupation;

his forces occupied the Rashidi chieftaincy (November 1921), northern 'Asir (between 1920 and 1923), and the Hijaz (in 1924 and 1925).

But even in the more orderly campaigns localized tribal engagements often determined the timing of fighting and the Saudi strategy. The Mutayr's engagement with Kuwaiti forces at Jahra in 1920 prompted Ibn Sa'ud's decisive intervention on that front. The rebellions of the al-'Aid clan in 'Asir caused recurrent Saudi punitive campaigns there. The massacre by the Mutayr in the Hijazi town of Ta'if in July 1924 led Ibn Sa'ud to adopt a strategy of slow conquest in the Hijaz, which involved long sieges of local towns.

Owing to tribal activities, the Saudis turned conquered provinces into arenas of conflict. Saudi tribes often engaged in raids against the local population and sometimes the neighboring territories of Iraq and Transjordan. The regions of northern Hijaz, al-Jawf (north of Jabal Shammar), and northern Najd, bordering Iraq and Kuwait, were arenas of continuous tribal conflict for several years. In this respect tribal involvement rendered the new arenas unruly and turbulent under formal Saudi rule.[9]

Tribal values were also noticeable in the initial process of consolidation. Thus, one of the means that Ibn Sa'ud and other members of the Saudi family employed was intermarriage with different nomadic and urban families. H. St. John Philby, the British emissary who was sent to Ibn Sa'ud in late 1917 and later became his adviser, noticed that Ibn Sa'ud fully exploited the Wahhabi right to marry four women. By divorcing and remarrying frequently, he and his relatives were able to bind many tribes to the Saudi family.[10] Another device was the successful and positive image Ibn Sa'ud projected for himself and for his chieftaincy. It was based on the successes of pro-Saudi forces in some initial clashes with Sharif Husayn's forces, on Ibn Sa'ud's liberal allowances of booty, and, before 1920, on low taxation. Ibn Sa'ud's image compared favorably with Sharif Husayn's arbitrary attitude toward tribes in the region after the revolt, and this brought the Saudi chieftaincy many supporters among these tribes. In binding tribal groups through blood ties and booty, tribal structures and practices were not altered.

A more earnest attempt at consolidation was the formation of the Ikhwan. Since 1912, but particularly since 1916, tribal groups were settled in predesignated sites, or *hujar*. The groups were supposed to fulfill some specific aims to advance consolidation: the unruly 'Utayba, Harb, Mutayr, Qahtan, and other tribes were expected to sell their camels and sheep, abandon their traditional nomadic habits, which in the past had been conducive to raids and defections, and become sedentary. By adopting agriculture and joining a religious revivalist movement, these tribes were also supposed to develop a new sense of cohesion and loyalty typical of a community of believers and to proselytize other tribal groups in the revivalist Wahhabi creed in order to extend pro-Saudi support. In addition, Ibn Sa'ud sought to benefit from their military skills by turning them into a standing army, known as the Ikhwan, in service to the state.[11] Although some Western observers depicted this venture as Ibn Sa'ud's "orchestrated attack on human nature,"[12] the real nature of the Ikhwan was more complex and exemplifies the wide spectrum of tribal values and the significance of tribal power in the Saudi conquest movement.

The Ikhwan possessed three main qualities: traditional military prowess, religious fervor, and detachment from restraining official positions. They had a key role in Saudi expansion and consolidation, featuring prominently as one of the three Saudi columns that defeated the Rashidis. The Ikhwan were part of the forces of Faysal, Ibn Sa'ud's son, in 'Asir and of the main Saudi force that occupied Ta'if and Mecca in the Hijaz. Moreover, as pioneers, zealous proselytizers, and promoters of sedentarization, the Ikhwan were also the center of Saudi nonmilitary expansion.

But a superstructure of sedentarization, religious revivalism, and army duties imposed on a tribal infrastructure inevitably generated certain unpredictable results. Thus, the evolution of the Ikhwan movement was neither controlled, uniform, or complete. The salient groups of the movement, belonging to the Mutayr, Qahtan, 'Utayba, and 'Ujman tribes, did not become fully sedentarized but rather maintained their tribal structure and their nomadic raiding habits. They combined tribal *'asabiyya* and unruliness with revivalist zeal. The easily adaptable traits of revivalism, such as external changes in life-style and dress, along with its violent zeal, rendered the Ikhwan both appealing and forceful. The movement spread beyond Ibn Sa'ud's reach to the gulf shores, the Rub' al-Khali desert, and the southern regions of Transjordan and Iraq.[13] This uncontrolled expansion generated raids unauthorized by Ibn Sa'ud and conflicts with neighboring states and populations of the new territories. Furthermore, consolidation of the new provincial populations was carried out through forced proselytism, which prevented solidification of the new provinces in the Saudi state. The Ikhwan's activities also generated an interelite struggle in the Saudi hierarchy. Because they had no traditional position in the Saudi power structure but depended instead on the prestige of their ideological goals, Ikhwan leaders grew as a "wild" pressure group, unrestricted by the limitations that bound established groups, such as the *'ulama'* and members of the Saudi family. The Ikhwan tried to make Ibn Sa'ud enforce policies of Wahhabi revivalism, notably in education, throughout the realm.[14] The Ikhwan's relations with Saudi *'ulama'* and urban elements became strained; Ibn Sa'ud had to replace their religious instructors in the *hujar*, and in 1919 he asked the senior Najdi *'ulama'* to issue a *fatwa* (legal opinion) that "Ikhwanist" Islam was not superior to ordinary Wahhabi practice. Ikhwan power was thereby weakened in the capital.[15]

The process of expansion generated new challenges for the Saudi chieftaincy. Some newly conquered populations were disloyal to the Saudis: the Shammar in the North were infiltrating into Iraq, and the Hijazis had difficulty adapting to the Saudi regime, with its revivalist religious creed and nomadic, austere political culture, which was quite different from the urban, rather mercantile life-style of the Hijaz. There were clashes with neighboring states: raids by the Ikhwan and counterraids against them by Transjordanian, Iraqi, and Yemeni tribes entangled Ibn Sa'ud in disputes with the Yemeni imam and the Hashimite rulers of Transjordan and Iraq. Moreover, the Saudis faced the problem of regulating their relations with British and other European powers. The British loomed behind Hashimite rule in Transjordan and Iraq. The Muslim subjects of Great Britain and other European states were pilgrims of the Saudi-administered hajj. In addition, the struggle between new and more traditional elements within the elite required the establishment of a stable government.

The control of new territories, although costly to the Saudis, also offered new economic opportunities. The British subsidy to Najd, which began modestly during 1917 with the sum of £5,000 per annum, reached tens of thousands of pounds sterling in the early 1920s but stopped in mid-1924 owing to British frustration with the collapse of the Kuwait Conference (designed to achieve a comprehensive frontier settlement in the region) and the need to cut inflated war expenses.[16] The decline and ultimate loss of this subsidy forced the Saudi leader to seek new sources of revenue. By contrast, the Saudi claim on the lion's share of Kuwaiti customs taxes levied on Najdi tribes trading in Kuwait's port enabled Ibn Sa'ud to establish and regulate new trade routes for his tribes; it also whetted his appetite for income extracted through customs. The ventures of American businessmen such as Charles Crane and Frank Holmes, who began searching for minerals in the gulf area in 1922, further stimulated Ibn Sa'ud's interest in developing his state's economy, which by the mid-1920s benefited from hajj revenues of nearly £100,000 per annum.

To cope with the challenges and opportunities of occupation, Saudi authorities strengthened the state attributes of their chieftaincy. For the first time a process of major centralization was undertaken that gave the Saudi entity one clear characteristic of a state, namely, the superiority of the central government over other groups and institutions in society.[17] Ibn Sa'ud's own position in society had grown since 1917. He was the only person to carry out the essentials of foreign policy vis-à-vis Britain, and soon he acquired the image of a trustworthy interlocutor with the British in his own society. Moreover, during expansion Ibn Sa'ud was regarded as both the leader of the Ikhwan and the defender of the traditional elites, such as the *'ulama'* and merchants, and of the newly occupied populations against the Ikhwan's wrath. As trusted mediator among all societal groups and as the architect of foreign policy, Ibn Sa'ud ceased being merely *primus inter pares*, as he and his ancestors had been in the former chieftaincies. He was crowned king of the Hijaz in 1926 and of Najd in 1927.

To infuse his leadership position with substance, Ibn Sa'ud created an administration. In contrast to Western experiences, which drew on mobile urban classes and class struggle as stimulants to centralized government, Saudi state bureaucracy resulted from the expedient practical calculations of the local leader. Ibn Sa'ud sought to tackle both the challenges in the new territories and the Ikhwan's unruliness. Several government offices were established after the occupation of the Hijaz. In 1931 they were incorporated into a council of delegates (*majlis al-wukala'*), which was united as a collective body before Ibn Sa'ud's death in October 1953 and reconstituted as a council of ministers (*majlis al-wuzara'*) in 1954 by his successor, King Sa'ud. Ibn Sa'ud also established a standing army for the Hijaz in the 1920s and recruited several Syrian and Egyptian advisers to provide expert opinion so that he could formulate policy unhindered by local interests. A consultative assembly (*majlis al-shura*) was founded in 1925, composed of Hijazi notables. Ibn Sa'ud's son, Faysal, chaired both the council of delegates and the consultative assembly.[18]

Increased centralization was directly connected to the expansion of government authority over the provinces. A new network of town governors, composed of Sa'ud family members, was installed in 1920–1921 and grew steadily. Less than a year after the occupation of the Hijaz, the Wahhabi code was made the law of the land throughout the country. Royal marriages bound notable families of the occupied areas to the Saudi center. A telegraph system and an initial network of roads, for the use of government cars, were built in the late 1920s. The government imposed higher taxes on Najdi tribes and forced them to trade only in the new ports of Jubayl and Hufhuf in the gulf, where high customs were exacted. Hence a combination of family rule, imposed religious norms, centralized economy, and technology were aimed at subduing the provinces.[19]

As government met new challenges, a new concept of territoriality developed. It evolved around the British-initiated frontier lines, which replaced the prevalent local concept of undemarcated frontiers set according to tribal grazing zones. The British introduced frontier lines following the occupation of the Rashidi territories, which brought the Saudis into contact with British-dominated Transjordan and Iraq in the north. They sought to secure tranquility among the pro-British rulers in the region. In the treaties of Muhamara (May 1922) and 'Uqayr (December 1922) Ibn Sa'ud had to forego his concept of flexible, undemarcated frontiers based on tribal grazing zones and adopt the European concept of a border line. During the Hada' and Bahra conferences in the fall of 1925 the agreements delimiting the frontiers of the Saudi state with Iraq and Transjordan were signed.[20] A vivid description of the collision between the imposed frontier line and the tribal frontier was given by a British spectator who witnessed the 'Uqayr conference. The British high commissioner for Iraq, Sir Percy Cox, called Ibn Sa'ud's "tribal-boundary idea" childish. Against the backdrop of the Najdi ruler's sobbing, Cox took a pencil and "carefully drew a boundary line."[21]

Following the Saudi occupation of Mecca in December 1924, Ibn Sa'ud had to abandon the erstwhile Saudi drive to conquer and expand, adopting instead the idea of regional peace with his neighbors. He also resorted to growing international cooperation to convince the British and Dutch governments, as well as other Arab and Muslim governments, that his country was safe for pilgrimage. In the 1930s Saudi Arabia signed treaties to demarcate boundaries and institutionalize neighborly relations with most of the surrounding states that recognized it. A new territoriality based on coexistence with other states within defined borders replaced the former expanding and fluid Saudi territorial concept. By relying on regional tranquility and a strong government, Ibn Sa'ud and his aides apparently aimed at turning the Saudi state into a center of pilgrimage and trade facilitated by a Hijazi urban elite.[22]

These changes created a complex interaction of state formation with tribal power and values. The new polity was antithetical to tribal power inasmuch as it tipped the former balance between tribes and central government in the latter's favor and introduced new internal structures and foreign policies that altered the character of the chieftaincy in which they had thrived. Tribal groups, notably the Ikhwan, assumed the role of advocates of the old polity amid the evolution of a new one.

Consequently, even before the occupation of the Hijaz there were reports that Ibn Sa'ud had tried to restrict Najdi tribes from going to markets in Kuwait and instead had directed them to the ports of al-Ahsa', which he was trying to develop. He also increased the already burdensome taxes imposed on his tribes.[23] Other reports indicated that Ibn Sa'ud's demand (as manifested during the Kuwait Conference) for a territorial corridor between Iraq and Transjordan was aimed not only at separating those two hostile Hashimite states but also at gaining a territorial advantage to the north of his turbulent tribes; this move would make it possible for him to engulf or at least control their grazing zones and hold them in check.[24]

The major Najdi tribes that formed the core of the Saudi tribal chieftaincy were opposed to the new polity because it precluded tribes from assuming positions in the state apparatus or from ruling the new territories. Thus, the leaders of the Ikhwan, Faysal al-Dawish of the Mutayr and Sultan Ibn Humayd of the 'Utayba, were not allotted governorships in the new administration following the occupation of the Hijaz despite their role in its occupation. Moreover, the centralization policies were a direct threat to tribal autonomy. Because of improved communications, transportation, and government machinery, tribes felt that their position as lords of the Najdi terrains and controllers of caravan routes would be curbed. Increased taxation, newly imposed trading centers, and the prohibition of raiding into other states seemed to be a direct attempt by the government to subjugate them economically. Ibn Sa'ud's growing contacts with the British, Hijazi notables, and foreign advisers were symbolic evidence that their ruler, once a follower of a tribal-state code and Wahhabi austerity, had separated himself from the old ways and become an adherent of alien practices.[25]

The opposition of the Ikhwan to Ibn Sa'ud during these years, therefore, should not be construed as having been motivated only by religious fanaticism, as many have suggested. Rather, the Ikhwan gave voice to the desire of Najdi tribes to maintain the Saudi state as a chieftaincy, in which internal tribal autonomy, freedom to raid, and rights to trade would be preserved. An Ikhwan commander, Faysal Ibn Shiblayn, expressed this motive clearly when he said in an interview with a British official that Ibn Sa'ud sought to curb "tribal autonomy to an extent unheard of."[26] Thus, the Saudi state developed two contradictory and competing systems: the centralizing Saudi government and the Ikhwan tribal version. Between 1927 and 1929 the Ikhwan challenged Ibn Sa'ud openly over the new principles of the Saudi state and competed for the support of the Najdi population; in a series of clashes in 1929–1930 he succeeded in defeating them.

Tribal rebellions continued on a smaller scale and against a different background in the 1930s. Agitated by the Hijazi Liberation Party
(Hizb al-tahrir al-hijazi), which sought to topple Saudi rule in the Hijaz, the Billi tribe revolted in the northern Hijaz in 1932, and 'Asiri
tribal groups followed suit in 1933. But the rebels were also motivated
by the heavy hand of Saudi centralization—high taxation, arbitrary
regional governors, and lack of governmental consideration—against
which they revolted. The government defeated the rebels easily, although the 'Asir revolt led to a Saudi war with Yemen in 1934, which
the Saudis also won.[27]

The emphasis on centralization, economic development, and regional peace did not produce a new, deeply penetrating value system.
The Saudi regime was in fact a patrimonial polity.[28] A strong personal rule emerged, governed by family ties and a personally picked
administration, whose functions were neither socially penetrating nor
institutionalized. The traditional, tribal fabrics of society remained
unchanged. The exercise of such a polity in itself emulated the classical pattern of Islamic empire building. The change in supreme authority, religious law, and economy epitomized the new polity and
left society unchanged. Sharif Husayn's polity after the Arab revolt
followed similar lines;[29] indeed, it probably served as a model for Ibn
Sa'ud, who encountered it after his occupation of the Hijaz. Ibn
Sa'ud and his aides were not prepared for more-substantial societal
changes. Continuous struggles against internal and foreign rivals occupied most of their attention and left little energy for such changes.

A continuous economic crisis had similar effects. Whereas the
state's revenues had increased from about £100,000 annually to £4–5
million after the occupation of the Hijaz—thanks to dues imposed
on pilgrims and on Hijazi profiting traders[30]—the world economic
crisis of the early 1930s dealt a severe blow to the Saudi economy.
The average annual number of pilgrims dropped from one hundred
thousand to between thirty thousand and forty thousand, generating
a parallel drop of 60–70 percent in Saudi income. The government
was also heavily in debt to foreign companies that had built some of
the new Saudi infrastructure. In contrast to conventional wisdom,
the striking of oil in commercial quantities in al-Ahsa' in 1938
marked no immediate substantial recovery of the Saudi economy.
During and after the war years low oil production (164,000 barrels a
day in 1946) generated minimal profits, leaving Ibn Sa'ud yearning
for American financial assistance. During the following years production grew fivefold, and the government's share of the contract
with the Arabian American Oil Company (ARAMCO) increased, such
that Saudi profits reached $56.7 million in 1950 and $110 million in

1951. Nevertheless, owing to inefficient state management (see below), ARAMCO still had to assist the government in securing arms and in building a railroad in 1946 to link the interior with the Red Sea.[31] As late as 1958, when Faysal undertook to reform the Saudi economy, the government was heavily in debt to New York banks ($92 million) and to other foreign lenders ($40 million). In addition, there existed an internal debt of 120 million Saudi riyals.[32]

In contrast to the limits of tribal power, tribal values prevailed in Ibn Sa'ud's polity; they suited the patrimonial regime, which left the old social structure intact. A dualism thus prevailed in Saudi state building. But whereas in the 1920s centralization and tribalism were alternative contending value systems, the next three and a half decades were dominated by centralizing and development policies that still encapsulated a simmering tribal infrastructure.

Encapsulation was articulated in several spheres of state formation. In governmental decision making, informal tribal practices loomed behind the bureaucratic procedures and institutions. There were several quasi-ministerial offices, a partially elected consultative council of notables in the Hijaz, and a system of regional governors. Yet reports indicate that real authority was vested in patrimonial, chieftaincylike institutions arising from the ruler's own authority, which was sparingly vested in what Philby called a privy council of several close advisers. The functions of this advisory council, which consisted mainly of Hijazi notables, were practically suspended in the 1930s. The ministers too had no collective responsibility, nor did they act collectively as a cabinet. Their personal responsibility to the king was paralleled by his personal selection of the members of the privy council, which included several of Ibn Sa'ud's sons, advisers, governors (notably the Syrian advisers Yusuf Yasin and Fuad Hamza, Philby, princes Faysal and Sa'ud, and Minister of Finance 'Abdullah Sulayman), and others.[33] This body was informally tied together and was based on chieftaincy codes. The religious practice of having a weekly audience with 'ulama', which was typical of the Saudi chieftaincy, complemented this arrangement.[34] Decisions were made haphazardly, mostly in response to Ibn Sa'ud's personal wishes.

The Council of Ministers of 1954 was to meet once a month and make decisions by a simple majority vote; no provision was made for the premiership of the council. This partial attempt to vest wider authority in a central governmental institution was intended as a substitute for the earlier patrimonial code. Sa'ud activated the council and became its premier, although he ignored or opposed its advice. It became a bastion for Sa'ud's opponents, notably his brother Faysal.[35]

Lacking institutionalization, Saudi state building hinged largely on the leadership of the king and suffered from the weaknesses of both Ibn Saʻud (until 1953) and Saʻud (until 1964). His charisma notwithstanding, Ibn Saʻud seems to have been struck by war-weariness following the Ikhwan's defeat or by temporary depression over the strain of fighting these former comrades, resulting in growing apathy toward state affairs. His spirit seemed to have recovered in the mid-1930s, but he did not resume full control over state affairs in the following decades. His last decade in power was overshadowed by illness and declining physical ability. Without his rigor and drive his aides did not indulge in as vigorous a state-building effort as might have been expected. His son Saʻud's conduct was marked by lavishness, hasty economic decisions, and oscillation between pro-Nasserist and pro-American foreign policies, which attested to unstable and ill-considered leadership.

The compromising dualism was most noticeable in economic administration, where the government's main concern focused on development. A budget that only included government expenditure was introduced in 1933. The search for natural resources (oil, water, and gold) was the government's main priority. Owing to the economic crisis of the 1930s and a lack of royal leadership in the next decades, however, there was no real differentiation between public and private purses. ʻAbdullah Sulayman acted more like a personal agent of the ruling family in a chieftaincy than like a state minister. He spent his time satisfying royal desires by borrowing first from one source, then from another to pay back the first. He also failed to prevent the smuggling out of the country of millions of Saudi silver riyals. The establishment of the Saudi Arabian Monetary Agency in 1932 was intended to standardize the Saudi currency and formulate a balanced budget. But Saʻud's lavish expenditure on palaces and luxury goods, and a failed business deal with Aristotle Onassis concerning the purchase of an oil fleet for Saudi Arabia, reflected a degree of continuity in chieftaincy practices.[36]

Encapsulation was also evident in the sphere of regional integration. Even though Ibn Saʻud proclaimed the foundation of the unified Saudi Arabian Kingdom (al-mamlaka al-ʻarabiyya al-Saʻudiyya) in August 1932, declared Saʻud as heir to the throne, and maintained the binding norms of Wahhabi law, the practices of social integration in the kingdom still resembled those of a chieftaincy. Differences among regions prevailed. The Hijaz provided the highest portion of taxes and constituted the new nerve center, where Ibn Saʻud's foreign advisers, Western businessmen in search of mineral resources, and wealthy local traders planned the economic future of the kingdom in the hope that their ideas would reach the members of the privy council. In contrast to the Hijaz's position, the people of Najd, the former hub of the state, felt relegated to an inferior position in the kingdom. The service of Najdi tribes in the state's military was a more effective means of integration, although it also caused frustration for Najdis whose desires for greater remuneration went unfulfilled (see below). The 'Asiris did not assume any leading positions, and only wealthy traders of al-Ahsa' and al-Qasim, such as the al-Qusaybi family or 'Abdullah Sulayman, were in positions equal to those of major Hijazi traders. In the 1930s British reports stressed the separation and particularism of these populations, characteristics fostered by economic crisis.[37]

In the 1940s new Hijazi separatist organizations (notably, in 1946, the Association of Hijazi Defense) emerged several times, and Shammar tribal shaykhs exiled in Iraq complained of Saudi discrimination exercised against their tribe in Saudi Arabia.[38] Thus, the level of integration did not exceed the most basic compliance with the system, and Saudi society remained separated along regional tribal lines.

Encapsulation also prevailed in regional administration, which was monopolized by branches of the Saudi family and its hand-picked aides and mainly sought to raise taxes and keep local tribal groups under control. To achieve these aims, the administration continued using chieftaincy tactics that focused on keeping tribes passive and loyal rather than channeling tribal power into new state-based organizations. Ibn Sa'ud (and Sa'ud after him) maintained the system of buying off tribes with subsidies. This system kept the tribes from intervening in state affairs yet ensured that they were sufficiently content and passive to be regarded as loyal. In addition, the official policy of taxation (*zakat*, denoting the religious term for alms) remained a means to maintain the obedience of peripheral tribes as late as 1954. Regional governors sent tax collectors among the tribes in specified seasons; there they collected a tax, paid in kind and collectively, according to the principles of religious law (*shari'a*).[39]

The only exception to these practices concerned the major Najdi tribes; these were occasionally called to perform their traditional military duty—for example, in suppressing revolts and in fighting the Saudi-Yemeni war in 1933–1934. The introduction of the White Army (or national guard), which was manned by sixteen thousand activists and thirty-two thousand reservists, and the smaller Royal Guard units, composed of untapped members of the major Najdi tribes, were designed to curb other forms of unrest.[40]

THE EFFECTS OF RAPID SOCIAL CHANGE

Another period of drastic change occurred in the late 1960s and 1970s during the reign of King Faysal. Like the changes of the 1920s, those of the 1960s came in response to new strategic and economic conditions in the regional and domestic arenas that challenged the existence of the Saudi state and prompted a restructuring of its polity. These changes, in turn, enabled Saudi Arabia to assume more state characteristics in various spheres and create a new mode of tribe-state interaction.

The encapsulated state that Saudi Arabia had become under King Sa'ud proved inept at meeting the new conditions within and around the kingdom. The arbitrary and unplanned process of decision making failed to cope with subversive activities generated by radical Arab nationalism and the impact of the Soviet-American rivalry in the Middle East. The failure of the government to stem radical tendencies was evident in the strikes at the depots of ARAMCO in 1953 and 1956. Sa'ud proved to be nebulous and vacillating in regard to regional affairs. During a visit to Washington in late 1957 he unexpectedly abandoned the friendly attitude he had shown toward Egypt's president Nasser, the leader of Arab radicalism, and adopted the Eisenhower Doctrine, thereby making him leader of the pro-Western, antiradical camp in the region. In 1958 he was even accused of instigating an attempt on Nasser's life. At the same time Sa'ud's arbitrary allocations of subventions to tribal chiefs (in order to still internal opposition), his fruitless involvement in the purchase of an oil fleet from Onassis, and the countless sums he invested in the building of desert castles all attested to an arbitrary, thoughtless manner of making decisions in domestic affairs as well.

Opposition among oil workers, uncertainty over the loyalty of tribes, and struggles among leading princes over how to deal with these issues pointed not only to weaknesses of decision making but also to anomalies in sociopolitical integration. The basic compliance among Saudi groups that had characterized the state of encapsulation was insufficient in establishing stability and cooperation in the 1950s. Moreover, despite increasing income from oil, a deficit in the state budget remained, illiteracy and health problems proliferated, and new public construction hardly met demand. The patrimonial, minimalistic administration was obviously insufficient.

Faysal (r. 1964–1975) sought to introduce change in two main respects. First, he focused on bureaucratization and institution building. Drawing on advice provided by a United Nations expert in 1960, by a Ford Foundation team in 1963, and by a team of specialists in

1964, and utilizing mounting oil revenues ($1 billion in 1970, $80 billion in 1980),[41] public administration was enlarged, modernized, and improved.[42] Second, Faysal sought to introduce technical modernization. In the words of 'Abd al-'Aziz al-Qusaybi, a former minister and a driving force of reform, "Adopting of some aspects of Western civilization is unavoidable if we wish to be delivered from our present backwardness. These include technology, the physical and social sciences, management procedures and the principles of scientific planning."[43] An infrastructure of modern systems of communication, transportation, health, and education was established to link the regions of the kingdom together and raise the living standard of its population.

Faysal and his aides did not, however, seek major sociocultural change. They were determined to maintain and even foster the role of Islam in society and did not envisage a new stratification, resettlement, and interregional immigration. A "social renaissance," in Faysal's view, meant the establishment of new educational institutions.[44] He adopted a bureaucratic outlook, attributing to the state a "causal role" in society,[45] namely, to activate and mold changes through the functions of an expanding administration. In Weberian terms Faysal sought to routinize the Saudi patrimonial polity.

The practice of informal decision making by members of the privy council endured, but they addressed only general policies. Government offices, which supervised an expanding bureaucracy, executed policies. The top advisers included Faysal's personal confidants, Rashad Far'un, Kamal Adham, and 'Umar Saqqaf; Ibn Sa'ud's brothers; top technocrats such as Zaki al-Yamani and 'Abd al-'Aziz al-Qusaybi (who also became ministers); the senior religious official, 'Abd al-'Aziz Ibn Baz; and other high-ranking 'ulama'. Faysal established a ministerial council of fifteen members, which grew to twenty-five members under his successors. The king and the crown prince presided over the council, making certain that administrative portfolios for planning, industry, electricity, and municipal and rural affairs were geared to development. As these offices were given to technocrats selected according to ability rather than mere trustworthiness, comparatively thoughtful policy-making was assured.

The establishment, in 1968, of a Central Planning Authority to facilitate orderly investment and construction marked the geographic expansion of governmental authority into new spheres of public activity. Although the appointment and function of provincial governors were still directly decided by the king (who picked them from the royal family and top technocrats), the four hundred thousand civil servants of the central government provided for a more standardized attitude toward the provinces. In terms of centralization Saudi Arabia achieved a high degree of state sovereignty. A welfare system, including standardized working hours, health services, and minimum wage laws, was applied in all quarters. The government extended its authority over institutions, which had hitherto been autonomous. A judicial system supervised by a ministry was founded in 1970; it included a twenty-member council, which incorporated both the *shari'a* and Western principles of law.[46] Manpower training gained first priority. Hundreds of thousands of pupils, including women, began to attend schools; tens of thousands of students attended universities in the kingdom or went to study in the West. Health centers and hospitals were established at every main settlement. Administrative reforms were accompanied by a growing number of economic activities. Apart from the oil industries, the government also encouraged the development of, and invested in, petrochemical plants. In turn, these industries, along with the buildup of infrastructural projects, produced growth in business enterprises such as hotels, insurance, airlines, catering, and construction.

Another sphere of reform concerned integration of the population. Following Faysal's initiative, the main cities of the kingdom, from the Red Sea to the Persian Gulf, were linked by air. State administration itself became the focus of integration, increasing the people's dependency on job training, health services, and welfare. In the physical and technical senses the population became more integrated.

Regional solidarity, which had in the past been the locus of traditional tribal identity, definitely eased. Tribes became less self-contained, more dependent on other populations in other regions, more closely linked by new communications, and more receptive to cooperative ideas. There was no new rise in empowered regional-tribal identities, and regional-particularist identities weakened.[47]

Unlike the changes of the 1920s, those of the later period did not concern just the political arena and power structure but the economic and social fabrics of society as well. By the mid-1970s government activities had spread throughout the realm and dominated all spheres of public life. There was a shift from economic subsistence to affluence, and many now enjoyed comfort, if not luxury. In the 1980s only about 35 percent of Saudi society was still living at subsistence level. A process of rapid urbanization evolved as the population moved from the rural agricultural and nomadic areas to cities, which became the centers of business, industry, and therefore affluence. The population of towns in the kingdom's central corridor grew by several hundred percent (for example, in Jidda, from sixty thousand in the 1950s to more than one million in the 1980s).[48] According to Donald Cole, the percentage of the population living as nomads—an absolute majority at the turn of the century—dropped to 25 percent; other reports say it fell to as low as 10 percent.[49] Habits and life-styles were also changing. The new work ethic focused on business and white-collar jobs rather than manual or trade work. New housing was built, and consumerism was on the rise. A rather egalitarian society had evolved into a stratified collective based on social classes and divided according to new skills and income. The royal family, whose members both enjoyed royal allowances and engaged in business, the senior *'ulama'*, and some major traders of nonroyal families now formed a large upper class; professionals and technocrats employed in government and in private businesses formed an emerging middle class; unskilled urban workers, nomads, the landless rural population, and most of the approximately two million foreign workers constituted a lower class.

In the second half of the 1970s it became evident that despite the blessings of modernization, the easing of physical burdens, free education, and health care, these dramatic changes in Saudi society had created serious problems. Although an expanding state administration could generate change, it failed to control its limits, that is, failed to provide symmetrical development and equal treatment to the different populations undergoing change. It also did not develop political outlets, parties, or representative bodies to articulate new political motives and drives. Moreover, Saudi state administration failed to supply accommodating cultural values, in terms of a new ideology, to make up for dislocations caused by change and to maintain a sense of orientation. The common denominator of these problems was a renewed sense of societal disintegration. The traditional intertribal and regional differences eased, but new problems of disintegration revolved around the new stratification, life-styles, and ecological divisions. Thus, tension ensued between a profligate upper class and the now rapidly emerging groups of ambitious technocrats and officials. As was the case in other Middle Eastern societies, these middle-class groups, which constituted 8 percent of the Saudi work force, became a potential opposition.[50] The legal right to accept commissions in return for promoting business led to a lavish life-style and conspicuous consumption. Ideological disorientation was fostered by the collapse of the traditional values of the once austere and egalitarian society. The importation of more than two million foreign workers to staff the vast construction projects created a totally new element in Saudi society. Public awareness of these new disparities heightened the opportunities for conflict in the kingdom.[51]

The negative side of modernization was particularly evident among tribal nomadic groups undergoing sedentarization and newly sedentarized tribespeople. The ecological integrity and political autonomy of tribes were eroded; in fact, tribes tended to disintegrate owing to sedentarization. Government pilot campaigns (at Wadi Sirhan, Harad, and Jabrin) mainly focused on the Shammar tribe in the north and on the Al-Murra in the south. Launched after severe droughts had beset these regions in the 1950s and 1960s, the campaigns were hardly successful. Lack of sufficient access to water resources and technical equipment, the difficulty experienced by large tribal groups (more than a thousand families in each case) in adjusting to settled life, and the residual disdain that certain tribal groups harbored toward agriculture prevented full sedentarization.

However, these campaigns generated a different, more complicated phenomenon of sedentarization: the abolition of the exclusive rights (*himma*) of an entire tribe in grazing zones. A 1968 law facilitated the allocation of smaller parcels of land to individual tribal members. With government technical and financial assistance, groups of small landowners emerged within the tribes. The enterprises of ARAMCO also produced tens of thousands of settlers.[52] Other tribal members preferred to exploit National Guard pensions, convenient government loans, and the opportunity to obtain casual employment in the booming cities while still maintaining a nomadic life-style. Yet they did so with modern aids, such as trucks, with education provided to growing numbers of youth, and with continuous access to part-time employment in cities. Urban centers thus functioned both as an attraction for sedentarization and as a source for the maintenance of nomadism, as tribespeople often mixed the two life-styles. Shirley Kay has observed that this process has taken the form of "semisettlement"; a Bedouin would spend some time as an unskilled worker in the city, then revert to nomadism with more income and a truck; but ultimately he would become fully sedentarized.[53]

The change in tribal settlement patterns had political and sociocultural implications as former tribal groups mixed with diverse social classes. On the one hand, tribal chiefs who acted as mediators between the central government and individual tribal members became large landowners and joined the upper class. On the other, many rank-and-file tribal members formed the bulk of the Saudi lower class. Nomads or lately sedentarized urban dwellers had difficulty adjusting to the new life-style. Devoid of sufficient skills, education, and income, tribal groups either settled in shacks on the outskirts of major cities or maintained a nomadic or agricultural life-style. The dissonance between their traditional ways and modernization led many to dissatisfaction with the new lavishness and Westernization, and they became alienated.

Still, tribal values and tribal elements continued to play an important role in state formation during a period of rapid social change and emerging affluence. This role did not, however, include agitating for the recurrence of the ancient state, the chieftaincy. The majority of the Saudi settled population (now the largest sector of the kingdom) supported the state and its new institutions. The making of a wealthy, centralized, and bureaucratized polity became an irreversible factor and was accepted as such by society. Diverse studies have shown how both nomadic and settled tribespeople took advantage of the improved health and educational facilities.[54]

Yet tribal values also eased the disparities that state administration had either created or failed to overcome. Tribal values functioned as modification devices that maintained a sense of familiarity and continuity in a society undergoing change. Their influence was evident in two spheres. In administrative and political life, tribal values compensated both for the creation of a formal and unfamiliar bureaucracy and for the absence of political parties in the kingdom. Leading figures, notably princes of the royal family or nonroyal high-ranking officials, established networks of support by associating with trustworthy people of their original tribe or others with whom they established cooperation. These associations provided political support for top leaders. In return, these elements regarded their highly empowered leaders as benefactors who could provide for their needs without their having to pass through unfamiliar bureaucratic channels. Such patron-client networks drew on tribal cooperation and familiarity for political support and for help in coping with the administration. In their ultimate form such networks created a large clientele dependent on the royal family. In Aziz al-Azmeh's words, "The Saudi polity tributarises other clan groups, no longer nomadic, and ties them . . . to the redistribution of Saudi wealth; for plunder is substituted by subsidy and the privilege of citizenship, such as the legal sponsorship of foreign business (*kafala*) is akin in many ways to the exaction of protection money (*khuwwa*). Thus tribalism becomes ascendant, not merely a *modus vivendi* or an additional structure of society."[55]

Tribal institutions also functioned as unofficial forums. The tribal *majlis*—the public audience of a Saudi *amir* with either his tribal elders, who function as secret advisers, or the public to adjudicate daily problems and grant petitions—served the patron-client groups or functioned as decision-making forums.

Ostensibly, then, tribal values limited and substituted for state institutions; in fact, they complemented familiar and adaptable procedures. Tribal values did not replace state administration but modified it, making it softer, easier to absorb. Thus, paradoxically, they became an important factor in spreading the authority of state institutions, particularly that of the top leaders. The importance of tribal values is also evident from the distinction Saudis make between *hukuma* (government) and *dawla* (state). They detest the *dawla*, the cold and estranged administration. But they sympathize with the *hukuma*, the leaders of the kingdom. This term encompasses the personal and clientele ties Saudis have with the royal family and other members of government.

Tribal values helped form identities, which in turn helped adapt to new state features. First, around the patron-client networks and other associations that developed in the towns,[56] among their new inhabitants, there emerged tribal associations, sometimes of mythical genealogy. These not only served administrative purposes but also helped overcome the unease of new social gaps by bridging them and somewhat neutralizing their effects on individuals. By forming groups based on ties of descent or profession, a familiar, supportive, quasi-tribal identity was recreated for these groups. As mentioned earlier, however, these groups were often led by government officials and princes, thereby strengthening their members' support of, and identity with, the kingdom. Indeed, the royal family itself formed a supreme coalition of twenty thousand members, representing not only notable families, as in the 1930s, but also support groups bound by common interests and royal intermarriage.[57]

Tribal values also formed an overall tribal ethos encompassing different groups that identified with tradition, austerity, conservatism, and religion. Interestingly, although tribal values contradicted Wahhabi norms in the 1920s and 1930s regarding sedentarization and termination of raiding, the improved regional relations of the Saudi kingdom encouraged the end of raiding and supported the forces of sedentarization. The differences between tribal values and Wahhabi tenets were therefore reduced. Moreover, in the wake of rapid change people of tribal descent could harmonize their tribal and Wahhabi values; in combination the two stood for familiar, common values, which helped modify the abrasive nature of change. Tribal values came to represent a general orientation to tradition.

Tribal values sometimes also had an opposite function—as norms of groups alienated from the modernizing government. Feelings of deprivation, poverty, and maltreatment were articulated in images of tribal fears—lack of water, failing agriculture, or sedentarization of youngsters.[58] In an allegorical novel about the beginnings of the oil industry in al-Ahsa', 'Abd al-Rahman al-Munif points to a similar sense of resentment toward government. He depicts the oil industry as the source of hardship for Saudi society. The title of the novel, *Cities of Salt* (*Mudun al-Milh*), suggests that the petroleum cities—in fact, the oil industry as a whole—do not rest on solid foundations deeply rooted in Saudi society and therefore might collapse.[59] Published in 1984, al-Munif's novel presumably expresses some of the resentment Saudis felt toward the emerging dislocations of the 1970s. Specifically, the book stresses the popular view that the once egalitarian, unstratified Saudi society had split apart and that its leaders had become estranged and oppressive.

Such attitudes found fertile ground among lower-class tribesmen who studied at the University of al-Madina in the 1970s. They were driven both by the ideological disorientation and social deprivation typical of some tribal groups during rapid development (their leader, Juhayman, was the nephew of Ibn Humayd, a renowned leader of the 'Utayba tribe of the Ikhwan in the 1920s) and by popular Muslim revivalist sentiments typical of the day, which had spread to Saudi Arabia with the arrival of guest workers from Egypt, Yemen, and Pakistan. Both sets of motives led them to regard the royal family as corrupt and obsolete. As a result, a few hundred tribesmen captured the Grand Mosque in Mecca on 20 November 1979 in an attempt to assassinate Saudi royal leaders and end their rule.[60] Even though this attempt proved futile (the rebels were defeated after several weeks of occupying the mosque), the predilection of tribesmen to reject the impact of change is noteworthy.

One significant countertactic has been the tendency of Saudi leaders to stress their tribal and religious background and to exploit accommodating tribal values by developing the identified tribal population as the common denominator in society. These attempts have been particularly evident during the reign of King Khalid (1975–1982) and King Fahd (since 1982).

Like the territorial expansion of the 1920s, rapid modernization posed unprecedented difficulties for Saudi state formation; it rent the socioideological fabric of the kingdom. In addition to the mosque incident, the Shi'i riots in al-Ahsa' in 1979–1980 and Riyadh's strained relations with the United States (the symbol of modernization) after the signing of the Camp David Accords attested to the fragility of Saudi state formation. Starting in the late 1970s, the Saudi government began to search for state-building mechanisms that could modify the pace and course of modernization. One was the development of rural, peripheral regions. Agricultural projects in 'Asir, petrochemical plants in the northern Hijaz and al-Ahsa' (notably the Yanbu' and Jubayl projects), and internal trade centers in al-Qasim

were emphasized.[61] The third five-year plan (1980–1985) was specifically designed to raise the rural living standard. The government actually wanted to reduce the pace of urbanization and reinforce the
confidence of nomads and villagers. King Fahd often praised the
moral rectitude and stability in rural areas that were mostly dominated by tribal values, as opposed to the corruption and instability
of the dynamic cities.[62] In this way Saudi leaders hoped to befriend
the rural population and develop a convincing common denominator
for the entire population.

Economic recession, generated by a sharp decline in oil sales, has
beset Saudi Arabia since 1982. It has further motivated the government to focus on an integrative state-building campaign to help minimize economic devastation. The private sector was encouraged to
finance many public projects to make up for declining government
funding. Middle-class businessmen could thus improve their role
and status in the kingdom.[63] By maintaining high subsidies on food,
free education, and health services, as well as continuous personal
contacts between lower-class elements and princes, the government
was able to increase the level of integration of lower-class, nomadic,
rural, and city-bound tribal groups.[64] By projecting the otherwise
broad budget cuts as a way of rationalizing public spending, the government sought to boost societal solidarity and support for its own
actions.

Tribal society and values thus exerted an intricate influence on
Saudi state formation during the twentieth century. As a military
and political power, tribes were a formidable instrument in the expansion of Saudi territory. Yet they failed to maintain a loosely
structured chieftaincy over the enlarged Saudi realm and were effectively challenged by a centralizing, development-oriented regime.
But the impact of the new government was felt most strongly at the
political and military levels. Tribal modes of behavior and values
prevailed in society alongside new state institutions and bureaucratic procedures; in fact, they commingled. As such, tribal values
sometimes loomed behind opposition movements and thereby
helped modify state policies. Their imprint is evident throughout the
Saudi kingdom—on its territorial setting, political regime, social
structure, and collective identity.

NOTES

1. Aziz al-Azmeh, "Wahhabite Polity," in Ian Richardson Netton, ed., *Arabia and the Gulf: From Traditional Society to Modern States* (Tatawa, N.J.,
1986), pp. 75–90; C. Moss Helms, *The Cohesion of Saudi Arabia* (London,
1981), pp. 29–75.

2. See, for instance, D. Holden and R. Johns, *The House of Saud* (London, 1981); L. P. Goldrup, "Saudi Arabia, 1902–1932: The Development of a Wahhabi Society" (Ph.D. diss., University of California, Los Angeles, 1971).

3. M. J. Crawford, "Civil War, Foreign Intervention and the Question of Political Legitimacy: A Nineteenth-Century Sa'udi Qadi's Dilemma," *International Journal of Middle East Studies* 14 (1982): 227–248.

4. Jacob Goldberg, *The Foreign Policy of Saudi Arabia, the Formative Years 1902–1918* (Cambridge, Mass., 1986).

5. Holden and Johns, *House of Saud*, pp. 23–38.

6. H. St. John B. Philby, *The Heart of Arabia* (London, 1923), pp. 92–96.

7. See Joseph Kostiner, "The Hashimite 'Tribal Confederacy' of the Arab Revolt, 1916–1917," in E. Ingram, ed., *National and International Politics in the Middle East: Essays in Honour of Elie Kedourie* (London, 1986), pp. 126–143.

8. See Brinton Cooper Busch, *Britain, India and the Arabs 1914–1928* (Berkeley and Los Angeles, 1971), pp. 164–268.

9. On Saudi occupation, see Amin al-Rihani, *Ta'rikh Najd wa-Mulhaqatihi* (Beirut, 1928); Muhammad al-Shahari, *Al-Matami' al-Tawwasu'iyya al-Sa'udiyya fil-Yaman* (Beirut, 1979); Sadiq Hasan al-Sudani, *Al-'Ilaqat al-'Iraqiyya al-Sa'udiyya 1920–31* (Baghdad, 1975).

10. Philby, *Heart of Arabia*, pp. 293–294.

11. See Joseph Kostiner, "On Instruments and Their Designers: The Ikhwan of Najd and the Emergence of the Saudi State," *Middle Eastern Studies* 21, no. 3 (July 1985): 298–323.

12. See K. Williams, *Ibn Sa'ud the Puritan King of Arabia* (London, 1938), pp. 63-64.

13. H. Wahbah, *Arabian Days* (London, 1964), pp. 128–129; H. St. John Philby, diary of political mission to central Arabia 1917–1918, vol. 2, Cairo to Riyad, 13 April 1918, *Philby Papers*, St. Antony's College, Oxford.

14. *Arab Bulletin*, no. 108, 11 January 1919, report by Philby, British Public Record Office (henceforth BPRO), FO 882/21; H. Dickson (British political agent in Bahrain and later in Kuwait), notes on the Akhwan Movement, 5 March 1920, FO IS/19/15.

15. Ibid., report by Gertrude Bell (British official at Baghdad), 23 August 1920, BPRO, FO 371/5061/E 3798.

16. The decision was made in 1923. Secretary of State for India to Viceroy, India, 18 April 1923, BPRO, FO 371/8937/E 4019.

17. Ronald Cohen, Introduction to Ronald Cohen and Elman Service, eds., *Origins of the State* (Philadelphia, 1978), pp. 1–20.

18. On the making of Saudi institutions, see F. Hamza, *Al-Bilad al-'arabiyya al-sa'udiyya* (Riyadh, 1961); see also Ghazi Shanneik, "Die Modernisierung des Traditionellen Politischen Systems," in Thomas Koszinowski, ed., *Saudi-Arabien: Ölmacht und Entwicklungs Land* (Hamburg, 1983), pp. 151–176.

19. Kostiner, "On Instruments."

20. R. O. Collins, ed., *An Arabian Diary: Sir Gilbert Falkinham Clayton* (Berkeley and Los Angeles, 1969).

21. Quoted by H. R. P. Dickson, *Kuwait and Her Neighbours* (London, 1968), pp. 273.

22. Political Agent in Kuwait to Resident, Bushire, 1 July 1929, BPRO, FO 371/13737/E 4330.

23. Political Agent in Kuwait to Resident, Bushire, 7 July 1923, BPRO, CO 727/5/40377; Political Agent in Kuwait to Resident, Bushire, 12 July 1923, CO 727/5/40377.

24. Ramadi to Air Staff Intelligence, 9 January 1925, BPRO, AIR 23/3.

25. Political Agent in Kuwait to Resident, Bushire, 1 July 1929, BPRO, FO 371/13737/E 4330; Kostiner, "On Instruments."

26. Political Agent in Kuwait to Resident, Bushire, 1 July 1929, BPRO, FO 371/13737/E 4330, includes an interview with an Ikhwan leader, Faysal Ibn-Shiblayn.

27. "Tentative Outline of the Historical Background of the War between Ibn Sa'ud and the Imam Yahya, 1933–1934," Sir Andrew Ryan Papers, Box 6/7, St. Antony's College, Oxford University.

28. Max Weber, *The Theory of Social and Economic Organization*, edited with an introduction by Talcott Parsons (Cambridge, Mass., 1984), pp. 346–352.

29. Kostiner, "Hashimite 'Tribal Confederacy.'"

30. Ryan to Henderson, 4 March 1931, British India Office Records (henceforth BIOR), L/P&S/12/2073, PZ 2449.

31. Holden and Johns, *House of Saud*, pp. 123–175; see also M. Abir, "The Consolidating of the Ruling Class and the New Elites in Saudi Arabia," *Middle Eastern Studies* 23, no. 2 (April 1987).

32. Faysal's Financial Reforms, March 1958—January 1960, 28 January 1960, United States National Archives (henceforth NA).

33. Notes on Saudi Arabia for Dr. Hugh Scott, 29 August 1944. Philby Papers Box 16/5.

34. Abir, "Consolidating of the Ruling Class."

35. Background and Implications of the Conflict within the Saudi Ruling Family, 1 April 1958, Intelligence Report No. 7692, NA.

36. Holden and Johns, *House of Saud*, pp. 179–197.

37. Joseph Kostiner, "The Making of Saudi Arabia" (manuscript in progress), chap. 3.

38. See Johannes Reissner, "Die Innenpolitik," in Koszinowski, ed., *Saudi-Arabian*, pp. 83–120.

39. The Eastern Reaches of al-Hasa Province, 31 January 1950, 886 2553/1-3150, NA; Muhammad al-Mana, *Arabia Unified* (London, 1980), p. 177.

40. Abir, "Consolidating of the Ruling Class."

41. Holden and Johns, *House of Saud*, pp. 255–357.

42. Abd ulrahman M. Al-Sadhan, "The Modernisation of the Saudi Bureaucracy," in Willard A. Beling, ed., *King Faisal and the Modernisation of Saudi Arabia* (London, 1980), pp. 75–89.

43. Ghazi Algosaibi, *Arabian Essays* (London, 1982), p. 13.

44. Extracts from Faysal's speech at Ta'if on 5 September 1963, in Gerald De-Gaury, *Faisal* (London, 1965), pp. 169–176 (appendix).

45. Lisa Anderson, *The State and Social Transformation in Tunisia and Libya, 1830–1980* (Princeton, 1986), pp. 270–279.

46. Holden and Johns, *House of Saud*, pp. 255–357; Helen Lackner, *A House Built on Sand* (London, 1978), pp. 60–69.

47. Soraya Altorki and Donald P. Cole, *Arabian Oasis City: The Transformation of 'Unayzah* (Austin, Tex., 1989), pp. 119–207, offer a long discussion on the effects of the market economy.

48. Shirley Kay, "Social Change in Modern Saudi Arabia," in T. Niblock, ed., *State, Society, and Economy in Saudi Arabia* (London, 1982), pp. 171–185.

49. Donald P. Cole, "Bedouin and Social Change in Saudi Arabia," *Journal of Asian and African Studies* 16 (1981): 128–149; P. A. Kluck, "The Society and Its Environment," in *Saudi Arabia: A Country Study* (Washington, D.C., 1984), pp. 57–132.

50. N. Safran and M. Heller, *The New Middle Class and Regime Stability in Saudi Arabia*, Harvard Middle East Papers, no. 3 (Cambridge, Mass., 1985).

51. M. Abir, *Saudi Arabia in the Oil Era* (Boulder, Colo., 1987), pp. 139–148; see D. Horowitz's discussion of group comparison in his *Ethnic Groups in Conflict* (Berkeley and Los Angeles, 1985), pp. 141–184.

52. Ugo Fabietti, "Sedentarization as a Means of Detribalisation: Some Policies of the Saudi Government towards the Nomads," in T. Niblock, ed., *State, Society, and Economy in Saudi Arabia* (London, 1982), pp. 186–197; A. H. Said, "Saudi Arabia: The Transition from a Tribal Society to a Nation" (Ph.D. diss., University of Illinois, 1982).

53. Kay, "Social Change."

54. Cole, "Bedouin and Social Change"; Taha al-Farra, "The Effects of Detribalizing the Bedouins on the Internal Cohesion of an Emerging State: The Kingdom of Saudi Arabia" (Ph.D. diss., University of Pittsburgh, 1973), pp. 204–208.

55. Al-Azmeh, "Wahhabite Polity."

56. Abir, *Saudi Arabia in the Oil Era*, p. 73.

57. Gary Samore, "Royal Family Politics in Saudi Arabia" (Ph.D. diss., Harvard University, 1985); see also Waddah Sharara, *Al-Ahl wal-Ghanima* (Beirut, 1981) pp. 171–207.

58. Motoko Katakura, *Bedouin Village* (Tokyo, 1977), p. 26.

59. 'Abd al-Rahman al-Munif, *Mudun al-Milh* (Dammam, 1982).

60. James Buchan, "The Return of the Ikhwan 1979," in Holden and Johns, *House of Saud*, pp. 511–526.

61. *Financial Times Supplement*, 5 May 1981.

62. See *Al-Mustaqbal* (Beirut), 31 March 1984; *Al-Sharq al-Awsat* (London), 29 March 1984.

63. *Wall Street Journal*, 20 December 1983.

64. *Al-Sharq al-Awsat*, 29 March 1984; *Al-Riyadh* (Riyadh), 14 September 1983; see also "Planning Minister Hisham Nazir's Outline for the Current Five Year Plan," Saudi Press Agency, 5 December 1983, published by Foreign Broadcast Information Service, 7 December 1983.

Imams and Tribes:
The Writing and
Acting of History in Upper Yemen

Paul Dresch

"The idea of the State has been under heavy criticism during the last decades," writes A. Passerin d'Entrèves. "Historians tend to consider the State a comparatively modern phenomenon, while some political scientists, for different reasons, reject the notion altogether as useless and out of date."[1] There are others, of course (classicists, perhaps, and lawyers), who consider the state very ancient; but part of the impetus for the present collection is that the state has been brought back in by those who put it out in the first place—the political scientists—and proposed as a concept of wide applicability. The growth of states is once again an obvious topic around which to organize multidisciplinary volumes. Yet it remains surprising how little the different disciplines agree on how to define or even characterize states. Some attention must be paid to the terms we use and to why we are using them.[2]

Many disciplines have something to say of states, but *state formation* is a concept worked out at length by archaeologists. The existence of particular states is deduced by them from external criteria such as settlement patterns or the geographic concentration of surplus produce, not from the modes of self-definition that are central to a lawyer's or historian's concerns.[3] Much the same is true of *tribe*. For most archaeologists, a tribe lies somewhere between bands and chiefdoms on a scale of complexity that culminates in states and empires. Little of this takes into account societies' capacity for self-definition; nor need it. The attraction of the term *state*, however, surely lies in the overlap of external criteria and internal (complexity, say, and legal sovereignty), in the area of obscurity to which d'Entrèves points. Only in one tradition can this overlap simply be assumed—the Western tradition, from which the disparate views of what a state comprises all derive. *Tribe* becomes the unmarked term, the archaic prestate or nonstate order that our own tradition lacks.

It is not the archaeologists' contention that all states have evolved from chiefdoms, and these in turn from tribes, or that the process at work is everywhere the same. But their operational concepts are readily assimilated by others to a folk sociology, which in part is shared by the inhabitants of the contemporary Middle East and many Western writers. A particular brand of anthropology, for example, associated with Marshall Sahlins, Elman Service, and Leslie White, concerned itself with "cultural evolution." It is this notion that Patricia Crone applied in her work on the tribe and the state in the Middle East.[4] Unfortunately, the anthropology in question tends to conflate folk sociology and operational concepts by equating history with evolution, and the results always haunt such discussions as the present one. Tribes are not only supposed to be simpler than states; often they are supposed to come first and to be less significant than states, in other words, to occupy a lower rung on the evolutionary ladder.

In Yemen, as in most Middle Eastern regions, this evolutionary axis does not hold. If tribes somehow lead to states, then states lead as often to tribes; and in any case they coexist over long periods. Henry Adams's discomfort with *Pteraspis*, that fossil sturgeon that seemed to evolve from nowhere and to nowhere, must be our discomfort too, as indeed it must be with most schemes of social evolution.

The temptation is to turn instead to a cyclical theory, particularly to that of Ibn Khaldun. As one scholar has said, however, "Ibn Khaldun may be a 'pessimist' or a 'determinist,' but his pessimism has a moral and religious, not a sociological, basis."[5] The argument is ordered always to final causes ("royal authority is the end/goal of group feeling"; "the end of civilization is sedentary culture"), not to the efficient causes in which sociology now trades. Without the philosophy and theology the cyclical theory is merely a summary of empirical events, particularly where the cycle is large—perhaps two peaks of power (that is, one repetition) in the whole of history. The choice between modes of causality overlaps with that between external and internal criteria, our terms and theirs.

Ernest Gellner's attempt to introduce efficient causes into short-term North African cycles by appealing to religious style and the relation of towns to countryside will be mentioned at several points in this essay so as to situate the Yemeni case. I should say at once, though, that I doubt all his insights are applicable generally: as Gellner himself notes,[6] the Yemeni Zaydis do not fit his thesis in some respects. His general writings on nationalism, however, fit the modern period very well, and it is within the ideology of this period that questions of tribes and state formation have their sense. Within the same ideology thrives the folk sociology of evolution, drawing for examples on as long a history as might be available.

TRIBES AND IMAMS

The tribes of Upper Yemen (roughly speaking, those of the dry, plateau area from San'a' northward) are territorial entities, and the vast majority of tribesmen are farmers who live in villages built of mud or stone.[7] The easy equation of tribes with pastoral nomads is inapplicable.[8] Tribes cannot escape the state by moving out,[9] and certain states based on Lower Yemen (whether the Sulayhids, Rasulids, or Ottomans) have sometimes shown how vulnerable tribesmen can be. The most defensible areas are those of the western mountains, where tribalism is weak in comparison with the plateau—or, to phrase things more cautiously, is quite differently organized. The rugged mountains of the west, which are heavily terraced, also provide a rich agricultural base. Lower Yemen, the mountainous southern part of what is now the Yemen Arab Republic, is agriculturally richer still, and the dominant theme in social affairs there is that of landlord and peasant. Lower Yemen is in effect nontribal, but many of the inhabitants of these southern areas, and of the western mountains, came originally from the arid north.

Village settlements in the north are grouped into sections and then into tribes; these larger elements are territorially defined and usually have clear borders between one and the next. The lines between tribes run arbitrarily across the landscape. They do not denote units of production or exchange; and were one to explain the tribes in functional political terms,[10] one should have to admit that the problems they contained or settled were the problems they produced in the first place. In the pre-Islamic period similar village communities were grouped quite differently, though on the same physical terrain and probably subject to similar ecology.

The sorghum, barley, and wheat that northerners grow is the property not of village communities but of particular families and men. Those who fail to maintain themselves move elsewhere in the country, to the west or south, and cease to be tribesmen. Those who succeed conspicuously (usually through association with a state of some kind) often move too. Hence the egalitarian aspect of land tenure and wealth in the tribal north is in part due to the fact that those who are exceptions to the rule move away and are defined out of the system. The major exceptions that remained in place were promi-

nent shaykhs whose wealth came largely from elsewhere in the country, to the west and south, where they or the states they bordered
held richer lands. Throughout the past millennium these figures can
be followed as their domains of influence in the north waxed and
waned; but the tribal divisions did not wax and wane with them,[11] a
point that differentiates this system rather clearly from many of
those in eastern Islamic Asia.[12]

Tribes are related to tribes, just as sections are related to sections
within tribes, and villages to villages within sections, by a rhetoric of
moral equality.[13] Regardless of population, wealth, or territorial extent, one tribe is conceptually the equal of any other tribe (there are
no client tribes, for instance), and disputes are resolved always in the
language of balance (mizan). The same goes for disputes between
men, whether they are structurally close in the tribal scheme (members of the same section, say) or structurally distant. Tribes are not,
however, corporate groups in either of the separate senses anthropologists sometimes muddle: they are not solidary units in an empirical
sense, nor are they in any sense legal personalities. The relation between individual tribesmen and the sets they fall into is not one of either automatism or prescriptive definition. Individual claims and
collective claims can contradict each other.

A man in this position who feels himself wronged but is denied
support by his tribe may leave and take refuge with the neighboring
tribe. His fellows are supposed to retrieve him and make amends.
Sometimes, however, he will become permanently part of the set he
joins, the moral redefinition being made by the slaughter of bulls, as
is done in parts of North Africa.[14] The morality all tribesmen recognize is indefinitely fragmented into separate spaces. Whether movement is temporary or permanent, it represents an avoidance of any
absolute judgment, a kind of moral particularism or pluralism. A
man who is wronged or does wrong in one tribe or section may move
to another like it, whereas a second man, involved in a dispute of the
same sort, may move in the opposite direction and in just the same
terms.

Were one looking for a single attribute that characterized tribalism in the present setting, it might well be this moral reciprocity that
turns on protection. Far from tribes cohering unthinkingly as
wholes around men at odds, men are constantly being moved back
and forth through the system and being "covered" for a time from
the view of their antagonists: the verb commonly used to describe
this action is tahajjaba, from the same root as the word for a veil or
for an amulet that covers someone from envious eyes. The tribal answer to men's general vulnerability is often temporary refuge. Simi-

lar concepts of covering pervade the whole ethnography and relate directly to a language of honor that applies to collective identities and to persons equally.

The importance of tribal divisions derives, as I have said, from a sensibility in which opposition and honor are salient, and the units are defined by moral contradistinction of the kind usually written of as balanced opposition.[15] According to tradition, two large blocs named Hashid and Bakil have descended from a pair of brothers. In the first bloc there are nowadays some seven major tribes, and in the second about fourteen, each with its distinct territory. Little is needed for the system to reproduce itself. A few names and some simple ideas are enough to provide the appearance of ageless continuity, and some of the major tribal divisions are ancient. The names of the largest divisions, Hashid, Bakil, and Hamdan, which comprises the other two, are in fact pre-Islamic; but full information on the tribes becomes available only in the early tenth century A.D. with the writings of al-Hasan al-Hamdani.

At the same time as we have this great fund of writing on the tribes (and in tribal terms), we have also the establishment of a major statelike tradition in Yemen, that of the Zaydis. The first imam arrived in 896, and the last one was overthrown only in 1962. The tradition has an attractive simplicity. The imam should be the best available of the Prophet's kin who successfully claims leadership and should "order the good and prohibit the evil," questions of circumstance notwithstanding. Justice is everything. The assertion of equality among men—albeit the imamate itself was reserved to the Prophet's descendants—and of the unity of men before God is central to the undertaking.

In Islamic law concepts of equality, such as 'adl and insaf, are largely concordant with the tribes' own interest in balance. Yet the stress on unity is, in abstract terms, antithetical to the tribal style of fragmented answerability. Vulnerability is not covered by temporary refuge. Instead, if one may impose the metaphor, the righteous seek safety beneath the imam's regal parasol. The rhetorical opposition between tribes and imams often turns, in fact, on something like sovereignty, as for example when Imam Ahmad b. Sulayman (c. 1140) applied the hadd (punishment) to a man under tribal protection, drawing enmity from the tribe in question but proclaiming that "even if we wished to pardon him, the punishment/right [haqq] is God's."[16] Although in practice they had always to trim their policy to local realities, imams before and since would not admit the validity of tribal autonomy and protection. One might think the Zaydis to that extent very statelike.

The imam had to be a *sayyid*, a descendant of the Prophet, but from the outset (c. A.D. 900) the *sayyids* and their supporters lived among the tribes and depended on tribal support. From at least 1150 (possibly much earlier) this support took the form explicitly of the *hijra*, which in Upper Yemen is an enclave under tribal protection where *sayyids* and scholars might live. The literate tradition, which Gellner associates with urban life,[17] was here being reproduced in small-scale centers scattered throughout the tribal countryside. Correspondingly, the North African distinction between a land of the state and a land of dissidence appears in the histories only partially and intermittently.

Set aside in their protected enclaves, and thus contained within the tribal scheme of fragmented answerability, the learned promoted their vision of union in allegiance to a just imam. The tribes, defined by contradistinction to each other, would sometimes accept this rhetoric on a local scale or rally on a massive scale to an imam who proclaimed the jihad against the ungodly. Two views of the world encompassed each other, taking precedence by rapid turns. It is only in the written histories that one moment of this dialectic seems subordinate to the other, and that is because the histories we have, from medieval times on, are all written by nontribesmen. It is therefore worth looking more closely at the start of the Zaydi venture, when two different styles of literature for a time overlapped.

Al-Hamdani's account of Hashid and Bakil (written c. A.D. 930–940) is composed in tribal terms, often designed to praise the tribal "lords" of his own day and organized in general around related conceptions of chivalry and genealogy.[18] The concern for conceptual equality, so marked in present-day ethnography, is visible also in this literature of a thousand years ago. The epithets of honor, for example, are numerous and are all comparatives and superlatives; but one cannot in fact rank the sets of people to whom these epithets apply, in large part because of the way the past is treated. To take an obvious example, several great men are each referred to as "lord of Hamdan in his time," but since no times are given, no ranking or sequence is implied. More generally, the tenth volume of the *Iklil* (the part of al-Hamdani's corpus most directly concerned with the northern tribes) is organized around genealogies, but the genealogies are not aligned with each other, and one cannot readily say whose ancestors were contemporaries of whose. There is only the simultaneity of each heroic encounter recorded in the form of battle days.

I will touch in a later section on how this eternal present in fact shifts through the years, but there is no temporal closure in al-Hamdani's scheme. A denial of hierarchy is accomplished primarily through the avoidance of a time scale, which might otherwise set in sequence the *akhbar*, or self-contained tales of tribal tradition. Although individual events in the Yemeni past are sometimes aligned with events in the wider world and thus could be dated if one wished, the *Iklil* itself does not give dates. The contrast with Zaydi literature is striking.

The Zaydi imamate was becoming established in Yemen at the time al-Hamdani was writing, and the near contemporary biography of the first imam (al-Hadi ila l-Haqq, d. A.D. 911) begins a historiographical tradition that continued until close to our own time. Within that tradition, as one might expect, dates are of immense importance, whether in the large biographical literature (both *sira* and *tarjama*) or in the chronicles and annals. Chronicles, in turn, are eminently political, whether ordered to a dynasty, tradition, or place. In all of them there is an appeal to shared experience, to a unity that exists in time through good and evil, the very opposite of tribal *akhbar* shorn of context and genealogies shorn of coordinate time.

To conceive of cycles, of good periods and bad (or indeed of any processual question such as state formation), requires reference to a shared standard, a conceptual center that Islamic chronology helped provide but that tribes place outside of their own traditions. Tribal literature of al-Hamdani's kind in fact soon died out. The tribes in any case have no unified story to tell, only the indefinitely fragmented body of heroic tradition. The time line that might inform our own theories of cycles, evolution, and so forth is not independent of our data but is intrinsic to the material and always to the statelike part of that material. We are engaged, inevitably, with a partial view that has already been abstracted from a reality that may well be more complex; and what counts as tribal is what learned histories leave as their residue. The learned histories, moreover, are themselves not cumulative. The moral frame within which imams judged others or were judged themselves took no account of changing circumstance, although the circumstances themselves were recorded carefully. Plainly there were good times and bad (no historical view of states and tribes would be possible were it not so), but no theory of progress or decline is evident, and no cycles are devised by indigenous theory.

To deal with changing circumstances by some cyclical theory of our own devising would require a great many epicycles. The first imam, for instance, took San'a' and pushed as far south as Dhamar, but by the end of his life he was again confined to the area around Sa'da, in the extreme north of the country. The influence of his immediate successors varied wildly, from leading armies reportedly eighty thousand strong to fleeing Sa'da for tribal protection in fear of their lives.[19] Some medieval imams ('Abdullah b. Hamza, d. 1217, is a clear example) were powerful figures, fighting off non-Zaydi movements based elsewhere in the country and consolidating their own power in fortresses, which suggest the presence of an obvious state. Many others, by contrast, were fugitives among the tribes, which left no trace of their presence except, at most, their scholarly writings. By external criteria the imamate seems to have been a state and then not a state almost year by year or even month by month.

THE IMAMATE AND ITS RIVALS AS STATELIKE ENTITIES

If we accept rough external criteria, we can say that there were states in Islamic Yemen before the Zaydi imams arrived, that is, before the final years of the ninth century. An obvious example would be the Yu'firid *dawla*, a dynasty based on San'a' and Shibam, which seceded from direct 'Abbasid suzerainty around 860. There were also great tribal families, the "lords" of Hamdan, who gave fixed allegiance to no one and, more important for the present purpose, to no set of ideas external to their own. Some of them were undoubtedly powerful, and they may well have taxed the tribes.[20] Certain of them recur in the histories for a long time afterward; the Al al-Du'am of Bakil, for instance, survive as *muluk* or sultans from the ninth century to the end of the twelfth.[21] In the medieval period we also find important new states or dynasties established by tribal leaders. The Bani Hatim and Bani Zuray' in the twelfth century are major cases. Such local dynasties were sultanates, holders of power by their own strong arms who nonetheless claimed validation from elsewhere, from Isma'ili and Fatimid movements in Lower Yemen and western Yemen or from powers even further off.[22]

The Bani Hatim (1099–1174) are of particular interest. Based in San'a', they could muster large armies and held at some periods nearly all of Upper Yemen, pushing the imams back to Sa'da and apportioning fiefs to the tribal nobles. In doing so, however, they left behind their own tribe. So did the Zuray'ids, based in Aden, at the far end of the country. Both dynasties in fact came from Yam, an Isma-'ili tribe of Najran (nowadays just inside Saudi Arabia), but Yam stayed where it was and did not, it seems, share in its kinsmen's dominance over other tribes: it was not quite like Ibn Khaldun's world, nor even like that of latter-day North Arabian tribal dynasties.[23]

One other point might be drawn from the Bani Hatim. They gave allegiance at first to the Isma'ilis and on their own ruled most of the north. When Ahmad b. Sulayman declared himself imam in 1137, the first full imam in about a century, they beat his forces soundly and for a decade afterward fought him throughout Yemen. Eventually, however, they recognized his suzerainty—but then again changed their minds. Their history illustrates what one sees quite often— immensely rapid shifts of the political map caused not by state formation or internal development of a state apparatus but by redefinition.

Instead of a discrete moment of state formation, what we have in medieval Yemen, as presumably in most of the Islamic Middle East, is a world in which general conceptions of legitimacy are already present from the outset. Since the rise of Islam, and very probably earlier, there is no need to invent the state in this sense. The theories are already present; or, in the archaeologists' terms, all our examples are of at least secondary state formation.[24] Not only are specific conceptions of a polity present, but so are writing, coinage, cosmologies, and much else that belongs to what in Middle Eastern terms is a very late cultural period. As a result, claims to legitimacy need not be confined to geographical units: one of the imams of the eleventh century, Abu Fath al-Daylami, made his da'wa (summons to God's law) in northern Persia and only appeared on the Yemeni stage seven years afterward.[25] The state need not grow or evolve in situ but can simply be declared and the shape of it filled in later.

Between the eleventh and sixteenth centuries Lower Yemen was the seat of several major dynasties (the Sulayhids, Ayyubids, Rasulids, Tahirids), which did not emerge from a tribal background or depend much on tribes for their strength. Some of them, however, struck north and subdued the tribes there, sometimes robbing the imamate of all but a rump of territory. The Rasulids, for instance, attacked Sa'da with five hundred cavalry and three thousand foot soldiers in 1268. In 1285 they granted much of the north as a fief to Hamzi Sharif, a descendant of the Prophet who, had he been inclined, might have appeared in quite other terms as an aspiring imam. Tribesmen who might otherwise have emerged as a local force to oppose the Rasulids appear instead as Rasulid soldiers at the far end of Yemen.[26] Only internal divisions around 1360 led the Rasulids to withdraw altogether from the north, but throughout the period the map of states kept changing for reasons only marginally attached to state formation.

In Upper Yemen the major statelike tradition was that of the Zaydis, which over time came to preempt all claims other than those made by states based elsewhere, usually Lower Yemen. This preemption of other claims was a matter of missionary work much more than of conquest or any discrete and permanent institution of coercion, which the Zaydis usually lacked.[27] Imams had instead to mobilize tribesmen against other tribesmen to "order the good and prohibit the reprehensible," whether the object of prohibitive action was an instance of some condemned tribal custom, a rival "summons" such as that of the Isma'ilis, or the claims of a rival imam, of whom there were sometimes several. It is the aim, rather than the means, that appears so obviously statelike.

Here, however, we encounter a problem. If one sets aside any external definition and uses "tribe" purely as a conventional gloss for *qabila*, as in fact I do here, one obscures very little—if only because in discussions of state formation, "tribe" is always the unmarked term. Yet to call the *da'wa* or *imama* a state is, I suspect, to misrepresent it. For one thing, which would catch the eye of a historian or an Arabist, it was not a *dawla* in the view of its own proponents, at least not at the beginning.[28] Even a *dawla* (a dynasty, a turn in power, such as that of the Rasulids) is not quite a state in the Western sense; nor yet is sultan, *khilafa*, or *mulk*. This is not an argument over external criteria and the extent to which cases might fit them. It is a matter of internal criteria that have a considerable effect on the shape of this problem.[29]

The etymology of the word *state*, going straight back to Latin *status*, is too simple to be helpful for comparative analytic purposes. The simplicity, of course, is deceptive in that one is dealing in any discussion of Western politics with medieval revivals of terms that had long been defunct;[30] and by the time the term *state* appeared in Europe, the reality had in any case emerged from a distinctive involution of church and secular *regnum*. Even so, the essence of the state in the Western tradition is legal. The state is constituted by law and is itself the source of law, which differentiates it radically from its Islamic counterparts: *quod principi placuit legis habet vigorem* is not something one could say in an Islamic context.[31] Power and right are combined in quite different ways.

The outcome of medieval experience and debate in Europe is a moral construction identified with a bounded community, a discrete collectivity having a past of its own and, potentially, a future. The connection of territory and history, established in large part by legal practice, is distinctive. Moreover, it is this part of our own cultural inheritance that inclines us to generalize our search for the state by assimilating history to evolution. We are all too ready to find a unified story of political development (of increased complexity, power, or order) repeated in ancient Mesopotamia, medieval Europe, Asia, or the Islamic East as if this moral of collective life might be confirmed almost anywhere.

Suffice it for the present purpose to note that no item in the pre-nineteenth-century Arabic political lexicon provides a really close parallel to our own key term.[32] The *umma* may be much like the medieval church as *respublica christiana*, with the important difference of lacking a papacy. The various sultanates and kingdoms (particularly those of Sunni inspiration), by contrast, were perhaps like the states of medieval Europe, "the police department of the Church,"[33] with the important difference that no inherited shape of general dominion was there to be filled (no Rome), and no argument was to be had over who were the Roman people that might bestow the vacated empire. Between the *umma* and the individual, however, there are no natural entities having legal or moral standing.

In most of Islamic history, political constructions are not by their nature coterminous with any bounded community. Regnal titles, whether in Sunni or Shi'i, western or eastern Islam, rarely identify the ruler with a social unit; instead of *duke of Anjou* and the like, we have typically *'izz al-din*, *sayf al-dawla*, and *imam al-muslimin*.[34] In the case of the Yemeni imams each full imam, like the earliest Islamic rulers, was simply *amir al-mu'minin*, setting no inherent limits to his dominion.

The first problem posed by the mismatch of Middle Eastern and Western concepts, therefore, is that of the unit whose formation or dissolution we might hope to explain. Which "state" is at issue, or are there only dynasties? Certainly, throughout the Islamic period there is a keen awareness, often manifest in the titles of history books, of Yemen as some kind of cultural unit. There are histories of particular towns. There are histories of traditions such as the imamate and of dynasties such as the Ayyubids and Rasulids in Lower Yemen. There is no necessary connection proposed between the forms of power and communal identities, however. The result is that from the point of view of a given community, power comes and goes (as imams, for instance, come and go from San'a'), whereas from the point of view of the power holders, the different areas of the country accede or dissent for what seem extraneous reasons. The process of state formation seems a contingency arising from the intersection of several otherwise autonomous histories. What is missing from the local tradition is an account of internal development, which, phrased in historians' or in lawyers' terms, would coincide with the progression of the archaeologist's model or that of the political scientist. The moral investment we ourselves may have in state formation as a generalizable process is not there.

The second problem, therefore, is that of the obvious quality the idea of state formation has for people in separate disciplines despite the myriad conflicting definitions they employ. If the complexity of Yemeni political formations comes and goes with the rapidity that written histories suggest, then in singling out state formation as a topic at all, we are in the position of someone who elects to analyze only the upstrokes on an irregular graph of spiky ups and downs.[35] It is as if only increasing complexity has a story to tell, thus mimicking our own constructions of national history. The accumulation of power and treasure seems almost a natural development of society itself. Indeed, accumulation and development can easily come to mean the same thing.

Many models of state formation as a process of accumulation deal with complexity as a matter of the selfsame links along which economic surplus comes.[36] Trade and tribute are often both the subject and the explanation, although their development may have implications unseen by those involved. The complexity is, as it were, visible. In the Yemeni case I doubt that mapping the lines of surplus accumulation would work well, and the complexity at issue seems instead to be located elsewhere—the "program" and the "output" are separate. Predictability, therefore, always fails us at the moment we need it, which is when things change.[37]

In passing, one might note that the classical cases of state formation in archaeology (or, more accurately, in the folk archaeology on which the rest of us draw; archaeologists themselves have moved on from the Tempelstadt) are precisely those where power and tribute seem integral to the state's self-definition: in other words, what I have distinguished as external and internal criteria are indeed fairly well concordant. Whether in Meso-America or the ancient Near East, the center seems a complex of temple and granary. People supposedly worked part of their land for the gods and defined the worth of their collective enterprise, whether willingly or not, by tribute to the conceptual center. The temples of Sumer or of the Maya and the granaries of Mohenjo Daro all come to mind. Imperial China no doubt offers a similar congruence of cosmology and wealth. In a small way, perhaps, so do the chiefdoms of Polynesia. Yet *zakat* (alms) does not work this way, and the Islamic state (if we admit its existence) is not a queen bee to be fed that the hive may prosper.

The Zaydis offer a particularly clear example, and we might contrast the ideally corpulent figure of a Polynesian chief with the ideal imam, whose scholarship and horsemanship suggest an altogether leaner model. A Zaydi imam should use none of the *zakat* for himself. He should control its collection and expenditure, but there is no need for it to move to any ritual or administrative center. No cosmology is at issue in where wealth goes. The law is at issue in how wealth is spent, but it can as well be spent in situ.

In the rise and fall of Zaydi state formation, I suspect, the productive base often does not change markedly, and many local units of control or organization do not change at all. Yet suddenly men allot their *zakat* to the care of a single man and not to local purposes or to the sink of their own dishonesty. How much produce is physically moved from place to place at different periods is unclear; what is clear is that command of large resources can appear and disappear rapidly. The factors encouraging the appearance of a powerful imam will be touched on in the following section, but the specialized and hierarchically organized agencies of control, which for an archaeologist might define a state, grow and wither just as fast as the patterns of payment.[38] There are plus and minus states of the system, and the switch is in part a matter of piety.

Although this sounds at first somewhat mystical, an appeal to the zeitgeist, the links that account for much of it (in other words, a large part of the program) are simply those that constitute the Zaydi tradition, links of teacher to student, of reader to author, of the learned and the pious to one another. These links are inscribed, as French theorists might say, not in the practice of exchange but in the literature of the Zaydi *madhhab*, and especially in the *tarajim* books where the biographical links of the learned with each other are carefully laid out. Literacy, no matter how restricted, makes an enormous difference.

Here perhaps is another difference from much of the literature on North Africa. The fragmentation of Islamic order since the maraboutic crisis is stressed by many who have written on the Maghreb. Local lines of *marabtin* (saints) and *ashraf* (claimants of descent from the Prophet) are depicted as largely independent, spiritually and morally as well as politically. On the surface each Zaydi *hijra* (flight) by itself may look similarly separate and singular; but in the Zaydi case, all these points are connected by the hierarchy of learning, as well as each being embedded in a network of tribal protection pacts.

Where such fragmentation has taken place, the form of something like a state can outlast its actual manifestations, the program rolling on intact through times when the output is thin or almost nonexistent. J. N. Figgis says of the state in medieval Europe that though it "might be a dream, or even a prophecy, it was nowhere a fact."[39] Something of the kind is true of most periods of Zaydi history, when the imams were unsuccessful or were oppressed by those they sought to order. The dream outlasted the facts, however, and was re-produced in an organized way by education carried on in the *hijras*. The politically labile imamate, which at times in the medieval period seemed on the verge of extinction (there were actually several inter-regnums), was a realization of ideas stored elsewhere, in the writings and connections of learned men whose beliefs were less vulnerable than any state apparatus and whose own apparatus of learning could reproduce itself if need be from a few severed fragments. Gellner mentions the dragon's-teeth quality of tribal leadership;[40] here we have a statelike idea with the same resilience.

Hence when Turkish invaders in the late sixteenth century crushed the north beneath violent maladministration and cruel taxa-tion, people did not have to bewail their fate in isolation, each area rebelling hopelessly by itself or turning to mystical consolation. Many people did precisely that (this was the period of great Zaydi po-lemic against the Sufis);[41] but the possibility was there of seeking someone who was just and vigorous, to whom all might send what tax they dared, and who could rally the tribesmen in little groups, as the chance arose, to produce in the end a guerrilla army. His com-manders, judges, and administrators were all on hand, could they only be persuaded of his worth and the chance of success.

THE QASIMI DYNASTY, STATE FORMATION, AND TRIBAL CHIEFS

The rapidity with which alliances were formed and altered at most periods has been stressed already. The muddle of fortune is given clear direction only by the Turkish occupation of the sixteenth cen-tury and the Zaydi riposte of the seventeenth century, when the Qa-simi imams (descendants of al-Qasim b. Muhammad, d. 1620) gathered armies from the northern tribes, drove out the invader, and conquered Lower Yemen, reaching for a time as far afield as Hadra-mawt. This momentous success illustrates a common theme in Mid-dle Eastern material, that of state formation running outward. A state bound to tribes invites instant collapse by ordering those tribes in situ but prospers when it leads them against the periphery, that is, against the richer areas that abut those arid zones where tribalism itself most prospers. The Islamic expansion is the paradigm case, and the Wahhabis an obvious example. In the Yemeni case the emerging state, under al-Mutawakkil Isma'il (1644–1676), moved its capital to Dawran, south of San'a' and outside the territorial system of northern tribes, though well placed to control tribal conquests southward at the Zaydi behest.

The career of al-Qasim, founder of the dynasty, who fought the Turks but did not live to see them beaten, again illustrates the general problem with conceptualizing state formation. Like many an imam before and since, he began his career as a fugitive (the gift of two muskets and three pounds of powder is treated by the chronicler as a turning point). By the end of his life he was wealthy.[42] He was known well for his generosity, which does not mean giving his last crust of bread in a gesture of piety but giving a great many loaves to his followers. The rapidity with which control of treasure is centralized and decentralized is striking.

The theory of legitimacy informing this was similarly singular and discontinuous. From the earliest days of Zaydism the imam was supposed to be recognized by something much like acclamation. The historian of al-Qasim's time draws together the prescriptive quotations on the subject, which begin with God's pledge to Abraham:

> "I have made you imam over people [put you before them]. . . ," and [God] would not grant the imamate afterward to any unjust person. . . . Whoever [of the Prophet's house] puts forward his summons is the imam to be rightly answered, as our imams, peace be on them, have said in their books. . . . Al-Hadi ila l-Haqq Yahya b. al-Husayn, peace be on him, said. . . the imam who must be obeyed and with whose word it is not permitted to differ is the pious man who fights in God's cause.[43]

It is the imam who is the issue, not the imamate as an institution defined by rules of succession or administrative structure. Indeed, neither of the latter two considerations forms any part of Zaydi theory. From one point of view, it would not be too much to call the imamate at many periods less a state than an antistate; and Zaydi rhetoric is shot through with this summons to a direct realization of God's law by adherence to a single powerful and pious figure.

That is by no means the whole of the reality. As Ibn Khaldun says, a da'wa unsupported by 'asabiyya (group feeling) will not succeed: 'Ali Al-Shami, for instance, claimed the imamate in 1686 and, as the biographer rather nicely puts it, his summons received "no answer whatever."[44] Yet 'asabiyya is not a matter simply of tribal solidarity, whereby one tribe might close ranks against another. Small fragments of a following each have their own 'asabiyya—sometimes forming on a tribal name, sometimes on that of a religious figure, sometimes on that of a tribal shaykh—but all overlap and can combine to form a powerful enthusiasm given the right setting. When an imam headed a rising against some outside power, the tribal and re-

ligious summons were scarcely distinguishable; and when, as with
the Qasimis, the fortunes of the holy war led imams into the richer
areas of Lower Yemen (which are predominantly Shafi'i; the tribes of
the northern plateau are nominally Zaydi), then the "warriors in the
cause of God" could be paid with land and treasure.

Little of tribal territory is productive agriculturally, and some
tribes (such as those of Jabal Barat in the extreme northeast, who
won a terrifying name for themselves as marauders in the eighteenth
and nineteenth centuries) are constantly on the margin of possibility
for growing crops at all. The country as a whole, even Lower Yemen,
has repeatedly been ravaged by drought and starvation. The imams
of the seventeenth and eighteenth centuries, however, were fortunate
in controlling both an agricultural tax base in Lower Yemen and
some part of the revenue from the ports at a time of comparative
prosperity from the coffee trade. A certain regal splendor became
possible. Indeed, the Qasimis traded gifts of fine horses with the Mo-
ghuls of India.[45]

The Qasimis, unlike most of those who came before them, are
characterized by their own chroniclers as a *dawla*, or dynasty, and
they established a recognizable "state," which probably borrowed
much of its style from the preceding Ottomans. They maintained
slave soldiers and a fairly elaborate court, both of which were run in
part by slave ministers. The ranks of governors, ministers, judges,
and doorkeepers swelled as the dynasty prospered, but the troops
who won their conquests were from the tribes, and the Qasimis relied continually on tribal support thereafter. The double character of
the state is aptly caught by M. S. Niebuhr, who mentions two great
leaders of the army in his day (mid-eighteenth century), one a slave
prince of the kind the Qasimis favored and the other a tribal
shaykh.[46] One of the concomitants of this double character is that the
major tribal families one deals with in ethnography nowadays all appear for the first time at a time of great, but fragmented, state power,
around 1710. It was the shaykhs who held the balance between rival
claimants to the imamate, of whom there were then several, and they
prospered accordingly.

The prosperity of these shaykhs was bound up with land they held
in the west and south, outside tribal territory. Some archaeologists
and anthropologists would see these external landholdings as chiefdoms or as minor examples of secondary state formation. They were
essentially tributary structures, extracting agricultural surplus. So
were certain self-styled principalities, the most important being that
of Kawkaban, ruled by a line of *sayyid* princes. On the other side of

the country were other principalities based on the towns of the Jawf. None of them, however, was conceived as the germ of universal dominion or royal authority.

Some tribal leaders were extremely powerful. Certain of them held large areas of Yemen (the al-Ahmar family of Hashid and the al-Shayif family of Bakil are good examples) and are sometimes referred to in Zaydi histories as sultans of the Arabs.[47] The most they attempted, however, was secession. The idea of extensive and legitimate domination had long ago been confined to learned traditions. What by external criteria may have been chiefdoms or even petty states (at least dynasties) were by internal criteria merely fiefs. To claim wider authority, a *sayyid* would bid for the imamate; and a non-*sayyid*, to grasp wider power, would back an imamic pretender.

By associating with successful imams, even lesser shaykhs became powerful, and certain families of them can be followed through the histories from reign to reign. Bayt Radman of Arhab, for instance, can be traced from the early eighteenth century right down to the present. One 'Ali Radman appears in 1724, accompanying the great scholar Ibn al-Amir to mediate between two rival imams.[48] By adhering to one of them, "he amassed great wealth [*amwal*, almost certainly land], which he distributed among his heirs before his death, leaving part of it [presumably as a family *waqf*] to meet what vicissitudes might befall them."[49] One of these heirs, Muhammad Salih, died fighting for a later imam against the tribes of Barat in 1782.[50] A century later a Turkish general wrote entreating the imam of his day and saying the imam could doubtless "scatter Bani 'Ali from Radman's fief [Bani 'Ali are Radman's own section of Arhab] but what if, God forbid, the forces of the Christian foreigners moved on Yemen?"[51] Evidently, the landed wealth in western Yemen remained. The family that the Turks suggested was the imam's potential enemy in fact appears on the imam's side two years later, in 1896, when it attacked a Turkish punitive column in Arhab itself.[52] It played an important part in Yemeni affairs after the Turkish withdrawal and indeed in the civil war of the 1960s. Examples of this kind could be multiplied, but are they part of the tribes or the state or both?

The answer lies always in the learned tradition, in the part of the total society that seems to analysts somehow statelike. For example, "Al-Hadi was one of the shaykhs of al-Nu'aymat, a tribe of Nihm, which itself is a well-known Bakil tribe. He used frequently to visit the Imam al-Mahdi Ahmad [1676–1681]...at al-Gharas, and al-Mutawakkil al-Qasim [1716–1727]...married his daughter. So he and his sons attached themselves to the service of al-Mutawakkil and moved elsewhere on government work."[53] Al-Hadi's son 'Ali al-Nihmi was put in charge of the stores of one of the San'a' palaces, and the family became, it seems, San'anis. The grandson, Ahmad 'Ali, "was one of the ornaments of his age. He loved that which is good, he was concerned to comply [with God's law], and he leaned toward the men of learning and probity, being charitable to the weak, true in his speech, and irreproachable in his beliefs."[54] Shaykhs who were not made learned persons through such absorption into literate hierarchies remained liable to be denounced as evil ones, tyrants, and servants of the *taghut* (devil). The "ignorance" of the tribes, much dwelt on by the learned, was reproduced as a confirmed tautology. Yet tribal leaders were the basis of the dynasty's strength.

The Qasimis found themselves trapped in legitimizing claims established by tribal force. They were also trapped between the tribal north, where armed strength still lay, and the agricultural south, on which northerners battened yet where much of the dynasty's wealth had somehow to be found:

> The prince who campaigns with his armies, who lives by pillaging, sacking, and extortion, disposes of what belongs to aliens; and he must be open-handed, otherwise the soldiers would refuse to follow him. And you can be more liberal with what does not belong to you or your subjects. . . . Giving away what belongs to strangers in no way affects your standing at home; rather it increases it. You hurt yourself only when you give away what is your own. There is nothing so self-defeating as generosity: in the practicing of it, you lose the ability to do so, and you become either poor and despised or, seeking to escape poverty, rapacious and hated.[55]

The problem was inevitably crystallized by the success of conquest. Those who had been outside the pale of righteousness in *dar al-harb* or *dar al-fisq* were now within the pale, in *dar al-islam*, and, in Machiavelli's term, ceased to be alien.

Al-Mutawakkil Isma'il (1644–1676) established considerable order throughout the country, but his constant demands for taxes from Lower Yemen stimulated serious criticism from the learned without satisfying the tribes he was paying.[56] Al-Mahdi al-'Abbas (1748–1775) won a fine name from the learned and from San'anis;[57] but elsewhere in the country his reign saw spectacular millenarian risings, and the Barat tribes fought him repeatedly for southern land or for payment to be made to them where they were. The tribal system persisted through all this turmoil, whereby rival imams could seek refuge in tribal territory and rally discontented tribes.

The attachment of different styles of Islam to different ways of life does not help us much in explaining this: a flux-and-reflux type of argument works poorly.[58] The imams and their supporters, living often among the tribes, denounced tribesmen constantly as poor Muslims and railed against many tribal practices as *taghut*, a term whose precise meaning would be hard to pin down but which is often taken to denote a work of the devil.[59] The learned all but defined their own status by making such condemnations, but they did so in situ; the city had no particular moral value for them, though learned and urban disdain for the tribes lined up readily when the imams, at various periods, held San'a'. It is also true that "puritan scholars" might leave the city and rally the tribes against an imam based there,[60] but it was nearly always a question of one puritan scholarly claim against another.

One should not discount the variation Zaydism itself showed. At times in the medieval period there were developments of the movement that by earlier or later standards were violently heterodox. Yet among the tribes a sober and scholarly Islam was promoted by the Zaydis at most times, which the tribesmen themselves seem usually to have matched in temperament, though not in literate accomplishment. Saints, tombs, and sorcery are in most periods a feature more of Lower Yemen and western Yemen. Northern tribesmen are routinely condemned not of undisciplined spiritualism but of cutting the roads, disobeying imams, and denying inheritance to women.[61] This standard framework of condemnation moved with the imams and tribes when they together took other parts of Yemen. So too did the terms in which tribes were rallied by learned persons.

As an example of a learned malcontent calling for tribal support against the imam of the day, we have 'Ali al-Kawkabani, who left San'a' for Barat in 1750 after quarreling with al-Mahdi al-'Abbas. When he arrived among the tribes, he circulated a poem:

> Tell the people of the desert and villages,
>   and him who sets out in noonday heat or the
>   nighttime,
> Who travels in the lands of God, through all the
>   wilderness and every trackless, bleak desert,
> In every part of the vast Tihama,
>   to Aden and Abyan and further:
> Blame upon him whose ears are stopped up when a rider
>   sets out to the people of the highlands or
>   lowlands,
> The religion of Mustafa [the Prophet] has died in our
>   times, and no one is seen to mourn for it or to
>   make amends.

I challenge you, did Muhammad's religion
    equate with the sins now committed?
Were there in his houses as in yours [the imam's]
    fabrics woven for kings of Rome or of Persia?
Did al-Hallaj have stuffed fabrics,
    from India, dyed like blossoming gardens?...
Were there treasures embroidered with silver and gold,
    seeming like life itself?...
Wake up, wake up and beware of the place,
    in which that which is hid from mankind will
    appear...
The Prophet had little...except for his bed,
    a mat with nothing between it and his body...[62]

The contrast is pointed between the supposedly corrupt imam with his luxuries and the frugal honesty of the Prophet, leaving little doubt that those "who travel in the lands of God," the indigent Bedouins, have more in common with the Prophet than with their ruler. There is nothing surprising about the style of such claims and their apparent affinity with tribal wishes; they are made in terms of equality and justice that match precisely the resentment of tribesmen at receiving less than what they think is their share of state patronage. The language of equality and justice is applicable to everyone and open to all.[63]

In practice there were seldom two clearly separable cultural registers, one tribal and the other statelike. Where a local *sayyid* called on his tribal protectors for support against others, he would be understood in terms of tribal justice as much as in terms of Islamic rectitude; where tribal interests were denounced as *taghut*, the tribe might respond that its aggressor was himself an un-Islamic tyrant. There were not even two clearly separate sets of people. Many of the scholars remained attached to, and protected by, tribes (indeed, their status was defined in largely tribal terms), whereas tribesmen of course had no doubt that they themselves were Muslims.

Tribes and state, therefore, do not refer to different things or groups. The apparent marginality of the tribes to history and their distinction from the state is largely the result of the scholars' self-definition, and it is easy to forget that the tribesmen, as much as anyone, are those making the history about which the scholars write. There cannot, however, be an alternative history of single tribes or sections as there can of, say, a town. Throughout the imamic period, though not explicitly noted in the literature, there continued to be a system concordant with that al-Hamdani wrote of, where units are defined by mutual contradistinction and change over time in specific ways.

A section that has some claim refused or ignored by its fellow sections may change tribes. No one physically moves. The territory and location of the section remain as and where they were, but the line between tribes A and B, which before ran along one side of the section's borders, now runs along the other. Whole tribes may transfer by the same means from Hashid to Bakil or vice versa. The practice is attested in al-Hamdani's works, where we are told numerous times of one tribe "entering" another; and the process of change can be followed through the toponymy of the last ten centuries down to our own time. At no point since at least the tenth century do we have named units on the plateau displacing each other by conquest. Tribesmen may flee one tribe for another, but the units themselves shift by recognizable quanta. When tribesmen migrate to dominate parts of Lower Yemen or even to settle there, the territory of the tribe itself does not expand to encompass their movement. Therefore, although tribesmen are certainly part of *histoire événementielle*, the tribes themselves, unlike the transient state, are not events.

Great men come and go; great deeds are done; people suffer or prosper;[64] but collective identities are not constructed in such a way that the story of a single tribe would have the slightest coherence. There are only the *akhbar*, or self-contained tales, which come in no particular sequence, and the moral equality of tribe against tribe, from which the tales derive their significance. The inequalities among men must be attached instead to a nontribal history such as that of a dynasty, leaving tribal identities themselves as a "part world." Yet the linear histories that produce this effect are themselves not those of a legal person, as the histories of Western states are. The Qasimis, for instance, became a dynasty or state (*dawla*) and later ceased to be one with surprisingly little formal comment. The successive imams are each assessed in the terms applied to imams before and after them (though the collapse of the dynasty is mourned when it happens), but the state as such receives no theoretical reflection.

The hierarchies of tribute, taxation, and largesse became quite elaborate under the Qasimis, although always liable to fragment as fiefs seceded under relatives of the imam, rival lines of *sayyid*s, or tribal shaykhs. The coherence of the links between these magnates was attributed always to the imam himself. His *hayba*, the awe he inspired, was in this regard much like the *virtu* of Machiavelli's prince.[65] Yet there was still nothing quite corresponding to *lo stato* in the sense of a circumscribed domain that might equally attach to a single man, a council, or some other sovereign body. The relation of the ruler to the area he ruled remained more like that of the medieval figures of Europe and their domains. The relationship was the more vulnerable, indeed, in that not only might the ruler be overthrown by external attack or internal rebellion,[66] but a rival claim might be made by Zaydis or non-Zaydis, which potentially was both these at once.

The Qasimi *dawla* collapsed in the nineteenth century, riven by intestine disputes but crippled particularly, one may guess, by the loss of the Red Sea ports following Wahhabi expansion further north. A period of disorder set in, known to the Yemenis as *ayyam al-fasad*, the time of corruption. Predictably, the blame for this disorder fell on the tribes rather than on the *sayyid*s who failed to agree among themselves on an imam or resolve their own differences. As the prominence of the dynasty lessened, that of the tribes increased, as if tribes and state were indeed quite separate alternatives, one of which gave way to the other. The impression is of the tribes spreading out into nontribal territory. Certainly there were large movements of people, driven by drought, famine, and plagues of locusts, but the impression of expansion is in large part illusory. Northern tribesmen had been associated with these nontribal lands already for two centuries. It was not that a borderline between tribes and peasants gave way as the state weakened but that the governance of the country as a whole collapsed.

The period of corruption ended with a second Turkish occupation in 1872, when the imams were pushed back to the tribal north. Toward the end of the century a new dynasty of imams, the Hamid al-Din, appeared and led the tribes against the foreign invader, besieging San'a' with tribal forces that by the standard of any tribal dispute were enormous. A truce in 1911 recognized the Imam Yahya's control of areas north of San'a'. Then, in 1918, the Turks were obliged to abandon Yemen; the imam led tribal armies toward the west and south, filling the vacuum, as it were; and in the course of the 1920s and early 1930s he conquered all of what is now North Yemen, repeating in part the Qasimi achievement of three hundred years earlier. The world in which he did this was not, however, that in which the Qasimis had lived.

The last imams, those of the Hamid al-Din (1918–1962), maintained very simple courts, ran the country by personal decision as far as possible, and established an unparalleled degree of order in the countryside by imprisoning an enormous number of hostages. As the century wore on, however, the idea of the nation-state increasingly took hold among Yemeni thinkers, an internalization of value relative to a particular community (the Yemeni "people") and at the same time a ranking against other units of the same kind ("progress" versus "backwardness"). Comparison and modernity were in the air. Emulation of other Arab nations and of the world beyond began to preoccupy first the intellectuals and then broader elements of the population, introducing a rather different time line than that constructed by the old order. The imamate came to be seen by some as what it could not have been at any earlier (prenationalist) period, namely, an anachronism; and when the last imam was overthrown, he was replaced not by a rival claimant to the same position but by the republic installed through the 1962 revolution.

At this point, where by the Yemenis' own estimation the premodern period ends, we should pause and take stock. What are we to make of this history? The imamate was conducted according to its own rules, which were not those of the nation-state or even of states in Europe around the time of the Renaissance. Nor do the definitions attached to the word *state* as a technical term in archaeology or political science apply readily. The state in this latter sense seems almost an epiphenomenon of Zaydi history. Yet the fact remains that the imamate seems to us not only to produce a state on occasion but to be somehow statelike, an obvious complement to tribalism, although we know that the two cannot be empirically separated. Even though tribal leaders at particular times have been more powerful than the imam or imams of their day, the tribes do not seem to us petty states.

I would suggest in all seriousness that what we intuitively recognize as statelike in such settings as this are formations with a unified political history of their own devising. Peasants, by contrast, we recognize as people whose history seems always to be the unwritten obverse of whoever dominates them: they, more than others, are the "people without history."[67] Tribesmen are a further category—not simply peasants with guns or spears. What we recognize as tribes in the Arabian setting (the *qaba'il* or *qubul*) are those units that are defined primarily against each other and that therefore have no single history but a plethora of fragmented *akhbar*, although their members are also involved in the events recorded by learned chronicles.

Ira Lapidus has suggested in his essay in this volume that the history of the Middle East cannot be told in a unified way from a tribal point of view. This is true because tribes are less important in many areas than some authors would have us think. Yet it is also true more generally (and perhaps more significantly) because in what we recognize as tribal there is something antithetical to unified narrative and thus to what we expect of states. Events may be related in several different modes, but only one of these, the learned version, presents the continuity from which processual forms such as state formation can be extracted. As always with human society, our material has been defined for us before we come to study it. To understand it fully would require working close to the grain of history and ethnography to determine how such definitions in fact were made in local terms. Questions posed in our own terms might best not be answered so much as carefully disassembled.

THE NATION-STATE IN THE MODERN PERIOD

I have stressed that the concept of the state is problematic when applied to Upper Yemen in the premodern period and is sometimes more a mote in the analyst's eye than a reflection of indigenous interests. This is not true of the present, when the Yemen Arab Republic plainly is a state, and one whose short but honorable history could be written in conventional terms. Let us start our consideration of the modern period, therefore, by sketching what has happened since the 1962 revolution and the demise of the imamate tradition.[68]

The last imam was ejected from San'a' by a coup of army officers, among them several men of tribal background. A civil war ensued between the royalists (backed by, among others, Saudi Arabia) and the republicans (backed, though for a long time also crippled politically, by Nasserist Egypt). From 1962 to 1967 the Yemeni civil war was often, despite Yemeni efforts, a battle by proxy between Riyadh and Cairo. The tribes were heavily involved in this, and the enormous expenditure of wealth by both sides passed mainly through the hands of tribal leaders, who, like those in Qasimi times, rallied the troops.

These families had been important, though largely inarticulate, in resistance to the Turks at the start of the century, but "after that time their political influence began to dwindle, and in Imam Yahya's day [1918 to 1948] this influence shrank considerably. However, their power revived again when both the republicans and the royalists recruited them in the late war, one of the results of which was that shaykhs on both sides took sensitive governmental posts, buttressed by both government hegemony and tribal power."[69] In the reconciliation at the end of the war (1969–1970), important shaykhs from both camps (along with many nontribal figures) were brought into first the National Assembly and then the Consultative Council. The idea of a governmental apparatus had been little developed under the last imams, and the appearance under the postwar republican regime of a body of men having both tribal standing and official rank was in large part new. The prominence of this apparent group has wavered considerably since 1970.

In the first few years after the war, governmental shaykhs were extremely prominent, and 'Abdullah al-Ahmar of Hashid, the most important of the tribal leaders, was speaker of the country's Consultative Council. Under President Ibrahim al-Hamdi (1974–1977), the council was dissolved and most, though not all, of the leading shaykhs were deprived of governmental office. The official style was not altogether lost, however, and were there space, one might pursue the way in which tribal documents in the postwar period incorporate the language of national politics. Nor was the influence lost that was based on tribal identity.

Throughout the late 1970s—through the assassination of al-Hamdi; then that of the ill-fated Ahmad al-Ghashmi, when the head of state seemed almost like Frazer's priest at Nemi; then the assumption of the presidency by 'Ali 'Abdullah Salih—North Yemen was plagued by rivalries between its immediate neighbors, South Yemen and Saudi Arabia. The tribes were in demand politically. Their allegiance to different powers and their changes of allegiance make a complex story if rendered in the conventional terms of international politics, and I have sketched part of it elsewhere.[70] The explicit internal divisions of North Yemeni politics, which were stimulated by external rivalries and flared up on occasion as minor warfare within the country, were only quieted by 'Ali 'Abdullah's defeat of the guerrilla movement in Lower Yemen during 1982.

Throughout the period 1975–1982 the tribes were militarily and politically in demand. And throughout the period the tribesmen, like many others in Yemen, were benefiting from a boom in remittances from emigrant labor. That boom has now ended. Oil has been found in eastern Yemen, with genuinely important implications for development planning. The disputes between neighboring states have for the moment subsided, and the years since 1982 have been far quieter in the tribal north than the previous five or six years. Tribalism has not, however, disappeared.

Some years ago I suggested that despite the power of tribal leaders, tribalism itself was still excluded from political debate, much as it had been, though in different terms, under prerepublican governments.[71] This has remained largely true. However, the rhetoric has not developed, as it then seemed likely to do and has done in many countries, in the direction of denouncing the tribes outright as a reprehensibly backward element of society. Indeed, the president, rather surprisingly by regional standards, has gone so far as to assert in an interview that Yemen is a tribal country.[72] On another front, Shaykh 'Abdullah of Hashid was quoted as affirming Yemen's democratic character and saying he himself would run for office in the reconstituted Consultative Council,[73] which suggests he conceived a fair chance of success in doing so. The game is far from over. What we must ask ourselves, however, is whether beyond the surface patterns of recent politics something has changed more fundamentally, something equivalent to the program I touched on earlier. An empirical account does not tell us what we want to know.

Approaches to modern state formation often run afoul of the illusion that tribes and states are things. The result, evident in some writing on the Yemeni case, is this: tribal leaders who hold governmental rank, for example, are counted part of the state; when they dissent they are quietly recast (without theoretical explanation) as tribal, and the state is thus whittled down to the military and the bureaucrats; when barrack-room politics rears its head, parts of the military too are quietly recast as nonstate; the bureaucrats then turn out to have views of their own, and the state is whittled down further still, with the result that it recedes indefinitely in front of the advancing analyst as if it were always to be found beyond the next hill or in the next office down the corridor. To escape this bind, we must recognize that the state is an idea just as much as an institution and that people may subscribe to several ideas in turn or, indeed, simultaneously, just as they have done in all periods. It is here that at least part of the program lies.

The ideas that define the modern period are distinctive: the ideology of transition is central,[74] and the subject of this transition is the "people," an entity to be molded by political practice yet whose existence is proposed as natural. The state, identified with the people usually in a rather Jacobin mode, is in effect the people militant. The people have a single history, usually marked by a decisive break with the past dark ages, a break that is brought about by a revolution; and all the so-called sons of the people share not just their past but also their present history and even a destiny.

This vision is promoted by the media, of course, but most of all by the apparently minor institution of primary schools. Long before central government exercises detailed control, the schools are what change perceptions in rural areas.[75] As Ernest Gellner long ago noted, one of the conditions "in which nationalism becomes the natural form of political loyalty" is "every man a clerk,"[76] or, in the Islamic world, "every man his own 'alim."[77] The serial identity of the newly educated, which fuels nationalist sentiment, also fuels funda-

mentalist religious sentiment. Both sentiments are evident in contemporary Yemen, and both persist in a newly generalized view of
social time and space.

Such a change of conception is required by the wider system of
nation-states in which the countries of the Middle East found themselves immediately after the First World War. There now must be a
state, whatever form it may take in the future. The modern system al-
lows no empty spaces on the political map. The beginnings of a new
sensibility are first visible perhaps slightly earlier, however, in
latter-day chroniclers' accounts of the years around 1900. Until then,
the entries concern Yemeni affairs almost exclusively. The struggle
of the righteous against the ungodly is recorded without regard for
what anyone outside the local system of reference may think. Suddenly items are mentioned in the foreign press—first, in an entry for
1896, accounts of such things as a landslide in America and the
death from disease of children in France; then a letter from the imam
to the Ottoman government quoted not just as a Yemeni document
but also as something printed in a Turkish newspaper; then Turkish
newspaper pieces on Yemen as reported to a Yemeni chronicler.[78] The
country, or its intellectuals, enters something perhaps akin to what
psychoanalysts call the mirror stage. Identity is established in part
by mutual observation of opposite numbers, a potentially endless set
of reflections among the elements of a nationalist world.

This attention to a world system and one's place within it has been
promoted among ordinary people in the last twenty years by travel
abroad, by the media, and by modern transport within the country.
Pluralism or particularism, so much a feature of the tribal scheme,
is being reevaluated, as it has been in such countries as Libya, Morocco, and Oman.[79] An important aspect of this process is precisely
the idea that the people have a single history and a national destiny.
As Dale F. Eickelman says of Morocco, "There is now underway a major transformation of the concepts of the past in which some elements of the traditional pluralism are rapidly disappearing.
Replacing it is a pluralism that is consciously elaborated into a system. . . . For all of society the subuniverse of meaning that is constituted by 'bookish' conceptions of history is increasingly creating a
'shock' with commonsense notions of the past."[80] E. L. Peters's remarks on Libya, although addressed to specifically religious institutions, deal in fact with this same phenomenon of particularism
encountering a vision of a general history and of a society among
others like it: "Particularism gives precedence to differences between groups of people. The development of a larger conceptual system of reference does not preclude particularism, but relegates it to

a subsidiary position."[81] The major question becomes how to accomplish this relegation, how to contain the local or particular within a national or supranational whole and not oppose them in a conflict only one can win. The question is posed in such a way, however, that the nation in the wider world and the tribes within the nation are almost inevitably connected. "Tribes and state formation" becomes a genuine and general question for the first time.

Despite the legal equality between states in international law, the nations rank themselves against each other within the language of development and underdevelopment. All are supposedly on the same trajectory. To that extent (insofar, for example, as I have just cited Peters on Libya or Eickelman on Morocco), one's own writing is always in complicity with a particular local view of what is happening—that the countries of the Middle East share a certain position in the world at large. Within that view the state seems of vital necessity as the locus of emulation. The conceptual whole of *lo stato* would be hard to avoid, and to deny its validity would, for those pinning their hopes on it, be treachery.

New problems replace the old, and the question of a time line, briefly touched on earlier, again becomes important in this modern setting. It was essential to the old tribal mode that persons or collective units not be commensurable, that they all conceptually be equals but that no standard exist to rank them impartially. Within the nationalist scheme, by contrast, persons or collective units such as sections or tribes now are commensurable and, unavoidably, are measured, often in terms of development and backwardness. They threaten to become not the prescriptive equals of the older scheme but elements that must struggle for equality or precedence as factions within a larger whole.

The government of North Yemen since 1982 has been attempting to include particularism, to find it a subsidiary position, by building a nationwide system of political involvement in the form of local and regional committees that culminate in a General Popular Congress. It is so far succeeding well. More generally, however, the problems to which this attempt responds, as indeed the existence of the state itself responds, are subtly different from those of the prerevolutionary period and quite typical of the modern world.

Unity of experience was previously constructed in a nontribal mode by learned chroniclers and biographers. The imagined community had no explicit boundaries, the particular links proposed between individual events or persons were presented as transient (unity of experience, as we said, had to be constructed), and changes of fortune were in a sense contingencies—more accurately, they were often attached to the will of God. The boundaries of the people, by contrast, are set from the outset. The unity of their experience is presented as given (pluralism, correspondingly, must now be consciously elaborated), while changes of fortune are taken to result directly from human action. A new cast of characters ("feudalists," "reactionaries"—now also rendered in supposedly Islamic terms) is established to explain the results. Elements within this national whole are now as likely as the nations themselves to be seen as backward or advanced, as liabilities or assets in national development. Not this tribe or that but tribalism at last appears on the conceptual map, and with it the question of tribes and state formation.

The analysis is made more difficult, therefore, by a final twist. The evolutionary scheme that most of us have abandoned—in part (and somewhat in al-Hamdani's tribal mode) so as not to rank ourselves against other cultures—has now been taken up by them. Nothing could nowadays be more common intellectual currency in the Third World, perhaps particularly in the Middle East, than nineteenth-century anthropology. Al-Majalla's interview with the Yemeni president, which I mentioned earlier, is worth quoting briefly because the interviewer's question seems so obvious to many:

> "To what extent has Yemen succeeded in moving from the stage of tribalism [marhala al-qabaliyya] to the state stage? And can it be transformed from [several] tribes into one tribe?" [The president replied firmly]: "The state is part of the tribes, and our Yemeni people is a collection of tribes. Our towns and countryside are all tribes. All the official and popular apparatuses of the state are formed from the tribes (or tribesmen)."

In fact, large parts of Yemen are not really tribal in the sense discussed here. Nevertheless, the president's reply motivated the interviewer, or his editors, to headline the whole article, of which this is a minor fragment, "Yes, We Are All Tribesmen."[82]

The questions I have posed about the relation between tribes and state thus run parallel to those posed by people within the system. The Yemenis themselves have cause to look over their history in a mode quite different from that of imamic times: indeed, the blossoming of a new historiography in Yemen in recent years has been remarkable. Yemenis too now face the temptation to separate tribes from states conceptually, contrast them, and then set them in order by assimilating history to evolution as if one stage would lead to the next. From that point would follow certain projects of politics. The idea of state formation corresponds to genuine compulsions in modern thought, affecting Middle Easterners as much as us, and these compulsions are not those of the premodern period. Their analysis would depend not on the history of particular tribes and states in the area (as if empirical continuities and change were the key) but specifically on the modern conjunction in which the relation of tribes to states in general has become a question and from which their history would not be written.

The world in which this is true is one where not just the state but the nation-state as well is the norm both morally and statistically. What place the fragmentary language of tribes might acquire within this world is a question best left to the authors of some Arabic *Leviathan* or *Essay on Civil Society*. Yet the tribes are not simply things, groups, or forces in this context. They are part of a system of ideas that can be reworked and no doubt will be. The differences among men, which tribalism always represented as the imamate-proclaimed subjection to a single law, must be dealt with somehow if the state is to prosper. If such differences are not included willingly, then they appear in the form of factions. The Arabic word for these, *tawa'if*, is very old. The sense such factions have, though, is largely new. They are the opposite not of organization generally but specifically of the unitary state as conceived in the modern period, and tribes as such are not the most important.

Patricia Crone suggests that tribes and states are not sequential stages but alternative answers to the problem of security. There is a great deal of truth to this notion, though the two entities often cannot be empirically separated. It is also true that those who hope tribal egalitarian values in the Middle East will by themselves ease a "transition to democracy" are likely to be disappointed. Yet the suggestion that tribes and the modern state are both "avowedly egalitarian, both espouse mass participation," perhaps obscures the main question now faced by those involved.[83] Certainly, large numbers of men sometimes turned out when tribe was pitted against tribe. Certainly, also, tribes are as egalitarian as Weber's rational state and its sovereign law that applies to everyone. Nevertheless, the individualism of the tribal scheme was predicated, and still is, on its indefinite divisibility. That of the nation-state, by contrast, is predicated on an absolute moral unity. The serial individuals who make up the people are potentially a mass in a way that tribes never were or could be; and the prince who aimed entirely to abolish tribes in favor of a simple identity between state and people would face problems concerning which neither Machiavelli nor Ibn Khaldun provides adequate guidance.

NOTES

The present paper has benefited greatly from discussion with Walter Armbrust, Michael Fahy, and Andrew Shryock, though it should be said in their defense that none of them agrees entirely with the approach taken. Particular thanks are due to Walter Armbrust for a draft translation of the poem quoted and to Robert Wilson for finding me the reference cited from *al-Majalla*. Thanks are also due to Henry Wright for numerous helpful and very patient criticisms. The faults are the author's.

1. Alexandre Passerin d'Entrèves, "The State," in Philip P. Weiner, ed., *Dictionary of the History of Ideas* (New York, 1973), 4:312.

2. Richard Tapper, ed., Introduction to *The Conflict of Tribe and State in Iran and Afghanistan* (London, 1983), pp. 10–11.

3. For an extremely useful discussion of state origins from an archaeologist's viewpoint, see H. Wright, "Recent Research on the Origins of the State," *Annual Review of Anthropology* 6 (1977): 379–397, and the references given there. See also H. Wright, "The Evolution of Civilizations," in David J. Meltzer, Don D. Fowler, and Jeremy A. Sabloff, eds., *American Anthropology Past and Future* (Washington, D.C., 1986). For useful indications, by contrast, of the views of an anthropologist committed to the idea of cultural evolution, see R. L. Carneiro, "Cross-currents in the Theory of State Formation," *American Ethnologist* 14, no. 4 (1987): 756–770.

4. Patricia Crone, "The Tribe and the State," in J. A. Hall, ed., *States in History* (Oxford, 1986).

5. H. A. R. Gibb, *Studies in the Civilization of Islam* (London, 1962), p. 174.

6. Ernest Gellner, "Flux and Reflux in the Faith of Men," in Ernest Gellner, *Muslim Society: Essays* (Cambridge, 1981), p. 82.

7. I have written about the tribes elsewhere (e.g., Paul K. Dresch, "The Position of Shaykhs among the Northern Tribes of Yemen," *Man* 19, no. 1 [1984]: 31–49; "Tribal Relations and Political History in Upper Yemen," in B. R. Pridham, ed., *Contemporary Yemen* [London, 1984]; "The Significance of the Course Events Take in Segmentary Systems," *American Ethnologist* 13, no. 2 [1986]: 309–324) and have tried to keep to a minimum the repetition here of points made earlier. Many of the subjects touched on in the present essay are dealt with at greater length in a monograph entitled *Tribes, Government and History in Yemen* (Oxford, 1989). For an overview of relations between tribes and the imamate, see R. B. Serjeant, "The Interplay between Tribal Affinities and Religious (Zaydi) Authority in the Yemen," *al-Abhath* (Beirut) 30 (1982), special issue, "State and Society in the Arab World," ed. Fuad Khuri, pp. 11–50.

8. Crone, "Tribe and the State."

9. Gellner, "Flux and Reflux," p. 20.

10. Gellner, "Flux and Reflux," pp. 30, 33, 37.

11. Dresch, "Position of Shaykhs," pp. 31–49.

12. Tapper, Introduction to *Conflict of Tribe and State*.

13. Dresch, "Significance of the Course," pp. 309–324.

14. Gellner, "Flux and Reflux," p. 72.

15. The sense best attached to the phrase *balanced opposition* in the Yemeni case I have discussed elsewhere (Dresch, "Position of Shaykhs," pp. 31–49; "Significance of the Course," pp. 309–324). For the present purpose it is enough to note that the phrase does not imply a balance of power, nor is kinship of central importance. From the existing anthropological literature it is easy to assume that a "tribe is . . . a society which relies on descent for political integration. Descent generates groups over and above the level required for production and allocation of property rights" (Crone, "Tribe and the State," p. 51). The language of shared ancestry is certainly important in the Yemeni case (it expresses the idea of shared honor), but it is not elaborated with detailed descent lines. In fact, the number of rural Arab societies with elaborate genealogies in anything like the patrilineal African mode is probably tiny, and too much academic discussion still labors under the assumption that Middle Eastern tribes are really organized as depicted by the great Umayyad schemes of shared descent, which themselves, of course, were the product of a growing state.

16. Yahya b. al-Husayn, *Ghayat al-Amani fi Akhbar al-Qutr al-Yamani*, 2 vols., ed. Sa'id 'Abd al-Fattah (Cairo, 1968), p. 298.

17. Gellner, "Flux and Reflux."

18. The major sources are a geography of the Arabian Peninsula (Al-Hasan al-Hamdani, *Sifat Jazirat al-'Arab* [1968]) and a ten-volume work called *Al-Iklil*, of which four volumes survive and one, the tenth (Al-Hasan al-Hamdani, *Al-Iklil min Akhbar al-Yaman wa-Insan Himyar*, vol. 10, ed. Muhibb al-Din al-Khatib [Cairo, 1948]), deals with the tribes of Hamdan. The relation between genealogy in this latter work and the actual organization of Yemeni tribes remains moot.

19. Muhammad Zabara, *A'immat al-Yaman bi-l-Qurn al-Rabi' 'Ashar*, 3 vols. (Cairo, 1956), 1:61, 67.

20. See D. T. Gochenour, "The Penetration of Zaydi Islam into Early Medieval Yemen" (Ph.D. diss., Harvard University, 1984), p. 106 and passim.

21. Yahya b. al-Husayn, *Ghayat al-Amani*, p. 316; Zabara, *A'immat al-Yaman*, 1:108.

22. It cannot be overly stressed that Yemen was not isolated from wider movements in the Islamic world. The Zaydis may well initially have intended a general caliphate. Almost certainly the Fatimids did when they organized their movement in Yemen (see S. Jiva, "The Initial Destination of the Fatimid Caliphate: The Yemen or the Maghrib?" *Bulletin of the British Society for Middle Eastern Studies* 13, no. 1 [1986]: 15–26). Even disputes within a single movement of piety would occasionally be referred elsewhere, as for instance when the Zaydi imam al-Mansur 'Abdullah b. Hamzah attempted to suppress the Mutarrifis (a local division of Zaydism) and both parties wrote to the 'Abbasid caliph in Baghdad (Zabara, *A'immat al-Yaman*, 1:136). What moral relevance the 'Abbasids could have had for Zaydis is a mystery.

23. For a classic account of minor state formation in northern Arabia, see H. Rosenfeld, "The Social Composition of the Military in the Process of

State Formation in the Arabian Desert," parts 1 and 2, *Journal of the Royal Anthropological Institute* 95, nos. 1, 2 (1965): 75–86, 174–194.

24. Roughly speaking, primary state formation is that which takes place in a context of interacting prestate units; secondary state formation takes place in the interaction with existing states; tertiary state formation perhaps takes place in the interstices between states, on trade routes or the like, and so on. Once one has left the world of primary state formation, divisions of this kind soon become unwieldy because of the sheer variety of cases. I am inclined to use *secondary state formation* here as the unmarked term, the residual category containing all nonprimary states. In conversation, and to make clear just what one is up against in talking about states in general, Henry Wright suggested that were one to be drawn into unproductive taxonomic games of this sort, then Yemeni political formations would probably have to be dubbed something like fourth-generation tertiary states! Certainly, to compare the Islamic world with the protostates of ancient Sumer (Crone, "Tribe and the State") is to compare very different things.

25. Zabara, *A'immat al-Yaman*, 1:90.

26. Zabara, *A'immat al-Yaman*, 1:188, 201, 226.

27. Gochenour, "Penetration of Zaydi Islam," chap. 5.

28. Gochenour, "Penetration of Zaydi Islam," pp. 70, 84.

29. Let me make clear that I am not arguing against ever using the term *state*; after all, Machiavelli himself used it in describing the Ottoman Empire, which he took as the prime example of a state where all power and honor depended on the ruler, and the army's affections were more important than the people's (*The Prince*, trans. George Bull [Harmondsworth, Eng., 1961], pp. 45–46, 113). I am, however, concerned to ask what is involved in doing so. The term is heavily overdetermined, to say the least.

30. H. C. Dowdall, "The Word 'State,'" *Law Quarterly Review* 39, no. 153 (1923): 98–125.

31. The history of the term *state* is a vast subject, and the most useful discussions seem still to be such aging classics as O. Gierke, *Political Theories of the Middle Ages*, trans. F. W. Maitland (Cambridge, 1900). Yet the association of states and law is of central importance to even the most empirical approach. Hall, for instance, in a general conspectus of states in world history, argues that both the Islamic world and Christian Europe in the Middle Ages comprised separate, competing *regna* within a single moral space defined by religion (J. A. Hall, "States and Economic Development: Reflections on Adam Smith," in J. A. Hall, ed., *States in History* [Oxford, 1986], pp. 159–163). The Islamic states were ephemeral (these Hall depicts by broken circles) and the Christian ones less so (solid circles). Hall leaves the difference unexplained. The institution of positive law, strikingly absent in the Islamic cases, is not primarily a matter of strength or weakness but one of continuity in self-definition, a major source of those solid lines in Hall's diagram. A succession of dynasties form a single state, a bounded entity with a single history, a single story that might then be made cumulative. By contrast, most Islamic dynasties, subject to a supposedly changeless law, come and go without moral issue.

32. A. Ayalon, *Language and Change in the Arab Middle East* (New York, 1987), pp. 81–82.

33. J. N. Figgis, *Studies of Political Thought from Gerson to Grotius 1414–1625*, 2d ed. (Cambridge, 1916), p. 4.

34. Where the designation *is* territorial it seems to derive from somewhere else, such as from a caliph. There are parallels to be drawn between the Andalusian *muluk al-tawa'if*, for instance, and principalities within the Holy Roman Empire. To pursue the question would take us too far afield, but a distinctive part of the European experience is surely marked by the transition, discussed long ago by Maine, between the idea of a *rex francorum* and that of a *rex francie*. For comparisons between Christendom and parts of the Islamic world, see Gibb, *Studies in the Civilization of Islam*, pp. 36–38, and Gellner, "Flux and Reflux," pp. 42–44, 54–55.

35. The rather selective nature of theorizing on primary state formation has been noted by Crone, "Tribe and the State," p. 66. On a much smaller scale, discussions of secondary state formation have often something of the same character. Carneiro, for example, boldly asserts that "the reality of cultural evolution is no longer questioned" (Carneiro, "Cross-currents," p. 756), and if the comparison is between ourselves and the Lower Paleolithic, then perhaps there is something in what he says. On any shorter time scale the question is less simple. He says of a recent collection of papers, "They are not simple history. They make no attempt to present all the data, but only data carefully selected and arranged with a definite end in mind: to bring out a certain pattern. This pattern we call *evolution*, that is, an orderly progression moving in a certain direction" (p. 769). Historians too bring out patterns, but Carneiro can take account of the Frankish state as "compelling historical evidence of the directionality of evolution" while also saying, "Who would want to call the collapse of Rome 'evolution'?" (p. 757). Plainly, rather different stories emerge depending on whether one takes Rome and the Franks together or just the Franks. It also matters very much where one stands in the history (whether Boethius is speaking, say, or Charlemagne). The assimilation of history to evolution, which would make perfect sense to a modern Yemeni nationalist, would have made none at all to a Zaydi in the years around 1800.

36. Not all models do this by any means, and for a discussion of possible approaches see Henry Wright, "Recent Research on the Origin of the State," *Annual Review of Anthropology* 6 (1977): 379–397, or Carneiro, "Cross-currents," pp. 756–770. But I am thinking particularly of a tradition in anthropology exemplified by Friedman's elegant model of Burmese tribes and chiefdoms and neighboring minor states (J. Friedman, "Tribes, States and Transformations," in M. Bloch, ed., *Marxist Analyses and Social Anthropology*, ASA Studies, no. 2 [London, 1975]).

37. E. W. Ardener, "The New Anthropology and Its Critics," *Man* 6, no. 3 (1971): 449–467, esp. p. 456.

38. Wright, "Recent Research," p. 383.

39. J. N. Figgis, *Studies of Political Thought*, p. 13.

40. Gellner, "Flux and Reflux," p. 24.

41. Zabara, *A'immat al-Yaman*, 1:408; Nubdha, *Kitab al-Nubdhat al-Mushira ila Jumal min 'Uyun al-Sira fi Akhbar...al-Mansur bi-llah al-Qasim b. Muhammad*, photoreproduction of the manuscript (San'a', n.d.), pp. 79–399.

42. Nubdha, *Kitab al-Nubdhat*, pp. 96, 336.

43. Nubdha, *Kitab al-Nubdhat*, pp. 202ff.

44. Zabara, *Nashr al-'Arf li-Nubala' al-Yaman ba'd al-alf ila 1357 hijriyya*, vol. 2 (Cairo, 1958), p. 211.

45. R. B. Serjeant, "The Post-Medieval and Modern History of San'a' and the Yemen," in R. B. Serjeant and R. Lewcock, eds., *San'a': An Arabian Islamic City* (London, 1983).

46. M. S. Niebuhr, *Travels through Arabia and Other Countries of the East*, trans. by Robert Heron (Edinburgh, 1792; repr. Beirut, Librairie du Liban), 2:80, mentions al-Mas and Ahmad al-Hamer as generals of the imam's army. The first was a slave prince. The second was almost certainly al-Ahmar, paramount shaykh of Hashid, who is mentioned again as commanding "the mercenaries of Hashid wa-Bakil" (2:81). Both shaykhs and slave princes are discussed in some detail by Niebuhr (1:247, 340–341, 368; 2:51–52, 62, 78, 82, 89; and passim). For a discussion of the slave princes in particular, see H. al-'Amri, *The Yemen in the 18th and 19th Centuries: A Political and Intellectual History* (London, 1985), p. 23.

47. Zabara, *Nashr al-'Arf*, 2:336.

48. Zabara, *Nashr al-'Arf*, 2:507.

49. Zabara, *Nashr al-'Arf*, 2:273.

50. Zabara, *Nashr al-'Arf li-Nubala' al-Yaman ba'd al-alf ila 1357 hijriyya*, vol. 1, photoreprint (San'a', 1941), p. 198.

51. Zabara, *A'immat al-Yaman*, 1 (pt. 2): 160.

52. Zabara, *A'immat al-Yaman*, 1 (pt. 2): 201.

53. Zabara, *Nashr al-'Arf*, 1:194.

54. Zabara, *Nashr al-'Arf*, 2:7.

55. Machiavelli, *The Prince*, p. 94.

56. Serjeant, "Post-Medieval and Modern History," pp. 80–82.

57. Al-'Amri, *Yemen in the 18th and 19th Centuries*, pp. 3–7.

58. Gellner, "Flux and Reflux."

59. Serjeant, "Interplay," pp. 30, 44–45; Dresch, "Tribal Relations," p. 161.

60. Gellner, "Flux and Reflux."

61. Dresch, "Tribal Relations," pp. 163–164.

62. Zabara, *Nashr al-'Arf*, 2:242–243.

63. Gellner, "Flux and Reflux," pp. 44–45; Crone, "Tribe and the State," p. 76.

64. Dresch, "Tribal Relations," p. 160.

65. See, for example, the contrast between Zabara's account (*Nashr al-'Arf*, 1:496–497) of al-Hadi al-Hasan, where he quotes the line *fa-laysa li-sultan 'ala ahli-ha yad*, and his account (*Nashr al-'Arf*, 2:6) of al-Mahdi al-'Abbas, where he quotes al-Shawkani's verdict: *la-hu hayba shadida fi-qulub khassati-hi*.

66. Machiavelli, *The Prince*, p. 103 and passim.

67. Eric R. Wolf, *Europe and the People without History* (Berkeley and Los Angeles, 1982).

68. I shall keep my account brief here because Yemen's recent political history and the development of the present state apparatus have already been ably discussed, for instance, by J. E. Peterson, *Yemen: The Search for a Modern State* (London, 1982). See also several of the contributions to B. R. Pridham, ed., *Contemporary Yemen: Politics and Historical Background* (London, 1984).

69. Zayd b. 'Ali al-Wazir, *Muhawala li-Fahm al-Mushkilat al-Yamaniyya* (Beirut, 1971), pp. 150–151.

70. Dresch, "Tribal Relations," pp. 167–170.

71. Dresch, "Tribal Relations," p. 172.

72. *Al-Majalla*, no. 347, 1–7 October 1986, pp. 15–18.

73. *Al-'Arab*, 7 December 1987.

74. Ernest Gellner, *Thought and Change* (London, 1964).

75. Dale F. Eickelman, "Ibadism and the Sectarian Perspective," in B. R. Pridham, ed., *Oman: Economic, Social and Strategic Developments* (London, 1987).

76. Gellner, *Thought and Change*, p. 160.

77. Gellner, "Flux and Reflux," p. 43.

78. 'Abd al-Wasi'i, *Ta'rikh al-Yaman* (Cairo, 1928), pp. 163, 221–225.

79. E. L. Peters, "From Particularism to Universalism in the Religion of the Cyrenaica Bedouin," *British Society for Middle East Studies Bulletin* 3, no. 1 (1976): 5–14; Dale F. Eickelman, "Time in a Complex Society," *Ethnology* 16 (1977): 39–55; Eickelman, "Ibadism and the Sectarian Perspective."

80. Eickelman, "Time in a Complex Society," p. 53.

81. Peters, "From Particularism to Universalism," p. 13.

82. *Al-Majalla*, no. 347, 1–7 October 1986.

83. Crone, "Tribe and the State," pp. 64, 77.

Tribe and State: Libyan Anomalies

Lisa Anderson

In most of the modern Middle East the primacy of the state in the exercise of national political authority is acknowledged by governments and citizens alike. Fidelity to kinship ideologies and genealogies may supplement, subvert, or bypass state institutions at the national level or serve in their stead at the local level, particularly where state penetration is weak; but tribal loyalty is not ordinarily considered a legitimate alternative to the bureaucratic state as a mechanism for political conflict resolution and economic appropriation.

Among the few exceptions to this general proposition appear to have been the governments of Libya under King Idris, who ruled from 1951 until 1969, and Mu'ammar al-Qaddafi, who came to power in a military coup in 1969. Very different in foreign-policy posture, avowed economic orientation, and social and cultural policy, these regimes nonetheless shared a remarkably similar aversion to reliance on state institutions and ideologies for political legitimacy and loyalty. This aversion was a reflection of the weakness and ultimate failure of both indigenous and colonial efforts at state building in Libya during the late nineteenth and twentieth centuries. Far from being eroded by the growth of state institutions, tribal affiliations not only remained strong but also continued to present a genuine challenge to acceptance of the state as the primary vehicle for economic distribution and conflict resolution. Tribal imperatives were interpreted in different terms under the monarchy, which emphasized the cohesion and exclusiveness of kinship, and the revolutionary regime, which also embraced the more general principles of egalitarian participation and abhorrence of economic specialization; but both regimes turned to the idiom and reality of the tribe to win support and maintain authority.

This aversion to statehood and reliance on tribal ideologies reflected widespread sentiment in Libya, but it was the particular economic position of the country that permitted the translation of sentiment into policy. As Jacques Roumani, an astute observer of Libyan politics and social life during the twentieth century, has noted, "Oil riches and a small population permit [Libya] to avoid the need for a differentiated social structure to cope with the complexities of the modern age."[1] That Libyans should want to dispense with modernity was a legacy of their recent history; that they were able even to try was a product of their contemporary economy.

DEFINITIONS

Before examining Libya itself, it is worth spending a few moments on questions of terminology, for, as several of the contributors to this volume point out, the terms *tribe* and *state* are eloquent in their ambiguity. Most of the scholarly concern to correct (or at least examine) the attendant confusion has been addressed to the first of these terms, and for anthropologists, *what is a tribe?* is a well-worn question. Less familiar, but no less pressing, is the question *what is a state?* For the purposes of this essay, both terms may be understood as what Richard Tapper calls tendencies or situations.[2] That is to say, tribe and state are not mutually exclusive analytical categories but rather summaries of characteristics more or less present in any society at any moment.

It seems useful to start with the general proposition that all societies have mechanisms by which surplus is extracted and distributed and by which conflict is regulated. These mechanisms may be embedded in other expressions of social life, such as kinship, in which case questions of economic appropriation and conflict regulation are resolved on the basis of rights and obligations described in terms of descent and genealogy. By contrast, mechanisms for extraction, distribution, and regulation may also be represented in a structurally differentiated and specifically designated apparatus; such an apparatus is a state. The existence of a state implies that other aspects of social organization are also differentiated, as should be evident in reliance on impersonal contractual relations and the appearance of a complex division of labor and correspondingly elaborate social hierarchy. In societies where such characteristics are absent, a specifically designated structure for economic appropriation and conflict regulation is both impossible and unnecessary.

Within both the tribal and the state tendencies or situations there is, of course, great diversity. Both tribes and states frequently exhibit what may be characteristics exogenous to their underlying rationale. Insofar as tribes manifest differentiated structures for appropriation and conflict regulation, such as chieftaincies, or states rely on the ruler's kin to staff the administration, for example, it is the predominant tendency rather than the categorical and exclusive presence or absence of tribal or state attributes that must be considered as characterizing the society.

Although the two categories are not, therefore, in any rigorous sense mutually exclusive, since the nineteenth century Western social and political theory has treated tribe and state as inversely correlated. Implicit in the nineteenth-century idea of progress inherited by the Western development theorists of the postwar era is the notion that the modern state appears and develops at the expense of the tribe. Although Karl Marx, Max Weber, Emile Durkheim, and their various followers were all skeptical about the benign outcome of this evolution, few disputed its reality. Capitalism, division of labor, industrialization, bureaucratic domination, and social differentiation appeared to be inevitable challenges to the egalitarianism of primitive communism, the substantive justice of traditional authority, and the security of mechanical solidarity.

Thus it appears to be widely accepted that once capitalism and rational-legal bureaucracy have been unleashed, over the long run tribe and state can coexist only temporarily and uncomfortably. Indeed, insofar as they are both understood as mechanisms for the distribution of resources and the regulation of conflict, coexistence produces redundancy. What this essay is about, however, is the historical short run or, more precisely in the Libyan case, the twentieth century. It is here where the anomalies that challenge simple interpretations of change in the modern world are to be found. As it turns out, the triumph of the state, however much it may be inevitable, should not be heralded (or lamented) prematurely. As reexaminations of European history have reminded us, the victory of the state over alternative structures of political authority was neither quick nor easy. On the contrary, European history is littered with the corpses of empires—holy and otherwise—burgs, duchies, and leagues defeated by the embodiment of political authority sanctified in the Treaty of Westphalia and defined by Max Weber as a "compulsory political association with continuous organization [whose] administrative staff successfully upholds a claim to the monopoly of legitimate use of force in the enforcement of its order...within a given territorial area."[3]

In the three centuries after Westphalia the juridical basis of the international system, of which the state is the basic unit, was elaborated and exported throughout the world. With the founding of the League of Nations after World War I and, even more so, the establishment of its successor, the United Nations, after World War II, statehood was designated as the sole internationally recognized form of political authority. At that time less than a century of European influence separated many parts of the world from submission to forms of political authority profoundly different from the European-style state. Participation in the international system, however, dictated adoption of the regalia, if not the reality, of statehood. Territorial boundaries were drawn, or more likely inherited, from European imperial cartographic designs. Armies were recruited—and it should be remembered that the modern standing army is the archetypical embodiment of the functionally differentiated, hierarchical, bureaucratic, impersonal mechanisms of the state. Ambitious programs were announced, and sometimes implemented, to increase production, enhance infrastructure, develop economies, improve the quality of life, and otherwise dramatically alter the nature of societies around the globe. That these programs were undertaken in the name of states on behalf of citizens both strengthened the image of the state as the tendency of modernity, progress, and wealth and made it the focus of the bitterness of the disappointed, the frustrated, and the angry.

The fact that state formation and economic development inevitably entail damage to the beneficiaries of the old system, and rarely deliver goods and services to new and expectant recipients as smoothly and efficiently as promised, accounts in large measure for the failure of the state to take root as easily and completely as was expected by early theorists of development. For the new citizens who are angry and disappointed—those who were dispossessed, ignored, and neglected by the state's development planners—there have been numerous ideological alternatives. Like the American Shakers and English Luddites of the nineteenth century, the twentieth century has seen its share of movements of righteous withdrawal and refusal. Not least of these, in the Middle East and elsewhere, have been efforts to revive and sustain fidelity to ideologies and loyalties based on actual or putative ties of kinship in the face of the challenge from the state.

Were this the story in Libya it would certainly be worth telling, but it would hardly be unique or even unusual. Libya presents a variation on this common theme in that it is the state elites themselves— the government development planners—who display ambivalence toward the organization and ideology of the state. Possessing, if nothing else, the sanction of international recognition, these regimes nonetheless evinced profound distrust of the instruments in their hands, preferring to appeal to what they appear to have believed were the more reliable idiom and obligations of kinship. It is the how and why of this to which we now turn.

LIBYA'S ENCOUNTER WITH THE MODERN STATE

Like almost all the peoples of the Middle East, and with some justification, Libyans believe themselves to have been ill-served by the twentieth century. The area now known as Libya entered the century as the last North African province of the failing Ottoman Empire.[4] It had been exposed to the reform efforts of the Ottoman rulers since the middle of the nineteenth century, and although it was hardly a model province, neither was it a sleepy backwater. Indeed, it appears that the late nineteenth century was a period of relative peace and prosperity. Whether directly, as in western Libya or Tripolitania, or in conjunction with the Sanusi religious order in Cyrenaica, the eastern region, the Ottoman administration secured law and order and increased the provision of services such as education. Libyans participated in the Ottoman local government and provided many of the incumbents of the local administrative bureaucracy. At the same time, both because of the enhanced political climate and because of the increased importance of Libya as the last outlet of trans-Saharan trade after the French and British occupations of Tunisia and Egypt in the 1880s, merchants found themselves prospering. Local trade increased, pastoralism began to give way to settled agriculture, and tribal networks were supplemented, and partially supplanted, by links of economic interest and political ideology.

The Young Turk revolution of 1908 shook Libya, as it did the rest of the empire, and the Libyan political elite was thrown into turmoil as the supporters and opponents of the new regime battled for bureaucratic advantage. Well before the dust settled, the province was shaken again: in 1911 Italy declared war on the Ottoman Empire and invaded the North African territory. When forced to sue for peace a year later, the Ottomans did not acknowledge Italian sovereignty but rather gave the inhabitants "autonomy." In fact, Ottoman influence remained important in Libya until the closing days of World War I, by which time battles for control of the province among the Italians, the Ottomans, and provincial leaders had severely weakened the local administration and economy.

The aftermath of World War I saw a number of local efforts to create independent states in the territory, including the short-lived Tripoli Republic and the Sanusi government. The Sanusis, under the head of the order, Idris, found a protector in the British in Egypt, who briefly sponsored negotiations between the Italians and Idris. By 1922, however, the new Fascist government in Rome had decided to forego negotiation and undertake the military conquest of the territory. In one of the most brutal colonial wars of the twentieth century the Italians took control of the territory kilometer by kilometer, facing fierce resistance for more than a dozen years. Whole villages were uprooted, wells were poisoned, civilian settlements bombed, and captured resistance fighters hanged on the spot.

By the mid-1930s, when Italian control was finally undisputed, the Libyan population had been halved by famine, war, and emigration. Particularly significant was the loss of almost the entire educated elite and much of the entrepreneurial merchant class. Settled coastal agriculture and domestic trade had been disrupted, and many of those Libyans who did not find employment with the Italians returned to pastoralism. Whatever damage to the economic and social infrastructure built up by the Ottoman administration that remained to be done would be completed shortly: the North Africa campaigns of World War II left Libya in French and British hands after a series of long and destructive battles.

During the war the British in Egypt promised Idris, who had fled into exile in Cairo in 1922, that Cyrenaica would not be returned to Italian control if he would provide troops from among his followers to fight with the Allies. After the war this promise proved decisive in the debates over the future of Libya. The newly established United Nations was unable to agree on a suitable mandatory power, and so Libya became independent in 1951, with Idris as king. At that time it was the poorest independent country in the world: the million or so inhabitants disposed of an annual per capita income of about fifty dollars, and the literacy rate among adult males was about 20 percent.

THE MONARCHY

During much of the first half of the twentieth century Libyans found themselves forced to rely on ties of kinship *faute de mieux*. Other bases of social cohesion, such as economic interest and political ideology, rely on a market economy and state structure like that which had appeared briefly at the end of the nineteenth century, only to be destroyed. Many of the Libyans who had thrown in their lot with the new commercial and administrative networks at the turn of the century had seen their fortunes and families decimated, and the survivors drew the conclusion that the only reliable connections were those of kinship. The federal system with which Libya became independent was, therefore, a compromise between the demands of the international system for a state and the inclinations of a domestic population skeptical of the utility and reliability of bureaucratic administration and commercial exchange. The elaborate and expensive government, underwritten by the United States and Great Britain in return for military basing rights, had the advantage of permitting local politicians considerable leeway while giving the country the appearance of national unity.

Obviously, the demands of statehood—the maintenance of a civilian bureaucracy, for example, if only to serve as local interlocutor for foreign economic interests such as the oil companies—require a more complex and elaborate administration than can be sustained by tribal structures alone. Yet in the Libya of the 1950s there were few persons with skills, experience, or confidence in bureaucratic administration. The earlier efforts at state building—on the part of the Ottomans, the Sanusiyya, the Tripoli Republic, and even the Italians—to construct and maintain more elaborate administrations were all short-lived experiments that had ended in horrifying failure. Small wonder, then, that enthusiasm for the state-building venture was conspicuously absent, and that the ideology of kinship remained prominent in both the formal and informal workings of the government. At the formal level the importance of kinship was enshrined in the constitution, which stated that "the sovereignty of the United Kingdom of Libya is vested in the nation. By the will of God, the people entrust it to King Muhammad Idris al-Sanusi and after him to his male heirs, the oldest after the oldest, degree by degree."[5] Informally, of course, the rejection of the impersonal norms of the state went much further. Political parties were banned shortly after independence, and politics was the contest of family, tribal, and parochial interests, as networks of kinship and clan provided the organizational structures for competition. As Ruth First described it, "The inner conclave of the King and its parallel system of authority was unwritten in the constitution, but it was this court government of trusted advisors and confidants among the tribal nobility, together with a judicious selection of townsmen picked for their loyalty to the monarchy and their complicity with this system of patronage, that ran the political system."[6] Thus, rather than rely on recruitment based on ideological loyalty or administrative competence, the monarchy delegated authority to locally powerful families. Notable families consolidated their positions by intermarriage, and there were numerous prominent figures whose marriages better accounted for their appointment to government positions than did their qualifications. The

World Bank reported in 1960 that among the obstacles to economic development was "the prevailing attitude towards appointments to government jobs, which are frequently made on the basis of personal friendship or family connections rather than merit."[7]

In his still-unsurpassed study of the political elite of the Libyan monarchy, Hasan Salaheddin Salem distinguished between the tribe and the family as vehicles for recruitment into the political elite. Both were important during the monarchy: "The tribal element constituted an integral part of the political leadership during the period 1952–1969," and many Libyans believed that "several families controlled the country and determined the destiny of its people throughout the period." Indeed, among the adherents of this view was Idris's successor as the Libyan head of state, Mu'ammar al-Qaddafi: "In the heat of his campaign for his 'Socialist Union'. . . Gaddafi stressed the end of family rule and family influence in Libyan politics."[8]

The relationship between family and tribe is complex, for reliance on family may constitute compromise with the state. Although both reflect the importance of kinship, strictly speaking, tribal criteria for resource allocation and conflict regulation compete with those of the formal institutions of the state—the tax and welfare agencies, the police, and the courts. Attachment to the smaller-scale networks of family do not necessarily contradict and, in certain historical circumstances, may even complement those institutions. Family relationships may represent a conceptual bridge and social insurance policy in transitions from exclusive or nearly exclusive reliance on kin to participation in the more complex webs of commercial and political relations of commercial and administrative life.[9] In Libya, in both the late nineteenth century and again in the 1950s, the appearance of prominent families representing tribes marked the dilution of ideologically egalitarian tribal organization and the transition to market- and bureaucracy-based clientelism for distribution and regulation. Whether family politics is understood as merely an extension of, or a departure from, tribal organization, reliance on kin is in principle inconsistent with the impersonal norms of the bureaucracy and the market. Thus, as a compromise with the state, it must be understood as transitional, although of course—and here Libya's unusual wealth played a critical role—the transition may be quite prolonged.

By 1960 the contradiction had led to crisis. The king felt obliged to issue a letter to the heads of department throughout the state administration complaining that "matters have come to a climax, as have deafening reports of the misconduct of responsible state personnel in taking bribes—in secret and in public—and in practicing nepotism—the two [evils] which will destroy the very existence of the state and its good reputation both at home and abroad, as well as the squandering of the [country's] wealth in secret and in public."[10] Nepotism is only evil, of course, when nonkin criteria for favor or advantage (such as the formal equality, achieved competence, and objectively assessed merit associated with the bureaucratic state) are being violated. Thus, by making the favoring of kinfolk an evil, the king, perhaps in spite of himself, acknowledged the contradiction between the state and tribal tendencies.

Part of the reason why the mechanisms by which resources are allocated had become a major political issue was the discovery in 1959 of substantial oil reserves. Oil company exploration activities had already brought significant revenues into the Libyan economy; in less than a decade per capita income was to reach fifteen hundred dollars. The inability of the monarchy to address the "deafening reports of misconduct" or distribute the oil revenues on terms considered equitable by either state or tribal criteria eventually led to its demise. Its balance of state and tribal tendencies was probably inherently unstable, however. Unable by the facts of international politics to rely solely on tribal support, the regime was required to establish and maintain bureaucratic organizations, which, by their nature as state institutions, were supposed to be equally responsive to all individuals, defined not as tribal members but as citizens. In creating and fostering an ideology of legitimacy based on the formal impersonal relations of civil equality, government policy eroded the position of the tribes. Yet such state institutions were deeply mistrusted by large and important segments of the population, including the king. The successor regime would use increased oil revenues to sustain a reinterpretation of tribal obligations and state imperatives, which emphasized their intersection in an ideology of nationalism and egalitarianism.

THE REVOLUTION

That a conservative monarchy would be caught in the dilemma of trying simultaneously to win favor with the more traditional elements of society while promoting developments, both political and economic, that undermined the social base of traditional political organization is not unusual. It is a position shared by most monarchies, surviving and defunct, in the modern world. More unexpected perhaps is the extent to which this ambivalence is equally evident in the avowedly revolutionary regime that followed.

The Libyan monarchy never had the opportunity to resolve the contradiction between its dual attachments to tribe and state; it was overthrown in the military coup led by Mu'ammar al-Qaddafi in September 1969. That the monarchy was overthrown by military officers and that they chose to rule themselves rather than oversee installation of a new civilian government reflected, in Libya as so often elsewhere, the extent to which the military represented the archetypical and almost sole embodiment of formal impersonal hierarchy in the country. Qaddafi's near contempt for such military organization was not immediately evident; that he appreciated military power but not military hierarchy was to be suggested only later when he attempted to disband the army in favor of "arming the people." At the very outset, however, Qaddafi was obviously and profoundly ambivalent about tribes. Early on he made it clear that he was simultaneously opposed to tribalism as a principle of political organization and proud of his own origins in a saintly, though not noble or wealthy, tribe, the Qadadfa.

Almost from the start the new regime attempted to abolish tribal organization. In general, the other members of the ruling Revolutionary Command Council (RCC), who had made the coup with Qaddafi, held no particular brief for tribal loyalties. They themselves were not from noble or prestigious tribes, and they viewed the tribal support for the old regime as lending itself to counterrevolutionary and conservative politics. Thus, the regime decreed the abolition of the tribe as a legal institution and redrew the local administrative boundaries that had followed tribal lines so as to include sections of several tribes in each of the new administrative units. According to Omar El Fathaly and Monte Palmer, who conducted field research in rural Libya in the early 1970s, "this restructuring was followed, in turn, by the dismissal of all local officials including governors, mayors, and deputy mayors, most of whom had been tribal sheikhs or their relatives; and replacement by a new class of local administrators whose values and social origins were compatible with those of the RCC, that is, educated members of less prestigious tribes with no ties to the old elite structure."[11]

Nonetheless, despite the early efforts of the regime to eradicate political reliance on tribal affiliation and replace it with ideological loyalty, tribal relationships retained much of their importance. Indeed, within a decade of coming to power, and as his regime faced increasing political opposition, Qaddafi himself had fallen back on reliance on his own kinsmen. He had entrusted a cousin with his personal security, and two brothers, also his cousins, not only served as his personal envoys in sensitive foreign missions but also held important positions in domestic intelligence. Still another cousin was commander of the armed forces of the central region, which included the oil terminals and the disputed Gulf of Sidra.

Not surprisingly, the Qadadfa did not fail to take advantage of their privileged position to enrich themselves. By the end of the 1970s per capita income had reached eight thousand dollars a year, and even during the oil glut and fall in prices of the following decade revenues remained substantial for a population of little more than three million people. In an ironic echo of the king's earlier protests about nepotism, in the autumn of 1985, Qaddafi apparently decided his relatives' behavior merited a rebuke. In an unsigned article in the newspaper *Jamahiriyya*, which bore the unmistakable imprint of Qaddafi's own pen, the Qadadfa were warned, "Mu'ammar does not belong only to the Qadadfa tribe but is the son, the father, the cousin, and the uncle of all revolutionaries."[12]

The ambivalence illustrated in the inconsistent recruitment practices of the regime is also evident in Qaddafi's own writings. During the late 1970s he published the three slim volumes of what he called *The Green Book*, where he expounds the third universal (or international) theory, so called to distinguish it from both communism and capitalism. It is the basis of the *jamahiriyya*, or state of the masses, in which Libyans were supposed to be living and through which they were supposed to be ruling themselves. The first volume, *The Solution to the Problem of Democracy*, does not contain much explicit discussion of the issues of tribe and state, although the direct participatory democracy he advocates has struck many observers as reminiscent of tribal practices. Indeed, Jacques Roumani described the revolution as "a reassertion of hinterland culture in national life." As he put it, "politically, this means rejection of central authority and state institutions in favor of direct participation in the affairs of society, operating by consensus or mediation."[13]

The evocation of tribal relationships is more apparent in the second volume of *The Green Book*, on economics. Here Qaddafi advocates a sort of precommercial or subsistence-based "primitive communism." His own words are worth quoting at length:[14]

> The sound rule is: He who produces is the one who consumes. Wage workers are a type of slave, however improved their wages may be. The wage-worker is like a slave to the master who hires him. . . .

> The ultimate solution is to abolish the wage system, emancipate man from his bondage, and return to the natural law which defined relationships before the emergence of classes, forms of government, and man-made laws. . . .

Natural law had led to natural socialism based on equality among the economic factors of production and has almost brought about, among individuals, consumption equal to nature's production. But the exploitation of man by man and the possession by some individuals of more of the general wealth than they need are a manifest departure from natural law and the beginning of distortion and corruption in the life of the human community.

Land is no one's property, but everyone has a right to use it, to benefit from it by *working, farming, or pasturing* [Qaddafi's italics].

Qaddafi's notion of the natural economy has its parallel in his view of natural social organization. Once again, his own words, here from the third volume, *The Social Basis for the Third Universal Theory*, are worth quoting:

To the individual man, the family is of more importance than the state. . . . Mankind, as a matter of fact, is the individual and the family, not the state. The state is an artificial economic and political system, sometimes a military system, with which mankind has no relationship and nothing to do. . . .

A tribe is a family which has grown as a result of procreation. It follows that a tribe is a big family. Equally, a nation is a tribe which has grown through procreation. The nation, then, is a big tribe. . . .

Since the tribe is a large family, it provides its members with the same material benefits and social advantages the family provides for its members, for the tribe is a secondary family. What needs to be emphasized is that the individual might sometimes act in a disgraceful manner which he would not dare do in front of his family. But since the family is smaller in size, he can escape its supervision, unlike the tribe whose supervision is felt by all its members. In view of these considerations, the tribe forms a behavior pattern for its members which will be transformed into a social education which is better and more human than any school education.

The only apparent disadvantage of the tribe, from Qaddafi's point of view, seems to be that "tribalism damages nationalism because tribal allegiance weakens national loyalty and flourishes at its expense." The state, by contrast, has only one possible merit: it may be the political expression of nationalism. Indeed, as I have suggested elsewhere,[15] Libya's experience with Italian nationalism and monarchical corruption may be the best, perhaps the only, illustrations of Qaddafi's observation:

The national state is the only political form which is consistent with the natural social structure. Its existence lasts, unless it becomes subject to another stronger nationalism, or unless its political structure,

> as a state, is affected by its social structure in the form of tribes, clans, and families. It is damaging to the political structure if it is subjected to the family, tribal, or sectarian social structure and adopts its characteristics.

Qaddafi may well be correct that it is damaging to the state to be subjected to criteria of recruitment and legitimacy drawn from tribal society; if so, he himself is partly to blame for the weakness of the Libyan administration, the incapacity of its military, and the discontent of its citizenry.

Qaddafi hoped to transcend the contradiction between tribe and state through nationalism and egalitarianism. The nation, whose political form is a state, he construes as a big tribe, familiar and nurturing. Similarly, the equality implied in citizenship he understands as the egalitarianism of natural law and natural socialism. Over the long run, this resolution of attachment to tribal values, hostility to the state, and the demands of the international political economy is not markedly more stable than the vacillation of the monarchy between condemning and employing nepotism. What gave it staying power was the extent to which it captured popular sentiment and, through the idiom of nationalism and egalitarianism, gave it ideological respectability. Moreover, oil revenues attached immediate and tangible benefit to adherence to both nationalism and egalitarianism; what were in fact very conservative positions were, so interpreted, neither embarrassingly reactionary nor materially costly.

Eventually, however, the stagnant, if not reactionary, implications of Qaddafi's ideology, combined with declining oil revenues, produced concern about the future among many Libyans. Maintenance of the delicate balance between tribe and state has consumed the energies of the regime and, for all its professions of revolutionary fervor, it has done little—indeed, given its ideological agenda, can do little—to foster sufficient political and economic development to guarantee that the current high standard of living will be sustainable when oil runs out in the twenty-first century.

TRIBE AND STATE

We have seen how the independent Libyan regimes, in their different ways, confounded tribe and state and how such amalgamation may influence Libya's future since it does not bode well for conventional nation-state formation and development. The final question here is *why*—why has Libya been unusually vulnerable to the nonstate, or even antistate, political ideologies of tribal life, and why does the transition postulated by the development theorists seem to have been suspended here?

The answer to the first part of the question has already been suggested: Both the monarchy and the revolutionary government drew heavily on tribal practices and ideologies in recruiting staff and justifying their rule because that is what they and their compatriots believed to be most trustworthy. The unusually strong emphasis on tribal relations and the explicit hostility toward state structures reflected the turmoil in Libya in the twentieth century and the resulting disappointment and distrust in the state.

If Libya's discontinuous experience with state formation during the twentieth century was unusually severe, however, it was not unique. What permitted the Libyan regimes to translate a sentimental longing for a mythical golden age when life was simpler into actual government policy was oil revenues. Jacques Delacroix provides a useful conceptual perspective from which to understand the impact of oil. He argues that in the absence of domestic extraction the principal function of the state is distributive; the relation between the elite and the mass is not the class relation usually associated with a complex division of labor, societal differentiation, and the hierarchical structure of the state. He suggests that as a consequence,

> other structures of social solidarity will have to be activated. Alternative structures are, by default, traditional structures. The more recently incorporated into the world economy a society, the more available are its traditional social structures. Hence, a distributive state ruling a recently incorporated society will experience a maximum of tribal, ethnic, and religious challenges.[16]

Traditional structures have more advantages than mere familiarity, however important that may be. Certainly in the Libyan case, the emphasis on kinship during the second half of the twentieth century was not due solely, or even principally, to the recentness of incorporation into the world economy. That might be enough to account for the reliance on kinship among conservative or traditional monarchies, but as Qaddafi's efforts to blend radical, revolutionary rhetoric with glorification of the tribe suggest, there is more to the Libyan case. The Libyan fidelity to kinship ideologies constituted a rejection of the state and a refusal to accept its criteria for social and political organization.

This refusal, as Roumani put it, to "cope with the complexities of the modern age" is a luxury afforded by oil. The transition from the tribal situation to the statehood dictated by the international system has been suspended, and the suspension prolonged, by oil revenues. No doubt Libya will eventually be forced to come to terms with its statehood, and only at that point will the true costs of today's refusal be apparent.

NOTES

1. Jacques Roumani, "From Republic to Jamahiriya: Libya's Search for Political Community," *Middle East Journal* 37, no. 2 (Spring 1983): 164.

2. See Richard Tapper's essay in this volume.

3. Max Weber, *The Theory of Social and Economic Organization* (New York, 1977), p. 154. On European state formation, see Charles Tilly, ed., *The Formation of National States in Western Europe* (Princeton, 1975); on the Middle East, see Lisa Anderson, "The State in the Middle East and North Africa," *Comparative Politics*, October 1987.

4. This discussion is based on the pertinent parts of Lisa Anderson, *The State and Social Transformation in Tunisia and Libya, 1830–1980* (Princeton, 1986).

5. Cited in Majid Khadduri, *Modern Libya: A Study in Political Development* (Baltimore, 1963), p. 189, who draws attention to a similar clause in the constitution of the defunct Iraqi monarchy.

6. Ruth First, *Libya: The Elusive Revolution* (Baltimore, 1974), p. 78.

7. International Bank for Reconstruction and Development, *The Economic Development of Libya* (Baltimore, 1960), p. 10.

8. Salaheddin Hassan Salem, "The Genesis of Political Leadership in Libya, 1952–1969" (Ph.D. diss., George Washington University, 1973), pp. 190–192.

9. Even for Ibn Khaldun, the decay of *'asabiyya* among rulers residing in cities is reflected first in their neglect of their distant kin. Much of the literature on clientelism stresses the use of the vocabulary of kinship and the creation of kinlike obligations—godparents, for example—among members of patron-client networks. See the essays collected in Steffen W. Schmidt et al., eds., *Friends, Followers, and Factions: A Reader in Political Clientelism* (Berkeley and Los Angeles, 1977).

10. The king's letter is cited in full in Khadduri, *Modern Libya*, p. 299.

11. Omar I. El Fathaly and Monte Palmer, *Political Development and Social Change in Libya* (Lexington, Mass., 1980), p. 58.

12. National Front for the Salvation of Libya, *Newsletter*, no. 44 (December 1985); for more detail on the Qadadfa in power, see Lisa Anderson, "Libya's Qaddafi: Still in Command?" *Current History* 86, no. 517 (February 1987), and the citations given there.

13. Roumani,"From Republic to Jamahiriya," p. 164.

14. There are numerous editions of Qaddafi's *Green Book*, each with slight variations in translation and without place or date of publication. Because the book is so short and the editions so various, page citations are usually considered superfluous.

15. Anderson, *State and Social Transformation*, p. 267.

16. Jacques Delacroix, "The Distributive State in the World System," *Studies in Comparative International Development* 15, no. 3 (Fall 1980): 11.

Conclusion: Tribes and States in Islamic History

Albert Hourani

The discussions in this volume range over a wide variety of subjects and ask questions which are interrelated in complex ways. It may, therefore, be useful to try to disentangle these questions, to ask them again, and to indicate the kinds of answers which emerge from the book as a whole.

Four kinds of questions have been asked. What is a tribe in the Muslim world? What is a state in the Muslim world? What has been the role of tribes in the formation of states as well as in their maintenance and destruction? What role has Islam played in these processes? That is, has it played such a role as to give them a specific nature which differs from that of what may seem to be similar processes in parts of the world where the people are not Muslims?

First of all, what is a tribe? The word can be used to indicate two kinds of entity, and these should be distinguished from each other. There is what might be called a natural phenomenon of rural society, whether pastoral or agricultural: the formation of more or less permanent cooperative groups, such as herding units or villages, because of the need for certain types of cooperation in the migration of pastoral groups, the operations of plowing and harvesting, the periodic redistribution of land, and sometimes defense. Such groups, bound together as they are by proximity and cooperative activities, tend also to be linked by kinship through either common descent or intermarriage. These kinship bonds arise because of the group's isolation from others, the need to keep land in a family, or the need to establish binding personal relations with those with whom one has common interests; kinship turns relationships of daily life and common interest into warm affective and moral bonds.

At certain times and places, however, there have existed larger units than village or herding group, and it is for these that the term *tribe* (or *fraction* of a tribe) has commonly been used. A tribe has certain characteristics. It has some kind of solidarity, which is intangible and may seem to disappear for a time but which is always present and may become effective in certain circumstances. These larger groups are not held together by genuine kinship; few people in illiterate societies know their ancestors more than three or four generations back or can extend their relationships beyond those whom they know personally or see frequently. Something similar to kinship, however, does exist in the larger unit: a myth of common ancestry, sometimes expressed in the tribal name. A tribe may be called the children (*awlad, banu*) of a common ancestor. To use such a name is to evoke not a rich structure of known and recognized relationships but rather a myth, which may or may not have any basis in fact. Even this myth may not exist, however. Lois Beck states that there is no idea of common ancestry among the Qashqa'i; another Iranian tribe, the Khamseh, would be a better example still, for it was formed out of five different groups having diverse ethnic origins and brought together in recent times. Among these larger units many have another characteristic, that of a more or less clearly defined territorial area of pasturage or cultivation. Paul Dresch has pointed out that the tribes he has studied in Yemen make boundary posts and whitewash them. Groups at this level, like the smaller ones, also have a concept of shared honor and a kind of leadership: the leading family does not have great or exclusive coercive power, but its authority is generally recognized and sought in moments of conflict or trouble. In such a family, and in the clan of which it is a part, the ties of kinship may be strong.

Some of the names of such tribes are known to be ancient. We find such names in the Maghrib, whatever they may mean: Sanhaja, Zenata, Masmuda. In Yemen, as Dresch has shown, the names of Hashid and Bakil go back hundreds of years. In the Sudan in the eighteenth century two tribal groups competing for land claimed descent from the Umayyads and 'Abbasids respectively; in the Palestinian countryside the conflicts of villages were expressed in terms of the tribal conflict of Qays and Yemen until the twentieth century.

The reasons for the persistence of these larger groups with their names and myths of origin can be indicated by making what may appear to be a digression. In states of the Muslim world before modern times there were three spheres of radiation from the cities, in particular the capital city. First, there was the city and its dependent hinterland, the area of direct administration and direct collection of taxes; it was in these areas that there appeared the phenomenon usually called land ownership, that is to say, claims to agricultural land by urban notables, recognized by urban law and enforced by urban government. Second, there were intermediate areas where the city and government could exercise control, not through officials but through intermediate powers to which the government gave recognition. The relationship of such intermediaries with the ruler was ambiguous and fluctuating. The intermediary would try to increase his power and defend it and even the ordinary people against the ruler; the ruler for his part would try to limit this power. Third, there was a further sphere of mountains, desert, and distant agricultural land, where a ruler could retain a certain influence by using his prestige or by such means of political manipulation as giving or withdrawing recognition or subsidies, but where, on the whole, taxes were not collected, urban law was not enforced, and urban claims to ownership did not exist.

If we consider each of these three areas in turn, we find that tribes, in the sense in which I have defined them, do not usually exist in the first, that of the city and its dependent countryside. There are some exceptions, however. When the town is small and on the fringe of the desert, it may be dominated by the ethos and organization of tribes, as was shown by A. de Boucheman in his study of Sukhna, a small town on the edge of the Syrian desert.[1] Again, if there is a breakdown of control in a town, or if important elements in its population live outside the urban order, a kind of tribalism may appear. Louis Massignon once made a tribal map of Paris and showed how Algerian immigrants settled in different parts of the city, tending to settle where their relations or those from the same districts lived and preserving a kind of tribal identity.[2] Fuad Khuri too, in his book *From Village to Suburb*, has shown how, even before the Lebanese civil war began in 1975, immigrants to Beirut from the mountain villages were forming almost the equivalent of tribal groups, identifying themselves in religious terms as Maronites, Shi'is, and so on; with the breakdown of order in Lebanon since 1975, these solidarities have taken on something of the nature and functions of tribes.[3]

It is in the second or intermediate area, however, that organized and permanent tribes with effective leaders can be found—tribes such as those described by Lois Beck in her book on the Qashqa'i, Gene Garthwaite in his writings on the Bakhtiyari, and Talal Asad in his work on the Kababish.[4] It is generally accepted that the government plays an important part in creating and maintaining tribal leaders in these areas, as the intermediaries through which its authority is exercised, and thus in creating tribes of this kind. In the

third area we find a different kind of tribal entity, that described by
Paul Dresch in Yemen, where tribalism is a language, a system of
ideas, symbols, or rituals, which may lie dormant for a time but can
be animated when it is needed, and where those recognized as the
heads of tribes do not have effective and permanent power so much
as an intermittent authority when conflicts have to be resolved or
some vital interest defended.

What is a state? This may seem to be a tedious and pedantic question, but it is an important one because the answer is relevant to the
way in which states have been formed in Islamic history. To define
the term simply, a state is an entity which has a recognized authority
claiming legitimate and exclusive power. The discussions in this
book show a wide spectrum of such entities and authorities and indicate how dangerous it is to generalize about states without making
further distinctions. At one extreme there have been authorities who
claimed legitimacy but had no effective power of coercion. The Zaydi
imams of Yemen are an example; the Ibadi imams in 'Uman and the
Maghrib might be an even better example, for according to Ibadi law
they were not supposed to have a standing army or any permanent
power since once they were no longer virtuous, they were no longer
legitimate imams and could not claim obedience. A second category
is that of states with wandering monarchies like those of medieval
Europe. These authorities had no permanent roots in the city and
had only a small bureaucracy, limited control of the agricultural surplus through taxation, and restricted power of coercion; they existed
by constant movement, political manipulation, and religious prestige. Examples of this type of state are Morocco until the end of the
nineteenth century, the Turcoman dynasties in eastern Anatolia in
the fifteenth century, and the Qajars in Iran until the reforms of the
nineteenth century took root. States of a third kind were bureaucrat-
ically organized monarchies with roots in a capital city and a chain
of dependent cities, an elaborate bureaucracy, a professional army,
and revenues from land and trade sufficient to maintain them. The
archetype of such monarchies is the Ottoman Empire, but other examples include Egypt from at least the Ayyubid period onward and
Tunisia at least from the time of the Hafsids. It may be that discussions of tribes and state formation tend to deal too little with this
third type of state and too much with what existed on the fringe of
the world of Islam. Almost nowhere in Islamic history, it seems, do
we find a state of a fourth kind, an authority with a clear and formally accepted territorial limit and a close traditional identification
with the civil society it ruled.

When we come to our third question, that of the role of tribes in the formation and life of states, the ambiguities of the term *tribe* appear most clearly. The question can be asked in several ways. First of all, have the armies with which conquerors have formed states come from rural people, and more particularly from nomadic pastoralists? On the whole, the answer is positive, for obvious reasons. Peasants and nomads are hardy and know how to ride horses and handle weapons; until the coming of modern medicine to urban areas, they were healthier than townspeople. The populations of towns were subject to plagues and diseases, which could kill a large part of them within months, whereas the countryside might produce a surplus of manpower to enlist in armies or replenish the urban population.

The fact that to a great extent armies were drawn from pastoralists and mountain peasants is not necessarily important in itself. It must be seen in the context of a second question: were tribesmen who were drawn into armies moved by a tribal *'asabiyya*, that is to say, a solidarity oriented toward the acquisition of power? In certain of the small states of Islamic history it may have been so, as when an army drawn from a single tribe, acting as a tribe and possessing a tribal solidarity, took over a small oasis town. Some of the small principalities of the Arabian Peninsula may have been formed in this way, although not all of them: the formation of the Saudi state, for example, was a more complex process than this, the product of an alliance between the ruler of a small market town and a religious reformer imposing their power and their view of the good life upon the nomads living in the *jahiliyya* surrounding them. It would seem, however, that larger states (with some possible exceptions) were created not by a tribe acting as a tribe but rather by the coalescence of different groups with an *'asabiyya* of a new kind. The point around which they coalesced might be a holy man or lineage; there are examples of this in Morocco and in Anatolia and Iran in the fifteenth and sixteenth centuries. Ira Lapidus is probably right, however, in stating that most large states were formed by a warlord, a military leader, or elites gathering around themselves elements drawn from the countryside and given a new kind of *'asabiyya*, that of men following a leader toward the seizure of power.

The *'asabiyya* of a conquering army might indeed subsume a number of tribal *'asabiyya*s. That seems to be true of the first Islamic conquest, when the caliphs and political elites of Mecca and Medina created an army in which tribal loyalties still existed within the new kind of *'asabiyya*. It was true also of the second Saudi state created by 'Abd al-'Aziz and of that abortive attempt to create a state known

as the Arab or Hashimite revolt. This last would repay study by a social historian or anthropologist: T. E. Lawrence's *Seven Pillars of
Wisdom* may be flawed as a revelation of his own motives and
actions, but it is a vivid illustration of the way in which a conquering
army was formed out of tribal elements, infused with a new kind of
solidarity, and launched to conquer a chain of towns on its way toward a capital, Damascus.

Even if tribal solidarities helped create states, did they also help
maintain them? Some dynasties tried to preserve the *'asabiyya*
which had enabled them to obtain power. This was true of the early
caliphate and, to some extent, of the Saudis and of the Hashimites in
Jordan; but, as Fuad Khuri has shown, if the *'asabiyya* of a tribe or
the sense of kinship of a clan remained strong once a state had been
founded, it was mainly as a mechanism for the distribution of power
and wealth. In general, Ibn Khaldun was right to suggest that the
first solidarity, which had led to the acquisition of power, tended to
dissolve. Sometimes the ruler took an active part in dissolving it;
that a ruler should rid himself of those by whose support he had
risen was a lesson that the founders of great Islamic states did not
need to learn either from Ibn Khaldun or from Machiavelli, although
both of them wrote of it.

Once firmly established, most dynasties tried to create a new kind
of *'asabiyya*, that of a household, an army of slaves or mercenaries,
and a bureaucracy. The officials of the bureaucracy were often taken
over from the previous dynasty. They were the permanent element in
Islamic states, the educated elites who kept the papers and accounts
and would serve any ruler; there is an article by Jean Aubin about
the way in which the Safavids enlisted the elite of Isfahan and other
cities into their service.[5] The creation of a mercenary or slave army
took place even in principalities formed by tribes. The history of central Arabia has shown this process in modern times as well. Once the
Ibn Rashid dynasty established itself in Ha'il, it tried to form a loyal
army; Nuri Sha'lan of the Ruwala also gathered around himself men
who had served in the Ottoman army, slaves, and anyone who would
give him personal loyalty. This is one essential aspect of the process
of maintaining a state, that of creating an alliance of interests between the dynasty and the urban population. In what may appear to
be a paradox, having risen to power by the use of soldiers from the
countryside and desert, the dynasty, if it wished to endure, would
change alliances and try to create a link with the population of the
city.

What role, if any, have tribes played in the destruction of states?
There are examples in Islamic history of well-established, bureau-

cratically organized states which were not destroyed for centuries; a kind of circulation of elites took place, but the basic structure of control remained. This is true, for example, of Egypt from the time of the Ayyubids until the end of the eighteenth century. In other instances, however, states grew weaker and were replaced by others, and one of the signs foreshadowing their end was the shrinking of the area of control and the encroachment of tribes upon the hinterland of the city. The most famous example of this process in Islamic history is that of the migration of the Bani Hilal tribe in the Maghrib. Writing of this event, Ibn Khaldun said that the Arabs destroyed everything they touched. There has been much discussion of this migration in recent years. Jacques Berque, Michael Brett, and others have shown that to a great extent the invasion of Bani Hilal and the destruction it caused is a myth; but it is a powerful myth, which conveys something of the fear of city dwellers as they looked out upon the world of the Bedouins advancing upon them.[6]

Our final question is that of the role of Islam in these processes. In the fourteen centuries of Islamic history, over an area stretching from Morocco to central Asia, it is certainly possible to find examples of Islam providing the impulse to expansion and being the unifying force of a coalition oriented toward the acquisition of power: the first caliphate, the Almohads in the Maghrib, the *sharifs* of Morocco, the Safavids in Iran, and the Mahdiyya in the Sudan during the nineteenth century. In all such movements, however, it would need a subtle analysis to distinguish the religious from other motives, and it would be dangerous to regard them simply as movements of religious fervor. In general, the role of Islam does not seem to have been as important in the first phase of the creation of dynasties as in the second, that of making them permanent. This is something else Ibn Khaldun pointed out: religion becomes important when a dynasty wishes to consolidate itself and give strength to its alliance with urban interests. On the scale of the state, religion takes the place of kinship as creator of a moral bond. The signs of Islamic sovereignty tended to supersede the older signs of tribal leadership; religious law, the *shari'a*, became important not only as the source of a claim to legitimate authority but also as an essential element in the life of the city, a guarantee of those shared expectations of behavior without which urban life, tradition, and civilization could not flourish. A dynasty which wished to remain had to make use of such symbols, uphold the *shari'a*, and honor the men who interpreted and administered it.

Intermingled with Islamic ideas and symbols of kingship, however, were other ideas and images drawn from an ancient ideal of human society, that of the ruler chosen by God to keep the world on its axis and maintain the harmony of the social order. Ira Lapidus has shown how the ruler, once he had established himself, adopted the imperial style, which to a great extent was that of the Sasanians and Byzantines. The duality of the Islamic and imperial styles can be seen above all in the way in which the Ottoman sultans depicted themselves; here, as in so many ways, the Ottoman Empire marks the apex of Islamic history. The Ottoman ruler was *padishah*, ruler of the world, but also sultan, upholder of the *shari'a*, and servant of the sanctuaries of Islam, and he claimed legitimacy in both capacities.

Neither the Ottoman sultan nor any other ruler could wholly control the expressions of religious belief, however. Islam could also justify opposition to rulers, but this happened mainly in the cities, when at moments of crisis or revolt there might be heard the great word that has run through the whole of Islamic history, *zulm* (tyranny). In general, tribal revolt and opposition do not seem to have used the symbolic language of Islam. There are indeed examples of Islam, particularly in its Sufi form, providing the channel through which tribes could express their opposition to settled government, but on the whole it was the city and its rulers which were able to use the language of Islam against the tribe. For the rulers of the city, and for the men of religion who expressed the collective mind of the city, the tribesmen were the danger beyond the walls, the *jahiliyya* or religious ignorance, which could be driven back but might always return. Nowadays, as Paul Dresch has suggested, the ideology of nationalism is tending to replace, or give support to, the ideology of religion as a means by which the rulers and elites of the city try to maintain and justify control over the forces of society.

NOTES

1. A. de Boucheman, *Une petite cité caravanière: Suhné*, Documents d'études orientales de l'Institut Français de Damas, vol. 6 (Damascus, 1939).

2. Louis Massignon, "Cartes de répartition des kabyles dans la région parisienne," in *Opera Minora* (Beirut, 1963), 3:569–574 and plates.

3. Fuad Khuri, *From Village to Suburb: Order and Change in Greater Beirut* (Chicago, 1974).

4. Lois Beck, *The Qashqa'i of Iran* (New Haven, 1986); G. R. Garthwaite, *Khans and Shahs* (Cambridge, 1983), and "The Bakhtiyari Ilkhani: An Illusion of Unity," *International Journal of Middle East Studies* 8 (1977): 145–160; Talal Asad, *The Kababish Arabs* (New York, 1970).

5. Jean Aubin, "Etudes safavides. I Shah Isma'il et les notables de l'Iraq persan," *Journal of the Economic and Social History of the Orient* 2 (1959): 37–81.

6. Jacques Berque, "Du nouveau sur les Bani Hilal?" *Studia Islamica* 35 (1972): 99–111; Michael Brett, "Ibn Khaldun and the Arabisation of North Africa," *Maghrib Review* 41 (1979): 9–16, and "The Fatimid Revolution (861–973) and Its Aftermath in North Africa," in *The Cambridge History of Africa* (Cambridge, 1978), 2:631–636.

GLOSSARY OF MIDDLE EASTERN TERMS

Many of the terms below are defined according to their specific usages in the text. Because they appear in slightly different forms in each of the major languages of the Middle East (Arabic, Persian, and Turkish), only the spellings found in the text are used below. Some common terms associated with tribes, states, and religion in the Middle East have also been included.

'adl	equitable; justice
akhbar	self-contained tales of tribal tradition
'Alawi or Alawite	schismatic Shiʻi religious sect concentrated in northwest Syria
amir (pl. *umara'*)	lay ruler; prince; tribal chief
'asabiyya	group feeling or solidarity
'ashira	tribe
ashraf	claimants of descent from the Prophet
'asl	descent
aulad	patrilineage
ayyam al-fasad	time of corruption
badu	Bedouin or camel-herding pastoralists
baraka	supernatural blessing
bled el-makhzen	area administered by state in Morocco
bled es-siba	tribal areas beyond state control in Morocco
dawla	state; dynasty
fatwa	legal opinion
ghazi	holy warrior
gobek	patrilineage
hadd	legal punishment
hajj	pilgrimage

hamula	kinship group
haqq	legal right
hayba	awe-inspiring; reverence
hijra	flight; exodus
hokumat	area administered by state in Afghanistan
hukuma	government
ilkhani	paramount leader of tribal confederation in Iran
imam	prayer leader; spiritual leader
insaf	equality
'ird	honor
jahiliyya	era of ignorance associated with pre-Islamic times
jihad	holy war
jirga	tribal assembly
khayma	tent
khuwwa	protection tax paid to a powerful tribal group
madhhab	school of law
majlis	public audience with tribal shaykh
majlis al-shura	consultative assembly
majlis al-wukala'	council of delegates
majlis al-wuzara'	council of ministers
mamluk	slave soldier
marabtin	saints; holy men
marabtin-bil-baraka	petty saints attached to small tribal segments
mawali	clients; non-Arab converts to Islam
mizan	balance
mulk	sovereignty; royal authority
mulla	preacher
muluk	rulers
pir	Sufi master
qabila (pl. *qaba'il*)	tribe
qaum	kinship term in Afghanistan
ra'iyyat	Persian peasant
sayyid	descendant of the Prophet
shari'a	revealed law of Islam
shaykh	tribal chief
Shi'i	major Muslim sect
shirk	polytheism; idolatry
sira	biography
Sufi	Muslim mystic
Sunni	largest subdivision or sect in Islam
taghut	work of the devil
ta'ifa (pl. *tawa'if*)	faction

tariqa (pl. *turuq*)	religious (Sufi) order
tayfa	local tribal section
'ulama'	those trained in the religious sciences
umma	community of believers
uymaq	pastoral nomad in Iran
waqf	pious endowment
wolus	political community
yaghistan	tribal region in Afghanistan
zakat	alms
zulm	oppression; tyranny

CONTRIBUTORS

Lisa Anderson is Associate Professor of Political Science and Acting Director of the Middle East Institute at Columbia University. She is the author of *The State and Social Transformation in Tunisia and Libya, 1830–1980* (Princeton University Press, 1986).

Thomas J. Barfield is Professor and Chairman of the Department of Anthropology at Boston University. He is the author of *The Arab Tribes of Afghanistan* (University of Texas Press, 1981) and *The Perilous Frontier: Nomadic Empires and China* (Blackwell, 1989).

Lois Beck is Associate Professor of Anthropology at Washington University in St. Louis. She is the author of *The Qashqa'i of Iran* (Yale University Press, 1986) and *Borzu Beg: A Year in the Life of a Qashqa'i Tribal Headman* (University of California Press, forthcoming).

Steven C. Caton is Associate Professor of Anthropology at the University of California, Santa Cruz, and author of *"Peaks of Yemen I Summon": Poetry as Cultural Practice in a North Yemeni Tribe* (University of California Press, forthcoming).

Paul Dresch is University Lecturer in Social Anthropology and Fellow of St. John's College, Oxford University. He is the author of *Tribes, Government and History in Yemen* (Oxford University Press, 1989).

Ernest Gellner is the William Wyse Professor of Social Anthropology at Cambridge University. Among his many studies are *Culture, Identity, and Politics* (Cambridge University Press, 1987), *Muslim Society* (Cambridge University Press, 1981) and *Saints of the Atlas* (University of Chicago Press, 1969).

Albert Hourani is Emeritus Fellow of St. Antony's College, Oxford University. He is the author of numerous works, including *The Emergence of the Modern Middle East* (University of California Press, 1981), *Europe and the Middle East* (University of California Press, 1980), and *Arabic Thought in the Liberal Age, 1798-1939* (Oxford University Press, 1962).

Philip S. Khoury is Professor of History and Acting Dean of the School of Humanities and Social Science at the Massachusetts Institute of Technology. He is the author of *Syria and the French Mandate* (Princeton University Press, 1987) and *Urban Notables and Arab Nationalism* (Cambridge University Press, 1983).

Joseph Kostiner is Lecturer in the Department of Middle Eastern and African History at Tel Aviv University. He is the author of *The Struggle for South Yemen* (Croom Helm, 1984) and *South Yemen's Revolutionary Strategy* (Tel Aviv, 1989).

Ira M. Lapidus is Professor of History at the University of California, Berkeley. His books include *A History of Islamic Societies* (Cambridge University Press, 1988) and *Muslim Cities in the Later Middle Ages* (Harvard University Press, 1967).

Roy P. Mottahedeh is Professor of Islamic History and Director of the Center for Middle Eastern Studies at Harvard University. He is the author of *The Mantle of the Prophet* (Simon and Schuster, 1986) and *Loyalty and Leadership in an Early Islamic Society* (Princeton University Press, 1980).

Richard Tapper is Reader in Anthropology and Chairman of the Middle East Centre, School of Oriental and African Studies, at the University of London. He is the author of *Pasture and Politics* (Academic Press, 1979) and *The King's Friends: A Social and Political History of the Shahsevan Tribes of Iran* (forthcoming); he is also the editor of *The Conflict of Tribe and State in Iran and Afghanistan* (Croom Helm, 1983).

Bassam Tibi is Professor of Political Science at the University of Göttingen. He is the author of numerous works including *The Crisis of Modern Islam* (University of Utah Press, 1988) and *Arab Nationalism: A Critical Inquiry* (St. Martin's Press, 1981).

WORKS CITED

Abir, Mordechai. "The Consolidating of the Ruling Class and the New Elites in Saudi Arabia." *Middle Eastern Studies* 23, no. 2 (April 1987).
————. *Saudi Arabia in the Oil Era*. Boulder, Colo., 1987.
Abu-Lughod, Lila. *Veiled Sentiments: Honor and Poetry in a Bedouin Society*. Berkeley and Los Angeles, 1986.
Abun-Nasr, J. *A History of the Maghrib*. Cambridge, 1971.
Afshar, Haleh. "An Assessment of Agricultural Development Policies in Iran." In Haleh Afshar, ed., *Iran: A Revolution in Turmoil*. Albany, N.Y., 1985.
Ahmed, Akbar S. *Pakhtun Economy and Society*. London, 1980.
————. *Religion and Politics in Muslim Society*, Cambridge, 1983.
Ahmed, Akbar S., and David M. Hart, eds. *Islam in Tribal Societies: From the Atlas to the Indus*. London, 1984.
Akhavi, Shahrough. "State Formation and Consolidation in Twentieth-Century Iran: The Reza Shah Period and the Islamic Republic." In Ali Banuazizi and Myron Weiner, eds., *The State, Religion, and Ethnic Politics: Afghanistan, Iran, and Pakistan*. Syracuse, N.Y., 1986.
Algar, Hamid. *Religion and State in Iran*. Berkeley and Los Angeles, 1969.
————. *Studies in Eighteenth Century Islamic History*. Edited by T. Naff and R. Owen. Carbondale, Ill., 1977.
Algosaibi, Ghazi. *Arabian Essays*. London, 1982.
Altorki, Soraya, and Donald P. Cole. *Arabian Oasis City: The Transformation of 'Unayzah*. Austin, Tex., 1989.
Amirahmadi, Hooshang. "Middle-Class Revolutions in the Third World." In Hooshang Amirahmadi and Manoucher Parvin, eds., *Post-Revolutionary Iran*. Boulder, Colo., 1988.
al-'Amri, H. *The Yemen in the 18th and 19th Centuries: A Political and Intellectual History*. London, 1985.
Anderson, Benedict. *Imagined Communities: Reflections on the Origin and Spread of Nationalism*. London, 1983.
Anderson, Lisa. "Libya's Qaddafi: Still in Command?" *Current History* 86, no. 517 (February 1987).

————. *The State and Social Transformation in Tunisia and Libya, 1830–1980*. Princeton, 1986.

————. "The State in the Middle East and North Africa." *Comparative Politics*, October 1987.

Andreski, S. *Military Organisation and Society*. London, 1968.

Ardener, E. W. "The New Anthropology and Its Critics." *Man* 6, no. 3 (1971).

Arjomand, Said Amir. "Religion, Political Action and Legitimate Domination in Shi'ite Iran." *European Journal of Sociology* 20 (1979).

————. "Religious Extremism (Ghuluww), Sufism and Sunnism in Safavid Iran: 1501–1722." *Journal of Asian History* 15 (1981).

Asad, Talal. "Equality in Nomadic Systems? Notes towards the Dissolution of an Anthropological Category." In Centre Nationale de la Recherche Scientifique, *Pastoral Production and Society*. Paris, 1979.

————. *The Kababish Arabs*. New York, 1970.

————. "Market Model, Class Structure and Consent: A Reconsideration of Swat Political Organization." *Man* 7, no. 1 (1972).

————. "Political Inequality in the Kababish Tribe." In Ian Cunnison and Wendy James, eds., *Studies in Sudan Ethnography*. New York, 1972.

Aubin, Jean. "Etudes safavides. I Shah Isma'il et les notables de l'Iraq persan." *Journal of the Economic and Social History of the Orient* 2 (1959).

Ayalon, A. *Language and Change in the Arab Middle East*. New York, 1987.

al-Azmeh, Aziz. "Wahhabite Polity." In Ian Richard Netton, ed., *Arabia and the Gulf: From Traditional Society to Modern States*. Totawa, N.J., 1986.

Bailey, F. G. *Stratagems and Spoils: A Social Anthropology of Politics*. Oxford, 1969.

Banuazizi, Ali, and Myron Weiner, eds. *State, Religion, and Ethnic Politics: Afghanistan, Iran, and Pakistan*. Syracuse, N.Y., 1986.

Barfield, Thomas. *The Arab Tribes of Afghanistan*. Austin, Tex., 1981.

————. "The Hsiung-nu Imperial Confederacy: Organization and Foreign Policy." *Journal of Asian Studies* 41 (1981).

————. *The Perilous Frontier: Nomadic Empires and China*. Oxford, 1989.

Barth, Fredrik. "Nomadism in the Mountain and Plateau Areas of South West Asia." In *The Problems of the Arid Zone: Proceedings of the Paris Symposium*. Paris, 1962.

————. *Nomads of South Persia: The Basseri Tribe of the Khamseh Confederacy*. London, 1961.

————. *Political Leadership among Swat Pathans*. London, 1959.

Basilov, V. N. "Honour Groups in Traditional Turkmenian Society." In A. S. Ahmed and D. M. Hart, eds., *Islam and Tribal Societies*. London, 1984.

Batatu, Hanna. "Iraq's Underground Shi'a Movements: Characteristics, Causes and Prospects." *Middle East Journal* 35, no. 4 (1981).

————. *The Old Social Classes and the Revolutionary Movements of Iraq*. Princeton, 1978.

————. "Some Observations on the Social Roots of Syria's Ruling, Military Group and the Causes of Its Dominance." *Middle East Journal* 35, no. 3 (1981).

Bausani, Alessandro. "Religion under the Mongols." In J. A. Boyle, ed., *The Cambridge History of Iran*. Vol. 5, *The Seljuq and Mongol Period*. Cambridge, 1968.

Beck, Lois. "Islam in Tribal Societies." *Reviews in Anthropology* 18, no. 1 (Spring 1990).

———. "Nomads and Urbanites, Invited Hosts and Uninvited Guests." *Iranian Studies* 18, no. 4 (1982).

———. *The Qashqa'i of Iran*. New Haven, 1986.

Ben-Dor, Gabriel. "Ethnopolitics and the Middle Eastern State." In Milton J. Esman and Itamar Rabinovich, eds., *Ethnicity, Pluralism, and the State in the Middle East*. Ithaca, 1988.

———. *State and Conflict in the Middle East*. Boulder, Colo., 1983.

Berque, Jacques. "Du nouveau sur les Bani Hilal?" *Studia Islamica* 35 (1972).

Birge, J. K. *The Bektashi Order of Dervishes*. London, 1937.

Black-Michaud, Jacob. *Cohesive Force: Feud in the Mediterranean and the Middle East*. Oxford, 1975.

———. *Sheep and Land: The Economics of Power in a Tribal Society*. Cambridge, 1986.

Bloch, Ernst. *Subjekt Objekt: Erlaeuterungen zu Hegel*. 2d ed. Frankfurt-am-Main, 1972.

Bloch, Marc. *Feudal Society*. Chicago, 1961.

Bloch, Maurice, ed. *Marxist Analysis and Social Anthropology*. London, 1975.

Bosworth, C. E. "The Political and Dynastic History of the Iranian World (A.D. 1000–1217)." In J. A. Boyle, ed., *The Cambridge History of Iran*. Vol. 5, *The Seljuq and Mongol Period*. Cambridge, 1968.

de Boucheman, A. *Une petite cité caravanière: Suhné*. Documents d'études orientales de l'Institut Français de Damas, vol. 6. Damascus, 1939.

Boyer, P. *L'évolution de l'Algérie Mediane*. Paris, 1960.

———. *La vie quotidienne à Alger*. Paris, 1964.

Bradburd, Daniel. "Kinship and Contract: The Social Organization of the Komachi of Kerman, Iran." Ph.D. diss., City University of New York, 1979.

Brett, Michael. "The Fatamid Revolution (861–973) and Its Aftermath in North Africa." In J. D. Fage, ed., *The Cambridge History of Africa*. Vol. 2. Cambridge, 1978.

———. "Ibn Khaldun and the Arabisation of North Africa." *Maghrib Review* 41 (1979).

Breuilly, John. *Nationalism and the State*. Manchester, 1982.

Brooks, David. "The Enemy Within: Limitations on Leadership in the Bakhtiyari." In Richard L. Tapper, ed., *The Conflict of Tribe and State in Iran and Afghanistan*. London, 1983.

Brunschvig, R. *La Berberie Orientale sous les Hafsides*. 2 vols. Paris, 1940, 1947.

Buchan, James. "The Return of the Ikhwan 1979." In D. Holden and R. Johns, *The House of Saud*. London, 1981.

Bull, Hedley. *The Anarchical Society: A Study of Order in World Politics.* New York, 1977.

Bull, Hedley, and Adam Watson, eds. *The Expansion of International Society.* Oxford, 1988.

Burnham, P. "Spatial Mobility and Political Centralization in Pastoral Societies." In Centre Nationale de la Recherche Scientifique, *Pastoral Production and Society.* Paris, 1979.

Busch, Brinton Cooper. *Britain, India, and the Arabs 1914–1928.* Berkeley and Los Angeles, 1971.

Centre Nationale de la Recherche Scientifique. *Pastoral Production and Society.* Paris, 1979.

Carneiro, R. L. "Cross-currents in the Theory of State Formation." *American Ethnologist* 14, no. 4 (1987).

Caton, Steven C. "Power, Persuasion and Language." *International Journal of Middle East Studies* 19 (1987).

Chelhod, J. *Introduction à la sociologie de l'Islam.* Paris, 1958.

Cohen, Ronald, and Elman R. Service, eds. *The Origins of the State.* Philadelphia, 1978.

Cole, Donald P. "Bedouin and Social Change in Saudi Arabia." *Journal of Asian and African Studies* 16 (1981).

———. *Nomads of the Nomads.* Arlington Heights, Ill., 1975.

Collins R. O., ed. *An Arabian Diary: Sir Gilbert Falkinham Clayton.* Berkeley and Los Angeles, 1969.

Combs-Schilling, M. Elaine. "Family and Friend in a Moroccan Boom Town." *American Ethnologist* 12 (1985).

Coon, Carlton. *Caravan: The Story of the Middle East.* New York, 1951.

Cornell, V. J. "The Logic of Analogy and the Role of the Sufi Shaykh." *International Journal of Middle East Studies* 15 (1983).

Crawford, M. J. "Civil War, Foreign Intervention and the Question of Political Legitimacy: A Nineteenth Century Sa'udi Qadi's Dilemma." *International Journal of Middle East Studies* 14 (1982).

Crone, Patricia. *Slaves on Horses: The Evolution of the Islamic Polity.* Cambridge, 1980.

———. "The Tribe and the State." In J. A. Hall, ed., *States in History.* Oxford, 1986.

Crone, Patricia, and Martin Hinds. *God's Caliph.* Cambridge, 1987.

Cunnison, Ian. *Baggara Arabs: Power and the Lineage in a Sudanese Nomad Tribe.* Oxford, 1966.

"Current Political Attitudes in an Iranian Village." *Iranian Studies* 16, no. 1–2 (1983).

Davis, John. *Libyan Politics: Tribe and Revolution, Society and Culture in the Modern Middle East.* London, 1987.

Delacroix, Jacques. "The Distributive State in the World System." *Studies in Comparative International Development* 15, no. 3 (Fall 1980).

Dennett, D. C. *Conversion and the Poll Tax in Early Islam.* Cambridge, Mass., 1950.

Dickson, H. R. P. *Kuwait and Her Neighbours.* London, 1968.

Digard, Jean-Pierre. "Histoire et anthropologie des sociétés nomades: Le cas d'une tribu d'Iran." *Annales: Economies, sociétés, civilisations* 28, no. 6 (1973).

———. "On the Bakhtiari: Comments on 'Tribes, Confederation and the State.' " In Richard Tapper, ed., *The Conflict of Tribe and State in Iran and Afghanistan.* New York, 1983.

———. *Techniques des nomads baxtiyari d'Iran.* Cambridge, 1981.

Dowdall, H. C. "The Word 'State.' " *Law Quarterly Review* 39, no. 153 (1923).

Drague, J. *Esquisse d'histoire religieuse du Maroc.* Paris, 1951.

Dresch, Paul K. "The Position on Shaykhs among the Northern Tribes of Yemen." *Man* 19, no. 1 (1984).

———. "Segmentation: Its Roots in Arabia and Its Flowering Elsewhere." *Cultural Anthropology* 3 (1988).

———. "The Significance of the Course Events Take in Segmentary Systems." *American Ethnologist* 13, no. 2 (1986).

———. "Tribal Relations and Political History in Upper Yemen." In B. R. Pridham, ed., *Contemporary Yemen.* London, 1984.

———. *Tribes, Government and History in Yemen.* Oxford, 1989.

Dunn, Ross. *Resistance in the Desert.* Madison, Wisc., 1977.

Eickelman, Dale F. "Ibadism and the Sectarian Perspective." In B. R. Pridham, ed., *Oman: Economic, Social and Strategic Developments.* London, 1987.

———. *The Middle East: An Anthropological Approach.* 2d ed. Englewood Cliffs, N.J., 1988.

———. *Moroccan Islam.* Austin, Tex., 1976.

———. "Time in a Complex Society." *Ethnology* 16 (1977).

El Fathaly, Omar I., and Monte Palmer. *Political Development and Social Change in Libya.* Lexington, Mass., 1980.

Engels, Friedrich. *The Origin of the Family, Private Property and the State.* 1884. New York, 1942.

d'Entrèves, Alexandre Passerin. *The Notion of the State: An Introduction to Political Theory.* Oxford, 1967.

———. "The State." In Philip P. Weiner, ed., *Dictionary of the History of Ideas.* Vol. 4. New York, 1973.

Esman, Milton J., and Itamar Rabinovich, eds. *Ethnicity, Pluralism, and the State in the Middle East,* Ithaca, 1988.

Evans, Peter B., Dietrich Rueschemeyer, and Theda Skocpol, eds. *Bringing the State Back In.* New York, 1965.

Evans-Pritchard, E. E. *The Nuer.* Oxford, 1940.

———. *The Sanusi of Cyrenaica.* Oxford, 1949.

Fabietti, U. "Sedentarization as a Means of Detribalisation: Some Policies of the Saudi Government towards the Nomads." In T. Niblock, ed., *States, Society and Economy in Saudi Arabia.* London, 1982.

al-Farra, Taha. "The Effects of Detribalizing the Bedouins on the Internal Cohesion of an Emerging State: The Kingdom of Saudi Arabia." Ph.D. diss., University of Pittsburgh, 1973.

Fazel, G. Reza. "Tribes and State in Iran: From Pahlavi to Islamic Republic." In Haleh Afshar, ed., *Iran: A Revolution in Turmoil*. Albany, N.Y., 1985.

Figgis, J. N. *Studies of Political Thought from Gerson to Grotius 1414–1625*. 2d ed. Cambridge, 1916.

First, Ruth. *Libya: The Elusive Revolution*. Baltimore, Md., 1974.

Firth, R. "The Skeptical Anthropologist? Social Anthropology and Marxist Views on Society." In Maurice Bloch, ed., *Marxist Analysis and Social Anthropology*. London, 1975.

Fletcher, Joseph. "The Mongols: Ecological and Social Perspectives." *Harvard Journal of Asiatic Studies* 46 (1986).

———. "Turco-Mongolian Monarchic Tradition in the Ottoman Empire." In Ihor Sevcenko and Frank Sysyn, eds., *Eucharisterion: Essays Presented to Omeljan Pritsak*. Harvard Ukranian Studies, vols. 3–4, part 1. Cambridge, Mass., 1979–1980.

Fried, M. H. *The Evolution of Political Society*. New York, 1967.

———. *The Notion of Tribe*. Menlo Park, Calif., 1975.

———. "The State, the Chicken, and the Egg; or, What Came First?" In R. Cohen and E. Service, eds., *Origins of the State*. Philadelphia, 1978.

Friedman, J. "Tribes, States and Transformations." In Maurice Bloch, ed., *Marxist Analyses and Social Anthropology*. London, 1975.

Friedl, Erika. *Women of Deh Koh: Lives in an Iranian Village*. Washington, D.C., 1989.

Gallissot, R. *L'Algérie pre-coloniale: Classes sociales en systeme pre-capitaliste*. Paris, 1968.

Garthwaite, G. R. "The Bakhtiyari Ilkhani: An Illusion of Unity." *International Journal of Middle East Studies* 8 (1977).

———. "Khans and Kings: The Dialectics of Power in Bakhtiyari History." In M. E. Bonine and N. R. Keddie, eds., *Modern Iran: The Dialectics of Continuity and Change*. Albany, N.Y., 1981.

———. *Khans and Shahs: A Documentary Analysis of the Bakhtiyari in Iran*. Cambridge, 1983.

———. "Pastoral Nomadism and Tribal Power." *Iranian Studies* 11 (1978).

Geertz, Clifford. "Centers, Kings, and Charisma: Reflections on the Symbolics of Power." In Clifford Geertz, *Local Knowledge: Further Essays in Interpretive Anthropology*. New York, 1983.

———. "Common Sense as a Cultural System." In Clifford Geertz, *Local Knowledge: Further Essays in Interpretive Anthropology*. New York, 1983.

———. *Islam Observed*. New Haven, 1968.

Geertz, Clifford, Hildred Geertz, and Lawrence Rosen. *Meaning and Order in Moroccan Society*. Cambridge, 1979.

Gellner, Ernest. *Cause and Meaning in the Social Sciences*. London, 1973.

———. "Cohesion and Identity: The Maghreb from Ibn Khaldun to Emile Durkheim." In Ernest Gellner, *Muslim Society: Essays*. Cambridge, 1981.

———. "Flux and Reflux in the Faith of Men." In Ernest Gellner, *Muslim Society: Essays*. Cambridge, 1981.

———. *Muslim Society: Essays*. Cambridge, 1981.

————. "Notes Towards a Theory of Ideology." In Ernest Gellner, *Spectacles and Predicaments*. Cambridge, 1979.

————. *Saints of the Atlas*. Chicago, 1969.

————. *Thought and Change*. London, 1964.

————. "Tribal Society and Its Enemies." In Richard L. Tapper, ed., *The Conflict of Tribe and State in Iran and Afghanistan*. London, 1983.

————. "Tribalism and Social Change in North Africa." In William Lewis, ed., *French-Speaking Africa: The Search for Identity*. New York, 1965.

Gellner, Ernest, and Charles Micaud, eds. *Arabs and Berbers: From Tribe to Nation in North Africa*. London, 1972.

Gibb, H. A. R. "Constitutional Organization." In M. Khadduri and H. Liebesney, eds., *Law in the Middle East*. Washington, D.C., 1955.

————. *Studies in the Civilization of Islam*. London, 1962.

Gibb, H. A. R., and H. Bowen. *Islamic Society and the West*. 2 vols. Oxford, 1950, 1954.

Giddens, Anthony. *The Nation-State and Violence*. Berkeley and Los Angeles, 1987.

Gierke, O. *Political Theories of the Middle Ages*. Translated by F. W. Maitland. Cambridge, 1900.

Glassen, E. "Schah Isma'il: Ein mahdi der Anatolischen Turkmenen?" *Der Islam* 41 (1965).

Gochenour, D. T. "The Penetration of Zaydi Islam into Early Medieval Yemen." Ph.D. diss., Harvard University, 1984.

Godelier, M. "The Concept of the 'Tribe': A Crisis Involving Merely a Concept or the Empirical Foundations of Anthropology?" In Jack Goody, ed., *Perspectives in Marxist Anthropology*. Translated by R. Brain. Cambridge Studies in Social Anthropology, vol. 18. Cambridge, 1973.

————. *The Making of Great Men*. Translated by R. Swyer. Cambridge, 1986.

Goldberg, Jacob. *The Foreign Policy of Saudi Arabia, the Formative Years 1902–1918*. Cambridge, Mass., 1986.

Goldrup, L. P. "Saudi Arabia, 1902–1932: The Development of a Wahhabi Society." Ph.D. diss., University of California, Los Angeles, 1971.

Grabar, Oleg. *The Formation of Islamic Art*. New Haven, 1973.

Griswold, William J. *The Great Anatolian Rebellion, 1000–1020/1591–1611*. Berlin, 1983.

Grousset, René. *The Empire of the Steppes*. New Brunswick, N.J., 1970.

Hall, J. A. "States and Economic Development: Reflections on Adam Smith." In J. A. Hall, ed., *States in History*. Oxford, 1986.

al-Hamdani, Al-Hasan. *Al-Iklil min Akhbar al-Yaman wa-Insan Himyar*. Vol. 10. Edited by Muhibb al-Din al-Khatib. Cairo, 1948.

Hamza, F. *Al-Bilad al-'Arabiyya al-Sa'udiyya*. Riyadh, 1961.

Harrison, Selig. *In Afghanistan's Shadow: Baluch Nationalism and Soviet Temptations*. New York, 1981.

Helfgott, Leonard. "The Structural Foundations of the National Minority Problem in Revolutionary Iran." *Iranian Studies* 13 (1980).

──────. "Tribalism as a Socioeconomic Formation in Iranian History." *Iranian Studies* 10 (1977).

──────. "Tribe and Uymaq in Iran: A Reply." *Iranian Studies* 16 (1983).

Helm, June, ed. *Essays on the Problem of Tribe*. Seattle, 1968.

Helms, C. Moss. *The Cohesion of Saudi Arabia*. London, 1981.

Hinsley, F. H. *Sovereignty*. 2d ed. Cambridge, 1986.

──────. *Nationalism and the International System*. London, 1973.

Hodgson, Marshall G. S. *The Venture of Islam*. Vol. 1, *The Classical Age of Islam*. Chicago, 1974.

Holden, D., and R. Johns. *The House of Saud*. London, 1981.

Hopkins, J. F. P. "The Almohade Hierarchy." *Bulletin of the School of Oriental and African Studies* 16 (1954).

Hopkins, K. *Conquerors and Slaves*. Cambridge, 1978.

Horowitz, D. *Ethnic Groups in Conflict*. Berkeley and Los Angeles, 1985.

Hourani, Albert. "The Ottoman Background of the Modern Middle East." In Albert Hourani, *The Emergence of the Modern Middle East*. London, 1981.

Hudson, Michael C. *Arab Politics. The Search for Legitimacy*. New Haven, 1977.

Hymes, D. *Foundations in Sociolinguistics*. Philadelphia, 1974.

Ibn Khaldun. *Le Voyage d'Occident et d'Orient*. Translated into French by Abdesseiain Cheddadi. Paris, 1980.

──────. *The Muqaddimah*. Translated by F. Rosenthal. 3 vols. Princeton, 1958.

──────. *The Muqaddimah*. Edited and abridged by N. Dawood. Translated by F. Rosenthal. Princeton, 1967.

Idris, H. R. *La Berberie Orientale sous les Zirides*. Paris, 1962.

Inalcik, H. *The Ottoman Empire: The Classical Age*. New York, 1973.

──────. "The Rise of the Ottoman Empire." In M. A. Cook, ed., *A History of the Ottoman Empire to 1730*. Cambridge, 1976.

International Bank for Reconstruction and Development. *The Economic Development of Libya*. Baltimore, 1960.

Irons, William. "Nomadism as a Political Adaptation: The Case of the Yomut Turkmen." *American Ethnologist* 1:1 (1974).

──────. "Political Stratification among Pastoral Nomads." In Centre Nationale de la Recherche Scientifique, *Pastoral Production and Society*. Paris, 1979.

──────. *The Yomut Turkmen*. Ann Arbor, Mich., 1975.

Jenkins, R. J. "The Evolution of Religious Brotherhoods in North and Northwest Africa." In J. R. Willis, ed., *Studies in West African Islamic History*. London, 1979.

Jiva, S. "The Initial Destination of the Fatimid Caliphate: The Yemen or the Maghrib?" *British Society for Middle Eastern Studies Bulletin* 13, no. 1 (1986).

Johnson, Allen W., and Timothy Earle. *The Evolution of Human Societies*. Stanford, Calif., 1987.

Karpat, Kemal. "The Ottoman Ethnic and Confessional Legacy in the Middle East." In Milton J. Esman and Itamar Rabinovich, eds., *Ethnicity, Pluralism, and the State in the Middle East.* Ithaca, 1988.

Katakura, Mokoto. *Bedouin Village.* Tokyo, 1977.

Kay, Shirley. "Social Change in Modern Saudi Arabia." In T. Niblock, ed., *State, Society and Economy in Saudi Arabia.* London, 1982.

Keddie, Nikki R. "The Minorities Question in Iran." In Shirin Tahir-Kheli and Shaheen Ayubi, eds., *The Iran-Iraq War: New Weapons, Old Conflicts.* New York, 1983.

———. "Religion, Ethnic Minorities, and the State in Iran: An Overview." In Ali Banuazizi and Myron Weiner, eds., *The State, Religion, and Ethnic Politics: Afghanistan, Iran, and Pakistan.* Syracuse, N.Y., 1986.

——— *Roots of Revolution: An Interpretive History of Modern Iran.* New Haven, 1981.

Khadduri, Majid. *Modern Libya: A Study in Political Development.* Baltimore, 1963.

Khazanov, A. M. *Nomads and the Outside World.* Translated by Julia Crookenden. Cambridge, 1984.

Khoury, Philip S. "Islamic Revival and the Crisis of the Secular State in the Arab World." In I. Ibrahim, ed., *Arab Resources: The Transformation of Society.* London, 1983.

———. *Syria and the French Mandate: The Politics of Arab Nationalism, 1920–1945.* Princeton, 1987.

———. "The Tribal Shaykh, French Tribal Policy, and the Nationalist Movement in Syria between Two World Wars." *Middle Eastern Studies* 18, no. 2 (1982).

Khuri, Fuad. *From Village to Suburb: Order and Change in Greater Beirut.* Chicago, 1974.

Kluck, P. A. "The Society and Its Environment." In *Saudi Arabia: A Country Study.* Washington, D.C., 1984.

Kostiner, Joseph. "The Hashemite 'Tribal Confederacy' of the Arab Revolt, 1916–1917." In E. Ingram, ed., *National and International Politics in the Middle East: Essays in Honour of Elie Kedourie.* London, 1986.

———. "On Instruments and Their Designers: The Ikhwan of Najd and the Emergence of the Saudi State." *Middle Eastern Studies* 21, no. 3 (July 1985).

Koszinowski, Thomas, ed. *Saudi-Arabien: Ölmacht und Entwicklungsland.* Hamburg, 1983.

Krader, Lawrence. *Formation of the State.* Englewood Cliffs, N.J., 1968.

———. "The Origin of the State among the Nomads of Asia." In Centre Nationale de la Recherche Scientifique, *Pastoral Production and Society.* Paris, 1979.

———. *Peoples of Central Asia.* Bloomington, Ind., 1963.

———. *Social Organization of the Mongol-Turkic Pastoral Nomads.* The Hague, 1963.

Krasner, Stephen. "Approaches to the State Alternative: Conceptions and Historical Dynamics." *World Politics* (December 1984).

Lackner, Helen. *A House Built on Sand*. London, 1978.

Lambton, A. K. S. "Ilat." In *The Encyclopedia of Islam*. Vol. 3. 2d ed. Leiden, 1960.

———. *Islamic Society in Persia*. London, 1954.

———. "Quis Custodiet Custodes: Some Reflections on the Persian Theory of Government." *Studia Islamica* 5 (1956).

Lancaster, William. *The Rwala Bedouin Today*. Cambridge, 1981.

Lapidus, Ira M. "The Arab Conquests and the Formation of Islamic Society." In G. H. A. Juyboll, ed., *Studies on the First Century of Islamic History*. Carbondale, Ill., 1982.

———. *A History of Islamic Societies*. Cambridge, 1988.

———. "The Separation of State and Religion in Early Islamic Society." *International Journal of Middle East Studies* 6 (1975).

Laroui, A. *The History of the Maghrib*. Princeton, 1977.

Lattimore, Owen. *Inner Asian Frontiers of China*. New York, 1941.

Leach, E. R. *Political Systems of Highland Burma*. London, 1954.

Le Tourneau, R. "Sur la disparition de la doctrine Almohade." *Studia Islamica* 23 (1970).

Lewicki, T. "The Ibadites in Arabia and Africa." *Journal of World History* 13 (1971).

———. "La répartition géographique des groupements ibadites dans l'Afrique du Nord au moyen-age." *Rocznik Orientalistyczny* 21 (1957).

Lewis, Bernard. *The Arabs in History*. New York, 1966.

Lewis, Norman. *Nomads and Settlers in Syria and Jordan, 1800–1980*. Cambridge, 1987.

Lindholm, Charles. "Kinship Structure and Political Authority: The Middle East and Central Asia." *Comparative Studies in Society and History* 28 (1986).

Lindner, Rudi Paul. *Nomads and Ottomans in Medieval Anatolia*. Bloomington, Ind., 1983.

———. "What Was a Nomad Tribe?" *Comparative Studies in Society and History* 24 (1982).

Lockhart, L. "The Persian Army and the Safavi." *Der Islam* 34 (1959).

Loeffler, R. "Tribal Order and the State: The Political Organization of Boir Ahmad." *Iranian Studies* 11 (1978).

McChesney, R. D. "Comments on 'The Qajar Uymaq in the Safavid Period.' " *Iranian Studies* 14 (1981).

McGovern, William M. *The Early Empires of Central Asia*. Chapel Hill, N.C., 1939.

Machiavelli, N. *The Prince*. Translated by George Bull. Harmondsworth, Eng., 1961.

Mackerras, Colin. *The Uighur Empire*. Columbia, S.C., 1973.

Mahdi, Muhsin S. *Ibn Khaldun's Philosophy of History*. Chicago, 1957.

al-Mana, Muhammad. *Arabia Unified*. London, 1980.

Marx, Emanuel. *Bedouin of the Negev*. New York, 1967.

———. "The Tribe as a Unit of Subsistence." *American Anthropologist* 79 (1977).

Marx, Karl. *Pre-Capitalist Economic Formations.* Ed. E. J. Hobsbawm. New York, 1965.

Marx, Karl, and Friedrich Engels. *German Ideology.* 1846. New York, 1970.

———. *Über Religion.* East Berlin, 1958.

Massignon, L. "Cartes de répartition des kabyles dans la région parisienne." In *Opera minora.* Vol. 3. Beirut, 1963.

Mazzaoui, M. *The Origins of the Safawids.* Weisbaden, 1972.

Meeker, Michael. *Literature and Violence in North Africa.* Cambridge, 1979.

———. "Meaning and Society in the Near East: Examples from the Black Sea Turks and the Levantine Arabs." *International Journal of Middle East Studies* 7 (1976).

Migdal, Joel S. "A Model of State-Society Relations." In Howard Wiarda, ed., *New Directions in Comparative Politics.* Boulder, Colo., 1985.

———. *Strong Societies and Weak States.* Princeton, 1988.

Minorski, V. *Hudud al-Alam, 'The Regions of the World: A Persian Geography A.H. 372–A.D. 982.* London, 1948.

Montagne, Robert. *The Berbers.* Translated by J. D. Seddon. London, 1972.

al-Munif, 'Abd al-Rahman. *Mudun al-Milh.* Dammam, 1982.

Nagel, Joane. "The Ethnic Revolution: The Emergence of Ethnic Nationalism in Modern States." *Sociology and Social Research* 68, no. 4 (1983–1984).

Nakash, Yitzhak. "Fiscal and Monetary Systems in the Mahdist Sudan, 1881–1898." *International Journal of Middle East Studies* 20 (August 1988).

Napier, G. C. "Memorandum on the Condition and External Relations of the Turkomen Tribes of Merv." In *Collection of Journals and Reports from G. C. Napier on Special Duty in Persia 1874.* London, 1876.

Niblock, T., ed. *State, Society, and Economy in Saudi Arabia.* London, 1982.

Niebuhr, M. C. *Travels through Arabia and Other Countries of the East.* Translated by Robert Heron. Edinburgh, 1792. Repr. Beirut, Librairie du Liban.

Nikitine, Basile. "Les afshars d'Urumiyeh." *Journal Asiatique* 214 (1929).

Norris, H. T. *The Tuaregs: Their Islamic Legacy and Its Diffusion in the Sahel.* Warminster, 1975.

Nubdha. *Kitab al-Nubdhat al-Mushira ila Jumal min 'Uyun al-Sira fi Akhbar . . . al-Mansur bi-Ilah al-Qasim b. Muhammad.* Photoreproduction of manuscript. San'a', n.d.

Pareto, Vilifredo. *The Mind and Society.* New York, 1963.

Peristiany, J. G., ed. *Mediterranean Family Structures.* Cambridge, 1976.

Perry, John. "Forced Migration in Iran during the 17th and 18th Centuries." *Iranian Studies* 8 (1975).

———. *Karim Khan Zand: A History of Iran, 1747–1779.* Chicago, 1979.

Peters, E. L. "Aspects of Affinity in a Lebanese Maronite Village." In J. G. Peristiany, ed., *Mediterranean Family Structures.* Cambridge, 1976.

———. "From Particularism to Universalism in the Religion of the Cyrenaica Bedouin." *British Society for Middle East Studies Bulletin* 3, no. 1 (1976).

————. "The Proliferation of Segments in the Lineage of the Bedouin of Cyrenaica." *Journal of the Royal Anthropological Institute* 40.

————. "Some Structural Aspects of Feud among the Camel-raising Bedouin of Cyrenaica." *Africa* 32, no. 3 (1967).

Peterson, J. E. *Yemen: The Search for a Modern State.* London, 1982.

Petrushevsky, I. P. "The Socio-economic Condition of Iran under the Il-khans." In J. A. Boyle, ed., *The Cambridge History of Iran.* Vol. 5, *The Seljuq and Mongol Period.* Cambridge, 1968.

Philby, H. St. John. *The Heart of Arabia.* London, 1923.

Pipes, Daniel. *Slave Soldiers and Islam.* New Haven, 1981.

Piscatori, James P. *Islam in a World of Nation-States.* Cambridge, 1986.

Planhol, X. de. *Les fondements géographiques de l'histoire d'Islam.* Paris, 1968.

Pridham, B. R., ed. *Contemporary Yemen: Politics and Historical Background.* London, 1984.

al-Qurdawi, Yusuf. *Al-Hulul al-Mustawrada wa Kaif Janat 'ala ummatina.* 2 vols. Vol. 1, *Hatmiyyat al-Hall al-Islami.* Beirut, 1960.

Rahman, F. *Islam.* Chicago, 1979.

Rasheed, Madawi Al. "The Political System of a North Arabian Chiefdom." Ph.D. diss., Cambridge University, 1988.

Rashid al-Din. *The Successors of Genghis Khan.* Translated by John Boyle. New York, 1971.

Reid, James J. "Comments on 'Tribalism as a Socioeconomic Formation in Iranian History.'" *Iranian Studies* 12 (1978).

————. "The Qajar Uymaq in the Safavid Period, 1500–1722." *Iranian Studies* 11 (1978).

————. "Rebellion and Social Change in Astarabad." *International Journal of Middle East Studies* 13 (1981).

————. *Tribalism in Society in Islamic Iran 1500–1629.* Malibu, Calif., 1983.

Rex, John, and David Mason, eds. *Theories of Race and Ethnic Relations.* Cambridge, 1988.

al-Rihani, Amin. *Ta'rikh Najd wa-Mulhaqatihi.* Beirut, 1928.

Robinson, Maxime. *Mohammed.* Translated by Anne Carter. New York, 1971.

Rosen, Lawrence. *Bargaining for Reality: The Construction of Social Relations in a Muslim Community.* Chicago, 1984.

Rosenfeld, H. "The Social Composition of the Military in the Process of State Formation in the Arabian Desert." Parts 1 and 2. *Journal of the Royal Anthropological Institute* 95, nos. 1, 2 (1965).

Roumani, Jacques. "From Republic to Jamahiriya: Libya's Search for Political Community." *Middle East Journal* 37, no. 2 (Spring 1983).

Ryckmans, J. *L'institution monarchique en Arabie meridionale avant l'Islam.* Louvain, 1951.

al-Sadhan, Abd Ulrahman M. "The Modernisation of the Saudi Bureaucracy." In Willard A. Beling, ed., *King Faisal and the Modernisation of Saudi Arabia.* London, 1980.

Safran, N., and M. Heller. *The New Middle Class and Regime Stability in Saudi Arabia.* Harvard Middle East Studies, no. 3. Cambridge, Mass., 1985.

Sahlins, Marshall D. *Tribesmen*. Englewood Cliffs, N.J., 1968.

Said, A. H. "Saudi Arabia: The Transition from a Tribal Society to a Nation." Ph.D. diss., University of Illinois, 1982.

Salamé, Ghassan. Introduction to Ghassan Salamé, ed., *The Foundations of the Arab State*. London, 1987.

――――. *Al-Mujtama' wa al-Dawla fi al-Mashriq al-'Arabi*. Beirut, 1987.

Salamé, Ghassan, Elbaki Hermassi, and Khaldun al-Naqib. *Al-Mujtama' wa al-Dawla fi al-Watan al-'Arabi*. Edited and coordinated by S. E. Ibrahim. Beirut, 1988.

Salem, Salaheddin Hassan. "The Genesis of Political Leadership in Libya, 1952–1969." Ph.D. diss., George Washington University, 1973.

Salzman, P. C. "Does Complementary Opposition Exist?" *American Anthropologist* 80 (1978).

――――. "Ideology and Change in Tribal Society." *Man*, n.s., 13 (1978).

――――. "Tribal Chiefs as Middlemen: The Politics of Encapsulation in the Middle East." *Anthropological Quarterly* 2 (1979).

Samore, Gary. "Royal Family Politics in Politics in Saudi Arabia." Ph.D. diss., Harvard University, 1985.

Savory, R. M. *Iran under the Safavids*. Cambridge, 1980.

――――. "Principal Offices of the Safavid State." *Bulletin of the School of Oriental and African Studies* (1960).

Schmidt, Steffen W., Laura Guasti, Carl H. Landé, and James C. Scott, eds. *Friends, Followers, and Factions: A Reader in Political Clientelism*. Berkeley and Los Angeles, 1977.

Schneider, David. *A Critique of the Study of Kinship*. Ann Arbor, 1984.

Seale, Patrick. *Asad: The Struggle for the Middle East*. Berkeley and Los Angeles, 1989.

Serjeant, R. B. "The Interplay between Tribal Affinities and Religious (Zaydi) Authority in the Yemen." *Al-Abhath* (Beirut) 30 (1982).

――――. "The Post-medieval and Modern History of San'a' and the Yemen." In R. B. Serjeant and Ronald Lewcock, eds., *San'a': An Arabian Islamic City*. London, 1983.

Seton-Watson, Hugh. *Nations and States: An Enquiry into the Origins of Nations and the Politics of Nationalism*. London, 1977.

Service, Elman R. *Origins of the State and Civilizations*. New York, 1975.

Shaban, M. A. *Islamic History*. Vol. 1. Cambridge, 1971.

al-Shahari, Muhammad. *Al-Matami' Tawwasu'iyya al-Sa'udiyya fil-Yaman*. Beirut, 1979.

Sharabi, Hisham. *Neopatriarchy: A Theory of Distorted Change in Arab Society*. Oxford, 1988.

Sharara, Waddah. *Al-Ahl wal-Ghanima*. Beirut, 1981.

Sider, Gerald. "When Parrots Learn to Talk, and Why They Can't: Domination, Deception, and Self-Deception in Indian-White Relations." *Comparative Studies in Society and History* 29, no. 1 (1987).

Skocpol, Theda. *States and Social Revolutions*. Cambridge, 1979.

Smith, Anthony D. *The Ethnic Origins of Nations*. Oxford, 1986.

Smith, John M., Jr. "Mongol and Nomadic Taxation." *Harvard Journal of Asian Studies* (1971).

———. "Turanian Nomadism and Iranian Politics." *Iranian Studies* 11 (1978).

Snyder, Louis. "Nationalism and the Flawed Concept of Ethnicity." *Canadian Review of Studies in Nationalism* 10, no. 2 (1983).

Sourdel, D. *Le vizirat 'abbaside*. 2 vols. Damascus, 1959–1960.

Spittler, Gert. *Herrschaft über Bauern: Die Ausbreitung staatlicher Herrschaft und einer islamisch-urbanen Kultur in Gabir/Niger*. Frankfurt-am-Main, 1978.

Spooner, Brian. "Baluchistan." In *Encyclopaedia Iranica*. Vol. 3. Fascile 6. London, 1988.

Sprengling, R. "From Persian to Arabic." *American Journal of Semitic Languages and Literatures* 56 (1939).

Stewart, Charles C. *Islam and Social Order in Mauritania*. Oxford, 1973.

al-Sudani, Sadiq Hasan. *Al-'Ilaqat al-'Iraqiyya al-Sa'udiyya 1920–31*. Baghdad, 1975.

Sweet, Louise. "Camel Raiding of the North Arabian Bedouin." *American Anthropologist* 67 (1965).

Tapper, Richard. "Ethnicity, Order and Meaning in the Anthropology of Iran and Afghanistan." In Jean-Pierre Digard, ed., *Le fait ethnique en Iran et en Afghanistan*. Paris, 1988.

———. Introduction to Richard Tapper, ed., *The Conflict of Tribe and State in Iran and Afghanistan*. London, 1983.

———. "On the Bakhtiari: Comments on 'Tribes, Confederation and the State.' " In Richard Tapper, *The Conflict of Tribe and State in Iran and Afghanistan*. London, 1983.

———. "The Organization of Nomadic Communities in Pastoral Societies of the Middle East." In Centre Nationale de la Recherche Scientifique, *Pastoral Production and Society*. Paris, 1979.

———. *Pasture and Politics: Economics, Conflict and Ritual among Shahsevan Nomads of Northwestern Iran*. London, 1979.

———. "Raiding, Reaction and Rivalry." *Bulletin of the School of Oriental and African Studies* 48 (1986).

———. "Shahsevan in Safavid Persia." *Bulletin of the School of Oriental and African Studies* 37 (1974).

Tapper, Richard, ed. *The Conflict of Tribe and State in Iran and Afghanistan*. London, 1983.

Terrasse, H. *Histoire de la Maroc*. 2 vols. Casablanca, 1954.

Terray, E. *Marxism and 'Primitive' Societies*. New York, 1972.

Tibi, Bassam. *Arab Nationalism: A Critical Inquiry*. New York, 1981.

———. *The Crisis of Modern Islam: A Pre-industrial Culture in the Scientific-Technological Age*. Translated by Judith von Sivers. Salt Lake City, 1988.

———. "Islam and Arab Nationalism." In Barbara Stowasser, ed., *The Islamic Impulse*. London, 1987.

———. *Konfliktregion Naher Osten. Regionale Eigendynamik und Grossmachtinteressen*. Munich, 1989.

————. "Structural and Ideological Change in the Arab Subsystem since the Six Day War." In Y. Lukacs and A. Battah, eds., *The Arab-Israeli Conflict*. Boulder, Colo., 1988.

Tilly, Charles, ed. *The Formation of National States in Western Europe*. Princeton, 1975.

Valensi, Lucette. *Venise et la Sublime Porte: La naissance du despote*. Paris, 1987.

van Bruinessen, Martin M. "Agha, Shaikh and State: On the Social and Political Organization of Kurdistan." Ph.D. diss., Utrecht University, Netherlands, 1978.

————. "The Kurds between Iran and Iraq." *MERIP, Middle East Report* 16, no. 4 (1986).

Vatin, J. C. "L'Algérie en 1830." *Revue Algerienne* 7 (1970).

Voll, John. *Islam: Continuity and Change in the Modern World*. Boulder, Colo., 1982.

Vološinov, V. N. *Marxism and the Philosophy of Language*. 1929. Cambridge, Mass., 1973.

Wahbah, H. *Arabian Days*. London, 1964.

Wallerstein, Immanuel. *The Politics of the World Economy: The States, the Movements and the Civilizations*. Cambridge, 1984.

al-Wasi'i, 'Abd al-Wasi'. *Ta'rikh al-Yaman*. Cairo, 1928.

Waterbury, John. "An Effort to Put Patrons and Clients in Their Place." In Ernest Gellner and John Waterbury, eds., *Patrons and Clients*. London, 1977.

Watson, Burton. *Records of the Grand Historian of China*. Vol. 2. New York, 1961.

Watt, W. Montgomery. "The Decline of the Almohads." *History of Religions* 4 (1964).

————. *Islamic Political Thought*. Edinburgh, 1968.

————. *Muhammad at Mecca*. Oxford, 1953.

————. *Muhammad at Medina*. Oxford, 1977.

al-Wazir, Zayd b. 'Ali. *Muhawala li-Fahm al-Mushkilat al-Yamaniyya*. Beirut, 1971.

Weber, Max. *The Theory of Social and Economic Organization*. Edited and with an introduction by Talcott Parsons. Cambridge, Mass., 1984.

Welch, S. C. *A King's Book of Kings*. London, 1972.

————. *Persian Painting: Five Royal Safavid Manuscripts of the Sixteenth Century*. New York, 1976.

Wilkinson, John. *The Imamate Tradition of Oman*. Cambridge, 1988.

Williams, K. *Ibn Sa'ud the Puritan King of Arabia*. London, 1938.

Wilson, Mary C. *King Abdullah, Britain and the Making of Jordan*. Cambridge, 1987.

Wolf, Eric R. *Europe and the People without History*. Berkeley and Los Angeles, 1982.

————. "The Social Organization of Mecca and the Origins of Islam." *Southwestern Journal of Anthropology* 7 (1951).

Woods, John. *The Aqquyunlu: Clan, Tribe, Confederation*. Minneapolis, 1976.

Wright, H. "The Evolution of Civilizations." In David J. Metzler, Don D. Fowler, and Jeremy A. Sabloff, eds., *American Archaeology, Past and Future*. Washington, D.C., 1986.

————. "Recent Research on the Origin of the State." *Annual Review of Anthropology* 6 (1977).

Yahya b. al-Husayn. *Ghayat al-Amani fi Akhbar al-Qutr al-Yamani*. 2 vols. Edited by Sa'id 'Abd al-Fattah. Cairo, 1968.

Yapp, Malcolm. "Tribes and States in the Khyber, 1838–1842." In Richard L. Tapper, ed., *The Conflict of Tribe and State in Iran and Afghanistan*. London, 1983.

Yu, Ying-shih. *Trade and Expansion in Han China*. Berkeley and Los Angeles, 1967.

Zabara, Muhammad. *A'immat al-Yaman*. 3 vols. Cairo, 1956.

————. *Nashr al-'Arf li-Nubala' al-Yaman ba'd al-Alf ila 1357 hijriyya*. Vol. 1. Ta'izz, 1952.

————. *Nashr al-'Arf li-Nubala' al-Yaman ba'd al-Alf ila 1357 hijriyya*. Vol. 1. Photoreprint. San'a', 1941.

————. *Nashr al-'Arf li-Nubala' al-Yaman ba'd al-Alf ila 1357 hijriyya*. Vol. 2. Cairo, 1958.

INDEX

'Abbas, Shah, 42, 200
'Abbasids, 31, 34–35, 36, 37, 259, 304
'Abdullah, Shaykh, 277
'Abdullah b. Hamza, 259
Abraham, 266
Achaemenids, 171
Adams, Henry, 253
Aden, 259
Adham, Kamal, 241
'Adl, 313
Administrators: imperial, 34–35, 39, 41, 42; in Libya, 292, 297; Saudi, 233, 236, 240–42, 243; tribal, 34–35; in tribal states, 69, 109, 172–74. *See also* Bureaucracy
Afghanistan, 3, 4–5, 63, 153, 162, 201, 210–11
Africa: East, 62, 63 (*see also* Sudan); ethnicity in, 131; Islamization in, 136; Saharan, 43, 110; sub-Saharan, 10, 43, 166; West, 136. *See also* North Africa
Afshars, 199, 201
Aghlabids, 31
Agriculture, 193, 305; in Iran, 190, 192; in Libya, 292; in Saudi Arabia, 230–31, 244, 247–48; segmentary-lineage model and, 111–12; in Yemen, 254, 267. *See also* Pastoralism
Ahansal, 119, 120
Ahmad b. Sulayman, Imam, 256, 259–60
al-Ahmar, 'Abdullah, 276
al-Ahmar family, 268
Ahmed, Akbar S., 90, 96–99, 162
al-Ahsa', 226, 228, 235, 236, 239, 247
al-'Aid, 230
Akhbar, 258, 272, 274, 313

'Alawis/Alawites: of Morocco, 31, 36, 39, 41; of Syria, 17, 129, 138, 139–40, 142, 148, 149, 313
Algeria, 31, 40, 116
Algerians, in Paris, 305
Algiers, 40, 116
'Ali, Ahmad, 269
'Ali 'Abdullah Salih, 276
'Alim, 27
Almohads, 29–40, 309
Almoravids, 29, 31, 34
Amir/Umara', 226–27, 245, 313
Anatolia, 63, 170–71, 306; confederations in, 157, 159–60, 166, 176–77, 200; Ottoman Empire in, 39, 115, 116, 155, 176; religiopolitical leaders in, 32, 33, 39, 307; Sufism in, 32, 33, 39, 43; warrior chiefdoms in, 33. *See also* Turkish/Anatolian plateau
Ancestors. *See* Descent
Andalusians, 35
Anderson, Lisa, 3–4, 14, 17, 288–301
Andreski, S., 109
Ansar, 30
Anthropologists: cultural, 91, 133, 253; on religion, 133; theories of tribe and state formation, 3, 69–70, 74–104, 253, 280; and tribe concept, 48–62. *See also* Archaeologists
Aqquyunlu, 32, 60, 171, 177, 200
Arabia, 10, 28; Bedouins of, 153; conquest movements in, 12, 29–30, 39, 44, 229–39, 307; egalitarian tribal system in, 154–55, 159, 160–64, 180; Ibn Khaldun on, 154–55; pre-Islamic, 133; Islamic state formation in, 39,

Text: 10/12 Aster
Display: Aster
Compositor: Point West Inc.
Printer: Bookcrafters
Binder: Bookcrafters